Jagdgeschwader 301/302 "Wilde Sau"

Jagdgeschwader 301/302 "Wilde Sau"

In Defense of the Reich
with the Bf 109, Fw 190 and Ta 152

Willi Reschke

Schiffer Military History
Atglen, PA

Cover artwork by Steve Ferguson, Colorado Springs, CO.

Depicted is the artist's recreation of the 21 November 1944 mission over Merseberg, Germany, at the fateful instant when the author's 12./JG 301 *Sturmbocks* crossed paths with the 352nd Fighter Group elements out of the one-hundred plus 67th Wing Mustangs present that day. Records indicate that while sixty of his brethren were lost, the author in his Fw 190 A-8 "White 6" was the only "*Focke-Wulfträger*" of 12./*Staffel* to knock down a P-51 in meager retribution.

Book design by Robert Biondi.
Translated from the German by David Johnston.

This book was originally published under the title,
Jagdgeschwader 301/302 "Wilde Sau",
by Motorbuch Verlag, Stuttgart, 1999.

Copyright © 2005 by Schiffer Publishing Ltd.
Library of Congress Catalog Number: 2004108050.

Printed in China.
ISBN: 0-7643-2130-7

We are always looking for people to write books on new and related subjects. If you have an idea for a book, please contact us at the address below.

Published by Schiffer Publishing Ltd.
4880 Lower Valley Road
Atglen, PA 19310
Phone: (610) 593-1777
FAX: (610) 593-2002
E-mail: Info@schifferbooks.com.
Visit our web site at: www.schifferbooks.com
Please write for a free catalog.
This book may be purchased from the publisher.
Please include $3.95 postage.
Try your bookstore first.

In Europe, Schiffer books are distributed by:
Bushwood Books
6 Marksbury Ave.
Kew Gardens
Surrey TW9 4JF
England
Phone: 44 (0)20 8392-8585
FAX: 44 (0)20 8392-9876
E-mail: Bushwd@aol.com.
Free postage in the UK. Europe: air mail at cost.
Try your bookstore first.

Contents

Foreword

It has not always been easy living here in East Germany, separated from my *Luftwaffe* comrades. And the danger was great that I would forget the experiences and memories that connected me with *Jagdgeschwader 301* and *302*.

In the years since the war I have spent countless days and hours poring over my remaining documents and writings, always filled with the hope that I might preserve my experiences and thus part of the history of these two units which formed part of the Defense of the Reich.

There is little if any mention of these two *Jagdgeschwader* in the publications dealing with the air war over Germany.

Jagdgeschwader 301 and *302* were not among those units of the *Luftwaffe* that bore the names of heroic figures. Instead they were born out of the desperate situation in which the *Luftwaffe* command found itself as a result of the Allied air offensive against Germany. Both fighter units nevertheless displayed a will to defend the Fatherland and paid a price in blood that equaled that of any other unit.

I have strived to create a chronicle of *Jagdgeschwader 301* and *302* from my own experiences and those of my comrades and from surviving documents and reports.

My efforts are dedicated to all the members of these two *Jagdgeschwader*, those who survived the war but especially those who gave their lives for Germany in faithful fulfillment of duty.

Willi Reschke
March 1998

Introduction:
How I Became a Fighter Pilot

My first contact with aviation came at an early age. My hometown of Mühlow an der Oder was about fifteen kilometers as the crow flies from Guben airfield, which became home to a flight training school in the mid-1930s. With great interest I followed the steadily increasing flying activities and was soon able to identify the various types of aircraft. My desire to someday sit in and fly an aircraft myself grew day by day and remained with me through my school days.

When war with Poland began in September 1939, I had just one goal: to serve in the *Luftwaffe* and become a fighter pilot. In February 1940, at the age of eighteen, I joined the *Luftwaffe* as a volunteer. Soon afterwards I was sent to Leipzig-Paunsdorf to take the aircrew suitability test. After passing, I waited impatiently to be called up. Weeks and months passed, and all my schoolmates became soldiers. Soon I was the only member of my class still walking around in civilian clothes.

Finally, on 4 February 1941, I was ordered to join the Flight Training Battalion in Königsberg-Neumark. After basic training, however, only a very few were sent to the "Monte Rosa" Pilot Candidate Battalion. The majority, including me, initially remained at the same air base for technical training. There was no hope of flying anytime soon, and the disappointment was written on all of our faces. I was assigned to the navigation team under the direction of *Feldwebel* Lienert. It could have been worse. It was the job of the navigation team to use small pieces of magnet to correct the magnetic compasses with which the training aircraft were still equipped. This required a reference point on the ground that was directly north of one's own position. In the beginning this activity was quite interesting, but after a while it became boring, especially since it was not bringing me one step closer to my goal of becoming a fighter pilot.

In the spring of 1942 I was finally transferred to the "Monte Rosa" Pilot Candidate Battalion. The "Monte Rosa" was a ship in Stettin harbor that served as quarters for a pilot preschool and an NCO instructor company. As a rule, each course lasted three months, but again I proved to be an

The author as an Oberfeldwebel in April 1945. In September 1944 Willi Reschke went from I./JG 302 to III./JG 301, where he was assigned to the 9. Staffel. From march 1945 he flew the Ta 152 on operations as a member of the Stabsschwarm.

exception. When the British landed at Dieppe our course was transferred to Morlaix, where we received infantry training. This was another setback on my road to becoming a pilot that cost a lot of time. Everyone on the course was happy when we returned to Germany in the autumn of the same year. On arriving back from France the pilot candidates were transferred to various gliding schools. I went to the one in Thorn, West Prussia. There I trained on winch-launched gliders and only to Class B level.

Among those who took the course with me: *Obergefreiter* Hampel and *Gefreiten* Thomsen, Homola, Eckhard, Rühlicke, Thiele, Müller, Semisch, Woehe, Neander and Suckrow.

The glider course at Thorn ended at the beginning of 1943, and the students were all transferred to Pilot School 51 in Elbing. There we were again divided into groups. My flight instructor was *Unteroffizier* Hansen, who instructed us on the Bücker Bü 181 *Bestmann* training aircraft.

At 1403 hours on 8 February 1943, with my flight instructor, I took off on my first flight in a powered aircraft, a Bü 181 coded SB+LN. The flight lasted twenty-three minutes. I trained at Elbing until 11 February 1943, during which time I made all of twelve flights in the Bü 181. After these few days at Elbing the entire group was transferred to the part of *A/B Schule 9* (*A/B Schule* = elementary flight training school) based in Grottkau, Silesia. The other part was stationed at Neisse. At Grottkau we were joined by student pilots *Unteroffizier* Steck, and *Gefreiten* Seidel, Riek and Jeromin.

The group flight instructor was *Oberfeldwebel* Musiol, and my instructor was *Unteroffizier* Marten. I soloed on my 33rd flight. This happened at 0847 hours on 9 March 1943 in Bü 181 SF+WH. The flight lasted six minutes. In those days I often thought back to the times when, as a boy, I stood by the Oder and gazed intently at the aircraft flying in the airspace over the Guben airfield. I had achieved what I had then wished for so passionately. My flying training continued, and in addition to the Bü 181 I now flew the Focke-Wulf Fw 44 *Stieglitz* and Bü 131 *Jungmann*. I received my initial instruction in aerobatics and made my first instrument flight in the Junkers W 34 trainer. The training at Grottkau ended on 28 March 1943, and the group was sent to Neisse.

Pilot training continued at Neisse. There our flight instructor was *Unteroffizier* Wilk and group flight instructor *Feldwebel* Niessen. We trained on the Klemm Kl 35, Arado Ar 66, Fw 56 and Ar 96. We made our first formation flights, very many cross-country flights, and spent a great deal of time in aerobatics training. It was also there that the decision was made as to which type of flying we would be best suited when our training ended – and many failed on working the navigation computer, the tricky drift angle and calculation of a triangular course.

On 27 June 1943 it was all over: we could call ourselves pilots and pin the coveted pilot's badge on the left breast of our tunics. I ended my pilot training with 229 takeoffs and landings. Our group of students, which had begun training at Elbing, remained together until the end of training, and no one had been dropped. Now, however, the day had come when we would part ways. The majority went to bomber of fighter schools, only a few to reconnaissance or dive-bomber schools. For those selected to become fighter pilots, the next stop was the fighter preschool at Magdeburg-South, part of *Jagdfliegerschule 102* based in Zerbst.

My specialized fighter training began there on 25 August 1943. *Oberfeldwebel* Becher was the chief instructor of our newly formed group of trainees, and *Unteroffizier* Will became my instructor. Training at the fighter preschool was a rather more difficult affair and we flew a new aircraft type, the Heinkel He 51. Each day we practiced pairs combat flying, flying among the clouds, low-level flying singly and in pairs, and shooting at ground targets. At that time the city of Magdeburg had still been spared heavy air attacks and I will never forget our evenings in the Hozo Café with the Juan Lossers orchestra.

After the conclusion of training at the preschool, on 23 October 1943 we began training at *Jagdschule 102* in Zerbst. We were assigned flight instructors *Unteroffizier* Ihlenfeld and Geserich. Our chief instructor was *Oberfeldwebel* Perrey, and the *Kapitän* of the *3. Staffel* was *Oberleutnant* Neumaier. We were now to learn everything a fighter pilot would later need to know in combat. In the beginning we mainly flew the Ar 96, and the demands on the students were raised from flight to flight. Combat flying at altitudes between 2,000 and 3,000 meters, simulated air combat, firing at practice targets, low flying, and formation landings were all part of our daily training. On 5 January 1944 I was familiarized with the Bf 108 *Taifun*. On 7 January I was familiarized with and made my first flight in Bf 109 E "White 16". Takeoff at 1504 hours, landing at 1508—the flight lasted just four minutes, but what a flight. It is unlikely that any pilot will ever forget this step from trainer to fighter aircraft.

By this time we had become familiar with the airfield, and everyone had developed his own routine, only now everything happened much quicker: the points in a circuit marked in one's memory weren't right any more, the prescribed circuit altitude was quickly surpassed, and on approach the landing cross came up quickly, only the machine was too high for a landing. During the first circuit in the Bf 109, many a pilot sweat blood and water until the wheels touched the ground and he had safely rolled to a stop. It was a tremendous readjustment, but with each flight more things became routine and confidence grew.

The training program continued quite intensively. Each pilot was required to determine the limits of maneuverability of his machine at an altitude of not less than 3,000 meters. This procedure included a steep climb until the aircraft stalled, followed by a spin, and the control inputs needed to recover from it. Other focal points of the training were: formation flying, combat maneuvers, high-altitude flying, dogfighting and gunnery. As a crowning conclusion, several flights were carried out in the Bf 109 F, and on 27 February 1944 our training with *Jagdfliegerschule 102* at Zerbst ended. To what degree each man felt himself to be a well-trained fighter pilot is an open question, but all that separated us from combat was the replacement training unit. My comrades quickly packed their things and headed off to the replacement training group. I alone stayed behind in Zerbst, a fighter pilot with no combat experience. This was meant as a sort of reward, but for me it was shattering news: I doubted that I would ever get to fly a combat mission. Of the men in my training group, I only ever saw one again.

At about the same time as our fighter training was going on at Zerbst, a *Gruppe* of the single-engine night-fighters (*Wilde Sau*) was also based there. The unit, *III./JG 301*, was stationed at Zerbst from the end of 1943 until the end of March 1944. At that time I had no idea that I would one day be a member of this *Jagdgeschwader* myself.

On 1 March 1944 I was assigned my own group of trainee fighter pilots. I wasn't terribly happy about this, for I myself had been a student at the same airfield only a few days ago. All of the students in my group were *Unteroffiziere*, which meant that we were all of the same rank: Lehrack, Gomschoreck, Harings, Prohaska, Zens, Lederer, Doornkat, Schliewinski and Haag. We started over again with the Ar 96: hazard briefings, circuits, and fighter area briefings.

Fourteen days later I was suddenly ordered to report to *Staffelkapitän Oberleutnant* Neumeyer, who informed me that I was being sent to Instrument Flying School 110 in Altenburg, Thuringia. Was I to join a *Geschwader* of the "*Wilde Sau*", about which I had heard? After all, I had achieved excellent results in all of my night fighter suitability evaluations. On 21 March I began training under *Feldwebel* Ziehlsdorf in an Ar 96, carrying out instrument flights. The training program at the instrument flying school was very concentrated, which meant that we flew both day and night. The main emphasis was on flying beam approaches, and this was practiced over and over again in a Siebel Si 204 twin-engine trainer. Toward the end of the course, however, we flew the Bf 109 G-6 exclusively, to become familiar with this fighter type. On 15 April 1944 we reached our training objective and were released to the units by the *Kommandeur, Hauptmann* Falderbaum, then German aerobatics champion. On arriving back at Zerbst I received orders to proceed to *Ergänzungsgruppe*

Ost (replacement training group east) in Weidengut, Silesia. As a rule this was a straight path to an operational unit – but not for me, for in my luggage there was a letter addressed to me that read:

"After passing through the replacement training group return to the unit in Zerbst." Would I ever be transferred to a front-line unit? Why did I always have to return to the fighter school?

When I reached the replacement training group in Weidengut I found that I had arrived a day late. The flying groups had already been selected, but as it turned out this was a stroke of luck for me. I and a *Leutnant* Jüngling, who had also arrived late, found ourselves standing in front of the commander of the replacement training group, *Hauptmann* Wienhausen. After briefly considering what to do, the *Kommandeur* said, "I would like to go flying too, therefore I will be your instructor."

In the course of a student pilot's training, from beginner to accomplished pilot, the flight instructor has many opportunities to pass on knowledge which will have a lasting effect on the quality of a pilot. I can claim that *Hauptmann* Wienhusen was my flying stepfather. He had gained a great deal of front-line experience with *Jagdgeschwader 5*, which was then based in the far north. With the *Kommandeur* as our instructor, there were always aircraft available, and we flew as if we were at the front. We were initiated into all the tricks and secrets of fighter piloting. After each flight he debriefed us in a comradely fashion. Anyone who had failed to keep up received a firm dressing down, but there were also words of praise for good flying. After one such debriefing *Hauptmann* Wienhusen brought up the letter I had brought with me from the fighter school, and I was given the opportunity to explain my miserable situation – no prospect of joining a combat unit. The *Kommandeur* showed much understanding for my case and promised to help me.

On completion of my training with Replacement Training Group East I returned to Zerbst with my evaluation – and, I believe, a supplementary letter. I received my first disappointment when I arrived: *III./JG 301*, which I had hoped to join, was no longer based on the airfield. The next disappointment followed quickly, for I discovered that I had to take a new flying group to Stolp-Reitz for training. Prior to the transfer I once again reported to *Oberleutnant* Neumeyer and asked to be transferred to a combat unit. At this point the supplementary letter was brought up. Although I never learned what was in the letter, I got the feeling that it was a frame-up: flight instructors were badly needed, and everyone had to do his duty wherever he was sent. In the end, however, *Oberleutnant* Neumeyer promised to agree to my transfer to a combat unit as soon as he found a replacement for me.

Flying at Stolp-Reitz began on 10 May 1944. The flying group was a large one, with ranks from *Obergefreiter* to *Feldwebel*. The students' names were: Tietze, Lemmer, Podzuweit, Scheibel, Seeger, Mahlow, Kordas, Hieke, Puls, Nickel, Spor, Kaufmann, Zimmer, Grieb, Scholz, Klün, Käufelin, Zimmermann, Zoepke, Sachse, Karl, Schulz and Kraftzyk. The size of the class made one thing clear: *Jagdfliegerschule 102* in Zerbst was running low on instructors. In a few days we completed 100 flights. That was necessary to prevent the students from being idle for too long. For a change, our flying activities were moved to Bronkow, twenty-five kilometers south of Lübbenau near the Spree Forest. At that airfield I was involved in a number of incidents during flying activities. On 25 May 1944, while on a maintenance test flight in a Bf 109 F, I struck a barrage balloon tether cable. The balloon, which had broken free, had been reported to us. Apart from a scrape on the left wingtip, I got away unscathed. A few days later, while on a fighter area familiarization with a student, the carburetor flap of the Ar 96 I was flying stuck open, and the student and I were forced to make a emergency belly landing in the Spreewald. As well, there was a ground loop while landing at the airfield in Bronkow, luckily without damage. I must admit that my nerves were rather shot at that time and that perhaps provided the "Old Man" with the impetus to keep his promise and transfer me to a combat unit. While I might not have wanted to leave *Jagdfliegerschule 102* in Zerbst that way, at least the door to a combat unit was now wide open.

On 13 June 1944 I reported to Replacement Training Group West in Gabbert, West Prussia. In just three days I carried out twenty-one flights and training sorties. On 18 June I was on a train with *Oberfähnriche* Kolbe and Aschendorf and *Unteroffizier* Peters and Kraatz, transfer order in my pocket. We were on our way to join *I./JG 302* at Götzendorf near Vienna.

Chapter One

Creation of the Single-Engined Night-Fighter Force

In the early summer of 1942 *Major* Hajo Herrmann, holder of the Knight's Cross and *Kommandeur* of *III./KG 30*, was transferred to "Group T" of the *Luftwaffe* operations staff. There he was confronted with the problems of equipment procurement for the bomber and fighter units and had access to armaments production plans, even those of the enemy. During the course of meetings with *Generalfeldmarschall* Milch, Inspector-General of the *Luftwaffe*, and leading figures in the air force and the armaments industry, *Major* Herrmann developed the idea of employing single-engined fighters in the night-fighter role.

Convinced that the concept was valid, Herrmann approached senior officers in the *Luftwaffe* command, but his proposals were received with extreme skepticism. There were some officers who, like *Major* Herrmann, realized that Germany's air defenses were on a shaky footing, and most of his support came from them. Most, however, held only medium level posts. What brought about the change in attitude was the situation of the German night-fighter arm. The existing *Nachtjagd-geschwader*, which were equipped with the Me 110 and 410 and the Ju 88 twin-engined night-fighters, were no longer able to cope with the growing weight of the RAF's night-bombing campaign. Formation of a single-engine night-fighter *Geschwader* would be something completely new in the history of the *Luftwaffe*: first, however, the idea's feasibility would have to be demonstrated.

At Staaken air base near Berlin, a fighter aircraft was made available to *Major* Herrmann for night trials. In April 1943 he flew his first live mission. Herrmann intercepted a Mosquito over Berlin and opened fire at the enemy machine, although he failed to shoot it down. This partial success brought Herrmann increased support from several quarters, for it was recognized that it might be possible to increase the effectiveness of the night-fighter arm.

The Wild Boar, emblem of the single-engined night-fighters. There were three "Wilde Sau" units, Jagdgeschwader 300, 301 and 302.

Night-Fighter Test Detachment

Generalmajor Galland, Inspector of Fighters, made available several more fighter aircraft. *Major* Herrmann was now able to begin selecting a number of pilots with experience in instrument flying for his experimental unit. They included:

Major von Buchwald	Vaerløse Gunnery School	—
Hauptmann Müller	*I./KG 50*	Instrument instructor
Hauptmann Janssen	*III./StG 2*	Stuka pilot
Oberfeldwebel Hofer	Brandenburg-Briest Flight Instructor School	Bomber pilot
Oberfeldwebel Löfgen	Brandenburg-Briest Flight Instructor School	Bomber pilot
Oberfeldwebel Künnecker	Brandenburg-Briest Flight Instructor School	Bomber pilot
Oberfeldwebel Wirth	Brandenburg-Briest Flight Instructor School	Bomber pilot
Feldwebel Müller	Vaerløse Gunnery School	Night-fighter pilot

It may be said that the Night-Fighter Test Detachment was born in the period from 20 to 22 April 1943. A logbook entry dated 22 April reads: short orientation flight with takeoff and landing at Brandenburg-Briest, aircraft type Bf 109 B.

In the weeks that followed, the pilots practiced night takeoffs and landings, although a few attempts were made to intercept Mosquito bombers at night, as on 14 and 17 May. These practice missions were extremely demanding for the former bomber pilots, as taking off and landing the fast fighter aircraft presented them with problems they had never encountered before. Cooperation with the flak was very important and was not always easy. The detachment also had to test new equipment, including an IFF set and a new instrument landing system for the FuG 16.

On 3 June 1943 the test detachment moved from Brandenburg-Briest to Mönchengladbach to continue its training. During this entire period *Major* Herrmann visited one flak commander after another, seeking concessions from them to facilitate his missions. Several obstacles had to be overcome in working with the anti-aircraft guns. On the evening of 3 June *Major* Herrmann drove from his office in Berlin to Staaken air base and from there took off to join the pilots of his test detachment in Mönchengladbach. He was more or less obliged to be present when the unit began operations: he wanted to prove to the skeptics that it was possible to fly night intercept missions in single-engined fighters without close control from the ground.

RAF Bomber Command, led by Air Marshal Harris, cooperated with *Major* Herrmann in a way that was most unpleasant for the civilian population: on the night of 3-4 July 1943 Harris launched his infamous 1,000-plane raid against the city of Cologne.

Oberst Hajo Herrmann was originally trained as a bomber pilot and later commanded III./KG 30. In May 1943 he began experimental sorties with single-engined night-fighters. On the night of 3-4 July he achieved his first Wild Boar kill. He formed JG 300 in July 1943 and was named commander of the 30. Jagddivision and Inspector of Night-Fighters. JG 301 and JG 302 were formed a short time later.

That same night, at 0027 hours, *Major* Herrmann and his night-fighter test detachment took off from Mönchengladbach. Under heavy anti-aircraft fire, the fighters made contact with British heavy bombers in the Cologne and Mühlheim areas. When the mission was over, twelve heavy bombers had been shot down.

So as not to overlook the flak, the victories were shared between the fighters and the anti-aircraft guns.

The first successful pilots of the single-engined night-fighter force were:

Oberleutnant Karl-Friedrich Müller	0128 hours	Halifax	Cologne
Major Hajo Herrmann	0130	Lancaster	near Mehlen
Feldwebel Hans Müller	0131	four-engined bomber	S of Cologne
Oberfeldwebel Hofer	0137	four-engined bomber	Cologne
Oberfeldwebel Lönnecker	0155	four-engined bomber	Cologne
Hauptmann Ewald Janssen	0205	four-engined bomber	Cologne

On this night *Feldwebel* Hans Müller took off from Mönchengladbach at 0027 hours flying a Fw 190 A-4 bearing the code RP+IK. He landed at the same airfield at 0224 hours.

This mission also resulted in the first casualty for the single-engined night-fighters: after shooting down an enemy bomber, *Oberfeldwebel* Hofer crashed and was killed. The exact cause of the crash is not known. On the very next day *Major* Herrmann received verbal orders from the *Luftwaffe* High Command to form a single-engined night-fighter *Geschwader* with himself as *Kommodore*.

Jagdgeschwader "z.b.V. Herrmann" (Special Purpose Fighter Wing Herrmann)

The following entry appears in the war diary of *Luftgaukommando VII* in the monthly report for August 1943: "*Luftwaffe* Commander Center has ordered the formation of the Herrmann *Geschwader*, code name 'Wild Boar', effective 13 July 1943. By order of the *Luftwaffe* Commander Center, as part of the ground organizations needed to carry out this operation *Luftgaukommando VII* is to set up a command post with the code name '*Kniebis*'. The Special Purpose Fighter Wing Herrmann is in the process of being established with three *Gruppen*, with 'Herrmann' providing a cadre of personnel."

Something was happening in the affected command positions. Where there had been doubt and skepticism, now there was feverish activity. Directives and orders were issued in rapid succession to the affected departments, as if they had always been in favor of the "single-engined night-fighter" project.

An enormous amount of work had to be done at the beginning of the formation of the first single-engined night-fighter *Geschwader*, and if personality wasn't enough, one just had to bypass the chain of command. The greatest challenges were faced by the signals, technical and maintenance sectors. If possible, the pilots were to have a Class I or II Instrument Flight Certificate. This requirement essentially eliminated the pure fighter pilot. Most of the aircrew were therefore instructors or pilots from bomber, reconnaissance and transport units. This had the advantage of obviating the need for time-consuming instrument training and the pilots only had to be given conversion training on fighter aircraft. The disadvantage, however, was that the pilots, who lacked specialized fighter training, initially had difficulties with night takeoffs and landings. Losses during this conversion period were correspondingly high. The lack of specialized fighter training had even more drastic consequences during later daylight operations.

With the necessary pilots in place, the *Geschwader* also needed aircraft. This created serious difficulties in the early weeks as the *Luftwaffe*'s plans at that time did not include the formation of new *Geschwader*. Once again it was *Major* Herrmann who came up with a workable solution.

The *Gruppen* were transferred to bases housing day fighter units. These "piggyback" *Gruppen* used the day fighter units' machines for night sorties. It was – at least within the Defense of the Reich – the optimal utilization of existing materiel: two pilots fighting with one aircraft, one by day the other by night.

This system also had serious drawbacks, however, in particular with regard to servicing the aircraft. The question soon arose: should one mechanic be responsible for both pilots or should each pilot have his own mechanic, and if so, which should bear the main responsibility? Another problem was the equipment: wear and tear was doubled, and the number of hours between engine overhauls was reduced. There was also the question of who should be responsible for supplying spares and replacement aircraft, the day or night fighter arms. The sharing of aircraft could only be an interim solution, and there were frequent reminders that every coin has two sides.

The difficulties were mastered in spite of everything, and after a certain time the "piggyback" *Gruppen* became a thing of the past. By the beginning of 1944 each of the "*Wilde Sau*" fighter *Gruppen* had its own aircraft. The airfields at Lechfeld, Leipheim, Munich-Riem, Neuburg an der Donau, Schwäbisch Hall, Echterdingen, Fürstenfeldbruck, Bad Aibling and Ingolstadt, all within the area of *Luftgaukommando VII*, were developed into bases for the single-engined night-fighters with facilities for night operations.

Reserves of aircraft cannon were established for the "*Wilde Sau*" units at the fighter bases. By order of the *Luftwaffe* Commander Center a weather station was added to the staff of *Luftgaukommando VII* to provide weather information to the single-engined night-fighters.

24-25 July 1943

On this night the British attacked Hamburg, for the first time employing aluminum foil strips to jam German radars. The entire control system for flak and fighters was put out of action and the raid turned into a disaster for the defenses. Operating without ground control, the night-fighters managed to bring down nine enemy bombers, the anti-aircraft guns three.

The various offices of the *Luftwaffe* began clamoring for the fighters of the "*Wilde Sau*". Directions were even issued to the twin-engined night-fighter units to adopt the methods of the Wild Boars when the ground-based radars were put out of action.

The *Luftwaffe* command's hopes of a more effective defense against the enemy bombers operating by night now rested on *Major* Herrmann and his *Geschwader*. Even if the initial results were modest, the main thing was that something positive could be reported to the high command.

29-30 July 1943

On this night the British bombers again attacked Hamburg. The aircraft of *Jagdgeschwader "Herrmann"*, still in the formation process, shot down three enemy aircraft:

Unteroffizier Brinkmann	*7. Staffel*	0055 hr	heavy	Hamburg
Unteroffizier Brinkmann	*7. Staffel*	0057	heavy	Hamburg
Major von Buchwald	*III. Gruppe*	0110	heavy	Hamburg

In spite of this modest success, *Major* Herrmann was ordered by the *Luftwaffe* to immediately establish another single-engined night-fighter *Geschwader*. At the same time, *Jagdgeschwader* *"Herrmann"* was renamed *JG 300* *"Wilde Sau"*. All subsequent single-engined night-fighter *Geschwader* were given numbers in the 300s.

Chapter Two

Formation of
Jagdgeschwader 301 and *302*
"Wilde Sau"

Jagdgeschwader 301 "Wilde Sau"

The *Stab* of *JG 301* first appears in an extract from *Luftwaffe* operations staff situation maps dated 19 October 1943. The *Geschwader* was established in the area of the *30. Jagddivision* in Neubiberg.

The *Geschwader*'s first *Kommodore* was *Major* Helmut Weinreich, an experienced bomber pilot who had been decorated with the Knight's Cross. The *Geschwader* headquarters remained at Neubiberg for only a short time, soon moving to Frankfurt-Rhein/Main.

The *I./JG 301* was formed at Gardelegen in Sachsen-Anhalt, but soon afterward if transferred to Neubiberg in the area of the *30. Jagddivision*. *Hauptmann* Richard Kamp was placed in command of the *Gruppe*. Initially a "piggyback *Gruppe*", it shared aircraft with *JG 1* and *JG 11*.

The *II./JG 301* was established at about the same time at Altenburg, with personnel from the *10./JG 4*. The first *Gruppenkommandeur* was *Hauptmann* Count Resugier. At the beginning of November 1943 this *Gruppe* was renamed *II./JG 302*. *II./JG 301* was not reformed until the end of 1943, at Seyring near Vienna.

The *III./JG 301* was formed at Zerbst at the end of October 1943. The unit's first commander was *Hauptmann* Manfred Mössinger. Like so many of the pilots assigned to *JG 301*, Mössinger was not a fighter pilot, having previously served as a Stuka pilot.

JG 301's pilots were as varied a group as those of *JG 300*. They came from every branch of the *Luftwaffe*, although flight instructors and bomber pilots were particularly well represented. Some of the pilots came from *JG 300* and already had some experience in single-engined night-fighters – several had already scored victories. One such pilot was *Feldwebel* Hans Müller, who had been part of *Major* Herrmann's night-fighter test detachment. The percentage of trained fighter pilots was also higher, for in the intervening time many of the fighter pilots transferred to the *"Wilde Sau"* had been sent to *Blindflugschule 110* in Altenburg, earning their Class III instrument ratings.

*The Geschwader emblem of JG 301. This emblem appeared on only
a few of the Geschwader's aircraft at the time of its formation.*

Jagdgeschwader 302 "Wilde Sau"

JG 302, the last of the three *Geschwader* earmarked for the single-engined night-fighter role, was established in November 1943 with the formation of the *Geschwaderstab* (wing headquarters) at Stade. The headquarters later transferred to Berlin-Döberitz. The *Geschwader* was commanded by former Stuka pilot *Oberstleutnant* Manfred Mössinger, most recently *Kommandeur* of *III./JG 301* and for a short time *Kommodore* of *JG 301*.

I./JG 302 was established at Jüterbog by renaming *I./JG 301*. The unit's first *Gruppenkommandeur* was *Hauptmann* Richard Lewens.

The *Staffelkapitäne* were: *1. Staffel Oberleutnant* Herbert Petersen, *2. Staffel Hauptmann* Karl-Heinz Dietsche and *3. Staffel Oberleutnant* Heinz Seidel.

II./JG 302 was established at Ludwigslust by renaming *II./JG 301*. *Gruppenkommandeur* was *Major* Treumund Engelhard.

The *Staffelkapitäne* were: *4. Staffel Oberleutnant* Hans Gottuck, *5. Staffel Oberleutnant* Karl-Heinz Seeler and *6. Staffel Hauptmann* Friedhelm Höschen.

III./JG 302 was formed at Oldenburg by renaming the *III./JG 300*; *Gruppenkommandeur* was *Major* Ewald Janssen.

The *Staffelkapitäne* were: *7. Staffel Oberleutnant* Hans Uhse, *8. Staffel Oberleutnant* Friedrich Leimkühler and *9. Staffel Oberleutnant* Helmut Schlechter.

Initially a "piggyback *Gruppe*", it flew the aircraft of *I./JG 11* and *III./JG 11*. These machines were used both as day and night fighters. The ratio of trained and untrained pilots was brought into rough balance through the incorporation of units of *JG 300* and *JG 301* into *JG 302*. Pilots from bomber or transport units were increasingly becoming the minority. The initial mission of all three *Geschwader* was to combat the growing night attacks by British bombers against Germany cities and industrial facilities as part of the "*Wilde Sau*" single-engined night-fighter force.

Oldenburg, autumn 1943: Oberstleutnant Ihlefeld in conversation with officers of I./JG 302. In the foreground is Oberleutnant Herbert Petersen, Staffelkapitän of 1./JG 302.

Operations by the "*Wilde Sau*" *Geschwader* did not follow the "*Himmelbett*" method previously used by the twin-engined night-fighters. The RAF had introduced a new navigation aid, the H2S blind-bombing radar, which made it possible for the bombers to locate their targets at night. *Major* Herrmann responded by proposing a completely new defensive tactic. Instead of the blackout regulations, which were now completely useless, he proposed that German cities be illuminated and generously equipped with searchlights.

The bombers were often held in cones of searchlights for minutes at a time or were silhouetted against the brightly-lit background, making them visible to the night-fighters. Under such conditions close control from the ground would not be necessary.

Nothing in the *Luftwaffe*'s previous experience could indicate if and how the tactic could be employed successfully. It was a daring idea, and the near future would prove whether and to which extent it was correct.

Chapter Three

Jagdgeschwader 301 and *302* in Action

The first confirmed action by *Jagdgeschwader 301* took place during the night of 31 August-1 September 1943, when the *I. Gruppe* intercepted RAF bombers attacking Berlin. It is probable that the "Old Hares" flew this first mission, for at least one victory is known. *Feldwebel* Hans Müller of *2. Staffel* took off from Gardelegen at 2339 hours and at 0058 shot down a Lancaster near Berlin. When the mission was over he landed at Stendal at 0159 hours. His aircraft was "White 4", a Bf 109 G-4.

Feldwebel Hans Müller was one of those who had initiated his own transfer to *I./JG 301* after having differences with his *Staffelkapitän*. In the latter's absence he had himself transferred from one *Geschwader* to the other with the aid of the operations officer.

Training for night operations by the *Geschwader* was still in full swing. Every available aircraft was flown in all weather to bring the pilots and ground crews up to the required standard. Sweaty palms were standard during night takeoffs and landings, both difficult undertakings. The speed of the single-engined fighters during takeoff and landing caused problems for many pilots. Crash-landings were not uncommon, sometimes with fatal consequences.

3-4 September 1943

I./JG 301 took off to intercept British bombers which attacked Berlin at about midnight. There is no information on possible victories. While returning to base, *Feldwebel* Hans Müller ran low on fuel and was forced to divert to Werneuchen, landing there at 0203 hours. The ground was soft and the machine overturned. Müller was injured and his aircraft (Bf 109 G-4 "White 4", *Werknummer* 15 615) sustained 35% damage.

5-6 September 1943

On this night British bombers attacked Mannheim. *JG 300* and *JG 301* put up fifty-nine aircraft and three enemy bombers were shot down. These downings were confirmed as victories by the "*Wilde*

The Gruppe emblems of I./JG 302 and III./JG 301 were initially only applied on the engine cowlings of the units' aircraft.

Sau" in the war diary of *Luftgaukommando VII*. The bombers crashed near Bachenau, fifteen kilometers north of Heilbronn, near Huttenheim, twelve kilometers northwest of Bruchsal, and near Heidelberg.

The raid on Munich on the night of 6-7 September 1943 was a typical example of the problems in cooperating with the flak. Flak-free zones had been precisely laid down, with specific times and heights.

From 0025 hours above 7000 m,
from 0030 hours above 5000 m,
from 0035 hours above 3000 m,
from 0044 hours total firing ban,
from 0125 hours above 3000 m.

The anti-aircraft searchlights illuminated the cloud cover (8/10 overcast), creating an effect that the night-fighter pilots called the "Shroud". Above this "shroud" the silhouettes of the enemy bombers were plainly visible to the fighter pilots. An examination of the individual times shows that the flak commanders had passed on the positions of "*Wilde Sau*" fighters to their batteries as soon as they received them. Nevertheless, there were pilots who ignored everything and lived up to the title of "Wild Boar". In many instances, too, the flak continued firing in spite of the restrictions, seriously jeopardizing the pilots' safety.

20-21 September 1943

British bombers attacked the Reich capital in a raid that lasted from 0318 to 0415 hours. Berlin was already being bombed, but *I./JG 301* at Gardelegen had still not received operational orders. Not until about 0340 hours, much too late, did the *Gruppe* take off. It is impossible to tell from surviving records whether contact was made with the enemy. It is also not known if enemy action played a part in the *Gruppe's* losses.

The *2. Staffel* reported that *Leutnant* Hans Kirsch had encountered problems with the engine of his Bf 109. The engine failed while he was attempting an emergency landing at Brandenburg-Briest and the aircraft came down in a wood. The pilot survived the crash with a femoral fracture.

Feldwebel Richard Meyer was killed when he crashed near Neubrandenburg for reasons unknown. A subsequent investigation into the cause of the crash failed to turn up anything.

Feldwebel Hans Müller landed back at Gardelegen ten minutes after taking off. Once again mechanical trouble was the cause.

22-23 September 1943

All three *Gruppen* of the newly-formed *Jagdgeschwader 301* were committed against a force of RAF bombers that attacked Hanover on this night. The *Gruppen* took off from their airfields at Gardelegen, Altenburg and Zerbst. The area of operations extended from Hanover to the North Sea. It was the first large-scale night mission by the *Geschwader* and its most successful to date. Eleven victories were claimed – a considerable success for the single-engined night-fighter force, one that underlined the correctness of its tactics.

Feldwebel Erich Teubner of *8./JG 301* reported shooting down a Lancaster west of Hanover at 2226 hours. At 2230 he claimed a second Lancaster fifty kilometers northwest of the city.

Feldwebel Anton Benning of *2./JG 301* shot down one Lancaster twenty kilometers southeast of Bremen at 2229 hours and a second northeast of Verden at 2235.

Oberfeldwebel Heinz Gossow of *1./JG 301* shot down a Lancaster south of Bremen at 2230 hours. It was his first night victory. After 340 missions as a bomber pilot he had now passed his baptism of fire as a member of the *"Wilde Sau"* night-fighters.

Oberfeldwebel Fleischmann of *7./JG 301* shot down a four-engined bomber west of Hanover at 2230 hours and a Mosquito near Oldenburg at 2400.

Oberfeldwebel Arthur Gross of *2./JG 301* sent a Lancaster to the ground northeast of Hanover at 2254 hours, while *Feldwebel* Herbert Chantelau of *3./JG 301* claimed a Lancaster shot down northwest of Hanover at 2303.

Oberfeldwebel Kurt Welter of *5./JG 301* shot down two four-engined bombers, at 2304 and 2312 hours.

JG 301 also suffered its first combat losses during this operation: its first large-scale night action cost the *Geschwader* four pilots killed and two wounded.

Feldwebel Wilhelm Marten of *6./JG 301* was shot down by enemy fire west of Neuharlingersiel (Fw 190 A-4, WNr. 142 347, aircraft of *I./JG 11*).

Unteroffizier Gerhard Zirrgiebel of *4./JG 301* was killed when his aircraft crashed south of Husum (Fw 190 A-5, WNr. 410 273, aircraft of *I./JG 11*). *Unteroffizier* Herbert Kreuchen of *5./JG 301* also died in a crash south of Husum (Fw 190 A-6, WNr. 470 04?, aircraft of *I./JG 11*).

Oberfeldwebel Adolf Wiedermann of *7./JG 301* lost his life in air combat over Hanover while flying a Bf 109 G-6.

Oberfeldwebel Xaver Neumeier of the *1. Staffel* tried to close with an enemy aircraft through anti-aircraft fire. His aircraft was hit by an anti-aircraft shell but he was able to parachute to safety.

Over Verden an der Aller *Unteroffizier* Werner Dienst of *3./JG 301* collided with an unidentified aircraft and crashed. Dienst bailed out but was injured in the process.

23-24 September 1943

I./JG 301 at least must have been in action on this night, for there is a report that *Leutnant* Gerd Bernhard rammed a Lancaster. The location of the incident is not given in the report. There is no loss report for this action.

24-25 September 1943

Shortly before midnight elements of *I./JG 301* took off from Gardelegen to intercept Mosquitos, but as far as is known there were no claims or losses. A total of seventy-five *"Wilde Sau"* aircraft were active that night, however the records do not reveal whether or not they achieved any successes.

27-28 September 1943

The main target of the British bombers on this night was Hanover. All three *Gruppen* of *JG 301* saw action, a fact confirmed by victory and loss reports.

Feldwebel Herbert Herre of *1./JG 302* shot down a British bomber over Grosspeisen at 2303 hours, then at 2306 he claimed a Stirling shot down south of Hanover.

Oberfeldwebel Karl-Heinz Seeler of the *1. Staffel* brought down a Halifax over Geidingen at 2307 hours.

At 2308 hours *Feldwebel* Andreas Hartl of the *6. Staffel* shot down a British bomber west of Hanover, followed by a second at 2324.

Oberleutnant Sauter of the *Stab* of *II./JG 301* claimed a Lancaster shot down at 2323 hours.

Losses suffered that night were:

Feldwebel Heinz Radloff of *1. Staffel* crashed to his death while in action over the Leister district of Hanover.

Feldwebel Alfred Riediger of the *6. Staffel* was hit by return fire while attacking an enemy bomber. He was killed when his aircraft went down near Schneeren in the Wunstorf district. (Fw 190 A-4 "Yellow 4", WNr. 140 607, aircraft of *I./JG 11*)

Oberleutnant Josef Schür of *III./JG 301* was wounded in action near Celle. He had taken off from Zerbst in his Bf 109 G-6. There is no information as to where and how machine and pilot returned to the ground.

A regrouping took place within the *"Wilde Sau"* units during the period from the beginning of October until early November 1943. The reason behind this is not known, but it was probably associated with the formation of new *Gruppen* within the three single-engined night-fighter *Geschwader*.

At the beginning of November 1943, *I./JG 301*, then based at Jüterbog-Damm, was renamed *I./ JG 302*. At almost the same time, a new *I./JG 301* was established at Gardelegen.

II./JG 301, which was then at Ludwigslust, was renamed *II./JG 302*. The second formation of *II./JG 301* followed at Zerbst in early 1944.

III./JG 301, at that time stationed at Wiesbaden-Erbenheim, was renamed *III./JG 300*. *III./JG 301* was reformed at Zerbst in early 1944.

This shuffling of units within the *Geschwader* was later repeated. The exact reason for this has never become clear, which of course makes it more difficult to accurately follow and keep separate the histories of these *Jagdgeschwader*. A clear line is difficult to find in the period from October to November 1943, especially since the names of pilots suddenly appear in different *Staffeln* and *Gruppen*. In chronicling these units the researcher finds numerous cases of overlapping information during this period, a situation that is now almost impossible to sort out. On the other hand, it is possible to determine when the "piggyback" arrangement came to an end for the various units. *JG 301* shared aircraft with *JG 11* until the end of October 1943, after which it had its own machines. The *Geschwader* was initially equipped with the Bf 109 G-6, while the *Stab* only flew the Fw 190 A-7 at the beginning. At the end of December 1943, however, *II./JG 301* again became a "piggyback" *Gruppe*, sharing aircraft with *II./JG 53*. When the unit was reformed at Seyring in early 1944 it shared aircraft with *III./JG 27*.

The final weeks of 1943 saw the establishment of *JG 302*, the third and last single-engined night-fighter *Geschwader*. Although some sources state that the *Geschwader* was formed at the beginning of November 1943, this may in fact have taken place several weeks earlier. Proof of this may be found in the records of "*Wilde Sau*" missions in October 1943, in which pilots of *JG 302* took part. *JG 302* operated as a "piggyback" *Gruppe* until the end of December 1943, using aircraft of *JG 1* and *JG 11*, after which it was equipped with its own Bf 109 G-6 fighters.

3-4 October 1943

Records reveal that *II./JG 301* and *I./JG 302* took part in the defensive effort against British bombers which attacked Kassel on this night.

Oberfeldwebel Kurt Welter of *5./JG 301* claimed two more enemy bombers for his 3rd and 4th victories. He shot down two Halifaxes over Hesse at 2229 and 2241 hours.

Oberfeldwebel Kurt Emler of the *1. Staffel* claimed a Short Stirling shot down northwest of Hanover at 2204 hours, proving *JG 302*'s participation on this night.

JG 301 also formed part of the defense when the British attacked Mannheim on the night of 4-5 October 1943. Just one claim was made, a Short Stirling shot down by the *Kapitän* of the *7. Staffel*, *Hauptmann* Helmut Suhr, at 2243 hours.

8-9 October 1943

It is likely that only the *II. Gruppe* of *JG 301* saw any action on this night, although its area of operations is not known.

Leutnant Kummer of the *Stab* of *II./JG 301* reported shooting down a Lancaster at 0124 hours. *Oberleutnant* Karl-Heinz Seeler, also of the *II. Gruppe*, shot down a Halifax at 0127.

I./JG 302 reported that *Oberfeldwebel* Kurt Emler had shot down two Short Stirlings on this night. The two enemy bombers were shot down near the "Marie" radio beacon at 0117 and 0132 hours, and were Emler's second and third night victories.

Two engine mechanics of I./JG 302. The accomplishments of these men, the technicians and ground crews, cannot be overestimated.

On 13 October 1943 the aircraft flown by *Oberleutnant* Friedrich Amsink of *Stab/JG 301* overturned while landing at Munich-Riem, sustaining 40% damage. Amsink was injured in the accident. (Fw 190 A-6, WNr. 539 354, aircraft of *I./JG 11*)

The war diary of *Luftgaukommando VII* contains the following entry under 13 October 1943: "*9./JG 301* transferred from Altenburg to Bad Wörishofen".

18-19 October 1943

Two victories were claimed by *I.* and *II./JG 301* in a mission against British bombers attacking targets inside the Reich. *Hauptmann* Hans Gottuck of the *Stab* of *II./JG 301* shot down a four-engined bomber at 2024 hours.

Fahnenjunker-Oberfeldwebel Fritz Yung of the *1. Staffel* shot down his first enemy aircraft, a Lancaster, at 2243 hours.

19 October 1943

Hauptmann Richard Kamp, *Kommandeur* of *I./JG 301*, took off from Gardelegen for a radio test flight. On landing, his aircraft veered off course and overturned. Kamp survived, suffering a minor concussion and several contusions (Bf 109 G-6, WNr. 200 274).

I./JG 301's adjutant, *Leutnant* Benno Rehfeld, didn't lag behind his commanding officer in anything. Ordered to fly a number of circuits, he also encountered problems on landing: his aircraft

Feldwebel Heinz Hürdler of 1./JG 301 in September 1943 in front of the barracks in Gardelegen. He was killed in action near Breslau on 20 October 1943.

veered sharply and flipped over. Rehfeld was pulled from the machine with an injured shoulder (Bf 109 G-6, WNr. 188 818).

20-21 October 1943

RAF bombers attacked Leipzig in the early hours of the evening. Seven aircraft of *I./JG 301* took off from Gardelegen at 1950 hours. Only three returned. *Unteroffizier* Rudi Fischer of the *1. Staffel* was killed in action northwest of Gardelegen.

Feldwebel Heinz Hürdler of the *1. Staffel* did not return from this mission. Records indicate that he was lost near Breslau.

Leutnant Ludwig Wißgens of the *2. Staffel* went down with his Bf 109 near Peckfitz west of Gardelegen.

Unteroffizier Kurt Gross of the *3. Staffel* was killed in action near Solpke west of Gardelegen.

When the mission was over, *Feldwebel* Hans Müller of the *2. Staffel* landed at Zerbst. He returned to Gardelegen on the morning of the following day.

The Defense of the Reich claimed just ten enemy aircraft shot down on this night, another very unsatisfactory result. There are few victories by the single-engined night-fighters to report at this time. Most reports concerned losses, which were quite high on occasion. In the majority of cases it was impossible to determine the cause of a loss with certainty. As the "*Wilde Sau*" night-fighters were lone warriors, witnesses to victories were extremely rare.

22-23 October 1943

The RAF's targets on this night were the cities of Kassel and Frankfurt/Main. This time the night-fighter controllers succeeded in guiding the defending units to the bomber stream as the raid was beginning. This is reflected in the number of enemy aircraft shot down: the RAF lost forty-two bombers over Germany on this night. *JG 301* and *JG 302* both took part in this night action. An evaluation of claims suggests that the "*Wilde Sau*" units achieved their first significant success on this night. Cooperation between the pilots and the control center was improving daily, and the "*Wilde Sau*" pilots were becoming more comfortable in the night sky. *I./JG 301* took off from Gardelegen at 1940 hours and made contact with enemy bombers near Frankfurt and Kassel.

Fahnenjunker-Oberfeldwebel Fritz Yung of the *1. Staffel* shot down two enemy bombers between Kassel and Frankfurt in the space of barely fifteen minutes, at 2059 and 2112 hours.

Unteroffizier Gerhard Witt of the *2. Staffel* was also successful, shooting down a British bomber that crashed at 2114 hours.

Another bomber was downed by *Fahnenjunker-Feldwebel* Emanuel of the *1. Staffel*.

The most successful pilot on this night, however, was *Oberfeldwebel* Kurt Welter of the *5. Staffel*, who destroyed three four-engined bombers within the space of just twenty minutes, at 2104, 2114 and 2124 hours.

JG 301 did not escape without loss, however. *Feldwebel* Kurt Degenkolb of the *7. Staffel* lost his life in combat east of Kassel. He and his machine came down near Lutherberg, crashing beside a bridge on the Kassel to Hanover autobahn.

The loss of *Feldwebel* Horst Neumann of the *8. Staffel* was particularly tragic. He and his Bf 109 crashed within the city of Göttingen, landing in the Nikoleistrasse. Nothing is known of civilian casualties. *JG 302*'s participation in this action is confirmed by the success of *Oberfeldwebel* Paul Streuff of the *1. Staffel*, who claimed a Halifax shot down north of Kassel at 2102 hours.

Oberleutnant Josef Wolfsberger of the *5. Staffel* destroyed a Lancaster over Kassel at 2106 hours. *Oberfeldwebel* Ernst Haase of the *1. Staffel* shot down a Lancaster over Kassel at the same time. His aircraft was later hit by flak and crashed near Fritzlar. Haase parachuted to safety. (Bf 109 G-5, WNr. 15 965, aircraft of *III./JG 1*)

The following note appears in the war diary of *Luftgaukommando VII* under November 1943: "12 November, *8.* and *9./JG 301* are transferring from Wörishofen to Wiesbaden. 19 November, *8.* and *9./JG 301* have moved from Wörishofen to Wiesbaden. *3./JG 301* is moving from Gardelegen to Wörishofen."

These entries show how often the various *Staffeln* and *Gruppen* were moved from one airfield to another at the very time of their formation. They also confirm the suspicion that changes took place in the very first weeks of existence of these *Jagdgruppen*.

III./JG 301 moved to Rhein-Main and saw increasing action against the British night bombers. Most aircraft, like this Bf 109 G-6, were fitted with flame dampers. They also frequently carried additional armament in the form of two 20mm cannon mounted beneath the wings.

18-19 November 1943

For the first time in the bombing war against Germany, the British launched major raids against two German cities in one night. Air Marshal Harris sent 325 bombers to attack Mannheim and 402 against Berlin. The raid on Berlin was also the beginning of a series of raids intended to level the German capital and force Germany to its knees.

The night-fighter units committed against the raids succeeded in shooting down nine "*Viermots*" (four-engined bombers) over Berlin and twenty-five in the Mannheim area. Records indicate that the *Stab* and two *Gruppen* of *JG 301* took part in the defensive effort.

The *Geschwaderkommodore*, *Major* Helmut Weinreich, led his *Geschwader* into action on this night. At 2035 hours he shot down an enemy bomber, but his own machine was seriously damaged by return fire. Weinreich tried to nurse the damaged aircraft back to Rhein-Main airfield, but shortly before landing the engine exploded. The Focke-Wulf (Fw 190 A-5, WNr. 151 482) crashed near Szeppelinheim, at the south edge of the airfield, and Weinreich was killed.

Helmut Weinreich was born in Lenzen, near Elbing in East Prussia. He flew 320 combat missions as an *Oberleutnant* and *Staffelkapitän* in *III./KG 30* and was awarded the Knight's Cross on 22 January 1943. In the summer of 1943 he retrained on single-engined fighters and on 1 September assumed command of *Jagdgeschwader 301*. He was promoted to the rank of *Oberstleutnant* posthumously.

Fahnenjunker-Oberfeldwebel Yung of the *1. Staffel* was also successful on this night, shooting down a Lancaster for his fourth victory.

Oberfeldwebel Anton Benning of the *2. Staffel* shot down a Lancaster for his third victory.

The *7. Staffel* lost two pilots in this action. *Leutnant* Arno Schmidt crashed to his death near Lachen-Speyerdorf.

Leutnant Rolf Nedden was killed in action near Fischbach, west of Kaiserslautern.

After the death of *Major* Helmut Weinreich, *Major* Mössinger of *III./JG 301* was named the new *Geschwaderkommodore*. *Major* Siegfried Wagner assumed command of *II./JG 301*. In December 1943 *III./JG 301*, which was based at Wiesbaden-Erbenheim, transferred to Rhein-Main and in January 1944 to Zerbst.

22-23 November 1943

Nothing is known of *JG 301*'s activities on this night. *I./JG 302* did see action, however, and reported shooting down four enemy bombers.

Hauptmann Karl-Heinz Dietsche, *Staffelkapitän* of *2./JG 302*, shot down a British bomber at 2114 hours.

Hauptmann Heinrich Wurzer, *Staffelkapitän* of *1./JG 302*, claimed to have shot down a Lancaster.

Oberfeldwebel Kurt Emler of *1./JG 302* shot down two enemy aircraft in one night.

25 November 1943

Oberstleutnant Helmut Weinrich, the *Kommodore* of *Jagdgeschwader 301* who had been killed in action on 18 November 1943, was buried in Munich's Waldfriedhof.

Funeral procession for the Geschwaderkommodore of JG 301, Major Helmut Weinreich, in the Munich cemetery.

Oberleutnant Ernst Holtschmitt carries the decorations pillow. The honor company presents arms as the gun carriage bearing the coffin arrives at the gravesite.

25-26 November 1943

On this night British bombers attacked Frankfurt am Main. Twelve were shot down.

JG 301 and *JG 302* were among the units committed against the intruders. No victories by either unit are indicating in the surviving records. Losses, on the other hand, were very heavy, with seven pilots killed and two wounded.

Unteroffizier August Deumlich of *1./JG 301* was killed in an unexplained crash 4 km east of Gardelegen airbase (Bf 109 G-6, WNr. 410 224).

Feldwebel Erwin Seifert of *3./JG 301* crashed near Krückeberg after air combat.

III./JG 301 made contact with the enemy over Spessart and Odenwald, either bombers or long-range night-fighters escorting the RAF bombers. This encounter cost three pilots their lives.

Feldwebel Heinrich Schwarz of the *7. Staffel* crashed near Hessenthal.

Unteroffizier Ullrich Braun of the *8. Staffel* was hit in air combat and crashed near Spessart.

Unteroffizier Ernst Krieg, also of the *8. Staffel*, was shot down over the Odenwald near Kreidach.

JG 302 also suffered casualties.

Oberleutnant Hans Gottuck, *Kapitän* of the *4. Staffel*, was hit by enemy fire. He abandoned his doomed machine, striking his head on the stabilizer in the process (Fw 190 A-5, WNr. 180 925).

Unteroffizier Heinz Kotthaus of the *7. Staffel* was killed when his machine crashed near Wehnen/Oldenburg shortly after takeoff. The cause of the crash is not known.

Fellow *Staffel* member *Gefreiter* Hans Derksen suffered the same fate. He also lost his life soon after taking off from Oldenburg. It is not known if the two crashes were related.

Oberleutnant Friedhelm Leimkühler, *Staffelkapitän* of *8./JG 302*, was hit by flak at an altitude of about 4000 meters. His machine was still partially controllable and Leimkühler decided to risk a forced landing at a nearby airfield. He crash-landed at Dutztal, sustaining injuries in the process.

26-27 November 1943

A force of 407 bombers attacked the Reich capital in a raid that lasted from 2050 to 2230 hours. It is impossible to tell with certainty where and in what strength the two *Geschwader* saw action.

It is known, however, that *Oberfeldwebel* Ernst Haase of *1./JG 302* shot down a Lancaster at 2056 hours.

28 November 1943

Elements of *I./JG 301* transferred from Gardelegen to Munich-Riem with stops at Altenburg in Thuringia and Ingolstadt.

Chapter Four

A Change in Command
in Both *Jagdgeschwader*

As related previously, *Major* Manfred Mössinger assumed command of *Jagdgeschwader 301* after the death of *Major* Helmut Weinreich on 18 November 1943. *Major* Mössinger had been *Gruppenkommandeur* of *III./JG 301* with *Hauptmann* Otto-Ernst Hocker as adjutant. *Major* Mössinger was to command *Jagdgeschwader 301* for just a short time before taking over as *Geschwaderkommodore* of *JG 302*.

JG 301's next *Kommodore* was *Major* Ewald Janssen. Born on 11 October 1913 in Rüstingen near Oldenburg, in 1935 he trained as a Stuka pilot. Janssen gained his first operational experience with the Legion Condor in Spain and later fought in the campaigns in Poland and Western Europe. On the Eastern Front Janssen served as a *Staffelkapitän* in the *II./SG 1* and *III./StG 2* and in March 1943 was made *Kommandeur* of *II./StG 2*. A few months later he was transferred to the Defense of the Reich, retrained on single-engined night-fighters and on 13 June 1943 assumed command of *I./ JG 300*.

From the war diary of *Luftgaukommando VII*:

"1 December 1943, *Jagdgeschwader 301* established its command post in Munich-Oberföhring. 12 December 1943, *Stab/JG 301* at Munich-Oberföhring, *3./JG 301* at Wörishofen."

2-3 December 1943

During the night a force of about 400 British bombers attacked Berlin, dropping 1,886 tons of bombs on the city. Alerted in good time, the night-fighter command was able to place its units in favorable positions from which to attack. It is impossible to say to what extent *JG 301* took part in this action, but *III./JG 301* reported the loss of *Feldwebel* Gerhard Wieck of the 8. *Staffel*, who crashed near Hennef/Sieg.

According to reports, the *I.* and *II. Gruppe* of *JG 302* flew a successful mission, claiming the following victories:

Pilot	Unit	Time	Type	Location	Victory No.
Feldwebel Andreas Hartl	6./JG 302	2020	Heavy	Berlin	3
Oberfeldwebel Ernst Haase	1./JG 302	2026	Lancaster	E of Berlin	3
Feldwebel Kurt Becker	5./JG 302	2034	Heavy	Berlin	1
Feldwebel Andreas Hartl	6./JG 302	2038	Heavy	Berlin	4
Feldwebel Herbert Herre	1./JG 302	2039	Heavy	Berlin	1
Leutnant Erich Schölta	2./JG 302	2043	Stirling	NW Berlin	1
Oberfeldwebel Egbert Jaacks	3./JG 302	2056	Halifax	SW Berlin	1
Leutnant Alfred Körver	II./JG 302	2111	Lancaster	Berlin	1

In return for these successes *5./JG 302* suffered two casualties:

Oberfeldwebel Karl Dreissinger was injured when his aircraft overturned in a crash-landing at Lüneburg airfield (Fw 190 A-6, WNr. 550 754, aircraft of *I./JG 11*).

Feldwebel Gerhard Lenz lost his life in combat southeast of Garlitz, west of the city of Brandenburg (Fw 190 A-4, WNr. 147 086, aircraft of *I./JG 11*).

3 December 1943

Feldwebel Kurt Becker of *5./JG 302*, died in his machine southeast of Husum. The exact cause of the crash could not be determined (Fw 190 A-5 "Yellow 1", WNr. 155 868, aircraft of *I./JG 11*).

One day later *Oberfeldwebel* Hans Jatzak of *9./JG 302* was killed in a crash near Wildenloh. Once again the cause of the crash is not known (Bf 109 G-6, aircraft of *III./JG 11*).

10 December 1943

While on a night training flight, *Feldwebel* Günter Nehrlich of 6./*JG 302* crashed 15 km southeast of Kiel near the village of Postfeld and was killed. The cause of the crash is not known (Fw 190 A-5, WNr. 710063, aircraft of *I./JG 11*).

One day later *Feldwebel* Wilhelm Falkenberg of 9./*JG 301*, formerly of *2./Nahaufklärungsgruppe 41*, was killed in a crash on Rhein-Main airfield. In most cases, when an aircraft crashed during a night sortie for reasons other than enemy action it was impossible to determine the exact cause. Was it the pilots' lack of experience flying fast fighter aircraft, or was it nocturnal navigation that gave the pilots problems? At the time there was insufficient time to conduct lengthy investigations – the war demanded everyone's full attention.

16-17 December 1943

In the early evening Berlin was again attacked by British bombers. The only record of *JG 301*'s activities on this night is a note that *Oberleutnant* Georg Sucker of the *9. Staffel* was killed when his Bf 109 crashed near Lohrhaupten. It is not known if this loss was combat-related.

I./JG 302 was in action on this night and recorded two victories: at 1948 hours *Oberfeldwebel* Anton Benning of the *1. Staffel* knocked down a Lancaster for his third victory. Fellow *Staffel* member *Oberfeldwebel* Kurt Emler scored his sixth victory, shooting down a four-engined bomber at 2012 hours.

The *Geschwader* reported the loss of *Unteroffizier* Otto Kutschenreuther of *9./JG 302*, who went down east of Bad Zwischenahn (Bf 109 G-5, WNr. 15 940, aircraft of *III./JG 11*).

20 December 1943

On this night RAF Bomber Command's targets were the cities of Mannheim and Frankfurt and the surrounding industrial complexes. It appears that elements of both *Jagdgeschwader* took part in the defensive effort. There is no record of successes on this night, however losses were recorded:

9./JG 301: *Unteroffizier* Walter Schellner, bailed out near Wesermünde after being wounded.

5./JG 302: *Feldwebel* Josef Leimer, crashed near Oldersbeck southeast of Husum (Fw 190 A-5, WNr. 160 079, aircraft of *I./JG 11*).

5./JG 302: *Unteroffizier* Leonhard Palzkill, wounded in combat, bailed out near Brückenau close to Schweinfurt (Fw 190 A-6, aircraft of *I./JG 1*).

7./JG 302: *Feldwebel* Ernst Hauptmann, killed in a crash following engine failure, near Bokel not far from Oldenburg (Bf 109 G-6, WNr. 15 845, aircraft of *III./JG 11*).

On 21 December *Oberfeldwebel* Josef Löffler of *3./JG 301* was injured in a takeoff crash at Germersheim.

24 December 1943

The RAF attacked Berlin in a raid that lasted from 0330 until 0510 hours. Among the units that responded was *JG 302* , though probably only its *I.* and *II. Gruppe* saw action. The only victory claimed during this operation was by *Oberfeldwebel* Kurt Emler of the *1. Staffel*. He spotted a Lancaster above the burning city and at 0240 hours he was able to shoot it down. The *I. Gruppe* reported no losses on this night. The *II. Gruppe* was less fortunate, especially the *6. Staffel*.

Unteroffizier Gerhard Krögel was badly hit during combat and went down with his machine west of Ludwigslust (Bf 109 G-6, WNr. 27 082, aircraft of *7./JG 11*).

Feldwebel Gerhard Pietsch and *Unteroffizier* Helmut Meinersberger both went down in the Bf 109 G-6s near Jüterbog. It is not known if these two crashes were related to the action over Berlin (aircraft of *III./JG 54*).

4./JG 302 recorded a crash on 27 December: *Unteroffizier* Heinrich Kairies lost his life southwest of Ludwigslust.

29-30 December 1943

Only *JG 302* saw action on this night, and *Oberfeldwebel* Otto Pritzel of the *5. Staffel* shot down a bomber, his first victory with the "*Wilde Sau*".

Oberfeldwebel Albert Hachtel of *1./JG 302* was killed in action near Clausdorf southwest of Rostock.

On 30 December 1943 *4./JG 301* reported the crash of *Leutnant* Josef Nester at Seyring. Nester, who was injured, must have been part of the advance detachment assisting in the second new formation of the *Gruppe*. It was to be mid-March 1944, however, before the newly formed *Jagdgruppe* saw its first action. By that time the *Gruppe* was used more in the day fighter role than "*Wilde Sau*" night-fighter operations.

At the end of 1943 the majority of the *Gruppen* of these two *Jagdgeschwader* were still using the aircraft of day fighter units. Only *III./JG 301* and *I./JG 302* were even close to having enough of their own machines at this time. This fact is illustrated by the strength reports submitted by *JG 301* and *JG 302* on 31 December 1943. The *Luftwaffe* had been unable to provide the three single-

Pilots of JG 301 photographed at Rhein-Main in the winter of 1943-44. From left to right: Feldwebel Heinz-Walter Schellner, Gefreiter Ernst Peiz (killed in action near Pretzen on 26 November 1944), and Unteroffiziere Horst Hugenschutt, Herbert Seifert and Willi Schmidt (killed in action near Salzwedel on 25 February 1945).

engined night-fighter *Geschwader* with the necessary aircraft in the short time available. As 1943 came to a close, *JG 301* and *JG 302* had the following aircraft complements:

Stab JG 301	1 Bf 109 G-6, 1 Fw 190 A-7
I./JG 301	no aircraft
II./JG 301	3 Bf 109 G-6
III./JG 301	22 Bf 109 G-6
10./JG 301	10 Bf 109 G-6
Stab JG 302	2 Bf 109 G-6
I./JG 302	4 Bf 109 G-5, 27 Bf 109 G-6
II./JG 302	1 Fw 190 A-5, 1 Fw 190 A-6
III./JG 302	no aircraft

10./JG 301, which had not yet appeared on the stage, was to form a cadre for the formation of *IV./JG 301*. Exactly where this *Staffel* was established is not known, but its subsequent history is well known. Formation of the *Gruppe*, however, proceeded no further than the establishment of the *10. Staffel*.

A closer examination of the losses since the formation of the two *Geschwader* reveals that the pilots of the single-engined night-fighters actually faced two enemies: on the one hand the British bombers and on the other the weather and darkness. In the beginning, at least, the latter two were the most feared.

The fighters were actually quite capable of dealing with the enemy bombers, confirming *Major* Herrmann's proposal. The ability of men like *Oberleutnant* Pleva, *Oberfeldwebel* Seeler and *Feldwebel* Herre to shoot down as many as three bombers in a few minutes, demonstrated the effectiveness of the *"Wilde Sau"* night-fighters. The loss reports clearly show that weather and darkness were more problematic foes. From the very beginning, experts with the skill to descent through low cloud to reach their airfields were in short supply and became even rarer as casualties mounted.

Pilots without this experience and training began crashing with alarming frequency in bad weather or else failed to locate their airfields in spite of searchlight signals and radio beacons at the airfields assigned to the *"Wilde Sau"*. Many were forced to abandon their aircraft or risk forced landings after running out of fuel. Every *"Wilde Sau"* pilot forced to fly the Bf 109 faced another problem: this fighter was very prone to ground-looping during landing and takeoff unless the pilot reacted immediately. It is quite safe to say that there were very few pilots who flew the Bf 109 for any amount of time who did not encounter this problem at some time during takeoff or landing. Students at the fighter schools were told of this characteristic from the very first day, and a certain amount of experience was required to master this problem during takeoff and landing.

The majority of the crashes that injured or killed pilots in the period until the end of 1943 occurred during combat missions but were not due to enemy action, and the majority took place during takeoff or landing. In the most cases it was impossible to determine what had caused the accident, and those who could have explained them were usually no longer capable of doing so.

Winter 1943-44: Unteroffizier Horst Hugenschutt photographed with his Bf 109 G-6 while technical personnel service and inspect the aircraft.

The former bomber and transport pilots deserve to be recognized for their accomplishments in the "*Wilde Sau*" units. Just switching from the cockpit of a bomber or transport aircraft to that of a single-seat fighter in a short time was stressful enough. Even pilots with training and experience in instrument flying sometimes found it difficult to fly in the dark on instruments. Used to having a radio operator to share the workload, they now had to perform all the required functions themselves and could easily become overwhelmed in the unfamiliar confines of a fighter cockpit. It was not uncommon for pilots too end up too high on a night approach, resulting in a heavy landing, and this could have serious consequences, especially when flying the Bf 109.

As with all types of fighters, the single-engined night-fighter's success was measured against its losses. At this time, the balance of successes versus losses was in the red for the "*Wilde Sau*" units. Various factors undoubtedly contributed to this, especially the hurried formation of the 300-series *Geschwader* with little time between establishment of units. In the formation process the lines were often blurred. There were pilots who were transferred from *JG 300* to *JG 301* and on to *JG 302* within a matter of weeks. This is a significant factor, for it takes time to form a binding comradeship. As well, there are the inexplicable disbanding, reestablishment and renaming of the *Gruppen* of the three *Geschwader* soon after their formation. It is not always possible to determine when these took place, but they caused many interruptions in *Geschwader* life.

With the onset of winter, weather conditions deteriorated steadily and there was no visible increase in successes. Another factor that was impossible to ignore was the growing strength of American daylight raids. As a result, during 1944 the *Jagdgeschwader 300, 301* and *302* were increasingly used to defend against American bombers.

At the beginning of 1944 *Jagdgeschwader 301* and *302* were operational at the following bases:

Stab and *I./JG 301* at Neubiberg south of Munich,
II./JG 301 at Seyring south of Berlin,
III./JG 301 at Zerbst southeast of Magdeburg.

Stab/JG 302 at Döberitz near Berlin,
I./JG 302 at Jüterbog south of Berlin,
II./JG 302 at Ludwigslust south of Schwerin,
III./JG 302 at Oldenburg.

During the month of January 1944, according to a report from the staff of the *General der Jagdflieger, III./JG 302* received its own equipment. With its own aircraft, the unit ceased to be a "Piggyback *Gruppe*".

At about the same time, *I./JG 301* at Neubiberg received its own aircraft; all were Bf 109 G-6s.

2-3 January 1944

On this night the British attacked Berlin again, bombing the city from 0200 to 0420 hours. Among the night-fighter units that rose to defend the capital was *JG 302*.

Oberfeldwebel Eduard Ries of 2./JG 302 reported shooting down a four-engined bomber over the city.

Oberfeldwebel Kurt Welter of 5./*JG 302* claimed another bomber shot down at 0255 hours. *Feldwebel* Andreas Hartl of 6./*JG 302* reported a Lancaster shot down at 0256 hours.

There was only one loss on this night, but it struck *I./JG 302* particularly hard:

Oberfeldwebel Kurt Emler of the *1. Staffel*, one of the most successful single-engined night-fighter pilots so far, lost his life in combat. He went down with his Bf 109 G-6 near Maltershausen, 10 km west of Jüterbog. Emler had been with the *"Wilde Sau"* from the beginning and was transferred from *JG 300* to *JG 302* when that unit was established. He had claimed a total of seven four-engined bombers shot down during that time. He was buried with military honors in the cemetery in his hometown of Hermsdorf in the Riesen Mountains.

4 January 1944

Unteroffizier Gerhard Koch of 3./*JG 301* crashed to his death near Unterzeismering,two kilometers south of Tutzing, after his aircraft developed engine trouble (Bf 109 G-6, WNr. 20 445, aircraft of *III./JG 3*).

5 January 1944

Both *Geschwader* flew their first daylight operations on this day. Although there are no victory claims for this day, loss reports reveal that the units were engaged in combat.

Gefreiter Ernst Peiz of 8./*JG 301* bailed out of his burning machine after air combat. The injured pilot was taken to hospital in Belgium.

Oberfeldwebel Ernst Haase of *I./JG 302* was injured in a crash-landing at Stade (Bf 109 G-6, WNr. 410 691).

5-6 January 1944

Stettin was the target of the British bombers on this night, and *JG 302* was among the units that participated in the defensive effort, probably committing its *I.* and *II. Gruppe*.

Feldwebel Andreas Hartl of the *6. Staffel* claimed a Lancaster west of Stettin at 0341 hours.

Oberfeldwebel Kurt Welter of the *5 Staffel* brought down two four-engined bombers, at 0346 and 0411 hours.

There were also casualties, however: *Unteroffizier* Heinz Brändlein of the *6. Staffel* went down with his Bf 109 G-6 fifteen kilometers south of Stettin near Ferdinandstein. He was listed as missing until 10 January.

Unteroffizier Otto Steinhagen of 5./*JG 302* was wounded in action, but was able to parachute to safety and came down near the town of Berlinchen without further complications (Fw 190 A-6, WNr. 470 018).

6 January 1944

JG 302 was committed against American fighter and bomber units in the airspace north of Berlin. This is the second verifiable daylight mission against American forces by *JG 302*, and this type of operation was to become more common in the days and weeks that followed. The growing American daylight bombing campaign was to result in additional heavy burdens for the pilots of the Defense of the Reich, though this was not yet apparent in the early days of 1944. *JG 302* failed to score any successes in this its second daylight mission, but there were casualties:

Winter 1943-44 at Rhein-Main airfield: from left to right: Gefreiter Peiz, Unteroffizier Hugenschutt, Unteroffizier Seifert and Feldwebel Schellner.

Pilots of I./JG 301 at Neubiberg in January 1944, at which time the unit was still flying night-fighter missions. From left to right: Feldwebel Hans Müller, 2./JG 301; Oberfeldwebel Max Röhricht, 1./JG 301; Unteroffizier Willi Peterreit, 2./JG 301; Oberfeldwebel Buschgast; Unteroffizier Klaus Jacobi, 2./JG 301; Fahnenjunker-Feldwebel Fritz Yung, 1./JG 301; Oberfeldwebel Ernst Czymmek, 1./JG 301; Fahnenjunker-Feldwebel Heinz Grube, 3./JG 301; Unteroffizier Gerhard Witt, 2./JG 301.

Unteroffizier Thomas Braun of 2./*JG 302* went down with his Bf 109 G-6 near Potsdam.

Unteroffizier Eduard Ries of 3./*JG 302* was wounded in action against the Americans and obliged to make a forced landing near Küstrin after his machine's engine failed (Bf 109 G-6, WNr. 410 704).

7 January 1944

The following comment appears in the war diary of *Luftgaukommando VII*: "*I./JG 301* arrived at Neubiberg from Gardelegen." Logbooks also reveal that at least part of the *Gruppe* had transferred from Seyring to Neubiberg on 18 December 1943.

The *III./JG 301* intercepted American fighter and bomber units on this day and reported the loss of two aircraft.

Feldwebel Leonhard Stark of the *7. Staffel* was shot down near Heidelberg. Wounded, he managed to parachute from his aircraft as it went down.

Fellow *Staffel* member *Feldwebel* Fritz Utermark failed to return from this mission. He was shot down and killed near Worms.

On 9 January 1944 *Hauptmann* Klaus Komoss of the *Stab* of *III./JG 301* was killed in the crash of his Bf 109 near Frankfurt am Main. The cause of the crash is not known.

11 January 1944

Fahnenjunker-Feldwebel Heinz Grube of 3./*JG 301* was injured when his machine overturned during a crash-landing at Brandis airfield near Leipzig (Bf 109 G-6, WNr. 411 213).

JG 302 once again saw action against American fighter and bomber units on this day.

At 1327 hours *Oberfeldwebel* Hogobert Langelotz of the *3. Staffel* shot down a four-engined bomber. This was the first daylight victory attributed to *JG 302*.

JG 302 suffered no fatalities in this mission, however it did lose four aircraft, whose pilots were either injured or wounded.

Oberfeldwebel Heinz Gossow of the *1. Staffel*, a veteran bomber pilot who had been decorated with the German Cross in Gold, was shot down by enemy fighters near Nordweide and bailed out. Gossow sustained injuries while abandoning his machine and was taken to the dispensary at Jüterbog airbase (Bf 109 G-6, WNr. 20 599).

Leutnant Erich Reinke of the *3. Staffel* was wounded in combat with the fighter escort near Osnabrück.

Leutnant Helmut Steinmann of the *2. Staffel* was wounded in action over the Teutoburg Forest in the area of Hilter and was delivered to the military hospital in Bielefeld (Bf 109 G-6, WNr. 410 109).

Feldwebel Walter Schermutzki of the *4. Staffel* was injured in a forced landing near Grabow following engine failure. It is not known to what degree this was combat-related (Fw 190 A-6, WNr. 470 214).

14 January 1944

Bombers of the RAF entered German airspace in the early evening, heading for Berlin. The capital was bombed from 1900 until 2019 hours. *JG 301* and *JG 302* were both committed against this attack. It appears that neither unit achieved any successes, as the records only contain information on losses.

Several pilots of *III./JG 301* tried to follow enemy bombers through the flak barrage over Halle. The aircraft of *Unteroffizier* Paul Hengel was hit fly flak and shot down. Hengel was able to abandon his aircraft and was subsequently delivered to the *Luftwaffe* hospital in Halle-Döbeln. He died of his injuries a short time later.

The *I. Gruppe* of *JG 302* also took part in the night action with the same result: losses but no victories.

Oberleutnant Herbert Petersen, *Staffelkapitän* of the *1. Staffel*, was killed when his aircraft went down near Kamenz northeast of Dresden (Bf 109 G-6, WNr. 410 224).

Feldwebel Herbert Herre, also of the *1. Staffel*, lost his life near Markendorf east of Jüterbog. Born on 13 April 1920, Herre was from Baden-Baden and had been with the "*Wilde Sau*" since its inception. During the formation of *JG 301* and *JG 302* he had been transferred from *7./JG 300* to *1./JG 302*. With four victories, Herre was among the most successful single-engined night-fighter pilots.

20-21 January 1944

The first of several waves of British bombers reached the Reich capital at about 1900 hours and released its bombs over the city. The night-fighter units sent up to intercept the raid knocked down thirty-five British bombers. *JG 301* and *JG 302* both took part in this action.

Fahnenjunker-Feldwebel Fritz Yung of *1./JG 301* shot down a Halifax en route to Berlin. *Hauptmann* Helmut Suhr of *7./JG 301* shot down a Lancaster over Berlin at 1947 hours.

Feldwebel Eugen Bauer of *9./JG 301* was shot down and killed near Jüterbog. Bauer had served in the army's 109th Replacement Battalion before transferring to the *Luftwaffe* and receiving training as a fighter pilot. *Oberleutnant* Franz Amsink of *Stab/JG 301* was killed when his aircraft crashed ten kilometers north of the town of Kehlheim in Bavaria (Fw 190 A-7, WNr. 430 178). The cause of the crash is not known.

The aircraft of *Oberfeldwebel* Heinz Stahlhut of *Stab/JG 301* developed problems over Brandenburg. He was subsequently forced to abandon the machine near Welzow after the engine caught fire. Stahlhut was injured while bailing out but landed safely.

JG 302 was also in the air that night, trying to intercept the bombers attacking Berlin.

Hauptmann Heinrich Wurzer, *Kapitän* of the *1. Staffel*, claimed a Halifax shot down west of Berlin at 1924 hours.

Oberfeldwebel Siegfried Heintsch of the *1. Staffel* was killed in action near Pretzsch an der Elbe (Bf 109 G-6, WNr. 27 045).

Elements of the *Geschwader* were also in action on the following night. This is supported by a claim made by *Feldwebel* Andreas Hartl of the *6. Staffel*, who shot down a four-engined bomber at 2315 hours. On the afternoon of 21 January 1944, *1./JG 301* took off from Neubiberg to transfer to Jüterbog, arriving there at 1630 hours.

Late in the evening a large force of British bombers was reported approaching German airspace. The actual target was not Berlin, as the British tried to make the defenders believe, but Magdeburg. Among the night-fighter *Gruppen* sent to intercept the attackers was *I./JG 301*, which took off from Jüterbog-Waldlager at 2245 hours and landed at around midnight.

There is no information on victories or losses, which suggests that no contact was made with the enemy. At 0945 hours the next morning the *Gruppe* took off from Jüterbog to fly back to Neubiberg, landing there at 1120. On 23 January 1944 *Unteroffizier* Fritz Staff, a member of *9./JG 301*'s ground crew, was fatally injured. No further details of the incident are known.

28-29 January 1944

Berlin was once again the target of the RAF's night bombers. Both *Geschwader* saw action on this night.

At 0321 hours *Oberleutnant* W. Kucharsowski of *9./JG 301* reported shooting down a four-engined bomber, and a short time later *Feldwebel* Herbert Seifert of *8./JG 301* shot down a Lancaster.

I./JG 301 took off from Neubiberg at 0205 hours and subsequently lost two aircraft in the action over Berlin.

The distance between the two crash sites illustrates just how alone the pilots of the single-engined night-fighters were in the night skies over Germany.

Leutnant Albert Wolter, acting commander of the *1. Staffel* and *Gruppe* Technical Officer, was shot down three kilometers southwest of Finsterwalde.

Oberfeldwebel Ernst Cymmek, also of the *1. Staffel*, was fatally injured while attempting a forced landing 500 meters south of the Hödingen-Siestedt railway station. The two crash sites were about 240 kilometers apart.

As was standard practice in the single-engined night-fighter force, when a mission was over the pilot took out his air navigation chart and looked for the nearest airfield. Marked on the map were airfields specially set up for the *"Wilde Sau"*, with all the necessary data and symbols. For example, the airfield at Augsburg used as its recognition signal two vertical searchlight beams, Hamburg two beams forming a "V", and Münster two crossed beams forming an "X". The pilots had to know by heart these identifying features of night-fighter airfields, which were spread over all of Germany.

On this night, for example, *Feldwebel* Hans Müller of *1./JG 301* landed at Königsberg-Neumark, two hours after taking off from Neubiberg.

JG 302 also saw action on this night. *Oberfeldwebel* Kurt Welter of the *5. Staffel* and *Feldwebel* Andreas Hartl of the *6. Staffel* each shot down a Halifax.

Oberfeldwebel Eduard Ries of *2./JG 302* was credited with shooting down a four-engined bomber. The date is given as the night before, however this may have been a typographical error.

27 January 1944

Major Treumund Engelhardt, *Kommodore* of *III./JG 302*, was forced to abandon his aircraft near Pritzier after it developed engine trouble. He came down in a wood and ended up hanging beneath his parachute, which was caught on a branch. Holding onto another branch, he was able to release his harness. But the branch broke, and Engelhardt fell, suffering several injuries on striking the frozen ground. After recovering from his injuries he was transferred to another unit.

Hauptmann Heinrich Wurzer, Staffelkapitän of 1./JG 302.

30 January 1944

Daylight missions against American bombers were becoming more common for *JG 301* and *JG 302*. Such was the mission on this day, one of the first daylight operations by the two *Geschwader*.

Leutnant Heinrich von Alven of *I./JG 301* shot down a B-17 during this mission, however it is not known where the bomber came down.

Feldwebel Kurt Zschoche of *7./JG 301* failed to return; he was later declared dead, location unknown.

Oberfeldwebel Rudolf Kirchner of *9./JG 301* was shot down and killed near Deelen in Holland.

Hauptmann Heinrich Wurzer, *Staffelkapitän* of *9./JG 302*, shot down a Flying Fortress on this mission. It was one of the first victories over an American four-engined bomber that can be verified in the unit records.

The beginning of 1944 brought a change in operational roles for the Defense of the Reich's three "*Wilde Sau*" units, *JG 300*, *JG 301* and *JG 302*. They had originally been conceived solely as single-engined night-fighter units, but in the preceding months a rethinking process had taken place in the *Luftwaffe* command. The impetus for this was probably the victory-loss ratio, for at the end of 1943 only *JG 300* had more victories than losses. From this time on the star of the "*Wilde Sau*" night-fighter force, which had risen so meteorically, began to wane. With each new day it became more of a certainty: the single-engined *Geschwader* of the illuminated night-fighter force were gradually becoming day fighter units. The *Luftwaffe* command had decided to further strengthen the regular night-fighter *Geschwader*, equipped with the Bf 110 and Ju 88, to counter the night incursions by the British, whose strength was roughly unchanged.

There was no shortage of qualified pilots with which to pursue this idea, for the disbanding of bomber and transport units was making available experienced, well-trained pilots. Another and perhaps more important reason for this rethinking on the part of the *Luftwaffe* command was the steadily growing strength of the American daylight raids and the growing range of the enemy's escort fighters.

In considering a changed role for the "*Wilde Sau*" units, the *Luftwaffe* command was probably also influenced by the prospect of having three *Jagdgeschwader* capable of operating in bad weather. The decision to change the role of the "*Wilde Sau*" units had not yet been made at the beginning of February 1944, and consequently they continued to operate at night as originally conceived, but day sorties, so-called "exceptions", were now occurring at much shorter intervals.

The two *Jagdgeschwader* saw little action in the early days of February 1944, largely on account of bad weather, however this also forced the English to keep their bombers on the ground.

In spite of this operational inactivity *JG 301* did suffer losses. These were not due to enemy action and occurred during training sorties.

8 February 1944

Feldwebel Heinz Hoppe of *7./JG 301* crashed to his death near Barby, fifteen kilometers west of Zerbst. The cause of the crash is not known (Bf 109 G-6, WNr. 411 136).

Feldwebel Gerhard Friedrich of *8./JG 301* was killed when his Bf 109 G-6 crashed for unexplained reasons. The aircraft fell on the Lemsdorf housing estate in Kreuzbreite near Magdeburg.

10 February 1944

I./JG 301 and *II./JG 302* took off to intercept a daylight raid by American bombers. The records do not reveal where the two *Gruppen* saw action.

Leutnant Heinrich von Alven of *I./JG 301* shot down a B-17 Flying Fortress.

Hauptmann Heinrich Wurzer, *Staffelkapitän* of *1./JG 302* destroyed a B-24 Liberator.

The only known casualty is *Feldwebel* Theo Erstermann of *3./JG 301*, who was wounded and bailed out.

18 February 1944

At Neubiberg airbase, eighteen-year-old *Flieger* Edgar Köhler, a clerk in the headquarters company of *I./JG 301*, was badly hurt when he was pinned between two trucks while shoveling snow. He was taken to the *Luftwaffe* hospital in Munich with serious internal injuries and died the following day.

19-20 February 1944

The British attacked Berlin again, bombing the city from 0240 until 0435 hours. Above the city searchlights swept the sky, trying to assist the flak and fighters by illuminating enemy bombers. *JG 301* and *JG 302* were both committed – having to fill two very different and rapidly changing roles was now a fact of life for the two *Jagdgeschwader*.

Leutnant Glaas of *8./JG 301* claimed a Lancaster shot down over Berlin at 0420 hours.

Feldwebel Herbert Seifert of *8./JG 301* ran out of fuel and abandoned his aircraft 15 km west of Parchim near the village of Dütschow (Bf 109 G-6, WNr. 410 473). The injured pilot was taken to the *Luftwaffe* hospital in Parchim.

Several of *JG 302*'s pilots also enjoyed success on this night. *5. Staffel's* Kurt Welter, who had been promoted to *Leutnant* at the beginning of the month, shot down two Lancasters, at 0327 and 0416 hours. Another Lancaster was brought down by *Feldwebel* Anton Benning of *2./JG 302*.

Just 14 minutes after takeoff, the aircraft flown by *Oberleutnant* Helmut Schlechter, adjutant of *III./JG 302*, developed mechanical trouble which forced him to attempt an emergency landing at Oldenburg. The aircraft's undercarriage struck the roof of a hangar, causing it to crash, fatally injuring the pilot. (Fw 190 A-6, "White 5", WNr. 470 230)

Unteroffizier Walter Peuster of *7./JG 302* was shot down and crashed to his death near the town of Dübinghausen in the district of Nienburg an der Weser. (Bf 109 G-5, "White 5", WNr. 110 044)

Unteroffizier Adam Wittersheim of *6./JG 302* was wounded in air combat over Oranienburg and forced to abandon his crippled aircraft. (Bf 109 G-6, WNr. 410 081)

20 February 1944

Some aircraft of both *Geschwader* had still not returned to their home bases after the night mission, when orders came for a daylight operation against American fighters and bombers heading for central Germany.

Both *Jagdgeschwader* were being tasked more often to intercept American aircraft attacking targets within the Reich by day. The two units had their first encounters with the B-24 Liberator and B-17 Flying Fortress, both heavy four-engined bombers, and their escorting fighters: the P-38 Lightning, P-47 Thunderbolt and P-51 Mustang.

Initially these increasingly frequent daylight missions presented the *"Wilde Sau"* units with an almost impossible challenge. Former bomber and transport pilots still made up the bulk of the pilots in the *Staffeln*. These men had never been trained as fighter pilots, but now they were being called upon to fight it out with the American escorts. Within the *Geschwader* there was a mixture of pilots, those who preferred attacking bombers to fighters, and those trained fighter pilots who would rather avoid attacking the heavies and concentrate on the escorting fighters. In the beginning, when losses were unbearably high, it almost seemed as if this mixture could not be tolerated. Soon, however, it proved to be very beneficial, for the two groups learned from each other and this mutual learning was later reflected in successes.

Only the *I. Gruppe* of *JG 302* took part in the daylight action on 20 February 1944.

Hauptmann Heinrich Wurzer, *Staffelkapitän* of *1./JG 302*, shot down a B-17 in the fighting that took place on this day, while *Oberfeldwebel* Hugobert Langelotz of the *3. Staffel* sent down another west of Seese at 1310 hours.

As usual, these victories were offset by casualties. *Feldwebel* Erich Teubner of *2./JG 302* was shot down near Bernburg an der Saale and bailed out. He was taken to Reserve Hospital II in Strassfurt-Leopoldshall with minor injuries. (Bf 109 G-6, WNr. 411 433)

Feldwebel Herbert Chantelau of *3./JG 302* was wounded in air combat and came down by parachute near Rothleben near Dessau. He was taken to hospital in Köthen for medical treatment. (Bf 109 G-6, WNr. 411 770)

There is no record of successes by *JG 301*, whose *I. Gruppe* took part in this action. On the other hand the *Geschwader* reported several losses, an indication that effective tactics against daylight raids had yet to be worked out.

Major Walter Brede, *Gruppenkommandeur* of *I./JG 301*, struck a tree at Germersheim airfield and crashed. *Major* Brede was fortunate to escape with only minor injuries. (Bf 109 G-6, WNr. 411 228)

Oberleutnant Ernst Fischer, *Staffelkapitän* of *2./JG 301*, was fired on by German anti-aircraft guns in the Göppingen area. His machine was hit several times and Fischer was forced to bail out. (Bf 109 G-6, WNr. 411 226)

Feldwebel Friedrich Brüssel of *3./JG 301* failed to return from this day's mission. He and his Bf 109 G-6 were reported missing.

Einsatzkommando Helsinki (Operational Detachment Helsinki)

At the beginning of 1944 the ADD, the Soviet strategic bombing force commanded by Air Marshal Golovanov, received a direct order from Stalin to launch an intensive night campaign bombing campaign against Helsinki. The objective of the campaign was to exert pressure on Finland's political leadership in order to achieve a separate peace with that nation. Toward the end of 1943 Finnish signals intelligence had begun intercepting and monitoring Soviet Air Force radio traffic. The Finns took every possible measure to counter these attacks, including a request for German assistance. As the Soviet attacks on Helsinki would be made across the Gulf of Finland, on 5 March 1944 the German night-fighter control vessel *Togo* sailed from Kiel for Reval. The *Togo*, which was equipped with every available device for the detection of aircraft, arrived at the roadstead off Reval on 7 March. That same night it moved to its nocturnal anchorage forty-five kilometers east of Helsinki.

Bf 109 G-6 of "Einsatzkommando Helsinki" at Helsinki-Malmi in early 1944. This detachment from I./JG 302 was commanded by Hauptmann Dietsche.

Helsinki-Malmi airfield: ground crew service one of the detachment's aircraft. On the wing of the Bf 109 G-6 is Gefreiter Otto Faßdorf.

Bf 109 G-6 "Black 33" of I./JG 302 at Helsinki-Malmi airfield in early 1944. Note the yellow Eastern Front band on the aircraft's rear fuselage.

Helsinki-Malmi in April 1944: I./JG 302's operational detachment under the command of Hauptmann Dietsche. The emblem of the "Wilde Sau" Geschwader is clearly visible on the engine cowlings of these aircraft.

Fritz Yung as a Leutnant while serving with I./JG 301.

In the days that followed, the *Togo* spent each night at its anchorage and then moved back to the Reval roadstead during daylight hours. The special equipment on board the ship enabled it to control German night-fighters using both the illuminated (visual detection) and dark (radar detection) methods. In order to counter the expected Russian attacks, *I./JG 302* formed an "operational detachment" equivalent to a *Staffel* in strength. It was based at Helsinki-Malmi airfield from 13 February until 15 May 1944. According to Finnish records, "*Einsatzkommando Helsinki*" consisted of three officers, twelve NCOs, fifteen mechanics and seven armorers. The detachment's pilots were: *Hptm.* Richard Lewens, *Hptm.* Karl-Heinz Dietsche, *Hptm.* Rheindorf, *Ofw.* Fritz Dieckmann, *Ofw.* Arthur Gross, *Ofw.* Egbert Jaaks, *Ofw.* Hugobert Langelotz, *Ofw.* Xaver Neumeier, *Ofw.* Dieter Rusche, *Fw.* Kurt Nachtigall and *Uffz.* Werner Dienst. The Helsinki *Staffel* claimed two enemy aircraft shot down on the night of 16-17 February 1944 and four on the night of 26-27 February. The names of the successful pilots are not revealed by the surviving records. Finnish records do reveal, however, that the following German fighter pilots of "Operational Detachment Helsinki" were awarded the Finnish Pilot's Badge, probably recognition for shooting down Soviet bombers in the Helsinki area:

18 Feb. 1944	*Hptm.* Richard Lewens
26 Feb. 1944	*Ofw.* Egbert Jaaks, *Ofw.* Xaver Neumeier, *Ofw.* Dieter Rusche,
	Uffz. Werner Dienst
12 Dec. 1944	*Hptm.* Karl-Heinz Dietsche

No German losses were reported during these night missions in the Helsinki area.

21 February 1944

3./JG 301, which was based at Neubiberg at this time, reported an unusual incident: while carrying out a function test on an unserviceable wing cannon, a careless armorer caused the weapon to fire a single 20mm round. The shell struck *Gefreiter* Johann Angerer, tearing off his right arm. The injured man was taken to the *Luftwaffe* hospital in Munich-Oberföhring.

22 February 1944

From Neubiberg, *I./JG 301* was committed against aircraft of the American 15th Air Force flying from Italy. It was the first time the pilots of *JG 301* had met American bombers operating from bases in the south of Italy instead of Great Britain. This fact further complicated the situation of the units assigned to the Defense of the Reich, and rising losses began to have an effect on the *Staffeln*.

On this day *I./JG 301* engaged the enemy over the Austrian Alps. The "*Wilde Sau*" pilots had yet to discover the proper tactics for attacking formations of bombers, and so this mission was an unsuccessful one for the *Gruppe*.

In the course of the fighting, the *Kapitän* of the *1. Staffel*, *Oberleutnant* Walter Burghoff, was shot down twenty kilometers north of Salzburg. He bailed out, injuring his knee and right forearm. (Bf 109 G-6, WNr. 411 270)

Unteroffizier Heinrich Block of *2./JG 301* was shot down over the Hohen Tauer and forced to bail out. Block was fortunate to come down near the Alpine village of Penk in the valley of the Möll instead of in the surrounding high mountains. (Bf 109 G-6, WNr. 411 244)

I./JG 302 saw action over central Germany against American bombers attacking Magdeburg. After taking off from Jüterbog, the *Gruppe* first sighted the enemy west of Magdeburg. At that time the American escort fighters lacked the range to reach Magdeburg and the bombers had no fighter cover over the target area.

Hauptmann Heinrich Wurzer, *Kapitän* of the *1. Staffel*, shot down a B-17 for his sixth victory.

24 February 1944

III./JG 3 "Udet" had transferred from Bad Wörishofen to Leipheim at 1400 hours the previous day. At 1205 hours it took off on a mission over Austria. Flying with the *Gruppe* was *Feldwebel* Hans Müller of *1./JG 301*, who, together with several other members of the *Staffel*, had been with *III./JG 3* for several days, instructing the unit's pilots in instrument flying.

Flying his Bf 109 G-6 "Black 3", at 1255 hours *Feldwebel* Müller shot down a B-17 near Steyr. He landed at Wels at 1315. *Oberfeldwebel* Max Röhricht, a member of Müller's *Staffel*, was shot down and killed over Almkogel. (Bf 109 G-6, WNr. 411 225)

On this day *I./JG 302* also took to the air on a daylight mission against American heavy bombers. *Staffelkapitän Hauptmann* Wurzer was again successful, downing a B-24 Liberator.

I./JG 301 was in action again that night, and *Fahnenjunker-Oberfeldwebel* Fritz Yung of *1./JG 301* shot down a British bomber.

25 February 1944

For both *Geschwader* this was a period of transition from single-engined night-fighter operations to the day fighter role. Both units were now fully equipped with their own aircraft. The Bf 109 G-6 formed the backbone of both *Geschwader*, with a few Fw 190 A-6s operated by some *Gruppe* staff flights and *Staffeln*.

In the beginning *JG 301* and *JG 302* each consisted of three *Gruppen* each with three *Staffeln*, but a fourth *Staffel* was added as daylight missions against American bombers became more frequent.

I./JG 301 engaged American bombers with fighter escort, and *Feldwebel* Arno Müller-Leutert of *2./JG 301* reported shooting down a B-24 Liberator at 1320 hours.

Unteroffizier Werner Waldenberger of *Stab/JG 301* was shot down by enemy fighters and seriously wounded. (Bf 109 G-6, WNr. 411 455).

Feldwebel Hans Müller of *2./JG 301* struck a snowbank during takeoff. He was lucky and sustained only minor injuries. (Bf 109 G-6, WNr. 411 455)

28 February 1944

Feldwebel Hans Engfer of the *7. Staffel* was wounded in action over Zerbst during a night sortie. Engfer had enough strength left to land his Bf 109 safely. After recovering from his wounds he returned to the *Geschwader*, joining the *1. Staffel*.

1 March 1944

7./JG 302 conducted formation training in the Oldenburg area. During a flight maneuver *Unteroffizier* Giesbert Vöcking stalled out of a turn and crashed near Wittemoor, losing his life. (Fw 190 A-6, "Green 3", WNr. 470 212)

Leutnant Fritz Yung of I./JG 301.

2 March 1944

Major Ewald Janssen, *Kommodore* of *JG 302*, was transferred to *SG 4* effective this date. On the same day *Major* Kurt Peters was named the new *Geschwaderkommodore*.

There was a tragic incident involving a member *I./JG 301*'s headquarters company: in the washroom of the men's quarters *Oberfeldwebel* Paul Pfütze, an accountant and pay NCO, suddenly fell to the floor. He was taken to hospital in Munich-Oberföhring with a suspected case of poisoning. Pfütze died of a stroke the next day.

3 March 1944

During a daylight mission over western Germany by *I./JG 301*, *Fahnenjunker-Oberfeldwebel* Fritz Yung of the *1. Staffel* shot down a Spitfire. Daylight encounters with fighters and bombers of the RAF were becoming rarer, while the activities of the American bombers were increasing in strength and range day by day. The fighter units of the *Reichsverteidigung* were visibly surprised by the steadily increasing range of the American escort fighters. When the American daylight bombing campaign began, the airspace bordering the German Bight marked the limit of the escorts' range;

now the American fighters were capable of reaching central Germany, including Berlin and Dresden. The *Luftwaffe* had nothing with which to counter this situation, and the German fighters were finding it much harder to get to the bombers.

4 March 1944

American heavy bombers attacked targets in central Germany, and *JG 301* and *JG 302* were among the units that rose to intercept them. *I./JG 302* took off from Jüterbog-Damm and attacked B-17s over Havelland Lakes area.

For the pilots of *I./JG 302* the sight of the powerful bomber formations, fifty to seventy aircraft per group at this time, was very intimidating. As the *Geschwader* had not been able to gather much experience with such massive concentrations of defensive firepower in its few daylight missions, the attack on the bombers was hesitant.

The hail of tracer coming from the bombers surely caused many pilots to break off their attacks prematurely. The sight of this fireworks display and its psychological effects had to be overcome before an effective attack could be made, and it took time to overcome this mental hurdle.

And so on this day only *Oberleutnant* Heinz Seidel, *Staffelkapitän* of *3./JG 302*, was able to force a B-17 out of the formation north of Berlin.

Leutnant Karl Vogel, acting commander of the *2. Staffel*, was shot down by return fire from the bombers. He crashed to his death southeast of Rathenow near the village of Klein-Wulkow. (Bf 109 G-6, WNr. 411 474)

During this mission *I./JG 301* engaged P-51 Mustang escort fighters, one of which was shot down by *Fahnenjunker-Oberfeldwebel* Fritz Yung of the *1. Staffel*. There are no records of any losses by *I./JG 301* as a result of this action.

5-6 March 1944

Unteroffizier Josef Feist of *3./JG 302* failed to return from an intercept mission against nuisance raiders. A search was begun at daylight and his wrecked machine was found in the Spree Forest near Zerkwitz. (Bf 109 G-6, WNr. 110 239)

6 March 1944

The Reich capital experienced its first major daylight raid. A force of 609 four-engined bombers of the American 8th Air Force attacked the city at noontime. The units of the *Reichsverteidigung* that intercepted the attackers shot down seventy-two bombers and twenty-two escort fighters. The surviving records contain no reference to any operations by *JG 301* on this day.

The *I. Gruppe* of *JG 302* took off from Jüterbog-Damm to intercept the raid and made contact with formations of enemy bombers near Berlin, attacking at 1230 hours. Once again the *Gruppe*'s target was formations of B-17s.

Hauptmann Heinrich Wurzer, *Staffelkapitän* of *1./JG 302* brought down two B-17s in separate attacks.

Oberfeldwebel Herbert Stephan of the same *Staffel* sent down a B-17 at the same time.

There were also casualties, and *2./JG 302*, which was in the second attack wave, was hardest hit.

Feldwebel Erich Buhrig was shot down and killed near Hohen-Lobbese, southwest of Brandenburg. (Bf 109 G-6, WNr. 411 256)

Unteroffizier Kurt Pelz, a native of Berlin, was fatally wounded while defending his hometown and went down with his machine near Stendal. (Bf 109 G-6, WNr. 410 697).

8 March 1944

The skies over Germany were clear blue that morning, when approximately 350 bombers and 170 escort fighters of the 8th Air Force took from their bases in England to attack targets in Germany. The Americans set a direct course for Berlin. Among the defending units was *I./JG 302*. Taking off in good time, it intercepted the incoming bombers north of Magdeburg. To what extent the bombers still enjoyed fighter escort is not known, but there is nothing to suggest combat with escorting fighters.

In the ensuing fighting, the *Staffelkapitän* of *3./JG 302*, *Hauptmann* Karl-Heinz Dietsche, forced a B-17 out of formation northeast of Magdeburg at about 1330 hours.

A short time later, the *Kapitän* of *1./JG 302*, *Hauptmann* Heinrich Wurzer, shot down two B-24 Liberators from another formation of bombers.

Feldwebel Karl Männer of 1.*/JG 302* was killed in action on this day, however the exact circumstances of his death are not known. (Bf 109 G-6, WNr. 411 517)

12 March 1944

Unteroffizier Horst Wöstenburg of *7./JG 301* was killed in an unexplained crash near Magdeburg. (Bf 109 G-6, WNr. 160 059)

During formation training by *III./JG 302*, two of the unit's aircraft collided near Stendal and crashed. The two pilots, *Leutnant* Robert Wolfsberger of *5. Staffel* (Bf 109 G-6, WNr. 411 374) and *Unteroffizier* Otto Pritzl of *6. Staffel* (Bf 109 G-6, WNr. 410 916), parachuted to safety, sustaining injuries in the process.

14-15 March 1944

On this night *I./JG 301* was ordered into the air from Neubiberg to intercept British bombers.

Feldwebel Gerhard Koch of the *1. Staffel* shot down two Lancasters, at 2325 and 2335 hours. The machine flown by *Fahnenjunker-Feldwebel* Heinz Grube of *1./JG 301* swung on takeoff. The undercarriage sheared off and the machine ended up sitting on the runway, where it caught fire. Grube sustained injuries. (Bf 109 G-6, WNr. 411 516)

The aircraft of *Unteroffizier* Gerhard Witt of 2.*/JG 301* sustained severe battle damage over Steinbronn and crashed with the pilot still on board. Witt's body was recovered from the wreckage of his machine (Bf 109 G-6, WNr. 161 137).

At 2328 hours on the night of 16 March 1944, *Feldwebel* Franz Laubenheimer of the *1. Staffel* shot down a Lancaster.

18 March 1944

I./JG 301 was scrambled from Neubiberg to intercept American bombers and fighters approaching from the south. The enemy's principal targets were airfields in northern Italy and southern Germany.

The bombers of the American 15th Air Force were based on airfields around Foggia and were escorted by large numbers of P-38 Lightnings.

During fighting over the Munich area, *Fahnenjunker-Feldwebel* Fritz Yung of the *1. Staffel* shot down two Lightnings for his ninth and tenth victories. *Feldwebel* Franz Laubenheimer, also of the *1. Staffel*, was shot down and killed in the same action. He and his aircraft fell north of the Hubertus Lodge in the Ebersberger Forest. (Bf 109 G-6, WNr. 162 373)

Feldwebel Ludwig Schmutz of the *3. Staffel* was wounded in action and forced to take to his parachute. He reached the ground five kilometers east of the village of Haar near Munich. (Bf 109 G-6, WNr. 411 735)

Oberfeldwebel Karl Hausmann of the same *Staffel* was shot down and killed, crashing on the southern outskirts of Harthausen, fifteen kilometers southeast of Munich. (Bf 109 G-6, WNr. 411 238)

His aircraft badly damaged in combat, *Oberfeldwebel* Josef Grauvogel attempted to reach his home airfield; however, he was forced to make a crash-landing three kilometers west of Reichenau near Neukirchen and was killed. (Bf 109 G-6, WNr. 15 478)

During the night of 18-19 March, *II./JG 302* took off from Altenburg to intercept incoming British bombers. *Leutnant* Kurt Welter of the *5. Staffel* claimed two Lancasters for his 14th and 15th victories.

I./JG 301 – Pilots of the 1. Staffel at Neubiberg. From left to right: Feldwebel Heinz Emanuel, Hauptmann Hölzer (technical officer), Feldwebel Fritz Laubenheimer, Oberfeldwebel Ludwig Schmutz, Fahnenjunker-Oberfeldwebel Fritz Yung.

Feldwebel Ernst Lutz of the *4. Staffel* failed to return from this mission; his aircraft went down southwest of Salzwedel.

21 March 1944

III./JG 301 had meanwhile transferred to Seyring near Vienna and after first being renamed, the *Gruppe* was established for the second time. The reason for the renaming of various *Jagdgruppen* within the "*Wilde Sau*" *Geschwader* has never been fully explained. Changing the names of *Gruppen* and assigning them to different *Geschwader*, followed by the reestablishment of the same *Gruppe* in the previous *Geschwader*: all of this created unrest and affected the striking power and defensive successes of the *Jagdgruppen*.

Each new establishment resulted in *Staffeln* and *Gruppen* having to fly training missions, and it took time to establish a sense of unity and strength in the air. During one such training flight *Leutnant* Waldemar Göttert of *5./JG 301*, a former transport pilot and one of the *Gruppe*'s oldest pilots (age class 1905), flew into the ground near Seyring north of Vienna. He was taken to the nearest hospital with injuries to both legs. (Bf 109 G-6, WNr. 15 478)

I./JG 301 took off from Neuburg an der Donau on a night interception mission. Various elements of the *Jagdgruppe* were based there from 18 March to 25 April 1944, flying day or night missions as the situation required.

Soon after takeoff, the *Staffelkapitän* of *3./JG 301*, *Oberleutnant* Wilhelm Burggraf, was shot down and wounded by a British long-range fighter near Rohrenfels, eight kilometers southeast of the airfield. (Bf 109 G-6, WNr. 411 205)

Fahnenjunker-Feldwebel Fritz Brinkmann, who sometimes served as the *Gruppe* technical officer, also fell prey to a British long-range night-fighter, which shot up his aircraft as it rolled out after landing at Neuburg. Brinkmann was taken to hospital with bullet wounds in his left foot and right hand. (Bf 109 G-6, WNr. 411 232)

III./JG 301 also took to the air from Zerbst that night. Unfortunately it is not known if the *Gruppe* made contact with the enemy. *Unteroffizier* Georg Schleenbecker of the *7. Staffel* failed to return from this mission. It is not known where he was lost, and Schleenbecker is still listed as missing.

Chapter Five

The Formation of *IV./JG 301*

The *Luftwaffe* had been planning the formation of a *IV. Gruppe* for *JG 301* since the beginning of 1944. In February the plan became reality. The process began with the establishment of the *10. Staffel*, however this was to be the only *Staffel* of the *IV. Gruppe* for some time.

It is not known where the *Gruppe* was formed. At the time of its establishment there were probably still differences of opinion as to how it should be employed. How else can it be explained that the area of operations assigned to the *Gruppe*, consisting just of the *10. Staffel*, was not within the Reich but far away from the rest of the *Geschwader* in Romania.

Based in Romania, this so-called *IV./JG 301* was employed against daylight raids by American aircraft operating from Italy and was under the command of the *Jägerführer Süd* (Fighter Commander South). During the period in question the *Staffel* was commanded by *Oberleutnant* Hans Kretschmer.

Combat reports from this period detail claims and losses by the *IV. Gruppe*, but there is nothing to suggest the formation of an *11.* and *12. Staffel*. A memo stating that *IV./JG 301* was based at Ziegenhain on 28 November 1944 does not seem credible. It is quite certain that the *Gruppe* was disbanded in mid-1944. A new *IV. Gruppe* was established at the end of 1944, but more about that later.

One of the first records of the existence of *IV./JG 301* (*10. Staffel*) is dated 24 March 1944: on that date *Oberfeldwebel* Egon Gerz of the *10. Staffel* was killed when his machine crashed at Targsoroul-Nou airfield. (Bf 109 G-6, WNr. 20 441)

24-25 March 1944
British bombers were detected heading for Berlin: both *Jagdgeschwader* were sent aloft to intercept them.

The constant alternation between day and night missions placed a great strain on the pilots of the two *Geschwader*. On the one hand it meant constantly changing tactics, while on the other night operations still had priority, and it was on their criteria that pilots for the two units were ultimately selected. It was during this phase that the greatest demands were being made of the *"Wilde Sau"* units, and as it would later turn out, the unique mixture of experienced bomber and transport pilots with trained fighter pilots was particularly advantageous. Both sides had much to give to the other: from the bomber pilots came the coolness required to select the correct method of attack, and from the fighter pilots the offensive spirit.

JG 301 contributed two *Gruppen* to the defense on this night, *I./JG 301* from Neubiberg and *III./JG 301* from Zerbst. The weather conditions were very favorable for illuminated night fighting ("*Henaja*"), which meant that pilots less experienced in instrument flying also had an opportunity to be successful.

Oberfeldwebel Hans Todt of *2./JG 301* shot down two four-engined bomber on this night; the first, a Lancaster, went down at 2241 hours.

Feldwebel Robert Siegfahrt of *7./JG 301* shot down a Lancaster over Berlin at 2237 hours.

On the negative side, *Oberleutnant* Kurt Medinn of *8./JG 301* was lost. Hit by return fire while attacking a British bomber over Berlin, he went down with his Bf 109 G-6. Medinn was a native of Berlin.

All of *JG 302* saw action on this night. The *Stab* of *JG 302* took off from Döberitz, *I./JG 302* from Jüterbog-Damm, *II./JG 302* from Ludwigslust and *III./JG 302* from Oldenburg. The fighter control service ordered all of the *Geschwader*'s aircraft into the Berlin area, where there were numerous contacts with bombers en route to and leaving the target area.

Leutnant German Merz of *Stab/JG 302* scored his first victory on this night, shooting down a Halifax on its way to Berlin.

Oberfeldwebel Ernst Haase of *1./JG 302* also shot down a Halifax at about the same time; it was his fourth night victory.

Oberfeldwebel Anton Benning of *2./JG 302* destroyed a Lancaster at 2240 hours.

Feldwebel Andreas Hartl of the *6. Staffel* had a particularly successful mission: he shot down his first four-engined bomber at 2237 hours, and before the night was over he had brought down three more.

Leutnant Kurt Welter of *5./JG 302* also had a successful night. At 2244 hours he destroyed a Lancaster and soon afterwards shot down a second.

Leutnant Glass of the *9. Staffel* shot down a Lancaster at 2250 hours.

Oberfeldwebel Eberhard Kroker of *6./JG 302* knocked down an enemy bomber over Berlin at 2242 hours.

Oberleutnant Karl-Heinz Seeler of *5./JG 302* concluded *JG 302*'s series of successes on this night by shooting down a four-engined bomber at 2257 hours.

Born in Bleckendorf in the Wansleben District on 31 October 1920, *Oberleutnant* Karl Heinz-Seeler was transferred to *II./JG 302* on 24 November 1943 and became acting commander of the *5. Staffel*. As a former bomber pilot, he had been trained in instrument flying and among the aircraft he had flown were the Do 23, Do 17, Ju 86, Ju 52, Ju 88, He 111 and Bf 109. In the period from February 1942 until August 1943 he had flown a total of about eighty combat missions with *KG 5* on the Eastern Front.

JG 302's successes on this night did not come without cost, however.

Feldwebel Kurt Bemme of *1./JG 302* suffered engine failure and abandoned his aircraft near Niedergörsdorf southwest of Jüterbog. He sustained serious injuries while bailing out and was taken to hospital in Jüterbog. (Bf 109, WNr. 161 376)

Unteroffizier Wolfgang Kindhäuser of *5./JG 302* sustained injuries when his Bf 109 G-6 crashed on takeoff at Ludwigslust.

Oberfeldwebel Herbert Stephan of the *1. Staffel* was seriously injured in a crash-landing at Pretzsch. He was taken to hospital in Torgau.

29 March 1944

On this day the *I.* and *III. Gruppe* of *JG 301* were sent against bombers and fighters of the American 8th Air Force.

There is no information on the number of aircraft that took part, but the pilots involved had to change their tactics once again. Attacks by one or two fighters were not advisable; the only way to attack a combat box of bombers was to attack in wedge formation.

The pilots in the ranks of the *Staffeln* and *Gruppen* had yet to fully accept this method of attack, as they still had too little experience with it. Another significant factor in these daylight missions was the growing range of the American escort fighters: the P-38 Lightnings, P-47 Thunderbolts and P-51 Mustangs were accompanying the bombers ever deeper into German airspace.

This new state of affairs – battling enemy bombers and their escorting fighters simultaneously – presented the *Luftwaffe* and thus the fighter units with an almost impossible problem. It would take time to develop tactics that allowed the intercepting fighters to engage the bomber formations with a good chance of success.

At 1345 hours *Oberfeldwebel* Willi Kropf of *7./JG 301* shot down a B-17 Flying Fortress.

Unteroffizier Rolf Burghardt of *3./JG 301* shot down a second B-17 at 1344 hours.

Oberfeldwebel Willi Kropf was shot down by return fire while making a second attack on the B-17s. He was extremely lucky to get out of his doomed machine near Gardelegen. He landed heavily and suffered serious injuries.

Feldwebel Robert Siegfahrt of the *7. Staffel* was shot down and killed by American escort fighters. He and his aircraft came down near Magdeburg.

Oberfeldwebel Walter Blickle of *9./JG 301* was wounded in action and was forced to crash-land his badly damaged Bf 109 G-6 near Colbitz in the Magdeburg District.

The scale of *I./JG 302*'s participation in this action cannot be determined with certainty. All that is known is that the *Staffelkapitän* of *2./JG 302*, *Hauptmann* Karl-Heinz Dietsche, was injured when he crash-landed his shot-up machine in a field near Stendal. (Bf 109 G-6, WNr. 440 160)

30-31 March 1944

The RAF launched a night attack against Nuremberg. For reasons unknown *I./JG 301*, then based at Neuburg an der Donau, was not ordered up even though Neuburg was only ten minutes flying time from Nuremberg.

The German fighter controllers guessed wrong as to the RAF's target, and the three *Gruppen* of *JG 302* were ordered into the air from their bases south and west of Berlin. Based on the loss reports, they made contact with the enemy over Thuringia and Hesse.

Hauptmann Helmut Suhr, *Staffelkapitän* of *7./JG 301*, show down two Lancaster bombers over central Germany.

Oberfeldwebel Willi Rose of *9./JG 301* was killed in a crash near Straguth northeast of Zerbst. The cause of the crash is not known.

Also successful was *Hauptmann* Gerlach of *5./JG 302*, who brought down a British bomber at 0103 hours.

Unteroffizier Erwin Völkel of *7./JG 302* was shot down and killed over Hildburghausen.

Oberfeldwebel Friedrich Hill of *8./JG 302* was killed in the crash of his machine near Lischeid. (Bf 109 G-6 "Black 4", WNr. 411 460)

Increasingly, the *Geschwader* were being sent graduates from the flying schools to take the place of pilots lost in recent months. The schools tried to prepare the young pilots to carry on the unequal struggle. Night missions were becoming fewer, while the number of daylight missions was growing. Nevertheless, pilots from every type of unit in the *Luftwaffe* were still being transferred to *JG 301* and *JG 302*.

After a time the *Gruppen* reached a favorable ratio between "skilled" and "unskilled" fighter pilots, meaning those who had received specialized fighter training and those who had been trained for other roles. In later missions this arrangement was to prove very solid. These later missions were increasingly directed against daylight raids by the Americans, who now came with growing strength from the west and south. Such missions required the interceptors to engage the bombers and the escort fighters simultaneously, and among the pilots there developed a quite natural division of roles based on their training: those who preferred to attack the four-engined bombers and those who sought combat with the escort fighters.

Even the apparently easier task of engaging the American escort fighters was filled with risks, especially for the recently trained pilots, for the pilots in the enemy fighters were well trained and experienced. Each had at least 300 hours on type. The training received by their German counterparts could not compare to this, placing them at a distinct disadvantage in combat. As there were not as yet high-altitude *Staffel* to protect the fighters from being attacked from above by escort fighters, the individual *Staffeln* and *Gruppen* formed covering *Schwärme* (flights of four aircraft) for this purpose. As the number of enemy incursions grew week by week, with ever greater numbers of bombers and escort fighters, the *Luftwaffe* was forced to change its tactics. These changes will be discussed later.

1 April 1944

Leutnant Max Kreil of *I./JG 301* was forced to abandon his machine about thirty kilometers north of Passau after its engine failed, sustaining injuries in the process. (Bf 109 G-6, WNr. 161 392)

2 April 1944

There were major raids by the American 15th Air Force from Italy against the ball bearing factory in Steyr, Austria. The attack force consisted of thirteen bomb groups with 125 B-17 Flying Fortresses and 286 B-24 Liberators. The bomber stream was escorted by 107 P-38 Lightnings and forty-five P-47 Thunderbolts.

I./JG 301 from Neubiberg was one of the units that rose to intercept the enemy.

At 1115 hours *Hauptmann* Helmut Suhr, who had transferred from the *7. Staffel* to *I./JG 301* just the day before, shot down a B-17 near Steyr.

Fahnenjunker-Feldwebel Emanuel of *1./JG 301* attacked a B-24 in the same airspace at 1137 hours. The bomber caught fire and was forced to leave the formation, however Emanuel was unable to watch the B-24 crash.

All of the aircraft that took part in the mission returned to their base undamaged. There were no casualties.

4 and 5 April 1944

The first victory claims were received from *IV./JG 301*. The *Gruppe*, still consisting of just the *10. Staffel*, was based in Romania. There is no information concerning the *Staffel's* aircraft or personnel, however the surviving records do detail the unit's first successes (HSS = *"Herausschuß"*, or a bomber forced to leave the protection of its formation).

4 Apr. 1944	*Feldwebel* Gerhard Mett	*10./JG 301*	1400	B-24 HSS	Romania
5 Apr. 1944	*Feldwebel* Gerhard Mett	*10./JG 301*	1435	B-24 HSS	Romania
5 Apr. 1944	*Feldwebel* Gerhard Mett	*10./JG 301*	1440	B-24	Romania
5 Apr. 1944	*Feldwebel* Gerhard Zeisler	*10./JG 301*	1455	B-24 HSS	Romania
5 Apr. 1944	*Feldwebel* Gerhard Zeisler	*10./JG 301*	1505	B-24 HSS	Romania
5 Apr. 1944	*Oberfeldwebel* Hubert Ippoldt	*10./JG 301*	1544	B-17	Romania

Most of *10./JG 301's* missions were in defense of the vital oil refineries at Ploesti.

During a mission by *I./JG 302* on 5 April 1944, *Hauptmann* Heinrich Wurzer of the *1. Staffel* shot down a P-51 Mustang. This type of American fighter was appearing in growing numbers and this was probably the first time that *I./JG 302* encountered it. This first meeting did, however, offer a foretaste of the problems the Mustang would present the *Geschwader's* pilots in the future.

There is no record of losses among the participating aircraft on this day.

8 April 1944

All *Gruppen* of *JG 302* saw action against American bombers and fighters over Lower Saxony. *Jagdgeschwader 3, 11* and *54* also took part in the fighting in the Hanover – Brunswick area.

III./JG 302, which took off from Oldenburg, apparently approached the bombers unhindered and carried out several attacks. The pilots of the *7. Staffel* reached a favorable attack position and shot down four of the enemy.

Unteroffizier Günter Maeser of the *7. Staffel* shot down a B-17 at 1310 hours during the initial firing pass.

In the second attack, this time against a formation of B-24s, *Leutnant* Mess and *Feldwebel* Anton Gaißmeier, both members of *7. Staffel*, each forced an enemy bomber to leave the formation.

In the ensuing dogfight with escort fighters, *Leutnant* German Merz of the same *Staffel* shot down a P-51 Mustang.

JG 302 did suffer serious losses in this battle which left significant gaps in the ranks of the fighter pilots.

Oberfeldwebel Ernst Wick of the *1. Staffel* failed to return and was initially reported missing. This was later changed to killed in action. Where he crashed remains a mystery. (Bf 109 G-6, WNr. 411 126)

Feldwebel Andreas Hartl of the *6. Staffel* was pursued by several enemy fighters. He tried to escape the Mustangs at low level but failed. Hartl was shot down sixteeen kilometers east of Hanover and was unable to bail out. (Bf 109 G-6 "White 7", WNr. 411 994)

At the time of his death, *Feldwebel* Andreas Hartl was among the most successful "*Wilde Sau*" pilots, with thirteen night victories over heavy bombers. In spite of its success in this action, the *7. Staffel* also took significant losses. The outcome of the air battles over the eastern edge of the Lüneberg Heath was as follows:

Unteroffizier Günter Haeser was killed in action between Grohe and Wieren southeast of Ülzen. (Bf 109 G-6 "White 4", WNr. 26 050)

Unteroffizier Willibald Heymann was shot down near Schweimke northeast of Wittingen. (Bf 109 G-6 "White 6", WNr. 411 027)

Fahnenjunker-Feldwebel Gerd Setzermann went down near Wittendorf in the Gifhorn district. (Bf 109 G-6 "White 10", WNr. 411 366)

Between 1407 and 1425 hours a formation of fifty-two B-24 Liberators bombed the airbase at Oldenburg from a height of approximately 5,000 meters. The attack resulted in casualties on *III./JG 302*'s airfield, mainly among the ground personnel.

Clothing *Unteroffizier* Karl Kohlbrecher suffered a broken leg when he was struck by a collapsing wall.

Obergefreiter Karl Pflumm, a driver in the headquarters company, was seriously wounded by a bomb that exploded near the vehicle hangar.

Obergefreiter Fritz Brückner, an aircraft mechanic in the *7. Staffel*, was delivered to the reserve hospital in Kreyanbrück with serious injuries.

Flieger Willi Eggert, an armorer in the *8. Staffel*, was fatally injured by a bomb splinter. Later in the evening the *Gruppe* received news that *Unteroffizier* Kohlbrecher and *Oberfähnrich* Brückner had succumbed to their injuries.

9 April 1944

On this day *JG 302* saw action with its *I.* and *II. Gruppe*, which took off from Jüterbog and Ludwigslust respectively. *III./JG 302* had to remain on the ground as the damage to its runway caused by the previous day's raid had yet to be repaired.

The units were ordered against American bomber units heading for targets in central Germany.

The *Geschwader*'s fighters shot down seven four-engined bomber in this action, which must be seen as a considerable success for a daylight mission.

Oberfeldwebel Eberhard Kroker of the *6 Staffel* shot down two B-24s, at 1138 and 1145 hours.

Hauptmann Heinrich Wurzer, *Kapitän* of the *1. Staffel*, shot down two B-17s in the same area.

Oberleutnant Heinz Seidel, *Kapitän* of the *3. Staffel*, also shot down a B-17; it was his 2nd victory.

Oberfeldwebel Ernst Haase of the *1. Staffel* shot down a B-24 for his 5th victory.

Oberfeldwebel Ernst Wick of the *1. Staffel* shot down a four-engined bomber on this mission. The victory was confirmed by an airborne witness.

Oberfeldwebel Wick was lost on this mission, although the date was mistakenly entered as 8 April.

11 April 1944

The records contain very little information on the mission flown by *JG 302* on this day, just a list of victories. There is no indication where the fighting took place. By all indications, *III./JG 302* was still out of action on this day because of damage to its airfield. Based on the general information concerning the location of victories, the air fighting must have taken place in the airspace over Brunswick.

Victories claimed:

Oberfeldwebel Eberhard Kroker	*6./JG 302*	1119	B-24 HSS	Brunswick
Oberleutnant Karl-Heinz Seeler	*5./JG 302*	1120	B-24 HSS	Brunswick
Feldwebel Fritz Gnifke	*5./JG 302*	1124	B-24	Brunswick
Oberfeldwebel Ernst Haase	*1./JG 302*		B-17	Brunswick
Oberfeldwebel Artur Gross	*2./JG 302*		B-24	Brunswick

There is no information as to losses sustained in this operation.

12 April 1944

Major raid by the American 15th Air Force against aircraft factories in Wiener-Neustadt. At 1130 hours *II./JG 301* took off from Seyring airfield to intercept the American bombers and fighters approaching from the south. *III./JG 301*, which used the same airfield from 5 to 13 April, also took part in this mission. At almost the same time *I./JG 301* was ordered off from its base at Neubiberg.

Luftgaukommando XVII's air surveillance service reported that about 400 B-24 and B-17 bombers and approximately 100 to 120 P-38 Lightning and P-47 Thunderbolt escort fighters entered its airspace between 1135 and 1253 hours.

The intercepting fighters engaged the enemy over the mountains. At 1222 hours *Leutnant* Willi Esche of the *1. Staffel* shot down a B-24 Liberator south of Vienna.

At 1223 hours *Oberfeldwebel* Adolf Krista of the *8. Staffel* shot down another Liberator in the same area.

But these were the only successes and the outcome was in no way satisfactory. The pilots were still having difficulty adjusting to daylight missions and the resulting combat with enemy escort fighters. Nevertheless, one must pay tribute to them: having been trained as bomber pilots, they had to adapt to a fundamentally different type of flying, and they became better as time went on.

This action resulted in losses among the pilots of *JG 301*, losses that had to be made good.

Oberfeldwebel Thaddäus Wakonigg of the *4. Staffel*, a native of Styria, was shot down and killed by a Lightning southwest of Eisenstadt. (Bf 109 G-6, WNr. 412 045)

Fellow *Staffel* member *Unteroffizier* Rudolf Schneider was shot down and killed over Wiener-Neustadt. (Bf 109 G-6, WNr. 160 809)

After attacking a four-engined bomber, *Unteroffizier* Stefan Zeitlinger of the *6. Staffel* was attacked by a P-38 Lightning and wounded. He subsequently had to force-land his machine near Ödenburg in the high country and was taken to the nearest hospital. (Bf 109 G-6, WNr. 140 305)

Götzendorf near Vienna, June 1944. This Bf 109 G-6 with underwing cannon was flown by I./JG 302.

Feldwebel Kurt Lamm of the 6. *Staffel* was wounded by return fire while attacking a B-24 Liberator south of Oberpullendorf. His machine was wrecked in the forced landing that followed. (Bf 109 G-6, WNr. 410 088)

13 April 1944

I./JG 301 was scrambled from Neubiberg to intercept American units approaching from Italy. The result was a large-scale air battle over southwestern Bavaria in which the *Jagdgruppe* recorded successes and losses.

Unteroffizier Rolf Burghardt of the 3. *Staffel* shot down two Liberators at 1255 and 1311 hours, his 2nd and 3rd victories.

Oberfeldwebel Hans Todt of the 2. *Staffel* shot down another Liberator at 1255 hours.

Fahnenjunker-Oberfeldwebel Fritz Yung of the 1. *Staffel* engaged a P-51 Mustang, which he shot down after a lengthy struggle.

Reported losses:

Feldwebel Georg Scharein of the 1. *Staffel* was shot down in flames over Augsburg. Despite facial burns he was able to parachute to safety. (Bf 109 G-6, WNr. 162 412)

While attacking four-engined bomber, the aircraft of *Oberfeldwebel* Hans Dornhoff of the 3. *Staffel* was badly hit and he was wounded. He nevertheless succeeded in making a belly landing near Kirchdorf an der Iller, north of Memmingen. (Bf 109 G-6, WNr. 411 721)

Shortly after 1130 hours, *II./JG 301* at Seyring was ordered into the air against aircraft of the 15th Air Force approaching from Italy. The fighters flew southeast into Hungarian airspace and from there toward Budapest. The Americans' main targets were industrial facilities and Raab airfield, plus Budapest and its airfields. *III./JG 301* made contact with the enemy in the airspace south of

Budapest. The *Jagdgruppe* was unable to close with the bombers, however, as it was intercepted by escort fighters, P-38s and P-51s, within sight of the bombers.

Oberleutnant Kurt Jäger, *Staffelkapitän* of *4./JG 301*, failed to return from this mission. He managed to break through the escorting fighters to attack one of the bombers, however his aircraft was caught in the defensive crossfire and shot down. He went down with his machine southwest of Budapest near Rackeresztur-Ercsi at about 1300 hours. (Bf 109 G-6, WNr. 411 375)

15 April 1944

10./JG 301 was scrambled from Otopeni to cover the airspace over Bucharest-Ploesti as American bombers were heading toward the Ploesti oil fields. At 1215 hours, before the bombers reached their target, *Oberfeldwebel* Franz Menzel and *Feldwebel* Karl Unger each shot down a B-24 Liberator.

On this day *Oberfeldwebel* Rudolf Walther was injured when his aircraft crashed on takeoff. (Bf 109 G-6 "Black 4", WNr. 160 089)

The pilots of *JG 302* killed on 8 April 1944 were buried in the Hankenbüttel cemetery:

Fahnenjunker-Feldwebel Gerd Setzermann twenty-four years old born in Berlin
Unteroffizier Günter Haeser twenty years old born in Deutsch Krone
Unteroffizier Willibald Heymann twenty-three years old born in Meseritz/Warthe

17 April 1944

Oberleutnant Hans-Georg Kretschmer, *Staffelkapitän* of *10./JG 301*, took off from Bucuresti with his *Staffel* to intercept American bombers and shot down a B-24 Liberator. *Oberfeldwebel* Hubert Ippold had difficulties with his machine while taking off from Bucuresti and came down near the airfield boundary, sustaining injuries. (Bf 109 G-6 "Black 7", WNr. 20 424)

During a training mission from Jüterbog-Damm, the aircraft flown by *Unteroffizier* Herbert Kordas of *2./JG 302* suffered engine failure near Maltershausen, west of Jüterbog. The pilot suffered serious injuries in the ensuing forced landing. (Bf 109 G-6, WNr. 410 693)

18 April 1944

II./JG 302 took off from Ludwigslust to intercept American bombers and fighters coming in from the west. The *Jagdgruppe* received the order to take off in the early afternoon, and the surviving records make it impossible to determine precisely where the fighters contacted the enemy.

The *Gruppe* attacked a formation of B-17s, one of which was shot down by *Leutnant* Alfred Körver at 1432 hours for his second victory.

Oberfeldwebel Eberhard Kroker of the *6. Staffel* shot down another B-17 from the same formation at 1435 hours. It was his fifth victory.

The *Gruppe* suffered no losses on this occasion.

19 April 1944

It was still early in the morning when *I.* and *II./JG 302* received orders to take off from their airfields at Jüterbog and Ludwigslust to intercept incoming bombers. The main target of the Americans was industrial facilities in central Germany. Over Kassel the two *Jagdgruppen* made contact with the enemy. Taking advantage of a gap in the enemy's fighter cover, they attacked a formation of B-17s.

The attack took place at 1034 hours, and in spite of heavy return fire from the bombers, *Oberleutnant* Heinz Seidel, *Kapitän* of the *3. Staffel*, and *Oberfeldwebel* Artur Gross of the *2. Staffel* were each able to bring down a B-17.

Oberfeldwebel Eberhard Kroker of the *5. Staffel* scored effective hits on another B-17, setting it on fire and forcing it to drop out of formation. The Messerschmitts were then attacked by enemy fighters and Kroker was unable to watch the B-17 go down.

I./JG 302's losses were light:

Unteroffizier Thilo Beetz of the *2. Staffel* was shot down and killed near Wahlhausen in the Heiligenstadt district. (Bf 109 G-6, WNr. 411 394)

All of *III./JG 302*'s losses came from the *4. Staffel*:

Oberleutnant Willi Klein, *Kapitän* of the *4. Staffel*, lost his life in his Bf 109 G-6, WNr. 410 570, near Alberode.

Oberfeldwebel Karl Dreißinger crashed two kilometers south of Bönecke near Halberstadt, sustaining fatal injuries. (Bf 109 G-6, WNr. 411 737)

Far from the rest of the *Geschwader*, *IV./JG 301* once again saw action from the Targsorul-Nou and Otopeni airfields. At this time the *Jagdgruppe* still consisted of just the *10. Staffel* and there is no information to suggest that the *Gruppe*'s strength was increased. It is no longer possible to determine if the *Gruppe* was employed exclusively against the Americans or whether it also saw action against the Russians as the Eastern Front moved nearer. On 21 April 1944 it was recorded that *Oberleutnant* Hans-Georg Kretschmer shot down a Liberator at 1257 hours.

22-23 April 1944

Hans Müller's logbook reveals that *I./JG 301* took from Neubiberg on a night mission at 0118 hours. The mission ended at about 0200 and there is no record of victories or losses.

III./JG 302 also saw action from Oldenburg that night. Its records reveal that *Leutnant* Otto Schwamb of the *8. Staffel* shot down two British heavy bombers, at 0115 and 0120 hours.

The steady increase in daylight raids against the Reich from the west and south was forcing the *Luftwaffe* to frequently move the operational elements of both *Geschwader* to favorable airfields as the situation demanded. These transfers lasted only a few days, however the frequent moves make it impossible to determine with certainty from which airfields the units operated for every mission.

24 April 1944

American bombers and fighters entered the airspace over southern Bavaria and bombed the air bases at Oberpfaffenhofen and Penzing near Landsberg, destroying numerous aircraft on the ground. A number of escort fighters strafed the air base at Neuburg an der Donau. *Major* Brede took off with his *I./JG 301* at 1312 hours to intercept the raiders and a fierce air battle developed east of Munich. The *Jagdgruppe* was unable to outflank or break through the fighter escort to attack the bombers. Long before the *Gruppe* reached them it was attacked from above by enemy fighters, mainly P-51 Mustangs.

At 1345 hours *Feldwebel* Hans Müller of the *2. Staffel* shot down a P-51 over the Ebersberger Forest. *Feldwebel* Müller's Bf 109 "White 5" was damaged in the fighting and he was forced to get to safety as quickly as possible. He managed to reach Munich-Riem, where he made a belly landing at 1355 hours.

I./JG 301 at Neubiberg in April 1944. From left: unidentified Leutnant or Hauptmann; Fahnenjunker-Oberfeldwebel Fritz Yung, 1./JG 301; Oberfeldwebel Hans Schäfer, 2./JG 301; Feldwebel Hans Müller, 2./JG 301; Feldwebel Viktor Gstrein, 2./JG 301.

This was to be the *Gruppe*'s only success on this occasion, for a close formation is always at a disadvantage when attacked from above, and the *Gruppe* had to fly close formation if it was to attack the bombers with any hope of success. The pilots of the *Reichsverteidigung* were well aware of this of course but, as the bombers were always the prime target, they had to fly in close formation.

By this time the *Gruppen* were employing high-altitude flights to provide top cover, however they were far too few to keep the enemy fighters at bay. In the weeks that followed, therefore, the *Jagdgruppen* assigned to the *Reichsverteidigung* were bolstered by the addition of a high-altitude protection *Staffel*. This raised the operational strength of a *Gruppe* from three to four *Staffeln*.

24 April 1944 ended as a rather costly day for *I./JG 301*:

Oberleutnant Hans Tschauder of the *Gruppenstab* was shot down and wounded over Erding. He parachuted to safety.

Oberfähnrich Hans Schäfer of the *1. Staffel* was shot down near Markt Schwaben but was able to bail out safely. (Bf 109 G-6, WNr. 163 060)

Fahnenjunker-Feldwebel Fritz Yung of *1. Staffel* was shot down near Markt Schwaben and seriously wounded. In spite of his wounds he was able to abandon his aircraft and pull the ripcord. He was taken to hospital where one foot was amputated.

Fahnenjunker-Feldwebel Arnold Müller-Leutert of the *2. Staffel* was shot down and killed near Erding.

Feldwebel Herbert Kunzinger of the *3. Staffel* was unable to shake off a P-51 Mustang that got on his tail. He fell near Markt Schwaben south of Erding.

Neubiberg 1944: Fahnenjunker-Oberfeldwebel Fritz Yung of 1./JG 301 and Feldwebel Arno Müller-Leutert of 2./JG 301, who was killed in action over Munich on 24 April 1944.

Oberfeldwebel Ludwig Schmutz of the *3. Staffel* went down with his Bf 109 G-6, WNr. 411 245, near Piusheim.

Gruppenkommandeur Major Walter Brede landed at the Holzkirchen airfield with splinters in his face and neck.

24-25 April 1944

At this time *III./JG 301* was stationed at Großsachsenheim airfield, where it received orders to intercept British bombers heading for the Ruhr.

Oberleutnant Otto-Ernst Hocker of the *Stab* of *III./JG 301* claimed a Lancaster shot down at 0043 hours.

This is the only success contained in the records of this mission. It is impossible to determine whether any of the *Gruppe*'s losses on this day were linked to the night mission.

Feldwebel Paul Dettmer of the *7. Staffel* was killed in aerial combat; he was shot down south of Biblis. (Bf 109 G-6, WNr. 411 377)

Unteroffizier Werner Albers of the *8. Staffel* went down with his Bf 109 G-6, WNr. 440 990, after an engagement in the area of Großsachsenheim.

Leutnant Gustav Mohr of the *7. Staffel* was killed in a flying accident near Linz am Rhein. (Bf 109 G-6, WNr. 163 046)

26-27 April 1944

The logbook of *Feldwebel* Hans Müller of *1./JG 301* reveals that *I./JG 301*, at least, saw action on this night. He took off from Neubiberg at 0119 hours and landed at Biblis at 0243.

III./JG 302, which had moved to Vechta for a few days at this time, must have taken part in the night operation from there. *Leutnant* German Merz of the *7. Staffel* shot down a British bomber at 0259 hours. This time fits the time period that *I./JG 301* was in action from Neubiberg.

27-28 April 1944

I./JG 301 flew another night mission from Neubiberg, as recorded in the logbook of *Feldwebel* Hans Müller of the *1. Staffel*. He took off from Neubiberg at 0120 hours and landed back at the same field at 0307. It appears that none of the *Gruppe*'s aircraft made contact with the enemy, as there are no reported claims or losses for this mission.

III./JG 301 was also in the air on this night, taking off from Großsachsenheim. This is confirmed by a claim made by *Leutnant* Glaas of *8./JG 301* for a four-engined bomber shot down at 0238 hours. This timing fits the period that *I./JG 301* was airborne.

It cannot be determined if the loss of *Hauptmann* Franz-Wilhelm Gerig of *Stab/JG 302* was related to the night mission. Gerig and his Bf 109 G-6, WNr. 440 745, went down in the Flammersheimer Forest, ten kilometers southeast of Euskirchen, between 0200 and 0300 hours.

29 April 1944

American bombers with fighter escort took off from their bases in England to attack industrial targets in central Germany. *I.* and *II./JG 302* were among the units that intercepted the raid. *I./JG 302* took off from Jüterbog-Damm, *II./JG 302* from Stendal, where the *Gruppe* was based for a few days. Both *Gruppen* engaged the enemy over Lower Saxony, resulting in fierce fighting.

Bf 109 G-6s of I./JG 302 in front of the hangars of Jüterbog airbase south of Potsdam, photographed at the end of April 1944. On 9 May the Gruppe was transferred to Seyring near Vienna.

At 1104 hours *Oberleutnant* Karl-Heinz Seeler, *Kapitän* of the *5. Staffel*, shot down a B-17 over Brunswick. It was his fourth victory.

Oberfeldwebel Eberhard Kroker of the *6. Staffel* shot down a B-24 at 1118 hours, also over Brunswick. It was his seventh victory.

At 1130 hours *Feldwebel* Werner Dienst of the *3. Staffel* shot down a B-17 over Wolfsburg.

Soon afterwards *Oberfeldwebel* Ernst Haase of the *1. Staffel* sent a B-17 down in the Brunswick-Wolfsburg area. It was his seventh victory.

Oberfeldwebel Artur Groß of the *2. Staffel* also shot down a B-17 over Magdeburg. It was his sixth victory.

Oberleutnant Heinz Seidel, *Kapitän* of the *3. Staffel*, shot down a B-17. In the ensuing dogfight with the enemy escorts he also destroyed a P-51 Mustang. They were his fourth and fifth victories.

These successes were overshadowed by the death of *Leutnant* Erich Schötta of the *2. Staffel*, who was shot down near Celle in his Bf 109 G-6/U4, WNr. 440 590.

Both *Gruppen* of *JG 302* could rightly judge this daylight mission a success. The pilots in the *Staffeln* were now better adjusted to daylight missions and some had become specialists in attacking four-engined bombers, which encouraged the others. Combat with enemy fighters was still a problem and would remain so as long as the bomber formations remained the prime target.

30 April 1944

II./JG 301, which had been based at Seyring near Vienna from 13 February to 27 April 1944 and lived through its second establishment there, was moved to Targsorul-Nou in Romania on 29 April. The *Gruppe* was sent there to support *IV./JG 301*, which still consisted of just the *10. Staffel* and had been stationed in Romania since the end of February.

At first the entire *Gruppe* was based at the Targsorul-Nou airfield. Later the *Stab* and various *Staffeln* were stationed at different airfields:

— the *Stab* operated at times from Busherischte and Wrasdebna airfields,
— the *4. Staffel* from Targsorul-Nou and Mizil airfields,

— the *5. Staffel* from Wrasdebna and Busherischte airfields,
— and the *6. Staffel* from Targsorul-Nou.

The *Gruppe* and its technical personnel remained in this area of operations until the end of August 1944.

The *Gruppe*'s first victory in the new area of operations was achieved by *Leutnant* Rudi Wurff of the *6. Staffel* with the downing of a B-24 Liberator at 0940 hours on 30 April 1944.

Situation maps of the *Luftwaffe* High Command (OKL) at this time provide the following information: deployed within the area of the *7. Jagddivision* on 30 April 1944 were:

— *Stab/JG 301* at Schleissheim,
— *I./JG 301* at Neubiberg,
— *III./JG 301* at Großsachsenheim

This confirms that *II./JG 301* was no longer attached to the *7. Jagddivision* at this time.

3 May 1944

Feldwebel Walter Schulze of *9./JG 302* was killed during a training flight, crashing from a height of 800 meters near the village of Treune, five kilometers north of Brunswick.

Unteroffizier Josef Niedermeyer was killed in action during a mission over Romania by *10./JG 301*. There is no information on the precise location of or the nature of the combat in which he lost his life. (Bf 109 G-6, DR+EK, WNr. 20 189)

Oberfeldwebel Franz Menzel of the same *Staffel* destroyed a B-24 Liberator at 1408 hours on 5 May.

On 6 May *II./JG 301* took off from Targsorul-Nou to intercept enemy bombers entering Romanian airspace. The target was a formation of B-24s operating without fighter escort.

Leutnant Hans-Joachim Weber of the *6. Staffel* shot down a B-24 at 1135 hours. At 1145 hours *Oberfähnrich* Peter Brenner of the same *Staffel* attacked a B-24 and left it in flames.

7 May 1944

I./JG 301 took off from Jüterbog on a daylight mission about which little is known. The only information known with certainty is that a B-17 was shot down by the *Kapitän* of the *3. Staffel*, *Oberleutnant* Heinz Seidel. *Leutnant* Hans Kohler of *7./JG 301* was killed in a crash near Heimdingen, however this was not due to enemy action. The precise cause of the crash remains a mystery. (Bf 109 G-6/U4, WNr. 411 153)

8 May 1944

I./JG 302 flew its last mission from Jüterbog on this day. The next day the *Gruppe* transferred to Seyring near Vienna.

II./JG 302, which had moved to Salzwedel, also flew a daylight mission, directed against American bombers which flew from England to Lower Saxony.

The two *Gruppen* of *JG 302* met and engaged formations of B-17s in the Hanover – Brunswick area.

Oberfeldwebel Eberhard Kroker of the *6. Staffel* attacked a B-17, scoring effective hits. On fire, the bomber dropped out of formation. It was Kroker's 8th victory.

Oberleutnant Heinz Seidel, *Kapitän* of the *3. Staffel*, shot down a B-17 in this action for his 7th victory.

There were also casualties in this action: the loss of *Hauptmann* Friedhelm Höschen, *Kapitän* of the *6. Staffel*, was a particularly severe blow. Höschen was shot down and killed near Kleinstockheim south of Brunswick. (Bf 109 G-6/U4 "Red 10", WNr. 440 562)

Leutnant Alfred Körver, technical officer of *II./JG 302*, was shot down and killed near Wiesenhügel. (Bf 109 G-6, WNr. 411 153)

10 May 1944

I./JG 302 had transferred from Jüterbog-Damm to Seyring the day before. In the period that followed, it would be employed mainly against incursions from southern Europe by the American 15th Air Force.

On 10 May the *Gruppe* was scrambled against American fighters and bombers coming in from Italy. Over Lake Neusiedler the *Jagdgruppe* attacked a formation of B-24s which had apparently lost its fighter escort. While suffering no losses, *I./JG 302* achieved its first major success in its new operations. Details of individual victories appear below (position information from the fighter grid system):

Oberfeldwebel Anton Benning	*2./JG 302*	1126	B-24 HSS	Lake Neusiedler EP 1
Oberfeldwebel Egbert Jaacks	*3./JG 302*	1131	B-24	Lake Neusiedler EO 8
Leutnant Gert Bernhard	*2./JG 302*	1132	B-24 HSS	Lake Neusiedler EO 8
Hauptmann Heinrich Wurzer	*1./JG 302*	—	B-24	Lake Neusiedler EO 4
Oberfeldwebel Anton Benning	*2./JG 302*	1138	B-24	Sopron FO1/2
Unteroffizier Rudolf Diecke	*3./JG 302*	1150	B-24	Wiener Neustadt EN
Hauptmann Heinrich Eurzer	*1./JG 302*	—	B-24	Wiener Neustadt EN

The American bombers operating from Italy were mainly escorted by P-38 Lightnings and P-51 Mustangs. The P-47 Thunderbolt was increasingly being replaced by the Mustang. It was also apparent that the number of escort fighters was considerably lower than in the west. Nevertheless, they were always numerically superior to the intercepting German fighters. In his book *Der Einsatzflughafen Fels/Wgr. im Tullnerfeld*, Anton Handelsberger wrote:

"On this 10th of May 1944 the Americans' target was the Messerschmitt aircraft factory in Wiener-Neustadt. Taking part in the attack were 175 B-17 Flying Fortresses and 231 B-24 Liberators. Providing the fighter escort were 168 P-38 Lightnings, forty-eight P-51 Mustangs and forty-eight P-47 Thunderbolts.

"According to the evening report by *Luftgaukommando XVII*, the German side put up 159 fighter aircraft."

11 May 1944

Unteroffizier Günter Heinsen of *9./JG 302* was killed in a crash near Edemissen, north of Peine. Cause of the crash is not known. (Bf 109 G-6 "Yellow 1", WNr. 411 333).

Chapter Six

Changes in Both *Jagdgeschwader*

May of 1944 brought a variety of changes to *Jagdgeschwader 301* and *302*. A report by the staff of the *General der Jagdflieger* reveals that *10./JG 301*, which had previously consisted of personnel only, received its equipment at this time, even though it can be proved that the *Staffel* had been in action since at the beginning of April 1944.

Several sentences later, however, it is stated that the *Staffel* was being disbanded.

Another directive from the same staff brought with it enormous changes for both *Geschwader*: units were to be disbanded, renamed, reformed, with some measures overlapping. At the conclusion of these measures there were numerous absurdities with two shrunken fighter wings. Disbanded were:

Stab Jagdgeschwader 301,
III./Jagdgeschwader 301,
10./Jagdgeschwader 301 (victory and loss records indicate that it continued to exist until the end of July 1944),
Stab Jagdgeschwader 302,
II./Jagdgeschwader 302,
III./Jagdgeschwader 302.

At the conclusion of these measures the picture was as follows:

Stab/JG 301	disbanded
I./JG 301	unchanged
II./JG 301	unchanged
III./JG 301	in process of disbandment

Stab/JG 302	disbanded
I./JG 302	unchanged
II./JG 302	renamed *III./JG 300*
III./JG 302	disbanded

This process of reorganization was completed by the end of May 1944, but the changes it brought would only last a few months: in September 1944 there would be another reorganization.

13 May 1944

II./JG 302 took off from Salzwedel on one of its last daylight missions. The *Gruppe* engaged American bombers, with fighting in the area north of Berlin, over Mecklenburg and Pomerania. Once again the pilots faced an almost impossible task, for in terms of offensive tactics they still lacked sufficient experience for the battle they were forced to fight against the American bombers and escort fighters. It was often necessary to grapple with the escorts before getting to the main target, the bombers, and there were few opportunities to evade the American fighters.

This is probably the reason why the *Gruppe* recorded just a single victory, a B-17 shot down by *Oberleutnant* Karl-Heinz Seeler of the *5. Staffel* at 1421 hours. Losses, on the other hand, were considerable.

Unteroffizier Heinrich Amerkamp of the *6. Staffel* was shot down and killed over Dargun in Pomerania. (Bf 109 G-6 "White 4", WNr. 440 901)

The aircraft of *Feldwebel* Fritz Gnifke of the *5. Staffel* was badly damaged in combat. He made a forced landing near Niendorf, southeast of Teterow, and was taken to hospital with wounds. (Bf 109 G-6 "Red 7", WNr. 411 924)

Unteroffizier Werner Greskow of the *6. Staffel* was wounded in action over Demmin. He bailed out of his doomed machine. (Bf 109 G-6 "White 8", WNr. 440 702)

Unteroffizier Artur Mayer of the *4. Staffel* was wounded in combat with the fighter escort southeast of Levin and bailed out. (Bf 109 G-6 "White 7", WNr. 440 680)

17 May 1944

Oberfeldwebel Alfred Pelz was killed in an unexplained crash near the airfield at Seyring. (Bf 109 G-6, "Black 10", WNr. 110 054)

18 May 1944

There are few surviving documents concerning *II./JG 301*'s activities in Romania. It is impossible to say how closely the unit cooperated with the so-called *IV./JG 301*, which consisted solely of the *10. Staffel*. Loss reports and victory claims suggest that they operated separately.

At 1115 hours on this day *Leutnant* Hans-Joachim Weber of *6./JG 301* shot down a B-24 Liberator.

19 May 1944

II./JG 302 took off from Salzwedel and saw action in the Berlin area. *Unteroffizier* Heinz Sarnow of the *4. Staffel* took part in this mission. He was initially reported missing after combat over metropolitan Berlin, however his status was later changed to killed in action. (Bf 109 G-6, WNr. 411 514)

23-24 May 1944

II./JG 302 flew its last mission against British night bombers using the illuminated night fighting method, however the scene of the action can no longer be determined. What is known, however, is that *Oberleutnant* Karl-Heinz Seeler of the *5. Staffel* shot down two four-engined bombers. The two victories, recorded at 0216 and 0227 hours, were his 6th and 7th. Not long afterwards, *Oberleutnant* Karl-Heinz Seeler was transferred to *JG 7* at Brandenburg-Briest, where he retrained on the Me 262. He returned to action in the jet fighter and fell in combat with American escort fighters near Perleberg in early 1945.

II./JG 302 appears in the records again on 24 May 1944, with a report that *Leutnant* Jonny Kruse, acting commander of the *4. Staffel*, was killed in action over Berlin. The downing of three B-17s is also reported:

at 1108 hours *Unteroffizier* Hans Breurs of the *5. Staffel* shot down a B-17 northwest of Berlin, while *Feldwebel* Otto Pritzl of the same unit downed two of the American bombers in the same area at 1108 and 1118 hours.

One final report by *II./JG 302* is dated 28 May 1944: it states that *Unteroffizier* Hans Breuers of the *5. Staffel* was wounded in action north of Köthen and forced to take to his parachute.

This must also be seen as the date on which *II./JG 302* was disbanded; it was renamed *III./JG 300* at Salzwedel.

III./JG 302 was also disbanded at this time. It appeared in the records for a final time on 29 May 1944: *Oberleutnant* Hans Uhse, *Kapitän* of the *7. Staffel*, was killed in a crash following a midair collision over Völkenrode airbase near Brunswick.

From this point on *JG 302* consisted only of *I./JG 302*, which was based at Seyring, north of Vienna. The *Gruppe* operated from there against American incursions from southern Europe. In mid-June 1944 it moved to Götzendorf, south of Vienna, where it was to remain until the end of August 1944. *Gruppenkommandeur* at that time was *Hauptmann* Richard Lewens. The *Gruppe* retained its original composition for the first missions in the new area of operations, but at the beginning of June 1944 a fourth *Staffel* was added to the original three.

The new *Staffel* came from *JG 51 "Mölders"*, which was based on the Eastern Front. At the end of May 1944 this *Jagdgeschwader* released its *2., 7.* and *12. Staffel* to the Defense of the Reich. The *12. Staffel* commanded by *Oberleutnant* Ferdinand Kray joined *I./JG 302*.

With its experience in fighter-versus-fighter combat, the new unit was assigned the role of high cover for *I./JG 302*, protecting the remaining *Staffeln* against attack from above as they engaged the enemy bombers.

The *Staffel* included such successful fighter pilots as *Oberleutnant* Kray (16 victories), *Leutnant* Grumme (20), *Leutnant* Kirchner (7), *Leutnant* Stahl (2), *Leutnant* Hallenberger (1) and *Feldwebel* Dreesmann (9 victories).

I./JG 302 now consisted of four *Staffeln* with an average strength of fifty to sixty aircraft. The *Staffelkapitäne* at that time were:

1. Staffel: *Hauptmann* Heinrich Wurzer
2. Staffel: *Hauptmann* Karl-Heinz Dietsche
3. Staffel: *Oberleutnant* Heinz Seidel
4. Staffel: *Oberleutnant* Ferdinand Kray

In the period that followed, the reorganized *Jagdgruppe*'s operational strength grew steadily. It fell under the command of the *Jagdführer (Jafü) Süd*, *Oberst* Handrik. Handrik had won the Gold Medal in the pentathlon at the 1936 Olympic games. His control center used the codename *"Rosenkavalier"*. *I./JG 302* was not alone in the struggle against the American incursions from Italy. Initially it received very effective support from *II./ZG 1* based at Wels. The *Zerstörergruppe* was equipped with the Bf 110, which had proved extremely effective against heavy bombers. The American fighter escorts initially lacked the range to accompany the bombers all the way to their targets, but as their range increased, the effectiveness of the German twin-engined fighters was seriously diminished. Hopelessly inferior to the American fighters, the Bf 110 was withdrawn from the daylight intercept role. *I./JG 302* was not the only single-engined fighter unit in the area. A *Gruppe* of *JG 27* was based north of Vienna and the Hungarian 110th "Puma" Fighter Group operated against the American bombers from its bases around Budapest.

24 May 1944

On Wednesday the 24th of May 1944 the American 15th Air Force dispatched 128 B-17 Flying Fortresses and 438 B-24 Liberators from bases in the area around Foggia to attack aircraft production sites and airfields in the area of Vienna and Graz. The bombers were escorted by 148 P-39 Lightnings, eighty-four P-51 Mustangs and thirty-eight P-47 Thunderbolts.

Thirty aircraft of *I./JG 302* took off from Seyring to intercept the raiders. In the fierce fighting that ensued in the airspace south and west of Vienna the *Gruppe* scored its biggest success to date. The *Gruppe*'s victories on this day are listed below:

1008	*Oberfeldwebel* Janke	*3./JG 302*	B-24	N of Mittersdorf
1010	*Hauptmann* Heinrich Wurzer	*1./JG 302*	B-24	near St. Pölten
1013	*Leutnant* Gerd Bernhard	*2./JG 302*	P-51	SW of Vienna
1013	*Oberleutnant* Heinz Seidel	*3./JG 302*	B-24	S of St. Pölten
1013	*Unteroffizier* Werner Voss	*1./JG 302*	B-24	near St. Pölten
1014	*Oberfeldwebel* Artur Gross	*2./JG 302*	B-24	Wiener Neustadt
1015	*Oberfeldwebel* Paul Streuff	*1./JG 302*	B-24 HSS	near St. Pölten
1016	*Hauptmann* Richard Lewens	*Gr.Kdr.*	B-24	Wiener Neustadt
1016	*Oberfeldwebel* Artur Gross	*2./JG 302*	B-24 HSS	St. Pölten
1017	*Hauptmann* Heinrich Wurzer	*1./JG 302*	B-24	W of Vienna
1019	*Feldwebel* Jäschke	*2./JG 302*	B-24	SE of St. Pölten
1020	*Leutnant* Gerd Bernhard	*2./JG 302*	B-24	SW of Vienna
1022	*Feldwebel* Jäschke	*2./JG 302*	B-24	20 km S St. Pölten

This was an outstanding success for a relatively small number of fighters and was extraordinarily important for the morale of the entire *Gruppe*. Four of the unit's pilots achieved more than one victory.

The mission was also a success in terms of losses: two pilots were wounded and none killed. Unfortunately, this ratio of victories to losses would seldom be repeated.

Oberfeldwebel Egbert Jaacks of the *3. Staffel* was wounded in combat near Kindherz and was taken to hospital in Mittersdorf. He flew the Bf 109 G-6 "Black 38", WNr. 410 733.

Feldwebel Werner Dienst of the *3. Staffel* was wounded in the upper arm during combat near St. Aegid and was taken to hospital in St. Pölten. He flew Bf 109 G-6 "Red 35", WNr. 440 597.

Aircraft numbers as high as "35" and "38" were seldom seen on operational aircraft. It must be assumed that these machines had come from a fighter school and had yet to provided with more standard tactical codes.

29 May 1944

The American 15th Air Force launched a major operation against Wiener Neustadt and industrial facilities on the southern outskirts of Vienna. *I./JG 302* took off from Seyring to intercept the raid, which consisted of 563 B-24 and B-17 bombers with an escort of 171 P-38 and P-51 fighters. Other German units that took part in the defensive effort were *III.* and *IV./JG 27*, *II./JG 77* and *II./ZG 1*.

I./JG 302's initial assignment was to escort the Bf 110s of *II./ZG 1* from takeoff at Wels until they intercepted the bombers. Once it had completed this task, the *Gruppe* attacked the bombers. In the fighting over Lower Austria the *Gruppe* shot down three four-engined bomber and damaged four others so badly that they had to leave their formations – at the time this was characterized as an "*Herausschuss*".

Hauptmann Wurzer and his *Staffel* played a major part in this success. Wurzer himself claimed two *Herausschüsse*.

0949	*Feldwebel* Jäschke	*2./JG 302*	B-24	W of St. Pölten
0952	*Unteroffizier* Heinz Ropers	*1./JG 302*	B-24	10 km W Markersdorf
0954	*Feldwebel* Anton Benning	*2./JG 302*	B-24	S of St. Pölten
0954	*Hauptmann* Heinrich Wurzer	*1./JG 302*	B-24 HSS	S of St. Pölten
0954	*Oberfeldwebel* Fritz Dickmann	*1./JG 302*	B-24 HSS	E of Markersdorf
0955	*Oberfeldwebel* Paul Streuff	*1./JG 302*	B-24 HSS	near St. Pölten
0959	*Hauptmann* Heinrich Wurzer	*1./JG 302*	B-24 HSS	SE St. Pölten

The *Gruppe* reported one loss: *Unteroffizier* Roland Bever of the *2. Staffel* was shot down and killed near St. Pölten in his Bf 109 G-6 "Red 25", WNr. 412 400.

It was in May 1944 that *I./JG 302* made the actual breakthrough from a mixed day and night fighter unit with its enormous disadvantages to a capable, determined day fighter unit. The *Gruppe*'s path had been a difficult and costly one, as reflected in the numerous casualties during training flights and its early day and night missions.

Hauptmann Lewen's list of victories at this time was as follows:

18 B-24 Liberators shot down,
2 B-17 Flying Fortresses shot down,
8 B-24 Liberators forced to leave formation,
1 B-24 Liberator finished off,
1 P-51 Mustang shot down.

At this time the area of operations of *JG 302*'s sole remaining *Gruppe* extended from Budapest to Munich. It was committed against incursions by the American 15th Air Force from the south as well those by the 8th Air Force from the west. To strengthen the defense against the American incursions, the *Gruppe* was supported by other *Jagdgeschwader*, which proved very effective during this time.

31 May 1944

II./JG 301 and *IV./JG 301*, still represented by just the *10. Staffel*, continued to operate in Romanian airspace. On this day the 6. and *10. Staffel* took off from Targsorul-Nou against American bombers attacking targets in Romania in support of Russian forces advancing toward the west.

The German fighters were heavily engaged by the escort and *Feldwebel* Ernst Kiehling of the *10. Staffel* shot down a P-38 Lightning at 1006 hours.

The pilots of the *6. Staffel* positioned themselves behind a group of B-24s and attacked.

Leutnant Hans-Joachim Weber and *Unteroffizier* Walter Toldrian inflicted damage on two B-24s, which dropped out of formation. Time of these two *Herausschüsse* was 1025 hours.

Oberfeldwebel Max Salzgruber, also of the *6. Staffel*, shot down a Liberator at 1054 hours. It was his first victory.

While the *6. Staffel* suffered no losses in this action, the *10. Staffel* was forced to pay a heavy price in blood:

Unteroffizier Waldemar Blazeck was shot down and killed by P-38s near Romanesti (Bf 109 G-6, WNr. 163 089).

Feldwebel Fritz Gehrmann lost his life in combat with escort fighters near Bultea (Bf 109 G-6 "Black 8", WNr. 20 144).

Feldwebel Kurt Witschel was shot down by the fighter escort and crashed to his death west of Bucharest (Bf 109 G-6, WNr. 162 126).

Oberleutnant Hans Kretschmer, *Kapitän* of the *10. Staffel*, was wounded in action and obliged to force-land his badly-damaged Bf 109 G-6 "Black 5", WNr. 412 236.

1 June 1944

I./JG 301 remained at the airfields of Holzkirchen, Frankfurt-Eschborn and Langendiebach until mid-June 1944, when it was transferred to St. Dizier and Epinoy in France. From there it flew illuminated night-fighter missions again until the end of August.

II./JG 301 – together with the *10. Staffel* – remained in Romania, the former until August 1944.

III./JG 301 was disbanded at Großsachsenheim on 6 June 1944.

In the first days of June 1944, *I./JG 302* moved from Seyring to Götzendorf airfield southeast of Vienna. This field enjoyed excellent natural camouflage, and even the "old hares" found it difficult to pick out in the midst of the greenery.

6 June 1944

In Romania, *II.* and *IV./JG 302* were sent against American incursions. The location of enemy contact and the target of the attack cannot be determined from surviving records.

Feldwebel Gerhard Zeisler of the *10. Staffel* shot down a B-24 Liberator at 0915 hours. He was subsequently shot down himself and went down with his fighter (Bf 109 G-6, WNr. 412 255).

In the same engagement, *Leutnant* Wurff of the *6. Staffel* shot down a B-24 for his third victory.

9 June 1944

I./JG 302 flew its first mission from Götzendorf on this day. It had been preceded by a few days rest, during which the unit's pilots familiarized themselves with the local area. They quickly discovered that the airfield's natural camouflage made it extremely difficult to spot from the air, even for those familiar with the area. This mission marked the first occasion in which the *4. Staffel*, formerly *12./JG 51 "Mölders"*, flew with the *Gruppe* in the "high cover" role.

The fighter control center guided the *Gruppe* into the Munich area and contact with the enemy was made east of Vienna. The *4. Staffel*'s value as a high-altitude *Staffel* for the *Gruppe* was quickly demonstrated. It was able to engage the fighter escort, which was not overly strong, and distract it while the *Gruppe* closed with the formations of bombers. *Feldwebel* Rudolf Dreesmann, who had scored nine victories on the Eastern Front, got off to a good start with his new unit by shooting down a P-51 Mustang.

The *Gruppe* recorded a large number of successes in this action:

0958	*Hauptmann* Heinrich Wurzer	*1./JG 302*	B-24 HSS	S of Landshut
1000	*Feldwebel* Dieter Rusche	*2./JG 302*	B-24 HSS	near Freising
1004	*Oberfeldwebel* Artur Gross	*2./JG 302*	B-24 HSS	SW of Landshut
1004	*Oberleutnant* Heinz Seidel	*3./JG 302*	B-24 HSS	S of Landshut

I./JG 302 at Götzendorf . The Jagdgruppe's shortest and tallest technicians: Gefreiter Otto Faßberg, aircraft mechanic, and Obergefreiter Peter Claus, aircraft electrician.

3./JG 302 at Götzendorf , June 1944. Feldwebel H.W. Schellner and Oberfeldwebel Sepp Sattler enjoy the sunshine.

1004	*Feldwebel* Anton Benning	*2./JG 302*	B-24 HSS	near Wasserburg
1005	*Oberfeldwebel* Hugo Langelotz	*3./JG 302*	B-24 HSS	SE Landshut
1006	*Oberfeldwebel* Sepp Sattler	*2./JG 302*	B-24 HSS	SE Munich
1007	*Feldwebel* Kurt Nachtigall	*3./JG 302*	B-24 HSS	S Landshut
1008	*Oberfeldwebel* Artur Gross	*2./JG 302*	B-24 HSS	SW Landshut
1009	*Feldwebel* Anton Benning	*2./JG 302*	B-24	S Landshut
1010	*Hauptmann* Heinrich Wurzer	*1./JG 302*	B-24	S Landshut
1010	*Unteroffizier* Werner Voss	*1./JG 302*	B-24	S Landshut
1010	*Feldwebel* Rudolf Dreesmann	*4./JG 302*	P-51	S Landshut
1012	*Oberfeldwebel* Artur Gross	*2./JG 302*	B-24 HSS	SW Landshut
1013	*Oberfeldwebel* Dieter Rusche	*2./JG 302*	B-24	SW Regensburg
1015	*Unteroffizier* Rudolf Diecke	*3./JG 302*	B-24	N Salzburg
1015	*Oberleutnant* Heinz Seidel	*3./JG 302*	B-24	8 km S Landshut

I./JG 302 had achieved a major success: six four-engined bombers and one Mustang shot down directly and another ten Liberators damaged and forced to drop out of formation. With three *Herausschüsse*, *Oberfeldwebel* Artur Gross of the *2. Staffel* was the *Gruppe*'s most successful pilot on this day.

What made this victory so remarkable, however, is the fact that it was achieved without loss: this day would be unique in the history of *I./JG 302*. An explanation of the values assigned to victories is perhaps appropriate here, for by this time the *Luftwaffe* had introduced a point system for the fighter arm.

The shooting down of a four-engined bomber was worth three points; the location of the crash had to be given.

Crippling a bomber and forcing it to leave its formation, a so-called *Herausschuss*, counted for two points. In this case it was often impossible to name a crash location, as the damaged bomber might remain airborne for some time.

Finishing off a bomber crippled by an earlier attack was worth one point. Shooting down an enemy fighter aircraft also counted for one point. A pilot's point total was taken into consideration in the awarding of decorations and promotions.

A brief summary of *Oberfeldwebel* Artur Groß' flying career: born in Stuttgart on 7 April 1911, he joined the *Luftwaffe* in early 1936 and received his initial flight training in Freiburg. He learned aerobatics at the Nellingen flying school at the beginning of 1937. Gross completed his pilot training at Nuremberg in August 1939. He subsequently served as a flight instructor with the Kaufbeuren Flight Training Regiment and in June 1943 arrived at the fighter training school in Lachen-Speyerdorf.

From 13 to 28 July 1943 Gross was with *Blindflugschule 110* (instrument training school) at Altenburg. On 29 July 1943 he was transferred to *III./JG 300* at Oldenburg. On 26 November, after the formation of *JG 302*, he was transferred to that unit's *I. Gruppe*. From 9 February to 27 March 1944 he was a member of the Helsinki Operational Detachment and subsequently moved with the *Gruppe* via Jüterbog to the Vienna area.

11 June 1944

II./JG 301 and the numerically-weak *IV./JG 301* were still active over Romania, intercepting raids by units of the 15th Air Force operating from bases in Italy. The main targets for the Americans were the tank farms and oil fields around Ploesti. These attacks touched the nerve of fuel supply system, not just for the *Luftwaffe*, but for all of the German armed forces.

During a mission by the *10. Staffel*, *Feldwebel* Fritz Ebel succeeded in bringing down a P-38 Lightning at 0858 hours. Soon afterwards, at 0925 hours, *Feldwebel* Gerhard Mett shot down a B-24 Liberator. Given the size of the attack force, however, these losses were like drops of water on a hot stone.

The *5. Staffel* was engaged by Mustangs of the fighter escort and suffered heavy losses.

Feldwebel Günter Iffert of Thuringia was shot down and killed seven kilometers west of Bodewgrad, *Unteroffizier* Heinz Gerling southwest of Samokow. Both were buried in the military cemetery in Pankia near Sofia. (Bf 109 G-6, WNr. 411 988 and 162 309).

Feldwebel Paul Becker abandoned his badly damaged Bf 109 G-6 (WNr. 410 085) northwest of Bodewgrad and was injured on striking the ground.

Unteroffizier Hermann Erchen was wounded in combat with P-51s northwest of Bodewgrad and was forced to bail out. (Bf 109 G-6, WNr. 162 644)

12 June 1944

I./JG 301 had been transferred from the Reich to France and at this time was at St. Dizier airfield. The *Gruppe* would fly "*Wilde Sau*" missions from this base for some time.

The first night mission from this base resulted in two Wellington bombers shot down by *Hauptmann* Helmut Suhr.

Two days later *Feldwebel* Theo Estermann of the *3. Staffel* was wounded in action against British bombers near Etampes but was able to parachute to safety.

13 June 1944

The American incursions from the south were coming at ever shorter intervals. It was the beginning of a period of maximum effort for *I./JG 302*, and the strain on the technical personnel was particularly great. Not all of the machines that made it back to base after a mission were undamaged: many suffered bullet damage in the wings and fuselage during attacks on the combat boxes of bombers or in combat with enemy fighters. Maintaining a high level of serviceability required a maximum effort on the part of the "Black Men". They worked in the hangars and maintenance sheds all day and sometimes into the night, repairing all types of damage. Mutual trust and a good working relationship between the pilots and technical personnel were absolutely vital in achieving the highest possible serviceability rate.

The order to take off reached the *Gruppe* in the early morning, and the fighters were vectored into the airspace over Munich. The long condensation trails behind the bombers could be seen from a great distance and *Hauptmann* Lewens, who was leading the *I./JG 302* attack formation, had time to determine the most favorable moment to attack.

But the enemy could also see the condensation trails produced by the German fighters, and soon the fighter escort turned to intercept them. The *Gruppe* was unable to make a concentrated attack on the bombers as it had done with such success on 9 June, but despite the efforts of the escorting fighters some of its fighters got through to attack a formation of B-24s. In the ensuing battle, four B-24 Liberators and two escort fighters were shot down. Another Liberator was forced out of formation.

0955	*Leutnant* Ernst-Dieter Grumme	*4./JG 302*	P-38	near Landau
1010	*Unteroffizier* Gerhard Walter	*2./JG 302*	B-24	10 km SE Ingolstadt
1015	*Oberfeldwebel* Anton Benning	*2./JG 302*	B-24 HSS	near Pfaffenhofen
1032	*Oberfeldwebel* Hugo Langelotz	*3./JG 302*	B-24	1 km N Weidenbach
1032	*Feldwebel* Rudolf Dreesmann	*4./JG 302*	B-24	near Weidenbach
1032	*Oberleutnant* Heinz Seidel	*3./JG 302*	B-24	N Weidenbach
1042	*Oberleutnant* Ferdinand Kray	*4./JG 302*	P-51	near Landau

I./JG 302 also suffered losses in this action:

Unteroffizier Hans Ettinger of the *2. Staffel* was shot down and killed near Erding, roughly fifty kilometers from his home town of Taufkirchen. (Bf 109 G-6, WNr. 163 531)

Unteroffizier Horst Sennewald of the *4. Staffel* was overwhelmed by the fighter escort and went down with his Bf 109 G-6 (WNr. 412 670) near Straubing.

14 June 1944

4./JG 302 engaged P-38 Lightnings over Lake Balaton. *Leutnant* Ernst-Dieter Grumme shot down one of the twin-engined fighters in grid square HQ9-HR7. It was his second victory against western opponents.

16 June 1944

The American 15th Air Force sent a total of 658 B-17s and B-24s to attack oil refineries in the Vienna area and the refinery in Preßburg (Bratislava). The bombers were escorted by 234 P-38s, P-47s and P-51s.

The Bf 109 G-6s of *I./JG 302* were scrambled from Götzendorf. Some aircraft still bore the wild boar's head, the emblem of the *"Wilde Sau"*, on their engine cowlings. The *Gruppe* was vectored south into Hungarian airspace, and over Lake Balaton it engaged the American enemy. With their experience in dogfighting, the pilots of the high-altitude *Staffel* were once again able to shield most of the *Gruppe* from the American escorts, allowing it to attack a group of B-24s. The high-altitude *Staffel* shot down two P-51s and a P-38 and also attacked the bombers, *Leutnant* Hallenberg shooting down a B-24.

I./JG 302's tally in this action:

0940	*Feldwebel* Rudolf Dreesmann	*4./JG 302*	P-51	E Preßburg
0950	*Feldwebel* H.-W. Schellner	*2./JG 302*	B-24 HSS	W Komaron
0950	*Unteroffizier* Rudolf Diecke	*3./JG 302*	B-24 HSS	E Raab
0955	*Feldwebel* H.-W. Schellner	*2./JG 302*	B-24 HSS	SW Komaron

Unteroffizier Rudi Diecke of I./JG 302 with his Bf 109 G-6 at Götzendorf.

0957	*Hauptmann* Heinrich Wurzer	*1./JG 302*	B-24 HSS	S Komaron
0958	*Oberfeldwebel* Heinz Gossow	*1./JG 302*	B-24 HSS	S Komaron
1002	*Hauptmann* Heinrich Wurzer	*1./JG 302*	B-24	S Komaron
1003	*Leutnant* Ernst-Dieter Grumme	*4./JG 302*	P-38	W Budapest
1030	*Feldwebel* Kurt Nachtigall	*3./JG 302*	B-24	S Lake Neusiedler
1040	*Unteroffizier* Rolf Burghard	*3./JG 302*	B-24	Lake Balaton
1040	*Leutnant* Wilhelm Hallenberger	*4./JG 302*	B-24	S Galanta
1045	*Oberleutnant* Ferdinand Kray	*4./JG 302*	P-51	Lake Neusiedler
1055	*Oberfeldwebel* Ernst Schäfer	*2./JG 302*	B-24	S Lake Neusiedler

This was another outstanding mission, and the number of victories is proof of the *Gruppe*'s growing effectiveness, a result of the unit's discipline and excellent tactics. It was becoming one of the most successful day fighter units in the *Reichsverteidigung*.

Attacking the combat boxes of heavy bombers and tangling with the escort fighters inevitably resulted in losses, however:

The *Staffelkapitän* of *3./JG 302*, *Oberleutnant* Heinz Seidel, suffered a grazing head wound during combat over Györ and was taken to hospital in Raab for treatment. Seidel flew Bf 109 G-6 "Yellow 1", WNr. 440 291.

Unteroffizier Rudolf Diecke of the *3. Staffel* was wounded while attacking a Liberator over Szekesfehervar and had to be taken to hospital in Stuhlweissenburg. After recovering from his wound he rejoined the *Gruppe*.

Unteroffizier Heinz Ropers of the *1. Staffel* failed to return from this mission and was reported missing. He was never found and his fate remains a mystery. (Bf 109 G-6, WNr. 440 663)

20 June 1944

In the early morning hours of 20 June 1944 the train from Berlin carrying soldiers on leave arrived at Vienna's main railway station. Five pilots from the *Ergänzungsgruppe West* (Replacement Training Group West) in Gabbert got off the train; after a brief stop they continued on to Götzendorf to join *I./JG 302*. The five arrived at Götzendorf at about noon and reported to the *Gruppenkommandeur*, *Hauptmann* Richard Lewens.

The *Gruppenkommandeur*, a man of average height, slim with a rather pale complexion, made a calm and level-headed impression. In a soft but rather energetic voice, he informed the newcomers that the *Jagdgruppe* was currently committed against American incursions from the south. Before going into action they would be given the opportunity to fly training missions with veteran pilots to gain experience. Then he concluded by saying, "You are hereby welcomed into the *Gruppe* as comrades – add to the honor of the *Gruppe* through your determination and willingness to fight!"

The pilots received their assignments: *Oberfähnrich* Aschendorf, *Unteroffizier* Kraatz and *Unteroffizier* Reschke to the *1. Staffel*; *Oberfähnrich* Kolbe and *Unteroffizier* Peters to the *3. Staffel*.

The *1.* and *4. Staffel* were quartered in a barracks camp about one kilometer from the airfield. There we met the "*Spieß*" (senior NCO), *Hauptfeldwebel* Mai. When soldiers think of the Senior NCO, they usually associate them with loud talking or even shouting. How different it was there: all formalities were carried out in a comradely tone. In *Hauptfeldwebel* Mai's case, the expression "Mother of the Company" really was appropriate.

Unteroffizier Rudi Diecke of I./JG 302, later III./JG 301.

The *Kapitän* of the *1. Staffel* was *Hauptmann* Heinrich Wurzer. Later, in the *Staffel* ready room, we heard all about him from the pilots of the *1. Staffel*.

Members of the *1. Staffel* at that time:

Leutnant Leonhard Reinicke, *Oberfeldwebel* Heinz Gossow, Ernst Haase, Herbert Stephan, Fritz Dickmann, Xaver Neumeier, Paul Streuff, *Feldwebel* Gerhard Scholz and Müller, *Unteroffizier* Werner Voss, *Obergefreiter* Günter Angermann and *Gefreiter* Ludwig Herdegen.

Leutnant Richard Jüngling joined the *Staffel* one day after us. We knew each other well from the *Ergänzungsgruppe Ost* (Replacement Training Group East) in Weidengut, where we had flown together in *Hauptmann* Wienhusen's training group. Seeing him again reawakened memories of that time.

The *4. Staffel*, with which we shared the barracks, was the former *12./JG 51 "Mölders"*. The *Staffel* had only recently been attached to *I./JG 302*. Made up of trained and experienced fighter pilots, this *Staffel* flew high cover for the *Gruppe*. One of its pilots was *Obergefreiter* Max Pick, with whom I had served in the *3. Staffel* of *Jagdschule 102* at Zerbst. From him I learned that *Obergefreiter* Schulze had gone to *JG 51* from the same training group and had since been killed on the Eastern Front.

I./JG 302 at Götzendorf near Vienna: Unteroffizier Reschke and Obergefreiter Angermann at the 1. Staffel dispersal.

For the first few days I was with *I./JG 302* the weather was rather poor, therefore the flying was little different than at a school. We spent the next few days in training flights and aerial gunnery practice, and I was assigned to fly as wingman to *Oberfeldwebel* Haase.

The *Gruppe* was equipped with the Bf 109 G-6, equipped to carry a 300-l external tank. Although the *Gruppe* had originally been formed as a single-engined night-fighter *Gruppe* in the "*Wilde Sau*" *Geschwader*, the Wild Boar emblem was now only rarely seen on the engine cowlings of the unit's aircraft.

The training flights provided a constant reminder of just how effective the airfield's natural camouflage was. Situated in open country with no prominent landmarks in the area, one had to look hard to pick it out against the green surroundings.

When we weren't flying we spent time at the *Staffel* dispersals, and there we young pilots discovered something new and interesting: small cards bearing the silhouettes of aircraft, seen from different directions. One could stick these cards in a type of sliding caliper, and, using an outlined "Revi" (reflector sight), select the angle of deflection on the front side. One could then read the reverse side to find out if the selected angle of deflection was correct. This game was very instructive and I used it whenever I got the chance, hoping to gain confidence in deflection shooting through practice.

23 June 1944

Over Romania, *II./JG 301* engaged units of the American 15th Air Force from Italy.

The *6. Staffel* took off from Targsorul-Nou and became heavily engaged with P-51 Mustangs of the fighter escort over Bucharest. At 0940 hours *Oberfeldwebel* Max Sulzgruber shot down one of the Mustangs.

The *10. Staffel*, based at the same airfield, also took part in this engagement, for it reported the loss of Bf 109 G-6 "Black 10", WNr. 163 422. The aircraft was flown by *Unteroffizier* Friedrich Röglsperger, who was wounded in this action. His subsequent fate is not known.

The *6. Staffel* was in action again one day later, and *Unteroffizier* Helmut Brenner reported shooting down a B-24 at 0932 hours.

26 June 1944

On this day the 15th Air Force attacked the Moosbierbaum hydrogenation plant for the first time. A total of 157 B-17 Flying Fortresses and 502 B-24 Liberators carried out the attack, escorted by 321 fighters: 131 P-38 Lightnings, forty-six P-47 Thunderbolts and 144 P-51 Mustangs.

The American bomber stream initially flew along the Adriatic, then turned into Hungarian airspace. The bombers assembled over Lake Balaton and then entered the airspace of *Luftgau-kommando XVII* on a broad front between Lake Neusiedler and Malacky.

During breakfast with the pilots of the *1. Staffel* that morning, the "old hares" suggested that the sky would probably be "full of violins" (enemy aircraft) on this day. There was a beautiful sunrise that morning, with not a cloud in the sky. While still eating breakfast, we received the order to go to thirty-minute readiness. With the last bite still in our mouths, we all jumped up and climbed into the vehicle that was always kept in front of the quarters of the *1.* and *4. Staffel* to take us to the airfield.

From the expressions on the pilots' faces, one could see that they were worried. The older, more experienced pilots knew what lay in store for us, and one can imagine what we younger pilots looked like. The vehicle drove the pilots of the two *Staffeln* to the airfield, and the *2.* and *3. Staffel* arrived at about the same time. Shortly afterward new orders: fifteen-minute readiness. *Hauptmann* Wurzer gathered the pilots of the *1. Staffel* around him once again and issued final instructions. During this quick briefing the order came to go to cockpit readiness. The aircraft crew chief gave a few technical instructions, questions and answers passed back and forth, and the tension was noticeable in every word. Then the command post fired the "Smoke, Flash, Bang" (signal flare): the signal to take off.

The order to take off came at 0834 hours. On this day the *1. Staffel* consisted of two *Schwärme* (flights of four aircraft) and one *Rotte* (flight of two). The first *Schwarm* was led by *Hauptmann* Wurzer, the second by *Oberfeldwebel* Gossow. The pair was made up of *Oberfeldwebel* Haase and *Unteroffizier* Reschke.

For the first time I experienced a fighter takeoff by *Staffeln* from their dispersals. As this type of takeoff was never practiced at fighter school, for the new pilots of the *Gruppe* its was the first test in their new flying environment.

The first to take off was the *4. Staffel*, which was to provide high cover for the *Gruppe*. The remaining aircraft followed in the sequence *Gruppenschwarm*, *1.*, *2.* and *3. Staffel*.

In the Vienna area *I./JG 302* was under the command of the *8. Jagddivision*, whose control center was located on the Kobenzl near Vienna. This control center, codenamed "*Rosenkavalier*", checked in soon after our takeoff. A very pleasant female voice transmitted information on the incoming bomber formations.

"*Dicke Autos* (fat automobiles = heavy bombers) with *Indianer* (Indians = fighters) at *Hanni* (height) 7,000 meters in GO (fighter grid reference) approaching Vienna." "Rosenkavalier" issued instructions to our formation leader "*Jumbo Anton*": "Climb to 8,000 meters, *Caruso* (heading) 220 degrees." We received a steady stream of reports on the position of the bomber formation. When the *Gruppe* reached 7,000 meters it was given a new heading: 160 degrees. At that time the *Jagdgruppe* was southwest of Vienna in grid squares EN-EO. There we were joined by a group of Me 410s of ZG 26, which was based at the airfield at Seyring or Vienna-Schwechat at that time.

We reached our assigned altitude of 8,000 meters. Lake Neusiedler was clearly visible below us on the left. The last transmission from "*Rosenkavalier*": "Fat Automobiles with many Indians ahead of you to the left. Attack at will!"

And there they were: the first group of about twenty-five to thirty bombers, to the left of the *Gruppe* and about 800 meters lower. The next group was visible right behind it. They were B-24 Liberators, and the groups of bombers came ever nearer, lined up like a string of pearls. Thin contrails revealed the position of the escorts, P-51 Mustangs, above the bombers and at about the same height as our formation. From "*Jumbo Anton*" came the order, "Release drop tanks, attack!" The close formation made up by the *1.*, *2.* and *3. Staffel* made a slight left turn, positioning itself behind the first and second groups of bombers and about 800 meters higher. Our *Jagdgruppe*'s high-altitude *Staffel* was already engaged with the escorts and the twin-engined fighters were also trying to fight off the enemy fighters.

As our pair was flying on the extreme right of the attack formation, we had the farthest to fly to reach attack position behind the bombers. The lateral spacing between the attacking Bf 109s increased steadily, and our pair was forced ever farther to the outside. The aircraft flying the inside curve had already fired at the target and were diving away, while our *Rotte* still had to complete the last part of the turn to get behind the heavies. At that moment we had difficulty getting into a favorable firing position, but I understood my elements leader's effort to make our approach somewhat behind the first row of attackers. Before takeoff, we young pilots had once again been strongly reminded not to lose contact with our element leaders, and I struggled constantly to stay with him. It was probably for that reason that I failed to realize that we were already under fire from the bombers or escort fighters. Heavy blows shook my machine and I immediately tried to climb up to the left.

I must have done this so abruptly and clumsily, however, that I immediately found myself hanging in the air like a ripe plum. It was not an unusual flight situation, for I had practiced it often at the fighter school: it was followed by a stall and spin, but that was easy to get out of. But that was at the fighter school – here a merciless enemy waited!

My machine did spin, and my only concern at that moment was getting out of that unusual flight attitude. I therefore released the stick and applied opposite rudder – but though I had practiced and carried out this procedure many times, the aircraft continued to spin. I tried again, but without success. I tried everything: trim forward, throttle lever forward and back, trying to force the nose down a little farther to increase speed and control effectiveness. I never thought about abandoning the aircraft. With much difficulty, I finally succeeded in getting out of my miserable situation, but I had lost a tremendous amount of altitude. I was only at 1,000 meters: the spin couldn't have gone on much longer.

When I regained control of my machine, I was unable to detect any other aircraft in my vicinity. I looked to my right and saw several holes in the wing. As well, the entire starboard wingtip was gone. That explained why I had had so much difficulty getting out of the spin. My first combat mission was over before it had really begun. The reality was much different than one had imagined it.

I had to find somewhere to land, and quickly, and so at 0934 hours I touched down at Deutsch-Wagram airfield. From the air traffic control unit I reported to my *Staffel* in Götzendorf and received permission to fly my damaged aircraft back after the enemy aircraft had departed.

Not long afterwards I opened the door of the unit, and a pilot with a blood-smeared face walked in. I soon discovered that he was *Oberfeldwebel* Sattler of 2./JG 302. After shooting down a B-24 Liberator, Sattler had been engaged by two P-51 Mustangs. He brought down one of the Mustangs just beyond the airfield, but then he was himself hit and forced down near the airfield.

At Götzendorf I learned from my element leader *Oberfeldwebel* Haase that I had been attacked by a P-51 Mustang while turning to attack the bombers. Haase, too, had seen this too late. I had to admit, however, that I had not seen any Mustang.

On the evening of the same day the pilots of the *1. Staffel* gathered in the lounge in our quarters. Several pilots from the *4. Staffel* were also there. The main topic was the mission flown a few hours ago. The comments by the experts present revealed the following:

The *Jagdgruppe*'s attack on the command group of the incoming bomber force had forced it off course to the right, consequently the main battle area was moved east of Vienna into the area between Lake Neusiedler and Preßburg. The disadvantage of attacking the command group was that it was very heavily escorted, which precluded a mass attack from the very start.

They were not completely satisfied with *Rosenkavalier*'s control, for we were vectored onto the bombers at too sharp an angle: as a result the *Gruppe* had to make a left turn before attacking, causing the aircraft on the right side to lose contact. The aircraft lagging behind were attacked by enemy fighters, partially breaking up the close formation and weakening the attack on the command group.

That evening we also heard some very pointed statements by our comrades of the *4. Staffel*, who declared that the presence of the American fighters made it necessary for us to adopt a completely new approach. In addition to getting used to their numerical superiority, we had to cope with the obvious high level of training of the enemy pilots in the escort fighters, as the pilots of our own covering fighters were discovering.

An evaluation of the mission of 26 July 1944 reveals the following balance for *I./JG 302*:

0910	*Feldwebel* Rudolf Dreesmann	*4./JG 302*	P-51	near Preßburg
0922	*Oberfeldwebel* Sepp Sattler	*2./JG 302*	B-24	Deutsch-Wagram
0926	*Oberfeldwebel* Sepp Sattler	*2./JG 302*	P-51	Deutsch-Wagram
0938	*Feldwebel* Karl Vetter	*3./JG 302*	B-24	E Vienna
0940	*Oberleutnant* Ferdinand Kray	*4./JG 302*	B-24	E Vienna
0959	*Oberfeldwebel* Ernst Haase	*1./JG 302*	B-24 HSS	Lake Neusiedler
1010	*Unteroffizier* Karl-H. Bamberg	*2./JG 302*	B-24 HSS	near Sopron
1020	*Leutnant* Ernst-D. Grumme	*4./JG 302*	B-24 HSS	5 km S Lake Neusiedler
1020	*Unteroffizier* Karl-H. Bamberg	*2./JG 302*	B-24	Raab
1040	*Feldwebel* Anton Benning	*2./JG 302*	P-51	S Lake Neusiedler

This success was overshadowed by the loss of three pilots, all of whom lost their young lives on this mission:

Feldwebel Nachtigall and Oberfeldwebel Langelotz of 3./JG 302. Nachtigall was killed in action over Hungary on 26 June 1944. Langelotz died in combat at the end of April 1945 while serving with III./JG 301.

Feldwebel Hans Spielhagen of the *1. Staffel*, twenty-five years old, was shot down and killed by enemy fighters near Raspunka in Slovakia. (Bf 109 G-6, "White 9", WNr. 411 703)

Leutnant Peter Altmeyer of the *2. Staffel*, twenty-three years of age, went down with his Bf 109 G-6, WNr. 440 309, near Zistersdorf.

Feldwebel Kurt Nachtigall of the *3. Staffel*, twenty-six years old, failed to return from this mission. He was killed in action near Szcenc in Hungary.

The combat death of *Feldwebel* Kurt Nachtigall was an especially heavy blow for *Oberfeldwebel* Fritz Dieckmann of the *1. Staffel*. The two men had been friends for a long time and had served in the Helsinki detachment. It took long and intensive assistance from his comrades to bring Dieckmann out of the depths of depression.

The anti-aircraft guns stationed in the Vienna area damaged a B-17 so badly that it was forced to land a few kilometers from Götzendorf airfield. The pilots of course took advantage of the opportunity to examine one of the "Fat Automobiles" from the inside and outside. Of special interest, of course, was the armament, and one could observe many reflective expressions when it was discovered that the bomber had virtually no defensive blind spots.

During the inspection there was talk of the possibility of ramming a bomber, which came up in conversations between pilots now and then. There was little enthusiasm shown by the pilots, however: the weight and size of the aircraft compared to the tiny Bf 109 saw to that.

27 June 1944

I./JG 302 had not yet recovered completely from the previous day's mission: several aircraft were still unserviceable with battle damage. The enemy, however, paid this no heed and flew into Romanian airspace. A small formation of bombers separated from the main group and set course for Budapest, which resulted in a scramble by the *Jagdgruppe*.

Over Budapest it engaged a group of B-17 Flying Fortresses with a small fighter escort, and the high-altitude *Staffel* had little difficulty keeping the enemy fighters away from the main formation. This evidenced by the fact that three members of the high-altitude *Staffel* shot down four-engined bombers:

1020	*Oberfeldwebel* Ernst Haase	*1./JG 302*	B-17 HSS	E Budapest
1022	*Leutnant* Wilhelm Hallenberger	*4./JG 302*	B-17	near Budapest
1024	*Oberfeldwebel* Ernst Haase	*1./JG 302*	B-17	near Budapest
				11th victory
1025	*Oberfeldwebel* Eduard Ries	*3./JG 302*	B-17	NW Budapest
1025	*Leutnant* Ernst-D. Grumme	*4./JG 302*	B-17	10 km S Budapest
				25th victory
1026	*Oberfeldwebel* Herbert Stephan	*1./JG 302*	B-17	NW Budapest
1026	*Feldwebel* Rudolf Dreesmann	*4./JG 302*	B-17	Budapest
				14th victory

Six four-engined bombers were shot down in the space of six minutes and another so badly damaged that it was forced to leave formation. The latter most likely crashed later or was obliged to make a forced landing.

The *Gruppe* reported the following losses:

Leutnant Gerd Bernhard, acting commander of the *2. Staffel*, was fatally hit by return fire while attacking a B-17 and went down with his Bf 109 G-6 "Red 1", WNr. 440 309, near Demesed south of Budapest.

Unteroffizier Heinz Strissel of the *4. Staffel* was shot down by the bombers' defensive fire and went down with his Bf 109 G-6 "Black 3", WNr. 163 868, south of Stuhlweissenburg.

27-28 June 1944

On this night *I./JG 301* flew "*Wilde Sau*" night-fighter sorties over France. There is no information on victories, however that the *Gruppe* saw action is confirmed by a loss report:

Feldwebel Paul Henger of the *2. Staffel* was hit by enemy fire and his aircraft caught fire. The Bf 109 G-6, WNr. 441 114, hit the ground near Lallaing.

28 June 1944

II./JG 301 and *IV./JG 301*, which still consisted just of the *10. Staffel*, were in action over Romania on this day. It is no longer possible to determine the operation strength of the *Gruppe*, which operated in this area for a period of several weeks. It is suspected, however, that not all of the *Jagdgruppe*'s missions were against American heavy bombers operating from Italy. The Russian front was drawing nearer day by day, and it is likely that missions were also flown in support of German ground forces at this time.

The *Gruppe* claimed two B-24s shot down on 28 June 1944: *Oberfeldwebel* Max Salzgruber of the *6. Staffel* shot down a Liberator at 0948 hours.

Oberfeldwebel Franz Menzel of the *10. Staffel* also reported shooting down a B-24, at 0955 hours. Menzel was wounded in this engagement and had to force-land in his Bf 109 G-6 "Black 3", WNr. 160 211, at an unknown location.

Feldwebel Karl Unger of the *10. Staffel* was wounded in this action and had to abandon his aircraft. (Bf 109 G-6 "Black 10", WNr. 161 432)

29 June 1944

Bad weather lasting into the afternoon made it appear unlikely that any missions would be flown. Because of the many new additions, a change in tactics was carried out by the *1.* to *3. Staffel*. Each pilot was assigned a permanent tactical number. These numbers were repeated within the *Staffeln*, but were differentiated from the others by different colors. Color and number revealed the name of the pilot. Each pilot also had a permanent radio call sign.

From this time on I flew "White 6" and had the radio call sign "*Jumbo 12*". In spite of the successes of 26 and 27 June 1944, commanding officer *Hauptmann* Lewens was not entirely satisfied with his *Gruppe*. He therefore scheduled a mid-morning briefing followed by a practice mission. The focal points of the mission were a scramble from dispersals and the following of instructions throughout the flight. During the post-mission debriefing, it was once again stressed that we must maintain flying discipline during the flight to the target. *Staffel* and *Schwarm* leaders, in particular, were to see to it that these fundamental requirements for success were adhered to.

30 June 1944

Aircraft of the American 15th Air Force took off from Italy to attack industrial targets south of Budapest.

The individual *Staffeln* of *I./JG 302* received the mission order and the order to go to thirty-minute readiness while still in their billets. During the drive to the airfield one could again see new faces in the *Staffeln*. They had already received a briefing in their individual *Schwärme* so that everyone knew his place within the *Staffel*. On reaching the dispersals the pilots immediately went to their aircraft, and at 0757 hours flight control fired a flare, the signal to take off.

The *Staffeln* again took off from their dispersals, and from Götzendorf we flew southeast into Hungarian airspace. Everyone could hear the reports from *"Rosenkavalier"*; the American bombers were still south of Lake Balaton, flying north. As the distance to that area was significantly greater for us, the *Gruppe* had time to climb, and the pilots, especially the younger ones, had a chance to calm down and at the same time train their "Hunter's Eye". The *Jagdgruppe* consisted of about fifty aircraft and was an impressive sight in the cloudless sky. As we were flying in loose formation with greater than normal spacing between aircraft, it was possible to now and then cast a glance behind and look at the ground below.

"Rosenkavalier" transmitted a steady stream of reports on the position of the enemy aircraft, commenting that there were only a few "Indians" escorting the bombers. Between Bruck an der Leitha and Lake Neusiedler the *Gruppe* passed 6,500 meters as it climbed to 8,000 meters on a heading toward Lake Balaton.

The voice of the controller sounded repeatedly over the radio: "Fat Automobiles with a few Indians still heading north, approaching Budapest." This all sounded reassuring, but suddenly an excited, high-pitched voice rang out in my headset: "Indians from behind!" Immediately the entire formation became unsettled, with everyone trying to scan the area behind him. The commander of the high-altitude *Staffel*, *Oberleutnant* Kray, at once radioed that there were no enemy fighters in sight. The alarm proved to be a cruel joke – there really were no enemy fighters to be seen anywhere.

The formation flew on at a height of 8,000 meters and with the good visibility the condensation trails of the heavy bombers were sighted soon afterwards. The report by the controller was confirmed: above the bombers there were only a few escort fighters, P-38 Lightnings. Our *4. Staffel*, which was flying about 500 meters above our formation, had already moved slightly ahead of us, positioning itself to ward off a possible attack by enemy fighters. From formation leader *"Jumbo Anton"* (*Hauptmann* Lewens) came the order: "Jettison fuel tanks! Spread out slightly!" We flew over Lake Balaton in a wide left turn, which positioned us well for an attack on a formation of B-17s. After the intervals between us had increased somewhat came the order to attack.

Flying on the left side of the second attack column, I was able to observe the attack on the bombers by those in front of me, and for the first time I saw the tremendous defensive fire of these Flying Fortresses, which opened up while we were still far away. The first attack column had opened fire and the initial effects were clearly visible: several B-17s were smoking. I had already flipped up the lever on the stick for the machineguns and my thumb found the button for the cannon, when the first aircraft completed their attack and pulled up to the left. I took aim at a B-17 and saw that it was too small in my Revi, which meant that the range was still too great.

But who can control his nerves and remain calm during his first attack on a four-engined bomber, especially with tracer from the bombers' many machine-guns flying toward him? All by itself my finger pressed the machine-gun firing lever and the rattling sound of my own weapons was at first reassuring. The path of my tracer revealed that I had allowed too little deflection. Slight pressure on the stick – and my rounds were on target. A press with my thumb on the cannon-firing button confirmed the correct deflection and I could clearly see strikes on the left wing. But the B-17 was now looming huge before me, and fearing a collision I quickly pulled my "White 6" up and climbed away to the left. Before me I saw *Oberfeldwebel* Haase's "White 11" and in front of it several other of the *Gruppe*'s aircraft forming up for a second pass. A quick glance to the side revealed that several B-17s were smoking heavily. The aircraft I had attacked was smoking but still in formation.

Approximately half the *Gruppe* had formed up for the second attack, and the attack was made against the group that had just been attacked. Several of the smoking B-17s had dropped out of formation, but in the brief interval between attacks the bombers tried to close up the resulting gaps. Once again the Bf 109 G-6s dove on the group of bombers, trying to place their bursts in the fuselage and wings. I selected a B-17 and opened fire, and once again it began to smoke, but still it remained with the group. What happened to the first B-17 I had fired at was impossible to determine at that moment.

A first glance at my own machine revealed no damage, and since there was no sign of our fighters regrouping again, I landed my aircraft at Tapolca airfield on Lake Balaton at 1015 hours, after a total flying time of two hours and eighteen minutes.

My fuel tanks were as good as empty. Several more of the *Gruppe*'s fighters landed at the same airfield. They were immediately refueled and ordered back to Götzendorf. During refueling, I discovered that my machine had two bullet holes in its fuselage, but they were of no significance. I took off from Tapolca at 1040 hours and landed at Götzendorf at 1138.

That afternoon the pilots gathered in the barracks dining room, and there was a thorough evaluation of the mission. Flying discipline during the approach and climb and attack discipline gave no cause for criticism. Of note was the unanimous opinion that in spite of solid strikes, only a few of the B-17s we had attacked had smoked, and some of them had remained in formation. Many of the pilots were also of the opinion that it was entirely possible that, while some of the targeted bombers were forced to leave the protection of their formations, they may nevertheless have succeeded in returning to their bases in Italy.

The two B-17s that I left smoking were subsequently not recognized as *Herausschüsse*.

The *Gruppe*'s armorers had plenty to do on this day, for most of the aircraft had expended all their ammunition.

In comparison to the unconfirmed successes, losses were kept within bearable limits:

Oberfähnrich Siegfried Aschendorf of the *1. Staffel* was wounded in action and force-landed his Bf 109 G-6 "White 10", WNr. 441 466, south of Budapest.

The death of *Unteroffizier* Roland Müller of the *3. Staffel* near Nakonywald in Hungary, which appears on 1 July in the records, must probably be seen as related to the air battle against the 15th Air Force on 30 June 1944.

The records of this actions indicate that *Unteroffizier* Hans Kemmerling of the *2. Staffel* brought down a B-17 south of Spittel at 1000 hours.

At 1007 hours *Gruppenkommandeur Hauptmann* Lewens show down a P-38 Lightning north of Lake Balaton.

1 July 1944

For *I./JG 302* the morning passed with no alarm and thirty-minutes readiness, and the pilots enjoyed a few quiet hours until lunch. On such quiet days there was always the possibility of getting together for lunch with comrades from the other *Staffeln*. In this way the cadre of older pilots met those newly transferred to the *Gruppe* – and it is known that pilots make friends quickly.

Things were different for the "Black Men" – there was no rest. From mechanics to armorers to radio technicians, all were busy trying to repair machines damaged in combat. Every machine counted, for at that time the *Gruppe* was well off in pilots.

At this time there was also a call for puttied and polished aircraft. Every pilot wanted to fly one of these machines, because they were thirty to forty km/h faster. It was as if the entire *Gruppe* had a craving: ground crews worked on the aircraft, filling seams and polishing the finish. Not wanting to be left behind in the air, some pilots picked up steel wool and polished their own machines. In the end, however, there was no proof that doing so in fact increased one's chances of survival.

At 1504 hours in the afternoon the entire *Gruppe* was scrambled. It was vectored over the Vienna area to Lake Neusiedler but there was no contact with the enemy. The *Gruppe* command later announced that the scramble had resulted from an incorrect assessment on the part of the ground control center.

2 July 1944

A major air battle developed in the skies over Hungary on this hot Sunday morning. The 15th Air Force had sent 541 bombers to attack Budapest and another sixty-two bombers against targets on the border between Hungary and Yugoslavia. The number of escorting fighters was unusually high: 270 "Indians", P-38s and P-51s, were sent to protect the bombers from the German day fighters.

In addition to *I./JG 302*, the defending force included the Hungarian "Puma" Fighter Group commanded by *Major* Heppes, *II./JG 27* from Fels am Wagram, together with *I./ZG 76* from Seyring and *II./ZG 1* from Wels.

I./JG 302 took off from Götzendorf at 0927 hours. Once again there was a scramble from the dispersals, a typical fighter operation, but hard on the nerves. Often the last aircraft of one *Staffel* had not lifted off when the first machines of another *Staffel* came from the side. This was a peculiarity of fighter flying – and who was going to raise objections on the grounds of possible flight safety implications?

Immediately after formation leader *Hauptmann* Lewens reported the *Jagdgruppe*'s takeoff to "*Rosenkavalier*", the fighter controller began issuing heading instructions and information on the tip of the bomber stream. The enemy aircraft had already reached the area where the battle of 30 June took place. Control reported "Fat Autos" with many "Indians".

It was obvious that, wishing to avoid a repeat of the previous day's sightseeing flight, "*Rosenkavalier*" had issued the takeoff order rather late. As the formation climbed, the controller repeatedly urged the *Gruppe* to "step on it", which meant that we were too far away from the enemy and should hurry.

The repeated calls for speed was already rubbing the nerves of many pilots. Then the familiar high-pitched voice sounded in our headsets: "Indians from behind!" Just prior to this we had received a report of bombers with numerous escorts – and now this bone-chilling call. The formation immediately became unsettled, with everyone looking behind him. One *Schwarm* of the *4. Staffel*, which was flying in front of and above the *Gruppe*, immediately reversed course to screen the airspace behind us. One of the *Staffel's* aircraft suddenly went straight down and did not pull out of its dive. There was an icy silence as everyone in the formation followed the aircraft's path until it struck the ground.

Of course there were no "Indians" to be seen anywhere. The formation leader ordered everyone to close up. This shook the formation from the paralyzing silence that had gripped it during the crash of our comrade.

Long before the fighter formation reached the airspace over Budapest we could see pillars of smoke above the city, followed immediately afterwards by the formations of bombers already flying away towards the south. As we suspected, we had been ordered into the air too late. This soon proved an advantage for our "heavy *Gruppe*" however, for the leading escort fighters, probably surprised that no enemy fighters had been met in the target area, had turned south with the first bomber groups.

The familiar command "Jettison fuel tanks!" was followed immediately by the order to attack. The heavy bombers were B-24 Liberators. They had probably realized that they were about to be attacked, for far ahead the narrow condensation trails of the escort fighters made a 180 degree turn and came toward the *Gruppe*. In terms of numbers they were little stronger than our high-altitude *Staffel*, and a short time later our *4. Staffel* was locked in combat with the Mustangs.

By that time our "Heavy *Gruppe*" (a heavy *Gruppe* was one whose principal task was to engage the bomber formations) had taken up a favorable attack position behind the withdrawing bombers. The attack wedges had formed up, each pilot took one more look to see where the man next to him was so that there would be no interruptions during aiming, and then the target was picked up in the reflector sight. In that position it was no longer necessary to watch for Mustangs, as they did not attack within range of the bombers' guns.

Flying in the first attacking column this time, I was able to get a Liberator in my sights very early. As the *Gruppe* was attacking with a height advantage of about 500 meters, I could see the entire topside of the Liberator. Of course tracer bullets again reached out for me from the bomber formation, but it was a matter of overcoming my inner coward and learning lessons from my previous mission. My finger and thumb rested on the firing buttons as the Liberator grew larger in the illuminated circle. When it filled the reticle I pressed the firing button for the two 20mm MG 151s. I had aimed at the bomber's left wing root, and when I saw that my shells were on target I immediately fired the 30mm MK 108. The effects of these shells on the wing root were immediately visible: parts of the wing came away and flew toward my machine. As my shells continued to strike the target, a large fire developed quickly, with heavy smoke. With ever larger pieces of skinning coming away from the wing toward my aircraft, I broke off the attack and pulled up to the left. The Liberator did exactly the opposite: it rolled over to the left, went down burning, and soon afterwards exploded in midair.

I had time only for a brief look, for over the radio I heard the order to form up for a second attack. As I was not immediately able to spot "White 11", the aircraft of my element leader *Oberfeldwebel* Haase, I tried to rejoin the other aircraft as they reformed.

The thin condensation trails above us revealed that the fighter-versus-fighter battle was still in full swing. Far below on the ground, the first smoke columns were rising from downed aircraft.

The American escort fighters also failed to prevent the *Gruppe* from reforming for a second attack, and so it was much like the first. I used the same tactic as before, except that I was somewhat farther to the right when I commenced my attack on the Liberator. My shells began striking the rear of the fuselage, then I shifted my fire to the left inner motor and wing root. This time only a few pieces flew off the wing, and I moved in closer. From close up I was able to clearly see the strikes and the effect of my shells. I had the impression that the rear gunner was no longer firing.

A growing amount of smoke and flames emanated from the area of the left inner motor and wing root, and I broke off the attack with a half roll and dive. The Liberator went down immediately afterwards.

Still completely absorbed by the events of this air battle, I was suddenly forced to realize that all was not well with my "White 6". A look at the instrument panel told the tale: the coolant temperature was far too high. I had probably been hit in the radiators, but in the heat of battle I hadn't even noticed. Of course I now had to get down and land. I closed the throttle and descended in a shallow dive, all the while looking for an airfield and scanning for enemy fighters. As there were none, I was hopeful that I might find an airfield, and as long as I descended in a glide the coolant temperature would not rise significantly.

As Budapest lay to the northeast and there were several airfields in the surrounding area, I held course toward the city. But my altitude was diminishing steadily and, with no airfield in sight, I had to increase power. In a very short time the coolant temperature rose to a critical level and the idea of very soon sitting in a burning machine was not exactly pleasant. Therefore there was only one solution: throttle back, fuel cock off, and look out for a suitable place for a forced landing. In such cases it is always vital to decide quickly, and a soon afterwards I made a belly landing in a clover field. This is not a great feat of flying, but it does differ from a normal landing in that the aircraft comes to a halt in a few seconds.

When the Bf 109 G-6 stopped sliding, there was a loud hissing sound emanating from the area in front of my legs, therefore I undertook to get out of the machine as quickly as possible and put some distance between it and me. From a safe distance I observed my Bf 109 for a while, then lit a cigarette to calm my nerves. I couldn't help thinking about our comrades on the Eastern Front who often found themselves in such situations far behind the front, and who had to concern themselves with their own safety first and foremost. There was nowhere to hide in the open field in which I was standing. But I was in a friendly country, I had gained some experience, and had survived the air battle physically intact.

At that moment I had no idea what was going to happen, but I could already see people in the distance, approaching my landing site rather cautiously. I waved and they quickened their approach, and they told me that I had come down near the village of Erd, not far from Budapest.

A short time later an Hungarian policeman arrived, then a *Waffen-SS* patrol in a *Kübelwagen*. Everything was settled quickly: the policeman remained with my machine, and I took my parachute and drove to Budapest with the SS men. While driving through the streets of Budapest, in several places I saw fires being fought by the fire brigade and residents – but I also saw many onlookers, wandering the streets in large groups. The SS unit's base was quite near the Budapest-North railway station, and after a fortifying snack I set off for the station with my parachute on my shoulder. It was of course out of the ordinary to see someone walking the streets of the city with a parachute, but it did fit the events that had taken place over and in the city in the past few hours. A number of people looked at me in astonishment.

Within sight of the station an Hungarian policeman stopped me and asked to see my papers. I told him that I was a German airman and that he should accompany me to the station, where I would show my papers to the station guard. As we talked, a crowd gathered round us, but the policeman's reaction suggested he was willing to go with me to the station.

At that moment a member of the military police pushed his way through the crowd to where we were. I was hoping for support, but instead he struck me in the face with his fist and shouted, "You dog!" To those standing around, it had now become obvious that I was not a German pilot. The Hungarian policeman, who tried to protect me, was pushed aside, and more blows followed. Instinctively I tried to reach for my pistol, but my hands were pinned. My repeated shouts that I was a German airman did no good – they kept hitting me. Somehow I went to the ground and all I felt was a heavy weight pressing on me. Then all was still.

In the meantime, the following had happened: two men from Vienna, middle-aged and working for the *Wehrmacht* in Budapest as cooks, had observed the incident from the crowd. Both were convinced that I was a German pilot, but they first had to push through the crowd to intervene. One of the two threw himself on top of me to prevent me from being kicked and stepped on, while the other explained to the crowd their mistake. When I got up from the ground, there was again a *Waffen-SS* patrol before me. When I told them what had happened, they immediately went looking for the military policeman, but he had disappeared, probably driven away by his guilty conscience.

Instead of to the station, the SS patrol drove me to the hospital, where I was examined by a doctor. He discovered a number of blue spots – which later changed to other colors – but no internal injuries. That same afternoon I boarded a train and rode to Vienna.

On the train I had time to go over the events of the day in my mind once more. The air battle with the four-engined bombers, my puttied and polished Bf 109 in a clover field near Budapest, but the question that concerned me most of all: why hadn't the people in Budapest recognized me as a German airman? A look at my uniform gave me some idea: a blue-gray flight suit and leather jacket with no national insignia. How were the Hungarians supposed to know who I was?

The next morning I returned to my *Jagdgruppe* in Götzendorf. They already knew about my forced landing and my two heavy bomber kills: I had asked the SS unit to pass this on. I then reported to *Gruppenkommandeur* Lewens on the incident in Budapest. The information was passed up the chain of command and soon afterwards resulted in the issuing of a directive for pilots of the *Reichsverteidigung* to wear yellow armbands bearing the legend "German Air Force".

A major air battle in the skies over Hungary was now part of the past. Both sides had fought hard and had suffered heavily. The area around Budapest was pockmarked by craters made by downed aircraft of both sides.

After the battle in the Budapest area, *I./JG 302* reported:

14 B-24 Liberators shot down,

5 B-24 Liberators damaged and forced to leave formation,

2 P-51 Mustangs shot down.

Given the conditions facing the Defense of the Reich, the *Jagdgruppe* had achieved a considerable success.

1020	*Leutnant* Reiche	*3./JG 302*	B-24	10 km W Budapest
1020	*Leutnant* Ernst-Dieter Grumme	*4./JG 302*	B-24 HSS	10 km W Budapest
1025	*Leutnant* Fritz Bouldan	*3./JG 302*	B-24 HSS	SW Budapest
1025	*Feldwebel* Ernst Schäfer	*2./JG 302*	B-24	SW Budapest
1025	*Gefreiter* Walter Weinzierl	*3./JG 302*	B-24	SW Budapest
1025	*Unteroffizier* Willi Reschke	*1./JG 302*	B-24	SW Budapest
1025	*Unteroffizier* Walter Berlinska	*2./JG 302*	B-24	SW Budapest
1025	*Unteroffizier* Gerhard Walter	*2./JG 302*	B-24	SW Budapest
1027	*Leutnant* Horst Kirchner	*2./JG 302*	B-24 HSS	SW Budapest
1027	*Oberfeldwebel* Dieter Rusche	*2./JG 302*	B-24 HSS	SW Budapest
1028	*Unteroffizier* Walter Berlinska	*2./JG 302*	B-24 HSS	SW Budapest
1028	*Oberfeldwebel* Herbert Stephan	*1./JG 302*	B-24	SW Budapest
1028	*Feldwebel* Bausch	*2./JG 302*	B-24	SW Budapest
1029	*Unteroffizier* Willi Reschke	*1./JG 302*	B-24	SW Budapest
1030	*Oberfeldwebel* Ernst Haase	*1./JG 302*	B-24	1 km W Tordas
1030	*Unteroffizier* Günter Richter	*3./JG 302*	B-24	W Budapest
1030	*Leutnant* Richard Jüngling	*1./JG 302*	B-24	SW Budapest
1034	*Oberfeldwebel* Ernst Haase	*1./JG 302*	B-24	W Tordas
1040	*Feldwebel* Rudolf Dreesmann	*4./JG 302*	P-51	near Tata
1050	*Oberleutnant* Ferdinand Kray	*4./JG 302*	P-51	SW Budapest
1050	*Gefreiter* Walter Weinzierl	*3./JG 302*	B-24	SW Budapest

Leutnant Wilhelm Hallenberger of the *4. Staffel* claimed a B-17 shot down at 1215 hours south of Lake Balaton. It is highly likely that Hallenberger scored this victory after an en route landing at an Hungarian airfield on his way back to Götzendorf.

I./JG 302 also suffered heavily in this air battle over Budapest and the losses seriously thinned the ranks of pilots:

Oberfeldwebel Paul Streuff of the *1. Staffel* was shot down and killed near Martonvasar, south of Budapest. (Bf 109 G-6 "White 14", WNr. 411 860)

Oberfeldwebel Xaver Neumeier of the *1. Staffel* failed to return from this mission. His fate remains a mystery and he is listed as missing. (Bf 109 G-6 "White 2", WNr. 411 862)

Feldwebel Gerhard Scholz of the *1. Staffel* was killed in action near Erd, southwest of Budapest. (Bf 109 G-6 "White 9", WNr. 441 620)

Oberfeldwebel Adolf Krista of the *2. Staffel* attacked a Liberator but his machine was badly damaged by return fire. He tried to land the aircraft but was killed when the Bf 109 G-6 went down near Ercsi.

Unteroffizier Gerhard Walter of 2./JG 302.

Unteroffizier Hermann Lammers of the *3. Staffel* was shot down and killed over Ercsi. (Bf 109 G-6 "Yellow 12", WNr. 441 878)

Unteroffizier Rolf Burghardt of the *3. Staffel* was wounded in combat over Stuhlweissenburg. He landed his aircraft safely and was taken to hospital. (Bf 109 G-6 "Yellow 9", WNr. 441 643)

Unteroffizier Otto Wiedemann of the *4. Staffel* was shot down and killed by Mustangs near Laszlomajor. (Bf 109 G-6 "Black 12", WNr. 163 925)

Unteroffizier Kurt Ramlow of the *4. Staffel* was killed in air combat near Kiss. (Bf 109 G-6 "Black 1", WNr. 164 380)

Obergefreiter Max Pick was killed when his aircraft crashed from great height, coming down in the border area between Hungary and Austria. (Bf 109 G-6 "Black 6", WNr. 411 611)

After shooting down a B-24 south of Budapest, *Unteroffizier* Gerhard Walter of the *2. Staffel* was attacked by Mustangs and wounded. He was initially entered into *I./JG 302*'s records for this day as killed in action. After recovering from his wounds he rejoined his unit but was soon transferred to *JG 4*. Gerhard Walter survived the war and it was years before he could correct the error in the *Gruppe*'s records.

The records also show that *Feldwebel* Karl Vetter of the *3. Staffel* was killed in air combat on 3 July 1944. He should probably also be included among the casualties of 2 July 1944, as the *Gruppe* flew no sorties on 3 July.

There was much discussion about the crash of the Bf 109 following the call, "Indians from behind!" It turned out that it was the aircraft of *Obergefreiter* Max Pick of the *4. Staffel*.

I was especially close to him, as we had been in the same training group in the *3. Staffel* of *Jagdschule 103* at Zerbst.

Opinions differed widely: some claimed that the crash had been caused by the radio message – others thought he had lost consciousness due to a leaky oxygen mask. Strangely, nothing was heard from the "warner" in subsequent missions.

There were further discussions in *1. Staffel*'s mess that evening. The room was quite comfortably furnished, given our situation. On one side there was a sitting area with several chairs where games were played, mainly chess and cards. In the center of the room was a long table where we took our meals, and on the left next to the entrance there was a small corner bar with a good assortment of alcoholic beverages. In front of it were four bar stools that were usually occupied by thirst men. At the very front of the liquor shelf was Steinhäger: it was reserved for guests we wanted to get rid of quickly.

On this evening much of the talking was done by *Leutnant* Grumme of the *4. Staffel*, who had once again been involved with the Mustangs. Attacking in a steep dive, he had knocked a B-24 out of its formation, after which he went after the Mustangs. He failed to shoot any down, for he was so outnumbered that he had to concentrate on saving his own skin. The heavy odds explain the losses sustained by the *4. Staffel* on this occasion.

It was commonly known that fighter pilots are superstitious: when lighting a cigarette, no one would be the third to take a light from a comrade. Everyone had a talisman, and everyone had a certain day on which he would rather stay on the ground. In *I./JG 302* it had been determined that aircraft bearing the tactical number "12" failed to return from combat missions more often than those with other numbers. The *Gruppenkommandeur* subsequently made a decision worthy of Solomon: there would be no more aircraft with the number "12" in any of the four *Staffeln*.

3 July 1944

II./JG 301 and *IV./JG 301* flew another tough mission over Romania. The operational conditions faced by these two *Jagdgruppen* were becoming more difficult with each passing day: from one side the Russian Front was drawing ever nearer, and on the other side the Americans were strengthening their attacks in an attempt to destabilize the German front. It is no longer possible to say whether *II./JG 301* was still at its full operational strength of three *Staffeln* at this time, for the *Gruppe* had suffered heavy losses in recent weeks. All that the records do reveal is that *II./JG 301* and *IV./JG 301* were based together at Targsorul-Nou at this time.

While on a mission from there on 3 July 1944, *Feldwebel* Gerhard Mett of the *10. Staffel* shot down a Liberator at 1151 hours.

During the same mission, *Feldwebel* Fritz Ebel, also of the *10. Staffel*, brought down another Liberator at 1210 hours. These are the last known victories from this area of operations.

Another report states that one day later, on 4 July 1944, *Oberfeldwebel* Max Sulzgruber of the *6. Staffel* was wounded in action northeast of Ibanzeti and had to make a forced landing in his Bf 109 G-6 "Yellow 10", WNr. 163 402.

On the same day *Unteroffizier* Walter Toldrian, also of the *6. Staffel*, was wounded in action south of Hermannstadt but was able to parachute to safety. (Bf 109 G-6 "Yellow 7", WNr. 410 068)

4-5 July 1944

On this night *I./JG 301* flew an extremely successful night mission from Epinoy airfield in France against RAF bombers:

Unteroffizier Grätz of the *3. Staffel* shot down a four-engined bomber at 0115 hours.

Leutnant Willi Esche of the *2. Staffel* shot down a Lancaster at 0116 hours.

Feldwebel Martin Schulze of the *1. Staffel* brought down two four-engined bombers, at 0117 and 0128 hours.

Feldwebel Hans Engfer of the *1. Staffel* destroyed a four-engined bomber at 1009 hours.

Oberleutnant Ernst Fischer of the *2. Staffel* shot down two Lancasters, at 0135 and 0139 hours.

Unteroffizier Hans Zarm of the *1. Staffel* brought down a four-engined bomber at 0150 hours.

Feldwebel Georg Scharein of the *2. Staffel* downed a Lancaster at 0152 hours.

Leutnant Willi Esche of the *2. Staffel* shot down a second Lancaster at 0158 hours.

This night mission is also extraordinary in that the *Gruppe* suffered no losses.

At that time *I./JG 301* was the last *Gruppe* from the three *"Wilde Sau" Geschwader* still operating in the night-fighter role. All of the other *Gruppen* of *JG 300*, *JG 301* and *JG 302* had been withdrawn from night-fighter operations and had converted to the day fighter role, operating against American heavy bombers. They were occasionally used as all-weather units, as the pilots of these *Gruppen* were trained in instrument flying.

6 July 1944

At 0950 hours *I./JG 302* took off from Götzendorf on a mission over the Munich area. Together with the *Jagdgruppen* of *JG 300*, it was to intercept an American attack on the Bavarian capital. While en route, *"Rosenkavalier"* handed the *Gruppe* over to *"Leander"*, the control center in *Luftgau VII*. The change in call-signs was accompanied by a change in controllers. The pleasant female voice was replaced by a male voice with clear military diction.

Having put my "White 6" down in a clover field near Budapest, on this occasion I flew "White 8". Immediately after takeoff we headed west, and a glance to the left revealed the foothills of the Alps. As we flew west, *"Leander"* repeatedly urged us to increase speed. As our *Jagdgruppe* approached the Munich area, from far away we could see that the air battle was in full swing. The formations of B-17s calmly flew along, but otherwise it was impossible to tell friend from foe.

In spite of the activities of the escort fighters, we formed up for an attack on one of the bomber formations. We had already got rid of our external tanks and the attack wedge had formed up. Seconds later our high-altitude *Staffel* reported contact with the enemy and the "heavy *Gruppe*" was suddenly attacked by P-51 Mustang escort fighters from several sides.

This of course put an end to the close formation that was to have attacked the bombers. A fighter-versus-fighter battle developed in seconds, and my memories of it are not exactly clear. Our formation quickly broke up into pairs and fours, and it required some experience to keep one's head in such a mix-up. As a still rather inexperienced combat pilot, I stayed with my element leader *Oberfeldwebel* Haase and simply tried to remain with him and prevent any escort fighters from slipping in behind us unseen. Haase tried to position his Bf 109 G behind two Mustangs and I attempted to follow. I would have to keep my eyes open to get out of there in one piece. One always had to have a portion of luck in air combat, and I certainly had it on this day. Quite suddenly I found a Mustang right in front of me: it had flown into my flight path from the side and was itself at the apex of a turn. It was almost impossible to miss, and the bullets from my two machine-guns struck the machine dead center. A visible shudder went through the aircraft and the P-51 immediately rolled over and went down. I had of course lost sight of *Oberfeldwebel* Haase's "White 2" and so I followed the plunging P-51 for a distance. There were fighters at all heights, friendly and hostile, and I soon realized that someone was following me: a Mustang!

Now the dogfight began in earnest, but I wasn't the only one whose hands were full: all hell had broken loose in headphones of my flying helmet. Everyone was trying to pass on his observations and comments, but whether any of them were understood and acted upon is another question. My engagement with the second Mustang produced no result, except that a tremendous amount of altitude was lost. In the end we were both happy to be able to keep flying, and at 1115 hours I landed my "White 8" at the Neubiberg air base.

My engagement with the P-51 made me realize that, although the pilots of these machines enjoyed a formidable reputation, they were only human too. This air battle went the same way as many I would experience later.

The fighter combats took part in fighter grid square "EC", and although I indicated the area north of Starnberger Lake in my report, my victory claim was not confirmed. One simply had to live with it.

Almost all of the aircraft of *I./JG 302* involved in this mission landed at airfields around Munich, most of them at Neubiberg air base. The aircraft were refueled immediately, but there was no time for a second mission. At 1245 hours, therefore, the *Gruppe*'s fighters took off together and landed back at Götzendorf at 1406.

The surviving records hold no information on victories achieved in this engagement over Munich. It was purely a fighter-versus-fighter battle, which shows that the *Jagdgruppe* had again failed to fully exploit the tactic of the massed attack against bomber formations. Doing so would also prove difficult in subsequent air battles.

In spite of its meager success on this day, the *Jagdgruppe* had fought bravely, for *I./JG 301* reported just a single total loss for 6 June 1944. The loss was an extremely painful one, however: *Feldwebel* Rudolf Dreesmann of the *4. Staffel* was shot down and killed by P-51s over Munich (Bf 109 G-6 "Black 3", WNr. 413 498).

Feldwebel Rudolf Dreesmann, born in Apen near Oldenburg on 16 May 1912, had come to *I./JG 302* at the beginning of June 1944 when *12./JG 51* was transferred to Götzendorf from the Eastern Front.

By that time he had scored nine victories on the Eastern Front, and in his short time with *I./JG 302* he recorded another six. The loss of this capable fighter pilot left a huge hole in the *Gruppe*.

6-7 July 1944

I./JG 301 saw action on this night, and entries in *Oberfeldwebel* Hans Müller's logbook show that the *Gruppe* took off from Dechy airfield near Cambrai. The targets were once again English bombers penetrating French airspace. Although all the other *"Wilde Sau"* night-fighter *Gruppen* had long ago switched to daylight operations, *I./JG 301* continued to fly night missions exclusively, and would continue to do so until the end of August 1944.

Flying his Bf 109 G-6 "Black 12", at 0044 hours *Oberfeldwebel* Hans Müller of the *2. Staffel* shot down a Halifax over the Channel. He took off from Dechy at 0001 hours and landed there at 0113.

Feldwebel Gerhard Koch of the *1. Staffel* shot down two heavy bombers, the first at 0038 hours and the second at 0045.

Leutnant Horst Prenzel, also of the *1. Staffel*, claimed Lancasters shot down at 0136 and 0148 hours.

Leutnant Willi Esche of the *2. Staffel* destroyed a four-engined bomber at 0356 hours.

The *Gruppe* also suffered losses in this night action, however:

Oberleutnant Ernst Fischer, *Staffelkapitän* of *1./JG 301*, was wounded by return fire while attacking a four-engined bomber. He was forced to abandon his Bf 109 G-6, WNr. 163 236, over Crecy.

Unteroffizier Paul Werner of the *3. Staffel* was wounded in action over Jeuvoi and bailed out (Bf 109 G-6, WNr. 163 509).

A report dated 7 July 1944 states that *Leutnant* Kurt Welter of *II./JG 301* was transferred to *5./JG 300* in Romania.

7 July 1944

On this day the American 15th Air Force attacked the Blechhammer and Odertal hydrogenation plants in Silesia. Approximately 400 bombers with fighter escort set off on this mission, following two routes to the target.

On that Friday morning, 7 July 1944, the weather at *I./JG 302*'s base at Götzendorf made it seem unlikely that there would be any flying: there was low cloud with visibility of just a few hundred meters. The reports from "*Rosenkavalier*", however, suggested otherwise. A large force of enemy bombers had taken off from their bases in southern Italy in the early morning and were now heading north towards the *Gruppe*'s area of operations. Then the weather forecast was received, calling for an improvement in conditions at about 0900 hours. It looked like it was going to be a hot day, in the truest sense of the word, after all.

The number of available aircraft on this day shows just how badly the most recent missions had thinned the *Gruppe*'s ranks. The unit was below authorized strength in both aircraft and pilots. As well, on this day – for reasons which can no longer be explained – the *Gruppe* flew two separate missions of different strengths. The bombers' approach lay on a line between Vienna and Budapest, and almost exactly the same route had been chosen for their return flight. Based on the initial situation report by "*Rosenkavalier*" the *Gruppe* should have got airborne some time before, but for some reason takeoff was delayed.

By the time the first takeoff order was issued shortly after 0900 hours, most of the bombers attacking Blechhammer had already passed through the airspace east of Vienna, and the only contact with the enemy involved a group of B-17s that apparently formed the rear guard. These B-17s were attacked immediately. The attack was not terribly successful, with just two bombers shot down. The fighters were not far from their airfield and the majority of them landed back at Götzendorf. All aircraft were immediately refueled and prepared for a second mission. There was a short mission briefing, at which the pilots were told that they would fly the second mission in loose formation and that there was no high cover *Staffel* available. The ground control center had already reported several times that there were few escort fighters with the retiring bombers.

The takeoff order for the second mission came at 1133 hours. Formation leader on the second mission was *Oberleutnant* Ferdinand Kray, *Kapitän* of the *4. Staffel*.

I once again took off in "White 8", and soon after leaving the ground it suffered a fractured oil line, which covered my windscreen with a film of oil. I reported my situation to the formation leader, who immediately instructed me to land and then take off in *Oberfeldwebel* Gossow's machine. Gossow had been grounded for the day on account of a bad cold. The technical personnel apparently overheard his order, for when I reached the dispersal preparations were underway for me to switch aircraft. *Oberfeldwebel* Gossow advised me that when charging the weapons I should press down on the charging button until the indicator lamp came on.

Soon afterwards I was airborne again, this time in "Yellow 5". I soon established radio contact with the formation leader and was ordered to fly a heading of 080 degrees. I was to proceed to grid reference DO-DP and try to link up with the formation there at a height of 7,000 meters. When I arrived in the designated area I was able to read the formation leader loud and clear, but was unable to spot any of our aircraft. We reported our positions several times, then I heard the formation leader give the order to attack.

During my efforts to rejoin the formation, I spotted the first formations of enemy bombers. They were flying south, probably already heading for home. There was no sign of escort fighters anywhere, and so I flew over the bombers at a safe height, hoping to see my comrades as they attacked the bombers. There was no sign of them, our position reports must have been in error. What was I to do up here all alone? Attacking the formations – they were all B-24s – would have been madness. Gradually I came to the conclusion that I should head for home.

Then I spotted a straggler lagging far behind a group of bombers approaching from the north. I headed toward the formation to find out why the lone Liberator was so far behind the formation. Machines flying on their own like that were often a trap for an attacker, carrying extra guns instead of bombs. I moved in close but couldn't see anything suspicious, so I jettisoned my external tank and prepared to attack.

I made my attack from about 1,000 meters above, so that I had the entire top of the Liberator as a target area. I had no need to fear the defensive fire from the formation, for it was much too far away.

My approach was not unseen, however, for I came under fire as I rolled over to begin my attack. It was nowhere near as concentrated as the fire from a formation, and the first burst from my machineguns struck the fuselage in the area of the dorsal turret. I was about to switch my fire to the two starboard engines and wing, when my guns fell silent. A quick glance at the weapons status lamp showed no indication. I quickly recharged the guns and the indicator came on. My very high speed brought the Liberator quickly closer, and after hastily aiming and pressing the firing buttons I clearly saw shells striking the Liberator. But once again my weapons fell silent after just a short burst. Recharging the guns again was impossible at this stage, for the Liberator loomed huge before me. At that moment a word appeared in my mind like a flash: "Ram!"

As I was still slightly higher with plenty of speed, my first thought was to just strike the starboard fin of the Liberator and then pull away to the right. I closed to within a few meters of the Liberator,

7 July 1944 at Götzendorf: after ramming a B-24 Liberator, Unteroffizier Reschke returns to the Gruppe on foot with his parachute under his arm.

but I had not taken into account the airflow caused by its propellers, which seized my Bf 109. I struck the starboard fin and rudder somewhat lower than I had planned. As a result, my left wing was damaged as well as the propeller, but I did not realize this until my machine separated from the Liberator. The engine was still running, but the damaged propeller blades were causing the machine to vibrate very heavily.

When I looked at the left wing I quickly abandoned the idea of making a forced landing. My only choice was to bail out, something that the fighter school had not prepared me for but which I now faced for the first time. As it was becoming increasingly difficult to maintain control of the aircraft, I wanted to get out as quickly as possible. I disconnected the helmet leads, took off my oxygen mask and released the seatbelt. I pulled the canopy jettison lever but nothing happened. I pulled the lever again while pushing against the top of the canopy. My efforts were rewarded and I flew out of the machine with the canopy.

Seeing the ground from this height was nothing new, but seeing it without an aircraft, free in the air – that was a completely different feeling! I very soon reached for the ripcord and after the parachute deployed there was a wonderful silence. As the parachute had opened at 4,000 meters, it at first appeared to me that I was not getting any closer to the earth, but then little by little the objects under me became grew larger.

While still in my parachute I saw men gathering at my probable landing site and I remembered what had happened to me in the streets of Budapest. I landed in a sun-baked field and my return to earth was therefore anything but gentle. In the end, however, I suffered nothing worse than a split lip. The people who rushed to the scene were very friendly, and it turned out that I had come down quite near the town of Szens, on the Hungarian-Slovakian border south of Preßburg.

These people were soon joined by a *Leutnant* and a *Feldwebel* of the infantry who were serving as part of the station guard in Szens. Both had witnessed my attack on the Liberator with binoculars: I therefore had witnesses for my ramming victory. I learned that after I had rammed the Liberator it immediately went down in a spin and later broke up in the air. The two machines had come down just a little more than a kilometer apart, and the crash sites were marked by two pillars of smoke.

I waited for a long time at the station guardhouse in Szens until the train to Vienna arrived. I sat in the train with my bundled parachute and had plenty of time to reflect on all that had happened in the last few hours. Only then did I realize the risk I had taken up there. The sound of the collision will probably never leave my memory. The cockpit canopy had probably become jammed when I struck the Liberator, and I was quite certain that I had only caught the top part of the Liberator's fin and rudder. Seen from above, my aircraft's left wing had suffered only minor damage. What the wing looked like on the bottom I can only imagine.

When I stepped off the train in Vienna in the early hours of the following morning, I was quite certain of one thing: as far as I was concerned, anyone who wanted to ran could do so, but for me this chapter was closed forever. The chances of escaping with one's life were minimal and were out of all proportion to the courage required to put such a plan into action.

As Götzendorf was roughly halfway between Vienna and Lake Neusiedler, I had to use my legs again. I reached the airfield at about noon – another of the missing had returned. For lunch there was grilled peppers, which I ate for the first time in my life. My bedding, which had already been taken away, was silently returned. Of my comrades there was no sign: they had taken off on another mission in the late morning.

For *I./JG 302* the balance sheet after the two missions on 7 July 1944 looks like this: *Unteroffizier* Karl-Heinz Bamberg of the *2. Staffel* was fatally wounded while attacking a formation of bombers. He and his Bf 109 G-6 went down near the town of Malacky in Slovakia.

Obergefreiter Wilhelm Herfel of the *4. Staffel* was wounded in action near Bruck and had to be taken to hospital. He later returned to the *Gruppe* after recovering from his wounds.

Against these losses were the following successes:

0945	*Feldwebel* Heinz-W. Schellner	*2./JG 302*	B-17	30 km S Komarom
1025	*Gefreiter* Ludwig	*1./JG 302*	B-17 HSS	NE Preßburg
1155	*Unteroffizier* Willi Reschke	*1./JG 302*	B-24 downed by ramming	NE Preßburg
1200	*Leutnant* Ernst-Dieter Grumme	*4./JG 302*	B-24 HSS	SE Preßburg
1200	*Leutnant* Wilhelm Hallenberger	*4./JG 302*	B-24 HSS	SE Preßburg
1225	*Leutnant* Wilhelm Hallenberger	*4./JG 302*	B-24 HSS	near Komarom
1236	*Unteroffizier* Heinrich Reuter	*2./JG 302*	B-24	S Györ
1240	*Unteroffizier* Hans Kemmerling	*2./JG 302*	B-24	S Györ

Two female signals auxiliaries, Hildegard Täschner and Anneliese Mörs, saw to it that the *Jagdgruppe* was kept properly informed. Both had been members of the *Gruppe* since its formation and were highly thought of by all because of their participation in the life of the *Geschwader*. Bound to the *Geschwader* in good and bad times, both women had an uncanny sense for which information should go in which direction. This flow of information became a solid part of the comradeship within the unit. Both auxiliaries stayed with the *Gruppe* until the end of the war.

7-8 July 1944

As a *"Wilde Sau" Gruppe* operating over France, *I./JG 301* was extremely busy but also extremely successful. Though doubts still lingered in some *Luftwaffe* staffs about the creation of the *"Wilde Sau" Geschwader*, *I./JG 301* had silenced the critics by becoming the most successful single-engined night-fighter *Geschwader*. In night-fighter operations over France it was able to demonstrate a high level of readiness and achieve the success expected of it, often under the most difficult conditions.

On the night of 7-8 July the *Gruppe* was again ordered to intercept incoming British and American bombers. The *Gruppe* received the takeoff order shortly after midnight and its aircraft lifted off from Epinoy and Dechy airfields. The *Gruppenstab* and all three *Staffeln* took part in this mission. The majority of the intruders were Avro Lancaster and Martin B-26 Marauder bombers.

The pilots of the *"Wilde Sau" Gruppe* scored the following victories in the night sky over northern France and the Channel:

0110	*Feldwebel* Herbert Böwer	*1./JG 301*	heavy bomber	1st victory
0112	*Hauptmann* Wilhelm Burggraf	*Stab*	Lancaster	1st victory
0116	*Leutnant* Max Kreil	*Stab*	Lancaster	1st victory
0120	*Feldwebel* Hans Engfer	*1./JG 301*	Lancaster	2nd victory
0121	*Hauptmann* Wilhelm Burggraf	*Stab*	Lancaster	2nd victory
0121	*Hauptmann* Erich Wegener	*2./JG 301*	heavy bomber	1st victory
0125	*Fahnenjunker-Fw.* Viktor Emanuel	*1./JG 301*	Lancaster	3rd victory
0128	*Feldwebel* Joachim Hähnel	*3./JG 301*	Lancaster	1st victory
0133	*Leutnant* Alfred Hiller	*3./JG 301*	Lancaster	1st victory
0136	*Feldwebel* Manfred Gromoll	*3./JG 301*	Lancaster	1st victory
0138	*Leutnant* Willi Esche	*2./JG 301*	Lancaster	5th victory
0139	*Leutnant* Fritz Brinkmann	*1./JG 301*	heavy bomber	1st victory
0142	*Feldwebel* Hans Engfer	*1./JG 301*	heavy bomber	3rd victory
0143	*Leutnant* Fritz Brinkmann	*1./JG 301*	heavy bomber	2nd victory
0143	*Unteroffizier* Klaus Jakobi	*2./JG 301*	Lancaster	1st victory
0144	*Feldwebel* Herbert Böwer	*1./JG 301*	heavy bomber	2nd victory
0148	*Feldwebel* Manfred Gromoll	*3./JG 301*	Lancaster	2nd victory
0214	*Feldwebel* Georg Scharein	*1./JG 301*	B-26	2nd victory
0222	*Hauptmann* Helmut Suhr	*1./JG 301*	Lancaster	7th victory
0228	*Unteroffizier* Paul Werner	*3./JG 301*	B-26	1st victory
0237	*Oberfeldwebel* Heinz Günther	*2./JG 301*	B-26	1st victory
0244	*Feldwebel* Georg Scharein	*1./JG 301*	B-26	3rd victory

0246	*Oberfeldwebel* Josef Löffler	*3./JG 301*	Lancaster	1st victory
0250	*Feldwebel* Gerhard Koch	*1./JG 301*	heavy bomber	4th victory
0305	*Feldwebel* Martin Schulze	*1./JG 301*	B-26	3rd victory

This was the greatest night success achieved by the *Gruppe* to date and proved that the day of the single-engined night-fighter was far from over. *"Wilde Sau"* pilots required lengthy specialized training, however, which the general situation no longer permitted. The *Gruppe*'s only casualty on this night was *Unteroffizier* Paul Werner of the *3. Staffel*. After shooting down a B-26 Marauder he attacked another but was wounded by return fire and bailed out near Jeuvoi. This pilot's subsequent fate is not known.

8 July 1944

On Saturday, the 8th of July 1944, the bomber units of the American 15th Air Force took off from their bases around Foggia to attack targets in the Vienna area. Their primary targets were three oil refineries in the area surrounding Vienna and five airfields in Austria and Hungary. The bombers attacked the Korneuburg, Floridsdorf and Vösendorf refineries and the Markersdorf, Münchendorf, Zwölfaxing, Parndorf and Veszprem airfields.

The attack force consisted of 525 B-17 Flying Fortresses and B-24 Liberators, with an escort of 225 fighters, P-51 Mustangs and P-38 Lightnings. Most of the American bombers were B-24s, with only a few groups of B-17s.

It was a fact that German fighter pilots would rather attack a Liberator than a Flying Fortress. As a rule, one well-executed attack was sufficient to cause a B-24 to go down, but that was not always the case with a B-17. Two attacks were often required to down a B-17, and there were cases when a German pilot expended all his ammunition on a B-17 with no apparent effect.

I./JG 302 was ordered into the air from Götzendorf shortly before ten in the morning. On this occasion it was led by *Hauptmann* Heinrich Wurzer. Reports from *"Rosenkavalier"* revealed that the bomber formations, coming from the southwest, had bypassed Vienna to the east. The *Gruppe* subsequently met and engaged the enemy over Lake Neusiedler, east of Vienna, and in the Preßburg area. The *Gruppe*, which consisted of about thirty machines, fought an heroic battle in spite of the enemy's numerical superiority. Some of the fighting occurred over the unit's base, and the ground personnel were able to witness some of the action. It was even feared that the airfield would be bombed, but this did not happen. Perhaps it had something to do with the airfield's excellent natural camouflage.

The fighting over the unit's home airfield, witnessed firsthand by the ground personnel, made this day a special one in the history of the *Jagdgruppe*.

A number of pilots recorded victories in this action:

Obergefreiter Ludwig Koller of the *3. Staffel* shot down a B-24 Liberator east of Vienna at 1030 hours. It was his first victory.

Oberfeldwebel Herbert Stephan of the *1. Staffel* shot down a B-24 Liberator east of Vienna in grid square DO 1/4 at 1033 hours. It was his third victory.

Oberfeldwebel Fritz Dieckmann of the *1. Staffel* claimed a B-24 forced to leave formation (*Herausschuss*) northeast of Vienna at 1033 hours. It was his second victory.

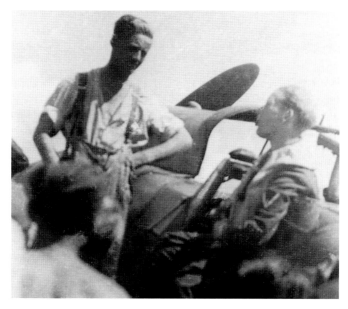

Götzendorf in July-August 1944: Gefreiter "Bubi" Blum of 1./JG 302 (right) in conversation with his crew chief, Gefreiter Stahlinger.

Unteroffizier Blum at 1./JG 302's dispersal at Götzendorf airfield in the summer of 1944.

Oberfähnrich Günter Kolbe of the *3. Staffel* shot down a B-24 northeast of Götzendorf at 1042 hours for his first victory.

Leutnant Reiche of the *3. Staffel* reported a B-24 damaged and forced to leave formation east of Vienna in grid square DO at 1045 hours. It was his third victory.

Oberfähnrich Walter Rödhammer of the *1. Staffel* shot down a B-24 northeast of Vienna at 1045 hours. It was his first victory.

Leutnant Horst Kirchner of the *2. Staffel* claimed a B-24 shot down east of Vienna at 1050 hours. It was his second victory.

Hauptmann Heinrich Wurzer, formation leader and *Kapitän* of the *1. Staffel*, brought down a B-24 east of Vienna at 1050 hours, followed by a second one minute later. They were his 25th and 26th victories.

Oberfähnrich Günter Kolbe of the *3. Staffel* reported a B-17 shot down northwest of Preßburg at 1055 hours, his second victory during this mission.

Unteroffizier Erich Reuter of the *3. Staffel* damaged a B-17 and forced it to leave formation southeast of Götzendorf at 1105 hours. It was his first victory.

Oberfeldwebel Ernst Schäfer of the *2. Staffel* shot down a B-17 southwest of Lake Neusiedler at 1120 hours. It was his third victory.

Other units that took part in the defense were *II./JG 27* from Fels am Wagram, *I./ZG 76* from Seyring and *II./ZG 1* from Wels.

These successes did not come without cost, however. The *Gruppe* reported the following losses:

Hauptmann Heinrich Wurzer, *Kapitän* of the *1. Staffel*, was wounded in the right arm and made a belly landing near Götzendorf airfield. This wound took him out of action for a lengthy period. (Bf 109 G-6 "White 1", WNr. 441 613)

Feldwebel Werner Voss of the *1. Staffel* was wounded in action near Preßburg and did not rejoin his comrades until the end of the year. On this day he was flying Bf 109 G-6 WNr. 441 625.

Twenty-year-old *Oberfähnrich* Walter Röhhammer of the *1. Staffel* was wounded in action near Untersiebenbrunn, east of Vienna and did not return to his *Staffel* until the final months of the year. (Bf 109 G-6, "White 16", WNr. 441 742)

The aircraft of *Unteroffizier* Heinrich Reuter of the *2. Staffel* was damaged in combat near Trautmannsdorf, southeast of Vienna, and he subsequently made a forced landing. (Bf 109 G-6, "Red 6", WNr. 440 950) After recovering from his injuries Reuter rejoined his *Staffel*; his subsequent fate is not known.

The only pilot killed on this day was *Unteroffizier* Kurt Zitzmann of the *2. Staffel*. He was shot down and killed while flying Bf 109 G-6 "Red 12", WNr. 441 900. It is not known where the aircraft crashed.

This day also saw the return from hospital of a number of pilots wounded in earlier air battles:

Oberfeldwebel Egbert Jaacks, wounded on 24 May 1944 near Kindberg,

Feldwebel Eduard Ries, wounded on 6 January 1944 near Küstrin, celebrated his return on 27 June 1944 with the downing of a B-17.

Feldwebel Werner Dienst, wounded on 24 May 1944 near St. Aegid.

The gaps in the ranks of the *Staffeln* were filled by young pilots from the fighter schools. Within a few days they would be confronted by the harsh reality of front-line service.

The "Men in Black": in the center is Prüfmeister Otto Schindler, on the left an unidentified Feldwebel, head of the workshop platoon, and on the right Feldwebel Adam Häublein.

Technicians of JG 301. From left: Feldwebel Stoll, Feldwebel Heinze and Oberfeldwebel Huber.

Unteroffizier Werner Stoll, technician.

The newcomers were: *Unteroffiziere* Willi Greiner and Hermann Dürr, *Feldwebel* Heinrich Dörr, *Obergefreiter* Walter Kugler and *Gefreiten* Erich Steidel and Christoph Blum.

Blum, a young blond man with curly hair and a very youthful face, appeared at the *1. Staffel* dispersal one day and introduced himself as a pilot, assigned to the *1. Staffel*. All of those present looked at him in astonishment: "Since when have they begun using children as pilots?", they wondered. None would have imagined that *Gefreiter* Blum was seventeen years old, though in reality he was three years older. In any case, from that day forth Blum was called "Bubi" (Sonny), and he cheerfully accepted his new nickname.

Many of the returning aircraft were damaged, and even minor damage, such as bullet holes in the fuselage and wings, had to be repaired. The "Black Men" under maintenance chief *Oberfeldwebel* Prell and technical sergeant *Feldwebel* Hercher often put in twenty-four hour days to ensure that the *Gruppe* was able to put the maximum number of aircraft into the air the next morning. The crew chiefs and their deputies were the true backbone of the ground crews; their tireless efforts often demonstrated to the others that the impossible could be achieved. We always relied on our "Black Men" and it is with gratitude and respect that I think of my own crew chief, *Obergefreiter* August Napiwotzki from Berlin. Unfortunately I never saw him again after the war. Not until 1966 did I discover his address in Hamburg, but by then he had been dead seventeen years.

9 July 1944

II./JG 301 and *10./JG 301* continued to operate in the Romanian theater despite the approach of the Russian Front. It is impossible to determine the exact type of operations flown by these units from the surviving records. There are no further victory claims by the *Jagdgruppe* from this period, however loss records suggest that its operations must have taken place under the most difficult conditions.

Unteroffizier Wilhelm Esser of the *6. Staffel* was wounded in the leg and arm by bullet fragments during combat with P-51s over Mizil airfield and was taken to the *Luftwaffe* hospital in Buzau. (Bf 109 G-6, "Yellow 5", WNr. 163 208)

This day was also a costly one for the *10. Staffel*:

Feldwebel Ernst Kiehling failed to return from a mission and was reported killed in action. Where he was lost is not known. (Bf 109 G-6, "Black 3", WNr. 165 043)

Oberleutnant Otto Kobert was shot down and killed in air combat and once again the location is not known. His aircraft's tactical number suggests that Kobert may have been leading the *Staffel* at this time. (Bf 109 G-6, "Black 1", WNr. 163 632)

Feldwebel Gerhard Mett was wounded in action, and his subsequent fate is not known (Bf 109 G-6, "Black 8", WNr. 412 236).

13 July 1944

In the late afternoon of 12 July 1944 two *Staffeln* of *IV./JG 3 "Udet"* under the command of *Oberleutnant* Horst Haase landed at *I./JG 302*'s airfield at Götzendorf.

Luftwaffe intelligence had discovered that a heavy attack from the south was planned for the next day. This was confirmed the following morning when intruders were reported approaching from the south. The probable target was given as Vienna, but in fact the bombers subsequently changed course south of Lake Neusiedler and headed for Budapest.

The takeoff order for *I./JG 302* and the two *Staffeln* of *"Sturmgruppe Moritz"* came at 1006 hours. As it had done in many previous operations, the *4. Staffel* took off first to provide top cover. It was followed by the Fw 190s of the *"Udet" Geschwader* and then the remaining *Staffeln* of *I./JG 302*. This was the first time that a mixed force of Bf 109s and Fw 190s had taken off from Götzendorf.

The entire force assembled in the airspace over Vienna and was climbing to altitude when *"Rosenkavalier"* issued instructions to turn southeast. This order came at the moment that the bomber formation changed course, turning toward Budapest instead of Vienna. This course change brought the mixed fighter formation quickly into Hungarian airspace, and contact with the enemy was made in grid square HQ near Veszprem.

The enemy force consisted of combat boxes of B-17s with many P-51 Mustangs guarding their flanks. In spite of the enemy's numerical superiority, the high-altitude *Staffel* was initially able to keep the escort fighters away from the *Jagdgruppe*, allowing the Fw 190s of *JG 3* to attack a formation of B-17s virtually unmolested. The attack was made out of a left turn at a relatively sharp angle. After the attack, some of the Fw 190s dove through the bomber formation and then broke right or left.

I./JG 302's attack was supposed to follow immediately, but the planned massed attack was foiled by the escort fighters and the *Gruppe* was forced to defend itself against the Mustangs. Only the first wave, which was already close behind the bombers, was spared attack by the escort fighters. As my machine was in the middle of the attack wedge, I was so bound up in the formation that I was forced to attack a B-17 flying in a lower formation. The first burst from my MG 131s was aimed at the tail gunner's position, which posed the greatest threat to me, then I shifted my fire to the left wing root and left inner motor with all guns. The effects were immediately evident: smoking heavily, the B-17 dropped out of formation, then went down in flames.

Even though it was stressed in debriefings and specified as a tactic before every mission, once again there was no sign of a massed attack on the bombers – the reality was much different. Fierce dogfights had broken out around the bombers, making a second attack impossible. The *Jagdgruppe* was prepared for this, however, and its performance was visibly better.

Our comrades of *IV./JG 3* left Götzendorf on the same day and flew back to Memmingen. Unfortunately nothing is known of this *Gruppe*'s victories or losses in this action.

It cannot be said that there was satisfaction in *I./JG 302* during the post-mission evaluation even though it had lost just one pilot killed: *Unteroffizier* Werner Mühlich of the *3. Staffel* was shot down near Enzersfeld, fifteen kilometers north of Vienna (Bf 109 G-6 "Yellow 11", WNr. 165 850).

That night in the *1. Staffel* mess, where the pilots of the *4. Staffel* also gathered to discuss the *Gruppe*'s mission, there was a perceptible sense of helplessness among the men. Authorized strengths were constantly being lowered and replacement aircraft and especially pilots could no longer keep pace with losses. With scarcely more than fifteen aircraft, screening the "Heavy Group" was far beyond the capabilities of the high-altitude *Staffel*. The steadily increasing number of escort fighters reduced the chances of a massed attack on the bomber formations. The ratio of losses to successes remained favorable, however this was merely proof of the determination with which *I./JG 302* was fighting.

After the *Kapitän* of the *1. Staffel*, *Hauptmann* Wurzer, was wounded in action on 8 July 1944, *Oberleutnant* Heinrich Ötteking assumed command of the *Staffel*. He was one of the few officers to join the *Gruppe* at this time and he strove to obtain forces with which to fill the gaps in the *Staffel*.

Ötteking also came to the *Reichsverteidigung* by way of several other units and his original training was not as a fighter pilot. His uncomplicated manner soon gained him the trust of the *Staffel*: he was a worthy successor.

14 July 1944

After several days of rest, on the night of 13 to 14 July *I./JG 301* returned to action from the airfields of Epinoi and Dechy; however, the *Gruppe* failed to repeat the success of its previous mission.

The only known results on this night are the downing of a Halifax by *Oberfeldwebel* Hans Todt of the 2. *Staffel*, and the wounding of *Feldwebel* Wilhelm Hähnel of the 3. *Staffel* while attacking a four-engined bomber northeast of Douai (Bf 109 G-6, WNr. 412 662).

At 0912 hours on 12 July, *I./JG 302* took off on an intercept mission under the command of *Gruppenkommandeur Hauptmann* Richard Lewens, and once again "*Rosenkavalier*" vectored it in the direction of Budapest. A large force of American bombers had taken off from bases around Foggia in southern Italy, B-24 Liberators of the 376th and 449th Bomber Groups and B-17 Flying Fortresses of the 463rd and 483rd Bomber Groups. The majority of the escort fighters were P-38 Lightnings of the 14th Fighter Group together with P-51 Mustangs. The P-38 J had more powerful engines and larger fuel tanks, and was able to remain airborne for up to twelve hours. *I./JG 302* met and engaged the first P-38s as it flew into the Budapest area from the west. Though the high-altitude *Staffel* immediately tried to tie up the escort fighters, it was unable to prevent other elements of the formation from being engaged by the Lightnings.

My crew chief, *Obergefreiter* August Napiwotzki, and my deputy crew chief had worked hard on my aircraft, filling seams and polishing it to a high gloss. It received its baptism of fire in this

Foe in countless missions, the Boeing B-17 Flying Fortress. This captured machine was photographed at Mannheim-Sandhofen airfield.

battle with the P-38s and came through with flying colors. I fired a burst at one P-38 and saw strikes, after which the aircraft fell away. I had no difficulty outturning the Lightning and getting into good firing position, but unfortunately this victory was not confirmed.

As the battle went on, *Hauptmann* Lewens succeeded in assembling part of the *Gruppe* and attacked a group of Liberators. I singled out one B-24 which immediately showed signs of strikes in the tail and right wing. I engaged my 30mm automatic cannon and sealed the Liberator's fate.

In the ensuing fight with P-51 Mustangs I was at a disadvantage from the beginning and I was never able to change this. My aircraft was hit, and I had no choice but to try my best to get down. I tried to land at an airfield near Budapest, but was unable to lower the undercarriage and was forced to make a belly landing. So much for my puttied and polished machine. Once again I returned to Götzendorf by train.

An evaluation of *I./JG 302*'s mission reveals more than our own losses. There are differing versions of the *Gruppe*'s successes on this day. While *I./JG 302* claimed the destruction of just one B-24 Liberator and one P-38 Lightning, American records in possession of George Punka of Budapest show the loss of three B-17s, two B-24s and five P-38s, all in the fighting over Budapest.

In action with *I./JG 302* over Hungary on this day was *II./JG 27* based at Fels am Wagram. It, too, engaged the enemy fighters and reported the loss of one pilot. There is no mention of victories. Consequently, it can be assumed that *I./JG 302* was responsible for downing more enemy aircraft than the records would indicate.

The following losses were reported:

Unteroffizier Erich Reuter of the *3. Staffel* was shot down and killed by enemy fighters near Budapest (Bf 109 G-6, "Yellow 8", WNr. 441 619).

Leutnant Ernst-Dieter Grumme of the *4. Staffel* lost his life in combat with enemy fighters near Budaörs. According to witnesses, Grumme shot down a P-38 at the beginning of the air battle but was then shot down by another Lightning.

Grumme had come to *I./JG 302* at the end of May of beginning of June 1944 with the then *12./ JG 51 "Mölders"*. He had recorded twenty victories on the Eastern Front. During his brief period with *I./JG 302*, Grumme scored eight more victories flying with the high-altitude *Staffel*, making him the most successful fighter pilot in the *Jagdgruppe* at that time.

Leutnant Grumme was extremely popular with his comrades on account of his easy-going, friendly manner. Often he sat in the mess with comrades of the *1. Staffel* and made no bones about his distaste for attacking bomber formations. He much preferred taking on the escort fighters, always stressing the different nature of the air battles in the west compared to those on the Eastern Front.

The death of *Leutnant* Grumme got under the skin of every pilot in the *Gruppe*; it was bad news for everyone. The next few evenings in the small but comfortable *Staffel* mess were not especially cheerful, instead the mood was reflective. It was some time before the *Gruppe* got over this loss.

16 July 1944

The American bombers and fighters from Italy came again, but the weather was generally unfavorable. Their targets were the city of Vienna and industrial facilities in Lower Austria. The attackers assembled over Lake Balaton at about 0930 hours and entered the airspace of *Luftgaukommando XVII* between

Lake Neusiedler and Preßburg (Bratislava). The approximately 400 bombers that made up the strike force were escorted by about 200 escort fighters, P-38 Lightnings and P-51 Mustangs, which screened mainly to the west.

At Götzendorf, *I./JG 302* received the order to take off a few minutes past 0900 hours. The fighters took off and climbed over the airfield. The exact operational strength of the *Jagdgruppe* on this day is not known, but could scarcely have been more than twenty-five aircraft. Contact was made with the enemy in the airspace southeast of Vienna. *"Rosenkavalier"* had positioned the *Jagdgruppe* well in spite of the adverse weather conditions. This time the *Gruppe* approached the bombers without hindrance and carried out a formation attack. The attack and subsequent combat produced the following results (FO = finished off a damaged aircraft; last number = running victory total):

1015	*Oberleutnant* Ferdinand Kray	*4./JG 302*	B-24	Vienna	21st
1020	*Oberfeldwebel* Heinz-W. Schellner	*2./JG 302*	B-24	SE Vienna	4th
1020	*Oberfeldwebel* Ernst Schäfer	*2./JG 302*	B-24	SE Vienna	4th
1020	*Oberfeldwebel* Fritz Dieckmann	*1./JG 302*	B-24	SE Vienna	3rd
1020	*Unteroffizier* Walter Scheller	*4./JG 302*	B-24 HSS	SE Vienna	1st
1021	*Oberfeldwebel* Herbert Göbel	*3./JG 302*	B-24 FO	Vienna	1st
1022	*Oberfeldwebel* Heinz-W. Schellner	*2./JG 302*	P-38	SE Vienna	5th
1022	*Oberfeldwebel* Herbert Stephan	*1./JG 302*	B-24 HSS	Vienna	4th
1022	*Leutnant* Horst Kirchner	*2./JG 302*	B-24 HSS	Vienna	3rd
1025	*Unteroffizier* Walter Berlinska	*2./JG 302*	B-24	Vienna	1st
1030	*Unteroffizier* Horst Wernecke	*4./JG 302*	B-17	Vienna	1st
1040	*Oberfeldwebel* Ernst Schäfer	*2./JG 302*	B-24 FO	SE Vienna	5th
1045	*Oberleutnant* Ferdinand Kray	*4./JG 302*	P-38	Vienna	22nd

The *Jagdgruppe* also suffered casualties in this action, however. In the current situation the loss of pilots was especially painful, as the flow of replacements was growing ever slower.

Leutnant Richard Jüngling from Linz, a member of the *1. Staffel*, failed to return from this mission and was later declared dead.

Oberfähnrich Fritz Braune of the *2. Staffel* was shot down and killed over Lake Neusiedler (Bf 109 G-6, "Red 11", WNr. 163 539).

Oberfähnrich Günter Kolbe of the *3. Staffel*, born in Königsberg, lost his life in combat over Lake Neusiedler.

All three pilots had been transferred to the *Gruppe* in the second half of June 1944. *Leutnant* Jüngling, who had been with me in the Wienhausen flight at the replacement training unit in Weidengut, had shot down his first B-24 Liberator on 2 July. While his name was not forgotten, his place would always remain empty.

Oberfähnrich Günter Kolbe had shot down a B-24 Liberator and a B-17 Flying Fortress in the area around Vienna on 8 July; now he was gone from our ranks forever.

I spent 17 July 1944 test-flying my new aircraft, which of course bore the tactical number "White 6". The practice of filling seams and polishing aircraft had been abandoned by this time, for the short operational lives of the aircraft made such time-consuming work unprofitable.

18 July 1944

On Tuesday, 18 July 1944, American bombers and fighters launched a major raid on targets in southern Germany. Among their targets were Memmingen and Holzkirchen airfields, bases used by *JG 300* and *IV./JG 3*.

At Götzendorf, *I./JG 302* received the order to take off at 0933 hours. Immediately after takeoff "*Rosenkavalier*" instructed us to head toward Munich. Control of the formation was soon transferred to "*Leander*". The controller ordered us to rendezvous with *JG 300* in the area east of Munich, but that unit had already engaged the enemy by the time *I./JG 302* arrived. Fierce dogfights had broken out on the flanks of the bomber stream between the Bf 109 Gs of *JG 300* and the escort fighters. Several groups of bombers had to withstand mass attacks by the Fw 190s of *IV./JG 3* and *II./JG 300* and there were already gaps in some formations. Those bomber groups that had escaped attack continued on toward their targets as it untouched by the events going on around them, leaving visible contrails.

I./JG 302, which had flown into the battle area unopposed, attacked a formation of Liberators which had moved into position beside the formations of B-17s.

Given the large number of escorts, P-51 Mustangs, it was clear from the beginning that the *Gruppe* would only be able to make one formation pass on the bombers. We therefore had to try and make this first attack count.

Once again, it was confirmed that a B-24 went down faster than a B-17. One pass was enough to send down my Liberator, which crashed quite close to Starnberger Lake. After the attack it initially looked as if the *Gruppe* would be able to make another formation attack on the bombers, but then there were the Mustangs again to foil this plan. They streamed into the combat area from all sides; as a rule, this resulted in a lengthy air battle. We were in no position to do this, for we had expended most of our fuel in the long approach and the subsequent attack on the bombers.

The rest of the battle was fought mainly in pairs, for increased maneuverability in the attack and defense. My "*Kaczmarek*" (wingman) on this day was *Obergefreiter* Günter Angermann, and we both had our hands full holding off the attacking Mustangs. In the course of this dogfight I got one of the many Mustangs in my sights and clearly saw the effects of my MK 108 cannon shells. Compared to a four-engined bomber, the expenditure of ammunition was minimal, but only those who emerged victorious from an air battle could make this determination. Many others never had the opportunity to do so.

After 122 minutes in the air, we landed at Neubiberg air base at 1135 hours. Other of the *Gruppe*'s aircraft had already landed there, and later the same day we flew back to Götzendorf, arriving there at 1735 hours.

This mission had clearly shown that there was two-way communication between the bomber formations and their escorting fighters. The proof of this was that there were no escort fighters in the immediate vicinity of the bombers before and during the *Jagdgruppe*'s attack on the bomber formation, as they were more or less engaged with the aircraft of *JG 3* and *JG 300*. Additional fighters must therefore have been ordered into the combat area, and only the bombers could have done this. All of the aircraft involved in the attack, bombers and fighters, may have used the same frequency.

The situation was much different in *Luftwaffe* units: there was absolutely no communication between *Geschwader*, which frequently proved extremely disadvantageous.

Unfortunately the absence of records makes it impossible to accurately evaluate *I./JG 302*'s mission on 18 July 1944. No list of victories and losses has survived. All that is known is that *Oberfeldwebel* Jaacks and *Feldwebel* Jaegels were reported missing in the first hours after the mission. It later turned out that both were in hospital with injuries.

I./JG 301 also saw action on 18 July 1944 in the skies over France. Once again it was a *"Wilde Sau"* night-fighter mission, however all that is known is that *Feldwebel* Hans Engfer of the *1. Staffel* was wounded in action over Changry.

19 July 1944

For *I./JG 302*, the 19th of July was much the same as the day before. The unit was placed on alert in the morning, and the mission order was not long coming. The order to take off was received at 0830 hours and once again the *Gruppe* immediately headed west in the direction of Munich. Those taking part were familiar with the route, and the landscape below was uniquely beautiful. No one had time to look, however. Everyone scanned the formation to see how many aircraft were taking part in this day's mission. The *Jagdgruppe* led by *Hauptmann* Lewens had only put up about thirty aircraft. While this was below authorized strength, the pilots considered it normal. The weakening of the *Jagdgruppe* from continuous action was not just the result of pilot casualties, which could not always be made good, but of aircraft losses as well. The technicians were not always able to keep all available aircraft serviceable.

The radio traffic between *"Leander"* and *"Jumbo Anton"* was not all that different from that of the previous day, and in the Munich area the pilots of the *Jagdgruppe* found roughly the same aerial situation as the day before. There was one small difference, in that only formations of B-17s could be seen and the number of escort fighters did not appear so great – although as we well knew, that could change quickly.

Well controlled by *"Leander"*, *I./JG 302* closed rapidly with the bombers. The formation leader had already given the order to jettison tanks and attack. With no interference from enemy fighters, the formation immediately attacked a group of B-17s. The attack took place in almost the same area as the previous day's battle: grid squares EC-ED between Munich and Starnberger Lake.

Once again I failed to shoot down a B-17 on the first pass; a second attack was required to bring down the bomber. This second attack happened very quickly, for the *Jagdgruppe* reformed immediately after the first attack. Just before the end of the second attack one of my guns stopped. I had used up a great deal of ammunition in the two attacks and the magazine had been emptied by the long bursts. With no ammunition there was no point in remaining in the air, so I landed at Munich-Riem airfield.

Several of our aircraft and some from other units had already landed there, and as we were to go up again, the ground crews immediately set about rearming and refueling the fighters. There was a short mission briefing for the pilots, given by a *Leutnant* from another *Jagdgruppe*, and then we took off again. Just fourteen aircraft took off on this second mission.

We were not far from the field after takeoff at a height of only about 1,000 meters, when my machine was shaken by a heavy jolt. Although I did not know the cause, it immediately became clear to me that I had only seconds to act. I therefore released my straps, jettisoned the canopy and jumped out. I pulled the parachute release cord as soon as I was clear of the aircraft. The parachute

Oberkommando der Luftwaffe
Chef f. Ausz. u. Diszpl. (V)   B e r l i n, den 4.11.1944
Az. 29 Nr.   951 /44

_____

An   1./J.G.302

Der   1./J.G.302

wird der Abschuß eines   amerikanischen Kampfflugzeuges vom Typ

Boeing B-17 "Fortress"   am 19.7.44   09.40 Uhr

durch   Uffz. Willi   R e s c h k e

als   zwanzigster (20.)   Luftsieg der Staffel ⎫ anerkannt,
                                                      Gruppe ⎭

                                       I. A.

B 5221. 9. 44. S

Victory confirmation for a Flying Fortress claimed shot down by Unteroffizier Reschke on 19 July 1944.

opened, and I swung just four or five times before striking the ground hard. As a result of the hard landing I was at first unable to release my parachute, but I was aware that everything was blurry. I rubbed my hand over my face and saw that it was covered in blood. This discovery must have shaken me to my senses: I stood up and released my parachute harness.

At that moment the first civilians arrived to render assistance, and they insisted that I lie down again. I probably passed out at that point, for when I came to I was lying on a stretcher. I was taken to a hospital on the outskirts of Munich. They placed me in a hallway for a short time, and on the litter beside me was a downed American airman who had also just arrived.

The examination revealed an injury to my left eye. My eyesight was not in danger, but I was ordered to remain in hospital for observation. Later that day an officer stationed at the airfield explained why I was in hospital: we had been attacked by low-flying Mustangs immediately after takeoff from Munich-Riem. Another pilot failed to get out of his machine.

My eye swelled up and turned all sorts of colors, but I was not confined to bed and could move about freely. In the hospital were soldiers from every branch of the service from every front.

The next day, 20 July 1944, brought the attempted assassination of Hitler, and as soon as the news was released a lively discussion broke out among the wounded. Reactions to the news differed widely – some rubbed their wounds before rounds so that the doctor would extend their stay in hospital. I was astonished at how shattered the morale of the troops already was.

Combat training by III./JG 301: in the foreground is Leutnant Schallenberg, behind him Stabsarzt Czaja and Oberleutnant Kirchner.

One thing worried me though: if I had to stay in the hospital for too long I would not return to my unit, instead I would have to go to the replacement training unit in Quedlinburg. During the doctor's rounds I tried to change his mind, convince him to release me to my unit, but in vain. I had almost given up hope of seeing my comrades in Götzendorf again.

One morning there was an air raid alarm, and all the patients who could walk had to find their own way to the bomb shelter. That was my opportunity: I quickly got dressed and, with my parachute under my arm, out the gate I went. Toward noon I boarded the train from Munich to Vienna. On my arrival in Götzendorf I was sent to see the medical officer, *Stabsarzt* Czaja, and I confessed to him what I had done. "What you did was out of line," said the medical officer, "but I will sort it out for you." *Stabsarzt* Czaja always had a soft spot for his men. His opinion: "It would be best if you disappeared from here for a few days, until the dust has settled." In the end I was even given a few days recovery leave.

It was impossible to overlook the fact that the Americans were growing stronger with each attack. While the bomber groups had become somewhat smaller, thirty to forty aircraft instead of the previous fifty to seventy, the number of groups in the formation had grown. The escorting fighters were now almost all P-51 Mustangs, and the P-38 Lightning was only rarely seen. As well, the ratio of bombers to escort fighters was rapidly approaching parity. The *Luftwaffe*, on the other hand, had to call upon all its resources to maintain operational strength, and this was only done by increasing

122

the output of new pilots from the fighter schools. This inevitably led to abbreviated training and a reduction in flying experience. When one considers that the American pilots had at least 300 hours experience on their operational aircraft, it is easy to understand the outcome of many air battles.

An assessment of the action in the Munich area on 19 July 1944 leads to the conclusion that *I./ JG 302* fought well in spite of its diminished operational strength.

The offensive tactics used against the bomber formations once again proved effective, and further lessons were learned from the successful attack. The *Gruppe* had gradually become one of the most successful anti-bomber units.

I./JG 302's successes on 19 July 1944:

0951	*Feldwebel* Bausch	*2./JG 302*	B-17	SW Munich	2nd
0955	*Obergefreiter* Günter Angermann	*1./JG 302*	B-17 HSS	SW Munich	1st
0956	*Oberfeldwebel* Ernst Haase	*1./JG 302*	B-17 HSS	SW Munich	14th
0957	*Unteroffizier* Willi Reschke	*1./JG 302*	B-17	Starnberg	8th
0958	*Oberleutnant* Ferdinand Kray	*4./JG 302*	B-17 HSS	S Munich	23rd
1005	*Oberleutnant* Ferdinand Kray	*4./JG 302*	B-17 HSS	Starnberg	24th
1006	*Leutnant* Wilhelm Hallenberger	*4./JG 302*	B-17	E Munich	7th
1013	*Obergefreiter* Walter Weinzierl	*3./JG 302*	B-17	Starnberg	3rd
1015	*Feldwebel* Heinrich Dörr	*4./JG 302*	B-17 HSS	Starnberg	1st
1015	*Unteroffizier* Klammer	*4./JG 302*	B-17 HSS	Starnberg	1st

This success was overshadowed by the loss of two pilots killed and two wounded. *Gefreiter* Ludwig Heerdegen of the *1. Staffel* was shot down and killed near Wolfratshausen (Bf 109 G-6, WNr. 165 523).

Unteroffizier Wilhelm Menke of the *3. Staffel* lost his life when he was shot down near Gartelsried, fifteen kilometers southeast of Aichach (Bf 109 G-6 "Yellow 19", WNr. 440 949).

Unteroffizier Paul Kraatz of the *1. Staffel* was wounded in combat near Eggenfelden, Lower Bavaria (Bf 109 G-6 "White 7", WNr. 165 604). He did not return to the *Staffel* after recovering from his wounds.

Unteroffizier Willi Reschke of the *1. Staffel* was shot down soon after taking off from Munich-Riem and bailed out. He was taken to Oberföhring Hospital in Munich with a head injury (Bf 109 G-6, "White 6").

It is appropriate to dedicate a few words to the radio procedures used by pilots in the *Reichsverteidigung*. A radio with transmit and receive capability was installed in every operational aircraft. The pilot wore a mesh flying helmet with integrated headset. A throat microphone was also part of the radio helmet. The transmitter was activated when the pilot pressed the transmit button on the joystick.

In action, fighter units were controlled by command agencies by means of radio; depending on the size of the operation this could be the fighter commander, the fighter division, or the fighter corps. Code-names and titles were assigned as a rule and were changed from time to time. In the summer of 1944, for example, "*Rosenkavalier*" was the code-name for the control center of the *Jagdfliegerführer Ostmark* (Fighter Commander Austria). At the same time *I./JG 302*'s call-sign was "*Jumbo*". The *Gruppenkommandeur* was "*Jumbo Anton*", and the other pilots used the call-sign "*Jumbo*" plus a number. My radio call-sign was "*Jumbo 12*".

The ground controller radioed instructions to the formation leader to guide him to the enemy. During this time the remaining pilots in the formation had to maintain absolute radio silence. Radio silence could only be broken when vital information had to be passed to the formation leader, for example the sighting of an enemy formation or an imminent attack by enemy fighters. When battle was joined, radio silence was lifted for everyone. Each fighter unit was assigned a discrete frequency, which was a disadvantage in battles involving more than one unit, as aircraft from different units were unable to communicate with one another. It was possible to exchange information through the controller, however this often proved too clumsy to properly coordinate an attack.

20 July 1944

Together with *II./JG 27*, which was based at Fels am Wagram, *I./JG 302* flew a mission against fighter and bomber units of the American 15th Air Force from Italy. The raid's targets were the Dornier factory in Friedrichshafen and Memmingenberg airbase near Memmingen. The Americans lost nine heavy bombers in this attack, including four that crashed in Switzerland. Another B-24 landed at Dübendorf, a Swiss air base, while a B-17 landed at Payerne airport on Lake Neuenburg in Switzerland.

Oberfeldwebel Fritz Dieckmann of the *1. Staffel* was shot down and killed near Kaufbeuren.

Unteroffizier Horst Pollak, also of the *1. Staffel*, was wounded in action. He did not return to the *Jagdgruppe* and his subsequent fate is not known.

There are very few clues to *JG 301*'s activities during this time. It appears that there was no longer a unified *Geschwader* command, and it is even suspected that the unit was disbanded for a short time. The reasons for this are obvious: with *I./JG 301* in France and *II.* and *IV./JG 301* operating in Romania, it was impossible to provide a centralized, unified command. Losses were beginning to affect both full *Gruppen* and replacements were urgently needed, but the general situation made this impossible.

I./JG 301 must have flown a mission over Belgium-Holland on 20 July 1944, for *Leutnant* Max Kreil was wounded in combat over The Hague and forced to abandon his machine (Bf 109 G-6, WNr. 163 411).

21 July 1944

Between 1020 and 1105 hours nearly 500 bombers of the 15th Air Force flew into the airspace over Brüx in northern Czechoslovakia. Their target was the hydrogenation plant at Maltheuren. The bombers were escorted by P-51 Mustang and P-38 Lightning fighters.

To meet this incursion the *8. Jagddivision* committed *II./JG 27* from Fels am Wagram, *II./ZG 76* from Seyring and *I./JG 302* from Götzendorf. *I./JG 302* made contact in the area of Wels an der Traun and engaged the enemy, despite being vastly outnumbered. *I./JG 300* later joined the attack northwest of Wels. *I./JG 302* made a determined attack on a formation of B-17s, and within thirteen minutes it shot down or forced out of formation ten four-engined bombers and one escort fighter. The successes in detail:

Pilots of 1./JG 302 photographed following a mission over Budapest in July 1944. From left: Gefreiter Heerdegen (killed in action on 19 July 1944), signals auxiliary Elfi Pößnecker, Unteroffizier Kemmerling and Gefreiter Ackermann. The pup in the center of the photo later became "Mustang", 1./JG 302's mascot, or Staffelhund.

1042	*Unteroffizier* Adolf Klärner	*4./JG 302*	B-17	SW Wels	1st
1043	*Leutnant* Horst Kirchner	*2./JG 302*	B-17	SW Wels	4th
1043	*Oberfeldwebel* Ernst Schäfer	*2./JG 302*	B-17	SW Wels	6th
1045	*Oberfeldwebel* Dieter Rusche	*2./JG 302*	B-17 HSS	SW Wels	4th
1045	*Unteroffizier* Willi Greiner	*4./JG 302*	B-17 HSS	SW Wels	1st
1045	*Feldwebel* Heinrich Dörr	*4./JG 302*	B-17 HSS	SW Wels	2nd
1045	*Feldwebel* Bausch	*2./JG 302*	B-17 HSS	SW Wels	3rd
1047	*Leutnant* Reiche	*3./JG 302*	B-17 HSS	SW Wels	4th
1048	*Oberleutnant* Ferdinand Kray	*4./JG 302*	B-17	SW Wels	25th
1049	*Oberfeldwebel* Ernst Haase	*1./JG 302*	B-17	SW Wels	15th
1055	*Obergefreiter* Walter Weinzierl	*3./JG 302*	P-38	NW Pürgg	4th

The *Gruppe*'s losses on this mission could be characterized as light – one pilot killed and one wounded – although every loss left a gap.

The acting commander of the 2. *Staffel*, *Leutnant* Horst Kirchner, was attacked by an escort fighter after shooting down a B-17. His aircraft badly damaged, he attempted a forced landing in a marshy meadow, however he and his machine (Bf 109 G-6, "Red 1", WNr. 441 784) sank immediately.

Leutnant Wilhelm Hallenberger of the 4. *Staffel* was wounded in action near Rietberg and was taken to hospital in Bacheringen (Bf 109 G-6, "Black 9", WNr. 441 656).

I./JG 301 flew a night mission in French skies on 21 July. The precise location of the action is not known, however the mission was apparently flown in inclement weather. *Leutnant* Horst Prenzel of the *1. Staffel* became lost and landed his Bf 109 G-6 "White 16" (WNr. 412 951) at Manston in England.

Feldwebel Manfred Gromoll of the *3. Staffel* suffered the same fate. He, too, became lost and put his machine down somewhere in England (Bf 109 G-6, "Yellow 8", WNr. 163 240).

Both pilots became prisoners of war and were interrogated by the English. The subsequent fate of the two pilots is not known.

For both *Jagdgeschwader* there followed several days with no action, and this unexpected break did the pilots of both units good, for the most recent missions had been extremely arduous. Days with no missions also benefited the technical personnel, allowing them to achieve maximum serviceability and then relax.

25 July 1944

The 15th Air Force launched a major raid against Linz and the Hermann Göring Works. The weather picture on this day favored an attack from the south and in the early morning hours a P-38 Lightning flew weather reconnaissance over Linz. The raid that followed involved 400 heavy bombers, B-24s and B-17s, with an escort of about 200 P-38s and P-51s.

To meet this attack, the *8. Jagddivision* mustered sixty-four Bf 109s and twenty-two Bf 110s. They were joined by two units from *Luftgau VII*, *I.* and *II./JG 300*, both equipped with the Fw 190 A-8.

Twenty-six fighters of *I./JG 302* took off from Götzendorf at 0952 hours and over Tullin they joined up with *II./JG 27*. The *JG 27* fighters were in part earmarked to provide high cover, while *I./*

Unteroffizier Hans Kemmerling of 2./JG 302. On 25 July 1944 he was killed in action south of Wiener-Neustadt.

JG 302 was to act as the "heavy" *Gruppe* and attack the bombers. While *II./JG 27* quickly became involved with the escort fighters, *I./JG 302* succeeded in making a massed assault against a group of B-24 Liberators in the airspace above Mariazell. A second attack on the bombers proved impossible, however, as P-51 Mustangs appeared on the scene and engaged the formation. The escort fighters were past masters at this type of attack on German fighters, for it was a simple matter to come down from above and get behind an enemy fighter that had just completed an attack on a bomber and was seeking to rejoin formation. For the fighter pilots of the *Reichsverteidigung* this was always the most critical moment of any mission. The American fighter pilots were quick to recognize this situation and of course exploited it.

The following is a summary of the successes achieved by the *Jagdgruppe*'s on this mission:

Leutnant Fritz Bolduan of the *1. Staffel* shot down a B-24 north of Mariazell in grid square EL at 1053 hours. It was his second victory.

Oberfeldwebel Dieter Ruscke of the *2. Staffel* also shot down a B-24 south of Mariazell at 1053 hours. The enemy aircraft initially left its formation on fire and subsequently crashed on grid square FL. It was his fifth victory.

Also at 1053 hours, *Unteroffizier* Jakob Laborenz of the *2. Staffel* sent a Liberator down in flames in grid square FL south of Marienzell. It was his first victory.

Once again at 1053 hours, *Feldwebel* Heinrich Dörr of the *4. Staffel* forced a Liberator to leave formation (*Herausschuss*) southwest of Vienna. It was his third victory.

Oberfeldwebel Herbert Stephan of the *1. Staffel* shot down a B-24 at 1058. The Liberator, which crashed in grid square EM, was his fifth victory.

Oberfeldwebel Ernst Haase, also of the *1. Staffel*, sent a B-24 down in flames at 1058 hours southwest of Vienna. The enemy aircraft crashed in grid square EL/EM and was Haase's sixteenth victory.

Feldwebel Heinz-Walter Schellner of the *2. Staffel* claimed a B-24 forced to leave formation at 1105 hours. The combat took place southwest of Vienna in grid square FM. It was his sixth victory. The *Gruppe* also suffered losses, and on this day they were heavy:

Fahnenjunker-Feldwebel Hubert Göbel of the *3. Staffel* was wounded in combat near Treptis. His wounds kept him out of action for some time.

While closing with the enemy bombers, *Unteroffizier* Hans Kemmerling of the *2. Staffel* was hit by defensive fire. He went down with his aircraft near Schwarzenbach, south of Vienna (Bf 109 G-6 "Red 6", WNr. 441 795).

Obergefreiter Ludwig Koller of the *3. Staffel* was shot down and killed by Mustangs near Kienberg, southwest of St. Pölten (Bf 109 G-6 "Yellow 9", WNr. 447 618).

Gefreiter Heinrich Pfeifer of the *3. Staffel* was killed when his aircraft went down near Boding following air combat (Bf 109 G-6 "Yellow 17", WNr. 155 697).

Unteroffizier Günter Richter was the fourth pilot lost by the *4. Staffel* on this mission: the twenty-year-old from Dresden was wounded in combat not far from St. Pölten and was taken to hospital there. On this day he was flying "Yellow 7", a Bf 109 G-6 with the *Werknummer* 440 687.

Oberleutnant Ferdinand Kray, *Kapitän* of the *4. Staffel*, was shot down and killed by Mustangs, also near St. Pölten. He was flying "Black 1", a Bf 109 G-6, WNr. 441 635.

With twenty-three victories, *Oberleutnant* Kray was one of the most successful pilots of *I./JG 302*. He and his *12. Staffel* of *Jagdgeschwader 51* had come from the Eastern Front at the end of May 1944, joining *I./JG 302* in the *Reichsverteidigung*. Though the German fighters were always outnumbered by the American bombers and their escort fighters, Kray's experience and skill had enabled him to shoot down five four-engined bombers and four escort fighters in a short time.

Oberleutnant Kray was the fourth *"Experte"* of the former *12./JG 51* to fall in the Defense of the Reich: *Feldwebel* Dreesmann, fifteen victories, killed on 6 July 1944, *Leutnant* Grumme, twenty-eight victories, killed on 14 July 1944, and *Leutnant* Kirchner, eleven victories, killed on 21 July 1944.

The loss of these four outstanding fighter pilots left a gap in *I./JG 302* that could not be filled. Their absence was sorely felt in subsequent missions, when it became apparent that the high-altitude *Staffel* had lost much of effectiveness and striking power. After Kray's death, *Oberleutnant* Hermann Stahl assumed command of the *4. Staffel*.

26 July 1944

Bombers of the American 15th Air Force based in Italy attacked the Ostmark-Flugzeugmotorenwerke in Wiener Neudorf. Also bombed were airfields in the area around Vienna suspected to house facilities of the Wiener-Neustadt-Flugzeugwerke. To meet this attack, approximately twenty-five Messerschmitts of *I./JG 302* took off from Götzendorf. They encountered the Americans between Vienna and Lake Neusiedler. In the ensuing fighting the *Gruppe* shot down three four-engined bombers for the loss of two of its aircraft.

Feldwebel Hubert Blomert of the *3. Staffel* shot down a B-17 at 1115 hours near Birkfeld in grid square GM/9. It was his first victory.

Gefreiter Walter Weinzierl of the *3. Staffel* shot down a B-17 at 1120 hours southeast of Aspern. It was his fifth victory.

At 1140 hours another B-17 went down in flames east of Lake Neusiedler, the first victory by *Gefreiter* Christoph Blum of the *1. Staffel*. It should be mentioned that this would not be his last. Later promoted to *Unteroffizier* and *Feldwebel*, his name would be closely linked with the *Gruppe*'s fortunes until the end of the war.

Unteroffizier Guido Buhl of the *4. Staffel* did not return from this mission; where he was lost is not known (Bf 109 G-6 "Black 5", WNr. 412 399).

After shooting down a B-17, *Feldwebel* Hubert Blomert of the *3. Staffel* was attacked by several P-51 Mustangs which shot him down in flames. Forced to abandon his plan to belly-land his crippled machine, he bailed out over the village of Schäffern. The injured pilot was subsequently taken to hospital in Pinkafeld. Blomberg later returned to his *Staffel* after recovering from his injuries.

27 July 1944

On this day the 15th Air Force's targets were industrial facilities in and around Budapest. The attack force consisted of 340 B-17 and B-24 bombers. The enemy aircraft reached the area south of Lake Balaton in the early morning hours heading for Budapest, which resulted in *I./JG 302* being scrambled from Götzendorf. The aerial fighting over Lake Balaton resulted in just two known victories: *Leutnant* Kapp of the *Gruppenstab* shot down two Mustangs, at 0930 and 0933 hours in grid squares HQ 7/8 and JQ 1/2. Kapp can only have been with *I./JG 302* a short time, for at the time none of the pilots knew his name. His two claims correspond almost perfectly with admitted American losses: two P-51s were lost over Lake Balaton on this day, and another south of Celldömölk. The loss of seven B-24 Liberators was also admitted. It may be assumed, therefore, that several other pilots of *I./JG 302* scored victories on this day, however there is no reference to them in the surviving records. I would like to suggest that there will probably always be gaps in the history of this *Jagdgeschwader*. The whereabouts and subsequent fate of *Leutnant* Kapp, for example, are a total mystery. There are other members of the *Geschwader* who were there briefly and then disappeared, before they became well known. *Unteroffizier* Herbert Eckert of the *4. Staffel* did not return from this mission. It is not known where he was lost, therefore he is still listed as missing (Bf 109 G-6, "Black 6", WNr. 441 666).

The desperate situation in which the *8. Jagddivision* found itself was already apparent. The division still had a significant number of units available to meet incursions from the south – *II./JG 27*, *I./JG 302*, *II./ZG 76* and in exceptional cases *IV./JG 3* and *I.* and *II./JG 300* – however none of them had an operational strength greater than 50%. As well, *II./ZG 76* was gradually being withdrawn from operations as losses became unbearable. The low operational strengths were not due to inadequate deliveries of aircraft, but a shortage of pilots. Although the training given by the fighter schools had been drastically shortened, the output of new pilots simply could not keep pace with losses. *I./JG 300* had also intercepted this raid, taking off from Bad Wörishofen. It attacked the bombers immediately after *I./JG 302*, and Lt. Günther Sinnecker of *3./JG 300* shot down a Liberator at 1000 hours. Sinnecker had been a member of *II./JG 302* until June 1944, transferring to *I./JG 300* when *II./JG 302* was disbanded.

28 July 1944

On this day *I./JG 302* again saw action over Bavaria, resulting in combats with the Americans between Hof and Neustadt an der Donau. *Gefreiter* Erich Steidel of the *1. Staffel* shot down a B-17 near Neustadt, however he was himself wounded and taken to hospital in Neustadt. After recovering from his wounds Steidel rejoined the *Staffel*. At 1005 hours *Feldwebel* Heinz-Walter Schellner of the *2. Staffel* succeeded in downing a Mustang northwest of Hof.

Once again there were losses: *Unteroffizier* Dieter Ratzow of the *1. Staffel* was wounded in combat with escort fighters over Neustadt and was put out of action for a long time. *Gefreiter* Walter Weinzierl of the *3. Staffel* was shot down and killed by enemy fighters near Neustadt. Weinzierl was one of the *3. Staffel*'s most successful pilots, having shot down two B-24 Liberators, two B-17 Flying Fortresses and one P-38 Lightning.

29 July 1944

The previous day's mission was still subject matter for discussion when, on the morning of 29 July, *I./JG 302* was ordered up from Götzendorf. American bombers and fighters were approaching Linz from the south, fighter control guided the *Jagdgruppe* to intercept. The hydrogenation plant in Brux and the Hermann-Göring-Werke in Linz had been attacked several times in the period from the end of June to the end of July 1944. This had resulted in fierce air battles, in which the *Zerstörergeschwader* based in the area, in particular, had suffered heavy losses. *I./JG 302* had initially been assigned to provide fighter cover for the unit, however by this date the *Zerstörergruppen* had virtually ceased operations. The heavy armament carried by the Bf 110 and Me 410 made them very effective against the heavy bombers, but they were too slow and cumbersome to dogfight with the escort fighters. At the end of July 1944 the *8. Jagddivision* withdrew the *Zerstörer* units from operations against the American air forces operating from southern Europe.

The *Jagdgruppe* made contact with the enemy southwest of Linz, and once again B-17s made up the bulk of the enemy bomber force. The constantly growing number of escort fighters made it increasingly difficult for the *Jagdgruppe* to even get to the bombers. On this day only a few pilots were able to brave the defensive fire of the B-17s to attack the bombers.

The first to get through was *Oberfeldwebel* Herbert Stephan of the *1. Staffel*, who at 1015 hours attacked a B-17. The enemy bomber began to burn, left formation and reversed course. It was Stephan's sixth victory.

At 1020 hours *Feldwebel* Heinrich Dörr of the *4. Staffel* shot down a B-17 in grid square MD southwest of Linz. It was his fourth victory.

At the same time *Oberfeldwebel* Ernst Haase of the *1. Staffel* attacked another B-17. On fire, it dropped out of formation. It was his seventeenth victory.

Also at 1020 hours, *Leutnant* Reiche of the *3. Staffel* brought down a B-17 in grid square MD-ME for his fifth victory.

The majority of pilots, however, were forced to fight off attacks by the P-51 escort fighters and were unable to attack the bombers.

Feldwebel Ernst Schäfer of the *2. Staffel* failed to return from this mission and his crash site is unknown. He lost his life in action after six victories.

Unteroffizier Horst Wernecke of the *4. Staffel* was also shot down and killed by P-51s. The records state that he crashed at Laucha, southwest of Leipzig. Why he went down so far to the north will probably never be explained. Wernecke's victory on 16 June 1944 had proved to be his last.

The early morning mission briefings – when the situation permitted – were among the high points in the life of the *Jagdgruppe*. In addition to the pilots, the heads of the technical services also attended. These meetings, which often lasted just a few minutes, were a reflection of the *Gruppe*'s operational strength. The ratio of "actual strength" in serviceable aircraft to "available number" of pilots was not always equal. There was usually a shortfall on one side or the other. As the war went on, the flow of replacement pilots slowed, and there were days when the *Staffeln* could put little more than a single *Schwarm* (flight of four) into the air.

An evaluation of the individual missions made one thing increasingly clear: the first three missions were the most dangerous for a new pilot. Almost fifty percent of new pilots failed to return from these first missions or ended up wounded in hospital. After the inexperience and fear of the first sorties, pilots tended to develop a certain recklessness, even overconfidence if they scored their first victory. Those who survived these first missions and kept a clear head had an improved chance of becoming "old".

The *Gruppe* was granted a respite in the final two days of July 1944. This applied less to the "Black Men", for they exploited this unexpected break to achieve maximum serviceability. On such days there was also a chance for pilots and ground crews to exchange ideas. Although relations between the technicians and fliers was always good, there were few opportunities for personal conversations, as official matters had priority. During one such conversation a pilot and crew chief discovered that they were from the same area and that their home towns were only a few kilometers apart.

An agreement within the *Gruppe* required that every pilot who recorded a victory be given a bottle of champagne from the stock above the bar. This tradition continued until early 1945. It was also an unwritten rule that the pilot share the bottle of champagne with the technical personnel responsible for his machine.

31 July 1944

On this day *10./JG 301* reported its final operation in Romanian airspace. It was a scramble into the Bucharest-Ploesti area. *Feldwebel* Fritz Ebel was wounded while flying Bf 109 G-6 "Black 12", WNr. 412 237.

The subsequent history of *IV./JG 301*, which still consisted of just the *10. Staffel*, is uncertain. It seems quite likely, however, that it separated from *II./JG 301* in the Romanian area of operations, for *IV./JG 301* appears again on 28 November 1944 at Ziegenhain. Its presence at this location probably coincided with the reestablishment of the *Gruppe*.

II./JG 301 remained in the Bucharest-Ploesti area, although it submitted no victory claims or loss reports for a considerable time.

5 August 1944

I./JG 302 was transferred out of Götzendorf either on the afternoon of 4 August or the early morning of 5 August 1944. It is to be assumed that the *Gruppe* was moved to Jüterbog, as it had been based there previously. The two victories recorded by *Oberfeldwebel* Heinz Gossow and *Gefreiter* Christoph Blum cannot otherwise be explained: each shot down a B-17 in grid square GE northeast of Magdeburg, the victories coming at 1241 and 1242 hours.

As no other victories or losses were reported, it is reasonable to assume that only the *1. Staffel* – to which both pilots belonged – moved on this day. This was not standard practice for the *Jagdgruppe*, however, and the reason for the transfer and its extent can no longer be clarified.

7 August 1944

In all of its previous missions and air battles, *I./JG 302* had fought bravely, and it had maintained a positive ratio of victories to losses. On this day the *Gruppe* once again engaged the enemy over Hungary, and for the first time losses exceeded victories. The *Gruppe* achieved just two successes in this engagement, which was played out between Lake Neusiedler and Lake Balaton.

At 1234 hours *Leutnant* Karl-Heinz Müller of the *2. Staffel* brought down a B-24 east of Lake Neusiedler in grid square EP/8.

And at 1235 hours *Gefreiter* Christoph Blum of the *1. Staffel* forced a B-24 to drop out of formation in flames east of Raab.

The losses suffered by the *Gruppe* on this day were all at the hands of the Mustangs.

Leutnant Fritz Boldenau of the *1. Staffel* was wounded in combat near Szombathely. He did not rejoin the unit.

Feldwebel Heinrich Dörr of the *4. Staffel* was wounded in combat near Pecel, Hungary. He returned to the *Staffel* after recovering from his wounds. *Unteroffizier* Paul Friedrich of the *2. Staffel* was shot down and killed by Mustangs over Györ.

Oberfähnrich Walter Rödhammer of the *1. Staffel* was also wounded in combat over Szombathely. He required a lengthy convalescence but eventually returned to the unit.

8 August 1944

From Epinoy airfield in France, *I./JG 301* took off on one of the last night missions by the *"Wilde Sau"* single-engined night-fighters. It had been almost a year since the formation of the *Gruppe*, and since then all of the single-engined night-fighter *Gruppen* had been removed from night operations and reassigned to the day fighter role. *I./JG 301* thus served in the single-engined night-fighter role longer than any other *Jagdgruppe*.

Oberfeldwebel Hans Todt of the *2. Staffel* shot down a Halifax on this mission, his last night victory.

The *Gruppe* also suffered two casualties on this night: *Leutnant* Willi Esche of the *2. Staffel* was shot down and killed over St. Pol-sur-Mer (Bf 109 G-6, WNr. 412 237).

Leutnant Alfred Miller of the *3. Staffel* failed to return. He was shot down and killed near Ledeghem (Bf 109 G-6, WNr. 162 263).

It was precisely at this time that I returned to Götzendorf airfield. The wound to my left eye had healed well and a few days convalescent leave had put the finishing touches on my recovery. I found myself once again standing before *Stabsarzt* Czaja, who in the meantime had turned my flight from hospital in Munich to the *Staffel* in Götzendorf into a very normal duty movement. I was thus spared having to go to the combat pilot assembly group in Quedlinburg, and at 1407 hours on 10 August I took to the air in my new "White 6". After completing this altitude flight, two hours later I took off to join my unit. Reunited with my comrades, I spent the first few hours catching up on what had gone on in my absence. There were not that many new faces, however some familiar ones were missing.

Oberfeldwebel Willi Esche during a skeet shoot or rabbit hunt on the airfield. In June 1944 he and Hauptmann Wegner went from 2./JG 301 to I./JG 301. Willi Esche, since promoted to Leutnant, was killed over France on 8 August 1944.

16 August 1944

On 15 August the American 8th Air Force sent a force of 200 Flying Fortresses with twice that number of escort fighters to attack Wiesbaden. Encountering bad weather about thirty kilometers from Trier, the attack force broke up into several groups, forcing the escort fighters to also divide their strength.

II./JG 300 and *IV./JG 3* operated together on this day and they easily evaded the escort fighters. The thirty-minute air battle over the junction of the Rhine and the Moselle west of Coblenz turned into a real massacre. Many B-17s went down, the lion's share falling to *IV./JG 3* under *Hauptmann* Moritz.

Another major raid from the west was expected for the following day, and in the late afternoon on 15 August *I./JG 302* flew from Götzendorf to Langendiebach near Frankfurt am Main. Takeoff was at 1750 hours, and the *Jagdgruppe* landed at Langendiebach at 2000.

On 16 August a large force of bombers from the American 91st Bombardment Group approached Halle. *I./JG 302* was scrambled from Langendiebach at 0858 hours and, together with a *Gruppe* from *JG 300* and the *Sturmgruppe* of *JG 3*, it waited for the incoming bombers. The other two *Jagdgruppen* were equipped with a mixture of Bf 109 G-6s and Fw 190 A-8s. Facing such an air battle, it was comforting to be part of such a potent force. Contact was made with the enemy over the Kassel area.

The escort fighters, P-51 Mustangs, were again very numerous, but faced with the strength of the German fighter formation they hesitated to attack. They flew past the German fighters at a respectful distance and tried to place themselves between the bombers and the attackers. *JG 300's* high-altitude *Gruppe* quickly recognized this tactic, however, and attacked the escort fighters. The "heavy" *Gruppe* immediately exploited this opportunity to attack the bomber formations. *IV./JG 3* and *I./JG 302* attacked two formations almost simultaneously.

Once again long streams of tracer from the bombers reached out toward the attacking aircraft, giving the pilots the feeling that they were standing in a shower. In those seconds one's nerves were stretched to breaking. The target firmly in the gunsight reticle, the tension did not ease until one pressed the firing buttons and the aircraft vibrated slightly under the hammering of the guns. As the angle of attack was almost the same on most firing passes, judging deflection became routine.

The *1. Staffel* formed the leading wave in *I./JG 302's* "heavy" *Gruppe*, and the first bullets from my two MG 131s were again aimed at the tail gunner. I had always had good luck with this tactic. I then adjusted my aim forward to the area of the wing root and inner motor. My strikes were on target and, with all guns firing, I closed to within about fifty meters of the B-17. It absorbed everything and showed little effect. I elected to break away sharply to the left, so as to be able to make a second pass as quickly as possible. As I turned back toward the bomber formation, however, I could see my B-17, also in a left turn, veering out of formation. My second attack achieved immediate results and the enemy bomber went down, trailing an increasingly long banner of smoke. The B-17 initially appeared to be under control and not until it reached about 4,000 meters was I sure that it was going to crash. I followed it down to confirm the crash site and saw it impact at the edge of a wood southeast of Kassel.

I paid more attention to the crash of the B-17 than I should have and consequently lost a lot of altitude. It was a widely-held view among us pilots that the feeling of approaching danger resides in the five letters on which one sits (*Arsch* = ass). I must have felt that warning feeling at that moment, for when I looked behind me I saw the belly of a Mustang, followed immediately afterward by a second. As I had slowed to match the airspeed of the doomed Boeing, I tried to regain some speed in a steep left turn so as to get out of my ticklish situation. I soon lost what little altitude I had and there began a low-level chase with me exploiting every bit of available cover. After a while I was relieved to find that the two Mustangs were no longer behind my Bf 109.

Finally, at 1040 hours, I landed at Nordhausen in the southern Harz. As soon as I had slowed after landing, I saw an officer come running up to my aircraft. He demanded that I take off again at once. Enemy bombers were flying overhead and he was worried that the presence of my Bf 109 might cause them to attack. I later learned that the man so determined to have no aircraft in the open on his airfield was the base commander. But after two hours in the air, my machine had to be refueled before I could take to the air again. The ground crew did not arrive immediately, however, and it was 1220 hours before I was able to take off again.

Leutnant Karl-Heinz Müller, Staffelkapitän of 2./JG 302. He was wounded on 16 August 1944 and never returned to the unit.

What had happened in the air battle over Kassel on this day? *IV./JG 3* made two attacks on the bomber group and shot down six B-17s. During a third pass *Oberleutnant* Tichy, *Kapitän* of the *13. Sturmstaffel*, decided to ram, probably because he had used up all his ammunition. Both aircraft, B-17 and Fw 190, went down over Abhausen. There were no survivors from either machine.

For *I./JG 302* the day's balance looked like this:

1000	*Obergefreiter* Walter Kugler	*3./JG 302*	B-17	SW Kassel	2nd
1000	*Leutnant* Reiche	*4./JG 302*	B-17	NE Kassel	6th
1001	*Oberfeldwebel* Heinz Gossow	*1./JG 302*	B-17	SE Kassel	4th
1001	*Unteroffizier* Willi Reschke	*1./JG 302*	B-17	SE Kassel	9th

Leutnant Karl-Heinz Müller, acting commander of the *2. Staffel*, was wounded while attacking a bomber formation over Kassel. It is not known whether he made a forced landing or parachuted to safety. Müller did not rejoin the *Jagdgruppe*.

Unteroffizier Walter Berlinska, also of the *2. Staffel*, landed at an airfield in Germany after the mission. On 17 August he took off to return to Götzendorf, but crashed near Heiligenstadt for reasons unknown. Berlinska had joined *I./JG 302* at the end of June 1944 and had achieved three victories since then.

All of the aircraft of *I./JG 302* that landed back at Langendiebach took off again at 1550 hours and flew back to Götzendorf. An en route stop was made at Regensburg as the aircraft carried no auxiliary fuel tanks. This lengthy excursion had not been particularly successful, although losses had been within acceptable limits.

18 August 1944

Following a mission over France by *I./JG 301*, *Feldwebel* Enno Hansen of the *1. Staffel* failed to return and was declared killed in action. His crash site is unknown (Bf 109 G-6, "White 7", WNr. 166 229).

During the course of *I./JG 302*'s operations briefings at Götzendorf, there was growing talk of a transfer and conversion to the Fw 190. Was this why so few replacement pilots were reaching the *Jagdgruppe*? The matter was discussed at length and opinions were put forward, but no one knew for sure.

In the hours of the late afternoon on such days we had the opportunity to go into Vienna. The city was just a short train ride from Götzendorf. As we had often flown over Vienna, we thought it would be interesting to explore the city on foot. As well, we were pleased to once again be among the civilian population, for often all contact was severed for weeks at a time because of our constant operations. Vienna had been bombed several times and damage could be seen from the air, but during our stroll through the city there was little evidence of it. The area around the Prater in particular had been spared: we were able to admire the giant wheel in its park-like setting, but one had to be lucky to see it in operation. In this peaceful setting it was possible to forget the war for a short time, only we found returning to reality difficult.

20 August 1944

On this day the American 15th Air Force struck the oil refineries in the protectorate. Other targets were Szolnok in Hungary and the Odertal refinery. For *I./JG 302* at Götzendorf the day began in the early morning, when we were placed on thirty-minute readiness. The order to take off came at 0845 hours. *Gruppenkommandeur Hauptmann* Lewens led our small force of about twenty aircraft into Hungarian airspace. The reason for the modest effort was not a lack of aircraft, rather a shortage of pilots. Every available pilot was in the air. No replacement pilots had been received. We no longer employed a high-altitude *Staffel*, anyway the experts that had made it up had all been killed or wounded by now.

We were therefore pleased when, as we were approaching Budapest, "*Rosenkavalier*" informed us that Hungarian fighters were waiting for us west of the city. The Hungarian "Puma" Fighter Group had been the subject of conversation among our pilots and we had occasionally met pilots from this unit when we landed at airfields in Hungary.

What no one had suspected before takeoff became a reality on this day: Hungarian Bf 109s were in fact waiting for *I./JG 302* west of Budapest. The Hungarian fighter group had about the same number of aircraft, and now everything looked a little better.

The *Jagdgruppe* was unable to communicate with the Hungarian 101st Fighter Group by radio, nevertheless the two units worked well together. From the beginning the "Puma" formation positioned itself above *I./JG 302*. Condensation trails from the approaching bombers were already visible south of Lake Balaton. The Americans, too, had changed their tactics. Instead of the large formations of more than fifty aircraft, they were more frequently coming in smaller groups of about thirty machines. P-38 Lightnings and P-51 Mustangs accompanied the bombers, which were mainly B-17s. Contact was made in the familiar area between Budapest and Lake Balaton. The Hungarians immediately engaged the escort fighters, and indication that they also preferred fighter-versus-fighter combat.

Under *Hauptmann* Lewens leadership, *I./JG 302* immediately took advantage of the situation and attacked one of the formations of B-17s. The pilots had gained in experience. Previous attacks on B-17s had shown them the bomber's most vulnerable spots and they tried to score hits as quickly as possible.

In my first attack on one of the B-17s I immediately fired at the rear gunner, for he posed the greatest threat. Only afterwards did I aim at the inner motor and wing root area. After several good strikes by MK 108 rounds the bomber began to burn. While swinging around for another pass, I saw that my B-17 had dropped out of the formation on fire.

I attacked a second B-17 and it soon began to smoke heavily, but just before I broke away my Bf 109 began making a familiar noise, one that threatened to make my heart stand still. A glance at the instruments revealed nothing, and the engine sounded normal, but an inner voice told me to find a place to land. Even as I was searching for a landing site, however, I realized that my Bf 109 was handling differently. I glanced at the right wing, and saw that the mechanical undercarriage position indicator was half extended. My search for an airfield became more urgent. I approached the Matjesfeld airfield near Budapest. On my first pass over the airfield they fired a red flare and subsequently displayed the large disc with the letter "R". This confirmed what I already knew, and now I had to decided between a wheels-up landing or one with the undercarriage down. I decided on a normal landing, hoping that all would go well. A belly landing would have meant returning home by train.

I banked the aircraft while on approach to land, hoping to cause the right undercarriage leg to lock down, and I touched down banked slightly to the left so that the left leg would absorb most of the impact. I touched down and began to slow, but then the right wing began dropping, resulting in the inevitable ground loop. Later that same day I boarded a train for the journey back to Götzendorf. That evening I was back among my comrades, albeit without my aircraft.

Because of the small number of available pilots, losses hit us twice as hard. *I./JG 302* suffered two significant losses in the air battle south of Budapest on 20 August 1944:

Hauptmann Richard Lewens, *Gruppenkommandeur* of *I./JG 302*, was shot down and killed by Mustangs near Pápa.

Oberleutnant Heinrich Ötteking, *Staffelkapitän* of *I./JG 302*, was killed by fire from the bombers near Bugyi.

According to the other pilots of the *Gruppenschwarm*, after the first attack on the B-17s *Hauptmann* Lewens headed toward the Hungarian Bf 109s, probably having mistaken them for his own machines. He became involved with the escort fighters and was shot down.

Richard Lewens had assumed command of *I./JG 302* at the time that the *Nachtjagdgeschwader 302 "Wilde Sau"* was formed. The unit fought with mixed success in the night-fighter role. After the switch to day fighting, Lewens molded his *Gruppe* into an efficient unit which enjoyed success against the American bombers and fighters. He had been awarded the Finnish Pilot's Badge in recognition of his service on the Finnish Front.

Oberleutnant Ötteking had only been transferred to the *1. Staffel* a few days earlier, assuming command after the wounding of *Hauptmann* Wurzer. He was killed on his first mission as *Staffelkapitän. Leutnant* Leonhard Reinicke was subsequently appointed acting *Staffel* commander (*Staffelführer*).

1./JG 302 achieved the following results on 20 August:

0945	*Unteroffizier* Willi Greiner	*4./JG 302*	B-17 HSS	S Budapest	2nd
0945	*Oberfeldwebel* Heinz Gossow	*1./JG 302*	B-17 HSS	S Budapest	4th
0945	*Unteroffizier* Willi Reschke	*1./JG 302*	B-17	S Budapest	10th
0945	*Oberfeldwebel* Herbert Stephan	*1./JG 302*	B-17	S Budapest	7th
0952	*Unteroffizier* Willi Reschke	*1./JG 302*	B-17 HSS	S Budapest	11th
0958	*Leutnant* Leonhard Reinicke	*1./JG 302*	B-24	NW Budapest	1st

But what were these few successes against the mass of incoming bombers? One must also take into account the aircraft shot down by the anti-aircraft guns, which were positioned in all important areas including major cities such as Budapest, Vienna and Munich, however the combined defenses were not sufficient to seriously threaten or deter the bomber stream.

As a rule the German fighters only attacked three or four groups of bombers, leaving the rest to carry out their attacks unmolested. This was a fact – at no time during the expanding air battles over Germany was the *Luftwaffe* able to inflict such losses on the enemy that they seriously threatened the bombing raids.

On the contrary: the pilots in the *Jagdgeschwader* assigned to the Defense of the Reich were increasingly forced onto the defensive by the enemy's escort fighters, whose numbers and radius of action grew steadily. As a result, the offensive nature of the fighter pilot came to mean little and losses became unbearable. None of this was able to crush the courage and fighting spirit of the pilots, however, and they continued to score to the end in spite of adverse conditions.

21 August 1944

On this day *1./JG 302* was sent on a mission which took it far beyond the airspace over Budapest, resulting in contact with enemy bombers near Debrecen. Few details are known, even though this mission took the fighter unit deeper into Hungarian airspace than ever before.

On this occasion the *Jagdgruppe* was led by *Oberleutnant* Hermann Stahl, former commander of the *4. Staffel*. Stahl was one of the last surviving pilots of the former *12./JG 51*.

The approaching bombers had a relatively weak fighter escort, allowing the intercepting fighters to attack with minimal interference.

Obergefreiter Walter Kugler of the *3. Staffel* shot down a B-17 at 1020 hours in the airspace southwest of Debrecen. It was his second victory.

The acting commander of the *1. Staffel, Leutnant* Leonhard Reinicke, shot down a B-24 Liberator southwest of Debrecen at 1025 hours. The enemy aircraft veered out of formation and went down in flames. It was Reinicke's second victory.

Also at 1025 hours, *Oberfeldwebel* Heinz Gossow of the *1. Staffel* attacked a Liberator from the same formation and left it in flames. It was his 5th victory.

There are no references to German losses, thus even these few victories were a success.

22 August 1944

In the late afternoon of 21 August 1944 Fw 190 fighters landed at Götzendorf, aircraft of *IV./JG 3* and *I.* and *II./JG 300*. Such an event always meant a heightened state of alert readiness for the following day.

By this time *I./JG 302* was in fact nearing the end of its strength and was only able to muster about half its authorized strength in men and machines. Such an unexpected reinforcement by comrades of *JG 3* and *JG 300* had a restorative effect, and everyone looked forward to the events of the coming day with a sense of relief.

There followed a rather long night with the men of the other *Jagdgeschwader*. The men of course took advantage of the opportunity to partake in such enjoyable hours. The visiting pilots included such notables as *Hauptmann* Wilhelm Moritz, *Oberleutnant* Horst Haase, *Feldwebel* Konrad Bauer and *Feldwebel* Rudi Zwesken. All were very experienced and had achieved success against the enemy bomber formations.

The next morning brought confirmation: the American 15th Air Force was launching a major raid on the Blechhammer and Odertal refineries in Silesia, as well as the Korneuburg and Vienna-Lobau refineries. Initial reports said that approximately 500 bombers with fighter escort were coming in over the Dubrovnik-Split area. There the bombers split up, with some heading in the direction of Upper Silesia and the rest setting course for the Vienna area.

The *Jagdgruppen* took off from Götzendorf airfield at 0900 hours. The pilots knew that a rough day lay ahead. Immediately after takeoff "*Rosenkavalier*" instructed the fighters to fly southeast toward Lake Balaton, out of Austrian airspace and into Hungarian. The combined fighter force made first contact with the enemy, B-24 bombers with a powerful escort of P-51 and P-38 fighters, in the airspace around Pápa north of Lake Balaton.

As there were too few high-altitude fighters to cover a massed attack on the bombers, the bulk of the fighter force had to break through the defensive barrier of the escort fighters. Inevitably, the aircraft on the flanks became involved with the escort, however the main force got through and attacked the B-24s. Some of the bomber crews were obviously not prepared for such a massive attack, for a number of B-24s jettisoned their bombs.

The first B-24s were soon going down in flames, shot down by the Fw 190s of *IV./JG 3* which formed the leading wave of the attack.

Flying on the outer left of the formation, my wingman *Obergefreiter* Angermann and I had become involved in a dogfight with P-51 Mustangs as we broke through the defensive screen. With its external tank long gone, at this altitude – more than 7,000 meters – the Bf 109 G-6 was at its best and equal to the P-51. It was always our numerical inferiority that prevented this equality from being exploited. Again and again we had to help each other out in order to keep the *Rotte* together. In such fighter-versus-fighter combats minutes can become hours, and it is often necessary to act instinctively. We had both finally learned that success did not always mean shooting down the enemy. In this action, the fact that we were both able to land safely back at Götzendorf at 1015 hours was a success.

As this action took place not far from Götzendorf, most of the aircraft landed there when the mission was over. The aircraft were immediately refueled and rearmed and made ready for the next sortie.

At 1225 hours the mixed fighter group was ordered off again. The area of operations was not far from the last, and the target was a group of B-17s on its way back to its base in Italy. In contrast to our last mission, this time the bombers were accompanied by just a few fighters, and we were able to make out attack without much interference.

We were back in the same airspace when the attack on the B-17 group took place. The vee-shaped attack formation had already formed up. I was in the first wave and had just reached a firing range of about 800 meters when a Fw 190 moved into position just off my left wing and stayed there. The other pilot and I briefly made eye contact and he gestured forward with his hand. We had the same target and opened fire on the B-17 almost simultaneously, taking both of the aircraft's wings under fire. Almost immediately, dark forms left the B-17. It was the crew abandoning the aircraft. Seconds later the B-17 blew apart under the combined fire from our two fighters, which were still in formation. This was a unique experience for me; I never experienced it again in subsequent missions. Not until I landed back at Götzendorf did I learn that the pilot of the Fw 190 beside me had been *Oberleutnant* Horst Haase, *Staffelkapitän* of *16./JG 3*. We congratulated each other on our success, which was then divided according to rank.

IV./JG 3 accounted for eight B-24s and one B-17 shot down. Casualties were one pilot wounded and one aircraft written off.

I./JG 300 shot down two B-24s and one B-17. Its losses totaled one pilot killed and one wounded.

II./JG 300 shot down seven B-24s, one B-17 and four P-38 Lightnings. Three of the *Gruppe*'s pilots were wounded.

This was to be *I./JG 302*'s last mission in Hungarian airspace, although none of the participating pilots had any inkling of this. It had been another mission flown with maximum determination and the pilots of the *Jagdgruppe* had fought bravely and successfully. For the pilots of *I./JG 302* the days of air battles over Hungary were over.

The *Gruppe* achieved the following successes on 22 August 1944:

0957	*Unteroffizier* Hermann Dürr	*4./JG 302*	P-38	near Pápa	1st
1000	*Unteroffizier* Willi Greiner	*4./JG 302*	B-24 HSS	near Pápa	3rd
1005	*Oberfeldwebel* Heinz Gossow	*1./JG 302*	B-24	near Pápa	6th
1005	*Unteroffizier* Christoph Blum	*1./JG 302*	B-24	near Pápa	4th
1005	*Unteroffizier* Hermann Dürr	*4./JG 302*	B-24	near Pápa	2nd
1250	*Unteroffizier* Willi Reschke	*1./JG 302*	B-17 FO	N Lake Balaton	12th
1250	*Leutnant* Leonhard Reinicke	*1./JG 302*	B-17 HSS	N Lake Balaton	3rd
1255	*Oberfeldwebel* H.-W. Schellner	*2./JG 302*	B-17	SE Vasegerszeg	8th

Losses on this day were acceptable, for the *Jagdgruppe* suffered just one casualty. Wounded while attacking a four-engined bomber, *Oberfeldwebel* Herbert Stephan of the *1. Staffel* was forced to crash-land his machine near Celldömölk. He was subsequently taken to hospital there. After recovering from his wounds Stephan rejoined the *Jagdgruppe*.

Oberfeldwebel Herbert Stephan, 1./JG 302.

For the mission on 22 August 1944 the *Gruppe* had once again mobilized every aircraft and serviceable aircraft. The success achieved on this day was good for morale. The pilots had become used to attacking increasingly powerful bomber groups with a steadily dwindling number of fighters. For a long time the number of replacements received by *I./JG 302* had failed to keep pace with losses, leading to the question: where will all this lead in the end? The constantly growing armada of escort fighters was a source of worry to the pilots. Many feared fighter-versus-fighter combat, in part because they lacked experience, but also because the enemy fighters were simply too numerous.

For the few replacement pilots that did reach the *Gruppe*, there was too little time to work them into the unit. It was virtually impossible to conduct training missions in even *Schwarm* or *Staffel* strength. As a rule the new men were given a few takeoffs and landings to get to know the airfield, and perhaps a maintenance test flight to familiarize them with the aircraft. For the most part the newcomers then flew these as their operational aircraft. The *Gruppe's* pilots still got together in the evenings, but the optimistic cheerfulness of earlier days was gone. The gaps in the individual *Staffeln* could no longer be concealed. The *1. Staffel* was down to just six pilots, and the other *Staffeln* were not much better off.

The word transfer began appearing more frequently in the information that reached the *Gruppe* in those days. An event on 23 August fed this rumor. Incoming American bombers were reported, but instead of being ordered to attack, the *Gruppe* was directed to proceed to the secondary airfield at Raffelding near Linz. Such an operation was called a *"Blindschleiche"* (slow worm), and was carried out when an attack on the home airfield was imminent. The pilots looked at each other in disbelief when the order was given, for they still had twenty aircraft with which to intercept the enemy – and they weren't used to being taken out of harm's way.

24 August 1944

On this day the 15th Air Force was sent to attack the oil refineries in Pardubitz, Bohemia.

I./JG 302 encountered familiar circumstances on this day. Unable to justify another *"Blindschleiche"* by the *Jagdgruppe*, the fighter control center ordered the *Gruppe* into the air at 0926 hours. The small group of about twenty fighters initially flew southwest into central Austrian airspace south of Linz. It was subsequently directed north, but there too it failed to find the enemy. The *Gruppe* landed back at Götzendorf at 1041 hours.

At 1157 hours *I./JG 302* was in the air again and was vectored northwest into the airspace over Bohemia and Moravia. While en route, the *Gruppe* was unexpectedly reinforced by *II./JG 300*. Although *"Rosenkavalier"* had promised that the two *Gruppen* would join up soon after takeoff, few were optimistic on account of the poor visibility. *II./JG 300* reached the formation just as it was making its first attack on a group of B-24 Liberators. Some of the *JG 300* pilots immediately joined the attack.

With no escort fighters in sight, the *Gruppe* quickly moved into attack position. For the veteran pilots the forming of attack wedges was already routine. Once again the white tracers reached out from the formation of Liberators, but we had to wait, for the range was still too great. These seconds of defenselessness were always difficult for the pilots, and nerves were not always strong enough to keep fingers off the firing buttons. As well, there was always the danger that one might be hit during this phase of the attack.

When we reached favorable firing range I was still slightly higher than the B-24s, and the first burst from my MG 151s struck the dorsal turret. Then the port inner motor was hit by shells from my MK 108. It was always impressive to see the effects of these projectiles. In a matter of seconds pieces of wing flew away and the engine belched smoke and flames. I was unable to complete the attack, for in the final phase my engine took a direct hit, which forced me to break off the attack prematurely. The B-24 was then finished off by *Feldwebel* Hubert Engst of *6./JG 300*, who was flying behind me.

I had initially planned to make a belly landing, but I was quickly forced to abandon this idea when smoke began filling the cockpit. My last option was to use my parachute, and soon afterwards I bailed out. As I had abandoned my aircraft at a height of more than 5,000 meters, I let myself drop for a while before pulling the ripcord. I was surrounded by an almost oppressive silence. But this silence was short-lived: suddenly I spotted two Mustangs, which circled quite close to my parachute. I hadn't seen the American fighters at first, and their sudden appearance came as an unpleasant surprise. The first Mustang circled my parachute and then flew straight toward it. I feared something terrible, for there had already been several examples of this. I cannot describe the thoughts that went through my head in the seconds that followed.

By the time I heard the sound of gunfire the bullets must already have been past me. I instinctively let my head and arms sag, and I was so frightened that I couldn't tell if I had been hit or not. When silence returned I looked around. There was no sign of the two Mustangs. I moved my arms and legs as best I could and felt no wounds.

When I reached the ground I quickly separated myself from my parachute and ran as fast as I could into the cover of some bushes. Driven by fear and helplessness, I could not resist the urge to get to safety. As was often the case in such situations, a cigarette worked wonders, and after a short time I bundled my parachute under my arm and began walking toward the nearest village. I had come down in Moravia, a few kilometers from the Austrian border.

Had the Mustang pilot really been such a poor shot, or had he simply aimed wide on purpose? Or was it in the end just a bit of luck needed to survive? Who could give the answer to such a question? There were numerous cases of pilots being attacked and killed while hanging in their parachutes.

I arrived back in Götzendorf the same day. In the meantime the die had been cast for *I./JG 302*. The entire airfield was a scene of hectic activity. Everywhere trucks were being loaded, large workshop trucks were being packed with tools and spare parts, and in the quarters everything was being packed and put in boxes. *I./JG 302* had flown its last mission from Götzendorf, transfer was now a reality.

Unfortunately, this last mission from Götzendorf had resulted in casualties and the number of pilots had been reduced further.

Unteroffizier Hermann Dürr of the *4. Staffel* was wounded in action during air combat over Indrichuv and was lost for several missions.

Unteroffizier Adolf Klärner, also of the *4. Staffel*, was shot down and killed near Wostoikowitz. He had only been with the *Gruppe* for a short time.

Oberfähnrich Sommer of the *3. Staffel* had only been with the *Gruppe* for a few days and lost his young life on his first sortie. He was shot down and killed near Neubistritz east of Budweis.

The *Gruppe* also registered a number of successes on this day:

At 1237 hours *Unteroffizier* Christoph Blum of the *1. Staffel* shot down a Mustang in grid square UL over Bohemia-Moravia. It was his fifth victory.

Leutnant Reiche of the *4. Staffel* shot down a B-24 at 1240 hours in grid square UL/4 near Neuhaus. It was his sixth victory.

At 1240 hours *Unteroffizier* Willi Reschke of the *1. Staffel* attacked a B-24 in grid square UK-UL near Neuhaus. The bomber caught fire and dropped out of formation. It was his 13th victory.

On the evening of 25 August 1944 there was a proper going-away party in the small makeshift mess of the *1. Staffel*. Everyone came who had been housed in these off-base quarters in the past weeks. The small bar just to the left of the entrance was always full. There was finally an opportunity to toast "Bubi" Blum's promotion to *Unteroffizier*. The youthful-looking pilot had fought bravely in the most recent actions.

Many of the comrades who had once been part of this circle were no longer with us. Many of us had lost our best friends forever. It was difficult, but there had also been good days there at the gates of Vienna. Fighting spirit and comradeship could not have been better, and for many it was tough to leave.

On this evening orderly *Obergefreiter* Trötscher made a special effort to prevent the mood from becoming too melancholy by keeping his "customers" happy, and he produced a number of surprises. In civilian life he had been a professor of astronomy, and now he looked after the welfare of the pilots before and after missions. And he was good at it. He had a knack for reminding young pilots that there were still beautiful things in the world.

It should also not go unmentioned that the *1. Staffel* was now the proud owner of a mascot, or *Staffelhund*. It was an Hungarian sheepdog, which either *Unteroffizier* Blum or *Obergefreiter* Angermann had brought as a puppy from Budapest in his aircraft. He was ceremoniously given the name "Mustang" but, well-fed by the *Staffel*, he grew very large indeed. We should have named him "Liberator".

Almost all of the pilots of *I./JG 302* who now left Götzendorf had been decorated with the Iron Cross, Second Class, and many had even received the Iron Cross, First Class. After the death of *Leutnant* Grumme, *Hauptmann* Wurzer and *Oberfeldwebel* Gossow were the only ones left with the German Cross in Gold – but they had won the decorations as bomber pilots.

26 August 1944

On this day the final reports were received from *I./JG 301* in the combat zone in France. *Hauptmann* Helmut Suhr reported shooting down a P-51 Mustang. The location of the combat is not known. One day later *Feldwebel* Martin Schulze of the *1. Staffel* was wounded in action near Cambrai, however he was able to escape by parachute from his Bf 109 G-6.

There are no further reports of operations by *I./JG 301* in France after this date, therefore 26 August 1944 is acknowledged as the date on which the *Gruppe* was withdrawn from action and transferred to Salzwedel in central Germany for a rest and refit.

Likewise there were no further reports concerning the activities of *II./JG 301* in Romania. There was just a report that *II./JG 301*'s technical officer, *Oberleutnant* Friedrich Seyffert, had been killed in action on the ground near Targsorul on 26 August.

It is no longer possible to determine with certainty what happened in this *Jagdgruppe*'s area of operations in the days surrounding 26 August. German and Romanian resistance had largely collapsed in the face of the advancing Red Army. An orderly withdrawal was out of the question, and entire German units were overrun by Soviet troops.

The speed of the Soviet advance also took *II./JG 301* completely by surprise, consequently it was not possible to move the *Jagdgruppe* in time. The heavy losses had reduced the *Staffeln* to a few pilots each, and in those critical days not all were successful in getting out of the danger zone with their aircraft. Proof of this is found in the fact that in the months that followed, the names of the pilots on strength with *II./JG 301* included few who had been with the *Gruppe* in Romania.

II./JG 301's technical personnel suffered a shocking tragedy during the retreat from Romania. Russian troops suddenly appeared at the edge of the Targsorul-Nou airfield, and the *Gruppe*'s ground personnel, in the midst of preparations for a move to central Germany, were forced to take up arms and fight their way out. Totally unfamiliar with this type of warfare, many of the *Jagdgruppe*'s technical personnel were slaughtered. Seventy-seven "Black Men" are known to have been killed or wounded at this time, however the majority are still listed as missing. The fate of these men remains a mystery to this day, and so the full story of this tragedy will probably never be known. As far as is known, *Obergefreiter* Ludwig Güsken was the only one to survive the rigors of the retreat. His story:

"On my birthday, 25 August 1944, I was NCO of the day and thus had the opportunity to get information on our situation. I was assisted in this by female signals auxiliaries who had been posted to our unit a few days earlier. The King of Romania had surrendered to the Russians on the night of 25-26 August 1944, and overnight our Romanian comrades in arms had become our new enemy. Romanians manned all the anti-aircraft positions in the Ploesti oil region, from 20mm *Vierlingsflak* to eighty-eights. We were completely surrounded by Romanians, who were well hidden in the cornfields.

A large number of Romanian officers on the Targsorul airfield were disarmed, and a general was taken as a hostage. The next day the airfield filled with female auxiliaries from the corps headquarters and soldiers from every branch of the service. II./JG 301 under *Hauptmann* Nölter was not at all prepared for this onslaught. Flatbed trucks were hurriedly converted transport out the female auxiliaries, with caterpillar tractors serving as prime movers. Later in the morning two Me 323 *Gigant* transports fitted out as flying workshops arrived. They were quickly stripped down and loaded with female auxiliaries.

So far there had been no fighting on the airfield proper and there were still no signs of a hectic retreat. This soon changed, however, and we were forced to watch as both *Giganten* were shot down by Romanian anti-aircraft guns as they climbed out in the direction of the Carpathians.

With the flatbed trucks fully loaded, we now tried to leave the airfield and get away from the front. But each time we tried to cross the cornfields we came under heavy fire from the Romanian anti-aircraft guns, which inflicted heavy casualties on the passengers on the flatbeds. Most of them were young female auxiliaries, and the wounded were left lying by the side of the road. The drivers of the prime movers could only keep driving, trying not to lose contact with the rest of the column. The column got as far as Mizil; we had no idea of our losses to that point.

There we received an incomprehensible order: "Save yourself if you can!" Before us lay the Carpathians, and no one had any idea of how we were supposed to get home. We set out in a Ford Taunus towed by a *Kübelwagen*, were wounded, repeatedly engaged in firefights, and drove only at night. Finally we reached Debrecen in Hungary. The signals auxiliary Rita Weiß, in particular, distinguished herself during our fighting withdrawal. She always procured the ammunition we needed and thus saved the lives of many comrades."

26 August 1944 was also not without significance for the pilots of *I./JG 302*: at 1736 hours the *Gruppe* took off from Götzendorf and headed for central Germany, landing at Magdeburg- East at 1930. The promised transfer was now complete.

27 August 1944

The previous evening, after landing at Magdeburg-East, *I./JG 302* was informed that it would be moving again the next day. At 0800 hours the *Gruppe* took off from Magdeburg and flew to Mörtitz, northeast of Leipzig, landing there at 0830. The *Gruppe* did not remain there long: at 1800 hours it took off again and at 1930 landed at Leeuwarden in Holland.

The mission order for the next day read: provide fighter cover over the Channel for a fleet unit which is to sail into Emden in the early morning. Only part of the *Gruppe* saw action, for the vessels had sailed through the Channel during the night and arrived early at the port of Emden. The pilots were visibly relieved, for many were anxious about flying over water. Before noon the *Gruppe* took off from Leeuwarden and at 1130 hours landed at Mörtitz.

Rumors persisted that the *Gruppe* was to be withdrawn from operations for a rest. Whether this would see the *Gruppe* convert to the Fw 190 remained an open question. In these days the aircraft were maintained by the airfield technical personnel, for the *Gruppe*'s own technicians were still somewhere on the road between Vienna and Central Germany. Living and operating on this airfield was unsettled anyway, and as the aircraft of another *Jagdgeschwader* were based there, no one really knew who was responsible for what.

29 August 1944

I./JG 302 would not have a chance to settle in at Mörtitz, for on 29 August orders were received to head back to the familiar territory in the south of the Reich. East of Regensburg the *Jagdgruppe* was guided to a rendezvous with elements of *JG 3* and *JG 300*. Such mutual support had been common in recent operations, but it was never explained just who was supposed to lead such a combined force. The inability of *Jagdgeschwader* to communicate with one another was always an insurmountable obstacle.

We came upon the enemy north of Linz, and *I./JG 302* formed the first wave. All of the pilots had experience in attacking the bomber formations and a certain standard had developed in the tactic of the attack wedge. We also knew the vulnerable spots of the B-17, with which we had to deal on this mission.

Once again I was in the first wave, and again the B-17s opened fire very early. This first phase of the attack was always a test of nerves: the pilot sat crouched behind his sight, while the target grew larger in larger in the gunsight glass. But he had to wait until the B-17 filled the reticle before opening fire. These seconds always seemed like an eternity, and one's nerves were stretched to the breaking point. It was always a relief when one's own guns began firing.

Again my first burst was directed at the tail gunner: he had the widest field of fire to the rear and posed the greatest threat to me.

After observing strikes in the tail turret my shells wandered right to the wing root and inner engine. The effects of the MK 108 rounds were always staggering: immediately after the first strikes pieces of the wing structure flew off and the engine began pouring smoke. This quickly turned to flames and the B-17 showed the first signs of dropping out of formation. Although I had not yet completed my attack and my rounds were dead on target, tracers from the man behind me were passing close to my Bf 109. Then the inevitable happened: there were several hard blows in the rear of my machine. I had been hit by one of my own people and I knew that I had to go down.

A glance behind revealed the extent of the damage: my tail surfaces had been badly damaged. The aircraft was extremely nose heavy. I tried to adjust the trim to compensate but was only partially successful. The normal control forces had changed drastically, and the aircraft reacted very slowly to rudder inputs. How long would my Bf 109 remain flyable with such damage? I had to decided whether to make a forced landing or bail out. An inner voice told me not to bail out, for the damaged elevators might not produce sufficient force to catapult me from the cockpit. I searched in vain for a suitable place to land, losing height all the while. My vertical speed indicator showed that I was in

29 August 1944: after combat with B-17s, Unteroffizier Reschke of 1./JG 302 made a forced landing in the Banor area. Here his aircraft ""White 6" is seen under guard by a Czech policeman and a member of the fire brigade.

a slow, steady descent, and this was confirmed by my altimeter. In the end my only choice was a belly landing.

As the terrain was quite hilly, I selected a clear slope with a gentle decline and made a belly landing there. Everything went much better than I had hoped. The gentle down-slope proved advantageous and resulted in a smooth touchdown. When I examined the tail surfaces of my aircraft I was truly grateful that I had my feet on the ground. Most of the skinning was gone and several ribs were badly damaged.

My forced-landing took place near Ungarisch-Brod in the Banor area of Moravia. I never did discover the identity of the impatient comrade whom I had to thank for the subsequent train ride.

At the same time that I was on a train for central Germany, *Fähnrich* Ludwig Bracht was on another train bound for the same destination. Transferred to *I./JG 302*, he arrived at Götzendorf the day after the *Gruppe* had departed. He returned the way he had come, and after a lengthy search he reached the *Gruppe* at Alperstedt near Erfurt. My rail journey first took me to Mörtitz and there I, too, learned that the *Gruppe* had moved on to Alperstedt. I was gradually getting fed up with rail travel, for because of one hour's flying time one often had to spend days traveling to return to his unit.

The results of the mission on 29 August 1944 were one B-17 forced out of formation at 1050 hours by *Unteroffizier* Willi Reschke of the *1. Staffel* in grid square UQ east of Brünn, and another B-17 shot down by *Oberfeldwebel* Heinz Nevack, also of the *1. Staffel*, at 1055 hours over Brünn.

The unit suffered no losses in this action. It was also the last action flown by the *Gruppe* under the designation *I./JG 302*.

It took several days for all the members of *I./JG 302* to find their way to Alperstedt, and to everyone's delight *Hauptmann* Heinrich Wurzer, who had been wounded in action near Götzendorf on 8 July 1944, had returned and assumed command of the *Gruppe* once more.

I./JG 302's fate was settled in those very first days at Alperstedt: the unit was renamed *III./JG 301* with the *9.* to *12. Staffel*.

The pilots of the old *I./JG 302* transferred to Alperstedt – scarcely more than twenty – formed the core of the new *Staffeln* of *III./JG 301*. At the same time the unit converted to the Fw 190 A-8. Some pilots regretted the change and had difficulties converting to the new type, having become used to the Bf 109 G-6. But there was also cheerful anticipation, for the reputation that preceded the Fw 190 was extremely promising.

The Defense of the Reich *Jagdgeschwader 302 "Wilde Sau"* had ceased to exist. It was now part of history.

Chapter Seven

Final Thoughts on *JG 302*

In the preceding chapters I have attempted to chronicle the most of the history of *JG 302*. This means, however, that I was unable to tell the complete story. It is a certainty that events occurred which are missing from the records or have simply been forgotten. I believe, however, that I have succeeded in compiling the significant events in the life of the *Geschwader*.

I do wish to take issue, however, with those who judge the men of this *Geschwader* based solely on their success in combat, while lacking sufficient knowledge about the fighter units of the *Reichsverteidigung* and the devotion, courage and fighting spirit of the men who served in them.

Every single member of *JG 302* – and this applies to pilots and technicians – selflessly gave his all in defense of the Fatherland. In the bitter air battles against a foe vastly superior in numbers, every pilot – from officer to NCO – heroically and selflessly stood his ground. There was never any sign of resignation, again and again combat was sought and often paid for in young lives. If this *Jagdgeschwader* failed to achieve the success by which it is often measured, it was primarily because of our political leadership. Anyone who declares war on dozens of nations, including the greatest empire in the world, cannot expect a few fighter wings to straighten out such madness.

I./JG 302 alone flew more than fifty missions against British and American fighters and bombers, and its area of operations extended over all of Germany and into Hungarian airspace.

At least 231 enemy aircraft were shot down in these missions, including 209 British and American four-engined bombers, twenty-one P-38 and P-51 escort fighters, and one Mosquito.

If one assumes that not every pilot was able to report the aircraft shot down by him, then the number of victories is probably higher.

At least 133 fighter pilots were members of *I./JG 302* during its existence. With a high degree of certainty, sixty-seven of these pilots were killed and forty wounded.

The fate of some pilots is still not known. Some wounded pilots returned to *I./JG 302* after recovery, or later to *III./JG 301*. There were also pilots who did not rejoin the *Gruppe* after being wounded, for example *Oberfeldwebel* Haase, *Unteroffizier* Kraatz and *Leutnant* Hallenberger.

During operations in the south, *I./JG 302* could be satisfied with the control provided by the two ground control stations *"Rosenkavalier"* and *"Leander"*, which always provided accurate information on the enemy's position and strength. Leadership of our own fighter unit was also excellent.

Chapter Eight

Self-Sacrifice - the Demise of *JG 301*

September to October 1944

Creation of the "*Wilde Sau*" single-engined night-fighter *Geschwader* had generated high hopes, but now there were only two left, *JG 300* and *JG 301*.

At that time the *Stab* and *II. Gruppe* of *JG 300* were based in the Finsterwalde south of Berlin, *I./JG 300* was nearby at Gahro, *III./JG 300* in Jüterbog south of Potsdam, and *IV./JG 300* at Reinsdorf east of Wittenberg.

For this *Jagdgeschwader*, too, night-fighter missions had long since become a thing of the past. It now flew only day fighter missions in the Defense of the Reich. The *Geschwader* command constantly strove to keep the units close together in order to maximize operational strength and striking power.

The situation was very different for *JG 301*. A few months after its formation, *III./JG 301* was disbanded or renamed, and in practical terms the *IV. Gruppe* consisted of just the *10. Staffel* – it was never expanded into a complete *Gruppe*. At this time the *I.* and *II. Gruppe* were based far apart in France and Romania. Completely on their own, they had little association with the *Geschwader* apart from the designation *JG 301*.

In September 1944, however, there was to be a fundamental change which was to give the *Gruppen* the feeling that they were part of a *Jagdgeschwader*.

The *Geschwaderstab* of *JG 301* was stationed at Stendal. The *Geschwaderkommodore* was *Major* Fritz Auffhammer, later promoted to *Oberstleutnant*.

I./JG 301 was based at Salzwedel under the command of *Hauptmann* Wilhelm Burggraf. *II./JG 301* was stationed at Sachau, southwest of Gardelegen, and was commanded by *Hauptmann* Rolf Jacobs.

On 10 October 1944 *III./JG 301*, which in September was still in Alperstedt, moved to Stendal. There *Hauptmann* Wilhelm Fulda became *Gruppenkommandeur*.

Right: Obergefreiter Ludwig Güsken (left), aircraft mechanic in II./JG 301, with a friend from the cavalry. Note the saber worn by the cavalryman. It was the only branch of the German armed services that permitted non-commissioned officers to carry a saber when not on duty.

Below
Alperstedt near Erfurt, September 1944: a group of III./JG 301 pilots photographed during the Gruppe's conversion to the Fw 190 A-8. From left to right, front row seated: Feldwebel Viehbeck, Flieger Daniel, Unteroffizier Ratzow, Feldwebel Rienth, Feldwebel Otto, and Oberfeldwebel Bäcker.

Second row seated: Stabsfeldwebel Böhme, Oberfähnrich Aschendorf, Oberfeldwebel Gossow, Feldwebel Müller, Hauptmann Franke, Obergefreiter Angermann, Obergefreiter Steidel and Feldwebel Tschorn.

Standing: Unteroffizier Prawitz, Fähnrich Bracht, Unteroffizier Berliner, Oberfeldwebel Döpel and Petersen, Feldwebel Reschke, Unteroffizier Schwaiger, Oberfähnrich von Alven, Unteroffiziere Fröhler and Kugler, Feldwebel Blomert, Unteroffiziere Scheller and Greiner.

A *IV./JG 301* was formed at Gardelegen at the end of 1944, commanded by *Hauptmann* Wilhelm Schmitz.

For the first time in the history of *JG 301*, the *Geschwader* and its *Gruppen* were together in a small area. The *Luftwaffe* command had removed the entire *Geschwader* from operations and it was now in the process of resting and reequipping. Replacement pilots were brought in to bring the *Staffeln* up to full operational strength, while at the same time the *Gruppen* converted to the Fw 190 A-8 or A-9 at their respective airfields. This process could not be achieved in a few days, for the pilots first had to become familiar with the handling characteristics of the Fw 190. As well, in every *Staffel* there were half-trained new fighter pilots who needed further instruction to make up for what they had missed at flying school.

The reestablishment of *III./JG 301* began at Alperstedt in September 1944, with the remaining personnel from *I./JG 302* providing a cadre of personnel for the new *Gruppe*. The twenty-two surviving pilots remained in their *Staffeln*, which were brought up to strength with new pilots. Only a few of the new pilots came straight from the fighter schools, the vast majority having previously flown reconnaissance aircraft, heavy fighters or bombers. Even instructors from flight training schools had been given a quick conversion course on fighters and now joined the *Gruppe*. These pilots in particular had a difficult time making the adjustment from training to the rough and ready life in a fighter unit.

Alperstedt was a second-line airfield with no paved runway. A level country road ran right through the middle of the airfield, and though it was no longer used it did present difficulties for the pilots during takeoff and landing. On the western edge of the airfield were several small makeshift hangars and a farm building. There were only enough quarters for the technical personnel, consequently the pilots and some of the technicians were quartered in the surrounding villages of Stotternheim, Alperstedt, Schwansee and Grossrudestedt.

Hauptmann Heinrich Wurzer remained *Gruppenkommandeur* during the conversion period.

The individual *Staffeln* were commanded by *Leutnant* Reinicke (9. *Staffel*), *Hauptmann* Dietsche (*10. Staffel*), *Oberleutnant* Herzog (*11. Staffel*) and *Oberleutnant* Sauer (*12. Staffel*). During the following months these commands would see several changes, for the great bloodletting in the Defense of the Reich was about to begin.

Many of the young pilots who joined the *Gruppe* were excited at the prospect of going into combat; they had no way of knowing that for many of them their first mission would also be their last.

At Alperstedt conversion to the Fw 190 A-8 began on 6 September 1944 and was complete by the end of the month. As this was a fundamental reorganization, the training program proceeded from circuit work through *Schwarm* and *Staffel* formation flying to massed *Gruppe* formations.

Conversion to the Fw 190 in fact proceeded quickly. This aircraft did not have the Bf 109's tendency to swing on takeoff and landing, and control forces were significantly less, which in some cases also meant better maneuverability. Rate of climb was better to 5,000 meters, but above that altitude it dropped off rapidly. The Bf 109 possessed a markedly superior performance at higher altitudes.

There were no accidents during the *Gruppe*'s conversion training, which reflected the high quality of the pilots. The number of flights per pilot varied, but on average it was about 20 takeoffs and landings.

Stendal, autumn 1944. Pilots of 11. and 12./JG 301 in front of a Fw 190 A-8. Standing from the left: Obergefreiter Straub, Unteroffizier Schrack, Unteroffizier Michaelis, Feldwebel Dörr, Unteroffiziere Dürr, Scheller, Greiner and Prawitz, Feldwebel Wißmann. Sitting from the left: Unteroffiziere Warnicke and Dederichs and Oberfeldwebel Bäcker.

During the reorganization at Alperstedt, Knight's Cross wearer *Leutnant* Karl Gratz of *JG 52* served as tactical advisor. He stressed how pilots should conduct themselves in fighter-versus-fighter combat, an indication that the *Luftwaffe* command had recognized this weakness. Many of the pilots serving in the *Reichsverteidigung* had never received specialized fighter pilot training. There is no way of knowing if this instruction provided the pilots with the desired advantages in later combats with escort fighters. Conditions and starting point were different in every air battle, and only experience could help the pilots survive.

After four weeks the *Gruppe*'s conversion period was over. For the pilots of the former *I./JG 302* this was a well-deserved and much-needed rest, but conversations revealed a certain unease about the coming return to operations. The *Gruppe* had to move once more before going into action, however. Its new base of operations was Stendal, and on 10 October the *Jagdgruppe* departed Alperstedt at 1620 hours, landing at Stendal at 1731. For some pilots the transfer itself was enough to put their nerves on edge, for one of the first things they saw at Stendal was three Fw 190s standing on their noses: three inexperienced pilots had misjudged their approaches to the airfield and made the acquaintance of the field beyond the airfield boundary.

It was another incident, however, that was to provide the subject of conversation in the days to come. *Oberfeldwebel* Karl Petersen of the *9. Staffel* and *Unteroffizier* Walter Kugler of the *12. Staffel* were delayed for a day at Alperstedt due to mechanical problems. Both departed the next day, but on reaching the Harz, Petersen inexplicably turned away to the west. He failed to arrive at Stendal that day and subsequent investigations into the whereabouts of aircraft and pilot turned up nothing. *III./JG 301*'s casualty list records that Petersen was injured in the crash of his Fw 190 A-8 "White 4", WNr. 682 011, on 11 October 1944, however no such information was received by the *Gruppe* in Stendal.

Stendal was a permanent *Luftwaffe* base with massive quarters, a control tower and three large hangars. The airfield was a few kilometers northwest of the city with clear approaches from all directions. The main runway was laid out in an east-west direction. There was a slight rise halfway down the runway, but this posed no problem for takeoffs and landings. The *Staffel* dispersals were located on the north and west sides of the airfield. The *Geschwaderstab* was situated on the west side of the airfield in an extension of the hangar area. The main gate was on the east side on the main road from Stendal to Osterburg. The quarters were on the north side of the airfield and were surrounded by trees. Among the buildings were the canteen and officers' mess.

The following pilots served with *III./JG 301* in the period that followed up to the end of the war, or were later transferred to the *Stabsschwarm* of *JG 301*:

9. Staffel	10. Staffel	11. Staffel	12. Staffel
Obergefreiter Angermann	*Unteroffizier* Ballwanz	*Unteroffizier* Alt	*Oberfeldwebel* Bäcker
Obergefreiter Bender	*Unteroffizier* Bandit	*Unteroffizier* Bellinghaus	*Feldwebel* Beck
Unteroffizier Berliner	*Feldwebel* Blomert	*Fähnrich* Bracht	*Flieger* Daniel
Stabsfeldwebel Böhme	*Feldwebel* Born	*Oberfeldwebel* Berming	*Feldwebel* Dörr
Feldwebel Blum	*Oberfeldwebel* Brand	*Unteroffizier* Burghardt	*Unteroffizier* Dürr
Oberfeldwebel Döpel	*Hauptmann* Dietsche	*Oberleutnant* Dreier	*Oberfähnrich* Fenkner
Oberfähnrich Aschendorf	*Unteroffizier* Konrad	*Feldwebel* Dienst	*Unteroffizier* Feltner
Oberfeldwebel Dademarsch	*Oberfähnrich* Fenkner	*Unteroffizier* Diecke	*Unteroffizier* Greiner
Unteroffizier Göthel	*Oberfeldwebel* Groß	*Feldwebel* Driebe	*Unteroffizier* Kugler
Oberfeldwebel Gossow	*Leutnant* Göbel	*Oberfähnrich* Fähnrich	*Oberfeldwebel* Krönke
Leutnant Hagedorn	*Leutnant* Frenzel	*Oberleutnant* Herzog	*Oberleutnant* Kranke
Oberfähnrich Hänsel	*Leutnant* Heinevetter	*Oberfeldwebel* Kabler	*Leutnant* Lüth
Leutnant Reinicke	*Oberfähnrich* Hörning	*Oberfeldwebel* Langelotz	*Leutnant* Reinhold
Oberfeldwebel Reschke	*Fähnrich* Hummel	*Oberfeldwebel* Jaacks	*Unteroffizier* Prawitz
Feldwebel Matter	*Oberfeldwebel* Jagels	*Oberfähnrich* Ludwig	*Oberleutnant* Stahl
Oberfähnrich Rödhammer	*Leutnant* Karioth	*Oberleutnant* Maul	*Oberleutnant* Sauer
Hauptmann Quednau	*Unteroffizier* Kordas	*Feldwebel* Ries	*Unteroffizier* Schendera
Obergefreiter Steidel	*Oberfeldwebel* Rusche	*Oberleutnant* Seidel	*Unteroffizier* Schrack
Oberfeldwebel Stephan	*Leutnant* Müller	*Unteroffizier* Michaelis	*Leutnant* Spies
Unteroffizier Schalk	*Unteroffizier* Marquard	*Feldwebel* Schellner	*Unteroffizier* Dederichs
Unteroffizier Schwaiger	*Unteroffizier* Reuter	*Unteroffizier* Moneta	*Unteroffizier* Scheller
Fähnrich Penzin	*Feldwebel* Schnier	*Feldwebel* Otto	*Leutnant* K.H. Mailer
Unteroffizier Fröhler	*Leutnant* v. Alven	*Oberleutnant* Teller	*Oberleutnant* Völker
Oberfähnrich Schindehatte	*Feldwebel* Tschorn	*Unteroffizier* Sonntag	*Oberfähnrich* Wiegeshoff
Feldwebel Thierling	*Oberleutnant* Kretschmer	*Leutnant* Tauscher	*Feldwebel* Wißmann
Feldwebel Over	*Oberfeldwebel* Sattler	*Feldwebel* Winter	*Oberfähnrich* Fay
Feldwebel Voss	*Feldwebel*Viehbeck	*Feldwebel* Rienth	*Leutnant* Reiche
Unteroffizier Ratzow	*Fähnrich*Voigt	*Unteroffizier* Warnicke	

12./JG 301 at Stendal, October 1944. Sitting on the propeller spinner is Unteroffizier Dürr. Below, from the left: Unteroffizier Scheller, a mechanic, Unteroffizier Greiner, Oberfeldwebel Bäcker. On the ground: Unteroffiziere Warnicke and Michaelis.

This list of names can make no claims to completeness. It is almost certain that the names of some pilots who were not with the unit long enough to become known are missing.

JG 301 and its three *Gruppen*, all of which had been increased to four *Staffeln* during its reorganization, were now based close together in central Germany, however any return to operations was initially out of the question. The men of the *Geschwader* became more aware of this with each passing day, and apart from a few maintenance test or training flights there was total inactivity. No reasonable explanation for this was offered from any quarter. In spite of the limited flight operations during this period there were several casualties, which may be more or less attributed to inattentiveness:

On 23 September 1944 *Feldwebel* Hans Engfer of the *1. Staffel* was killed when he crashed his Fw 190 A-8, WNr. 732 272, near Solbke during a training flight.

Also on 23 September, *Feldwebel* Georg Ertel of the *2. Staffel* was killed in a crash near Recklinghausen (Fw 190 A-8, WNr. 175 179).

On 9 October *Oberleutnant* Kurt Dittmann of the *3. Staffel* died in the crash of his Fw 190 A-8, WNr. 201 376, near Salzwedel.

On 13 October *Unteroffizier* Werner Malz of the *8. Staffel* was injured in a crash near Sachau (Fw 190 A-9, WNr. 734 039).

Feldwebel Georg Scharein of the *1. Staffel* was killed in a crash near Salzwedel on 16 October. The exact cause is not known. Scharein was an experienced pilot who had seen considerable action and had three victories to his credit (Fw 190 A-9, WNr. 202 398).

Also on 16 October, *Unteroffizier* Heinz Sturm of the *6. Staffel* was injured in a takeoff collision at Sachau. His aircraft (Fw 190 A-8, WNr. 350 236) sustained considerable damage.

On 21 October 1944 *Oberleutnant* Karl Völker of the *12. Staffel* took off from Stendal in his Fw 190 A-8 "Black 1", WNr. 681 801, on a training flight. Before beginning the flight he told his *Staffel* mates that he wanted to show them how to carry out a low-altitude roll in the Fw 190. He overestimated his piloting ability and crashed to his death. Völker was buried in the Stendal cemetery.

For *III./JG 301* the first weeks in Stendal brought a period of curious inactivity. Rested and at full strength, the *Jagdgruppe* was burning to get back into action – but nothing happened. Formations of four-engined bombers flew over the airfield to attack Berlin, Leipzig and Dresden. The pilots had to content themselves with watching the heavy anti-aircraft guns by the railway bridge over the Elbe near Tangermünde as they discharged well-aimed salvoes at the bombers high overhead and took a regular toll of the enemy. The morale of the pilots and technicians was not exactly good at this time: there were no more high points, and the recent reorganization seemed to have had no purpose. The depressed mood spread throughout the entire *Gruppe*, and even the *Gruppe* command had no idea how to keep the men's spirits up. One bright spot was *Obergefreiter* Trötscher, professor of astronomy, who could always find listeners eager for knowledge.

There should have been plenty of time to pass on to the new pilots theoretical and practical information for the coming operations, but instead they played pool in the officers' mess.

It also did little to raise the morale of the troops when, during the period of inactivity, *General der Jagdflieger* Adolf Galland arrived in Stendal wearing only the Spanish Cross. The differences that existed in the *Luftwaffe* command were now plain for all to see – and JG 301's inactivity was quickly linked with this.

Aircraft of 9./JG 301 at Stendal, November 1944. The pilots are sitting in their cockpits, waiting for the order to take off against the bombers and escort fighters.

Leutnante A.W. Hagedorn and Rolf Lüth of III./JG 301.

Stendal, October 1944. Unteroffizier Dederichs in front of his Fw 190 A-8.

Stendal, October 1944. From left: Feldwebel Reschke, Leutnant Göbel and Oberfeldwebel Ruscke.

Salzwedel, autumn 1944: Oberfeldwebel Hans Todt of 8./JG 301 following a successful mission in which he shot down a B-24.

Left: Knight's Cross wearer Oberfeldwebel Heinz Gossow of 9./JG 301. Gossow was a former bomber pilot who flew 340 combat missions with KG 3. He was transferred to I./JG 302 in the spring of 1944 and after the Gruppe was disbanded became a member of III./JG 301. Right:Stendal, 24 October 1944. Major Auffhammer, Geschwaderkommodore of JG 301, presents Oberfeldwebel Gossow with the Knight's Cross before the assembled personnel of III./JG 301.

The entries in my logbook provide the best proof of the inactivity in those days. There is just one flight recorded in the period between the transfer to Stendal on 10 October and 2 November 1944: a maintenance test flight on 20 October which lasted nine minutes.

Even after *General der Jagdflieger* Galland left the *Geschwaderstab* again, there was still no explanation for our inactivity. Words of explanation were no doubt offered, but we pilots could only shake our heads: why were we, a fully-operational *Jagdgeschwader* at the gates of Berlin, not in the thick of the fighting?

At that time *Hauptmann* Heinrich Wurzer, who had achieved twenty-six victories flying *"Wilde Sau"* night-fighter missions, was replaced as *Gruppenkommandeur* of *III./JG 301* by *Hauptmann* Wilhelm Fulda. Wurzer was transferred soon afterward and left the *Gruppe*. This decision also provoked heated discussion among the *Gruppe's* experienced pilots: in general the measure was not considered a good one.

Hauptmann Wilhelm Fulda had been awarded the Knight's Cross on 14 July 1941 during the campaign in the Balkans. He was decorated for his actions while leading a glider unit at the Isthmus of Corinth. He later became a fighter pilot during the formation of the single-engined night-fighter force. Since 26 November 1943 he had commanded *II./JG 301*. The records contain no information on his participation in operations during that period.

On 24 October 1944 *III./JG 301* had something positive to celebrate: before the assembled *Gruppe, Oberfeldwebel* Heinz Gossow of the *9. Staffel* was awarded the Knight's Cross by *Geschwaderkommodore Oberstleutnant* Auffhammer. It was a proud day for the *Geschwader*, for Gossow had truly earned this high decoration.

Oberfeldwebel Heinz Gossow had flown 340 bomber missions in Russia with *6./KG 3* and on 23 November 1942 was awarded the German Cross in Gold. In autumn 1943 he was transferred to single-engined night-fighters and flew fifteen night missions. He subsequently shot down twelve four-engined bombers by day and night. In keeping with fighter pilot traditions, that night in the mess there were numerous toasts offered to his Knight's Cross.

At the beginning of November there was an increase in flying activity, and everyone probably realized that the period of inactivity was about to be consigned to the past. It was not just the new pilots who were eager to prove themselves – the inactivity had gradually become too much for the veterans as well. The incursions by the Americans were proof that they were needed in the air. While everyone looked forward to the imminent return to action, there was also reservations, for it was common knowledge that more could have been done to prepare the newcomers for X-Day.

The American bombers came over almost daily, and even from the ground it was obvious that the number of escort fighters had increased even further. Only some of the pilots knew what that meant.

November 1944

On 2 November 1944 American bombers with fighter escort struck the Leuna hydrogenation plant near Merseburg, but once again the two Reich Defense *Geschwader*, *JG 300* and *JG 301*, remained on the ground. At Borkheide, south of Potsdam, *I./JG 300* was subjected to a strafing attack by P-51s and suffered heavy losses in aircraft.

On 3 November a *Schwarm* from *III./JG 301* took off from Stendal on a training flight. The mission over, the four fighters headed back to base. As they made their landing approach, the aircraft flown by *Unteroffiziere* Dieter Ratzow and Johann Schwaiger of the *9. Staffel* touched wings. Both pilots were killed when their machines crashed near the airfield perimeter (Fw 190 A-8 "White 8", WNr. 682 308 and Fw 190 A-8 "White 9", WNr. 681 897). In the days that followed, *III./JG 301* suffered further non-combat losses. On 7 November *Unteroffizier* Ludwig Vogel of the *8. Staffel* was killed when his Fw 190 A-8 "Blue 13", WNr. 176 080, crashed north of Rathenow.

On 19 November *JG 301* lost three pilots in non-combat-related incidents. *Unteroffizier* Anton Obermaier of the *5. Staffel* died in a crash at Sachau (Fw 190 A-9, "White 17", WNr. 205 083). *Leutnant* Harry Winkelhöfer of the *6. Staffel* crashed to his death near Solbke (Fw 190 A-9 "Red 2", WNr. 206 150). *Feldwebel* Franz Modrow of the *1. Staffel* was killed when his aircraft went down near Stendal during a training mission (Fw 190 A-9, WNr. 202 384).

It was now mid-November, and *JG 301* continued to watch the air war from the ground. While the *Geschwader* was able to demonstrate its numerical strength in a training mission, it was still denied the chance to prove itself in combat. In *JG 301*'s tactical formation the *III. Gruppe* was assigned the role of "heavy *Gruppe*". *I.* and *II./JG 301*, partly equipped with the Fw 190 A9/R, each provided two *Staffeln* for the high cover role, while the rest also served as "heavy *Gruppen*".

Fw 190 A-8 at the 12. Staffel's dispersal at Stendal airbase in the autumn of 1944. The name of the mechanic on the Fw 190 is not known. On the left is Unteroffizier Michaelis, the pilot with the dog is Unteroffizier Scheller, the two pilots behind him are Unteroffiziere Warnicke and Dederichs. In the next row are Unteroffiziere Prawitz and Greiner, and the blonde pilot on the far right is Unteroffizier Dürr.

Stendal in October 1944, photographed between the barracks and the mess. From left: Feldwebel Driebe, maintenance foreman Oberfeldwebel Prell, Luftwaffe signals auxiliary Hildegard Täschner, Oberfeldwebel Gossow, Oberfeldwebel Stephan, unidentified, Feldwebel Herrcher and Unteroffizier Blum.

21 November 1944

As on 2 November, a strong force of American bombers with fighter escort headed for Merseburg, but also for Osnabrück and Hamburg. 1,290 B-17 and B-24 bombers of the 8th Air Force had taken off from their bases in England, together with a fighter escort of 954 P-51 Mustangs and P-47 Thunderbolts. The Americans flew several different routes to their targets.

The pilots of *JG 301* sensed that the waiting was about to end. In the morning they were placed on alert, and the pilots waited for the order to take off, some standing by their aircraft, some sitting in their cockpits. Weather conditions were poor: 8/10 cloud with scattered shower activity. This was no obstacle to the pilots, for they were all trained in instrument flying. Nevertheless, they had been waiting for the mission order for a long time, and doubts began appearing here and there.

III./JG 301 was ordered into the air at 1055 hours, and there was a tangible sense of relief as the pilots advanced their throttles. The attack force formed up in the Gardelegen-Stendal area and what a sight it was: nothing but our fighters wherever one looked – when was the last time that had happened? As the formation climbed, the weather grew ever worse, with multiple cloud layers that made it difficult for the unit to maintain formation. The extensive cloud also made it impossible to see the approaching Americans at first. But when the control center gave the formation its first turn as it was still climbing, it became apparent that the *Jagdgeschwader* had been ordered off too late. Instead of flying toward the enemy on a southwest heading, it had been ordered to fly southeast, toward Magdeburg and Thuringia, suggesting that the first bomber formations had already passed that way. Contact was made with enemy fighters as *JG 301* approached Thuringian airspace east of the Harz. The high-altitude *Staffeln* of *I.* and *II./JG 301* were the first to engage the Mustangs, followed soon afterward by all the remaining fighters of the two *Gruppen.*

III./JG 301, which was flying somewhat lower, was spared the first attack by the escort fighters and flew on in close formation. Soon, however, the first vapor trails were seen at the Gruppe's two o'clock position, and Hauptmann Fulda, the Gruppe formation leader, decided to make a frontal attack on a formation of B-17s coming from the right. None of the pilots in this Gruppe had any experience with frontal attacks on bomber formations, and as the close formation attack was initiated much too near to the bomber formation, only the first few aircraft ended up in a favorable firing position. All of the remaining aircraft crossed with the B-17 formation at an ever-increasing angle: the success of the attack was thus zero.

A few of the fighters in the formation immediately turned and attacked the bombers from behind and slightly above. A quick glance to the rear confirmed that my wingman, Obergefreiter Bender, was still with me.

The Fw 190 A-8/R2 possessed tremendous firepower – two MG 131s (13mm) over the engine, two MG 151s (20mm) in the wing roots, and two MK 108s (30mm) in the outer wings. As a result, both inner motors of the B-17 I had selected were soon in flames and the aircraft fell out of formation trailing smoke. The escort fighters then intervened, coming from every direction, and consequently I was unable to make another pass at the B-17 formation. I saw a number of B-17s on fire and going down, but I could not locate my wingman. Once again there began the unequal battle with the escort fighters, and at times I had the impression that several were trying to shoot me down at once. But they also took the tracer from my guns seriously, and so I was able to disengage at a favorable moment. After almost two hours in the air, at 1251 hours I landed at Burg air base near Magdeburg.

The early attack by the escort fighters had the effect of splitting up the bulk of *Jagdgeschwader 301*, and the three *Gruppen* ended up fighting in different areas. *I./JG 301* was largely engaged in combats with the enemy fighters, and these extended over most of Thuringia, from Eisenach to far beyond Jena. *II./JG 301* also had to fight off attacks by the Mustangs, resulting in dogfights between Gotha and Eisenberg.

III./JG 301, the only *Gruppe* to close with the bombers, after which it too was engaged by the escort fighters, fought its battles from south of Magdeburg to the Altenburg area.

An evaluation of the mission by *III./JG 301* brought the following results:

It seems likely that the fighter control center initially misjudged the Americans' intentions, which explains the course assigned to *III./JG 301*. The order to take off was issued much too late for an attack on the Americans heading for Merseburg. As a result, the *Geschwader* was forced to approach the enemy from the side, seriously jeopardizing the element of surprise.

The massed frontal attack, a tactic it had never used before, was begun too close to the bombers. Consequently, the rear of the fighter formation could not attack from directly ahead; instead, it closed at an ever-increasing angle which seriously reduced its chances of scoring hits.

Another weak point, which was raised by the pilots of the last attack wedge in particular, was the flying behavior of the unit leader during course changes. When leading a fighter formation toward the enemy, the leader must strive to plan and execute all course changes correctly. If he does not, the result is a hopeless mix-up in the rear of the formation.

For *JG 301* this long-awaited mission had not gone as hoped. Many of the "Old Hares" were seen standing by their machines hanging their heads, because their fears had been realized. The lengthy period of rest and inactivity had had a negative effect on the *Jagdgruppe*, and the enemy had not been asleep – how else could one explain the overwhelming numbers of escort fighters?

On this day *I./JG 301* had borne the brunt of the fighter-versus-fighter battle and it is highly probable that all of this *Gruppe*'s losses were inflicted by the P-47s and P-51s. The *Gruppe* suffered heavily, losing twelve pilots killed or wounded. The *Geschwader* as a whole mourned numerous casualties:

The most painful loss of all was that of *Hauptmann* Wilhelm Burggraf, *Kommandeur* of the *I. Gruppe*, who was shot down and killed by Mustangs near Jena (Fw 190 A-9, WNr. 206 072).

Feldwebel Herbert Böwer of the *1. Staffel* was wounded in combat, but made it back to Stendal where he crash-landed (Fw 190 A-9, WNr. 202 374).

Gefreiter Johann Meindl, also of the *1. Staffel*, was wounded in combat and abandoned his aircraft near Groß-Möhring (Fw 190 A-9, WNr. 202 435).

Feldwebel Viktor Gstrein of the *2. Staffel* was shot down and killed by P-51s near Langensalza (Fw 190 A-9, WNr. 202 419).

Unteroffizier Klaus Jacobi of the *2. Staffel* was overwhelmed by the Mustangs and fell near Bökau (Fw 190 A-9, WNr. 202 379).

Unteroffizier Willy Peterreit of the *2. Staffel* lost his life in combat with Mustangs; he fell near Röhrensee (Fw 190 A-9, WNr. 202 319).

Stendal, autumn 1944 – landed safely! From left: Unteroffiziere Greiner, Warnicke, Prawitz (in the cockpit of the Fw 190), Scheller and Dederichs.

Stendal, November 1944. Pilots of 12./JG 301. From left: Unteroffizier Greiner, Unteroffizier Scheller, Oberleutnant Sauer, Unteroffiziere Warnicke, Dederichs, Prawitz, Michaelis, Obergefreiter Straub and Staffel mascot "Strubbel".

Unteroffizier Alfred Scholz, also of the *2. Staffel*, was wounded in combat and bailed out near Zeitz (Fw 190 A-9, WNr. 206 040).

Leutnant Hermann Engelhardt of the *3. Staffel* was also wounded in combat. He abandoned his aircraft over Pößneck (Fw 190 A-9, WNr. 202 244).

Obergefreiter Franz Harrer of the *3. Staffel* was shot down and killed by Mustangs near Jena (Fw 190 A-9 "Yellow 15", WNr. 202 241). He was buried in the Michaelis Cemetery in Jena.

Leutnant Klaus Pagel of the *3. Staffel* fell in air combat near Langensalza (Fw 190 A-9, WNr. 202 434).

Oberleutnant Heinz Weise, acting commander of the *3. Staffel*, was wounded in combat. Weise was able to abandon his machine, however he died before his parachute reached the ground near Klein-Lochmar (Fw 190 A-9, WNr. 202 448).

Unteroffizier Harry Rauch of the *4. Staffel* was shot down and killed near Sanne, not far from Stendal (Fw 190 A-9, WNr. 206 047).

Fahnenjunker-Unteroffizier Willi Heidenreich of the *5. Staffel* was one of the first to fall prey to the escort fighters. He came down somewhere in Thuringia, however the exact location has never been discovered (Fw 190 A-9, WNr. 350 238).

Wounded in combat with Mustangs, *Leutnant* Siegfried Heise of the *5. Staffel* took to his parachute and came down near Bendeleben (Fw 190 A-9 "White 7", WNr. 206 153).

Obergefreiter Ernst Hobby of the *6. Staffel* was shot down and killed by escort fighters over Eisenberg (Fw 190 A-9 "Red 12", WNr. 206 137). He was buried in the North Cemetery in Jena (Field 27, Row 3, Grave 2).

Oberfeldwebel Hans Wagler of the *6. Staffel* was wounded in combat near Könitz (Fw 190 A-9 "Red 7", WNr. 202 424).

Obergefreiter Willi Kempf of the *7. Staffel* was killed in action near Goldbach (Fw 190 A-9 "Yellow 16", WNr. 206 170). Kempf was buried in Goldbach Cemetery near Gotha (Grave 23).

Unteroffizier Herbert Bartenieck of the *8. Staffel* was injured when his machine went down near Neustadt following engine failure (Fw 190 A-8 "Blue 12", WNr. 176 071).

Obergefreiter Rudolf Bender of the *9. Staffel* was wounded while attacking a formation of bombers and was forced to land near Waldeck (Fw 190 A-8 "White 5", WNr. 682 008). Bender did not return to his *Gruppe*.

Oberleutnant Hans Kretschmer, acting commander of the *10. Staffel*, was shot down and killed by Mustangs near Wenigenlupnitz (Fw 190 A-8 "Yellow 1", WNr. 208 112). Kretschmer was buried in Eisenach cemetery. *Oberleutnant* Hans-Georg Kretschmer had been a member of *IV./JG 301*, serving as *Kapitän* of the *10. Staffel*, which made up the entire *Gruppe*. His victories consisted of two B-24 Liberators shot down over Romania.

The records contain very little information about successes by *JG 301* in this action. The only recorded victory is a B-17 shot down at 1205 hours south of Magdeburg. Reference is made to additional victories, however no names are attached.

The Americans admitted the loss of thirty-three four-engined bombers and fifteen escort fighters on this day, with twelve bombers and nine fighters lost over Thuringia.

The first mission after the reorganization had confirmed what some older, more experienced pilots had feared: the enemy was steadily gaining the upper hand in the air battle over Germany

Fähnrich Ludwig Bracht, 11./JG 301.

through his superiority in pilot training, technology and numbers. For a long time the general situation had hindered the training of pilots in Germany. Pilots arriving at operational units had just enough experience to take off and land a Bf 109 or Fw 190. There was no time to teach them how to handle a fighter aircraft in a dogfight. By comparison, the American fighter pilots had between 300 and 400 hours on the aircraft they flew in combat.

In the fierce air battles over Germany, only those who were masters of their aircraft stood a chance of survival. It was shown repeatedly that an inexperienced pilot stood the least chance of surviving his first few missions, and exceptions only proved this rule. From one mission to the next a pilot learned lessons and gained experience, and in the end those who survived were the ones who could fly well and assess any situation correctly and take the necessary action. Conquering one's fear played a major role in this: how else can one explain why several of the pilots who saw their first action on 21 November 1944 landed with full magazines? Fifty percent of the pilots who took to the air that day were going into combat for the first time.

Basically, however, they had done exactly as they were told. Although the entire airspace was filled with enemy aircraft, they were so fearful of losing their element leader that they didn't look at anything else. That was quite understandable to many: one simply had to learn to watch everything up there.

It was also noted that the bomber formations were even smaller than those in the south. As a result, our attack tactic had to be modified to suit the smaller formations. The attack wedge, which had formerly consisted of two *Schwärme* (flights of four), was now changed to one *Schwarm* and one *Rotte* (pair).

Attacks on bomber formations deviated decidedly from the general fighter pilot tradition. Of course fighter units in the *Reichsverteidigung* still employed the *Rotte* and *Schwarm*, and every *Rotte* and *Schwarm* leader still had his "*Kaczmarek*" or wingman. These formations then progressed to the *Staffel* and *Gruppe*.

For attacks on bombers, however, the attack wedge normally consisted of two *Schwärme*. The *Schwarm* leaders flew in the center of the wedge, with the other aircraft of the *Schwärme* echeloned to their left and right. When the bomber formations were reduced in size, the wedge was also reduced, to one *Schwarm* and one *Rotte*.

In such attacks the wingman was relieved of his covering role, for the enemy could only be in front. In such situations there were either friendly fighters behind or no one. There is no known instance of escort fighters attacking during an assault on a bomber formation, for the risk of being hit by the bombers' defensive fire was too great. For this reason the "*Kaczmarek*" abandoned his covering function and himself became an attacker. Prior to commencing the attack, the formation spread out so that each pilot could take aim at his own target. This explains why the fighters in the attack formation became separated after an attack.

At this time some of *JG 301*'s pilots flew with a gun camera mounted under the wing. It was activated by pressing the firing buttons and continued to run for four seconds after firing ended. This made the confirmation of claims much simpler, eliminating the often wearisome search for witnesses. In almost every instance the pilot had no time to worry about his kill, for ensuring one's own safety took precedence. Submitting a claim always involved a lot of paperwork, and it often took weeks to have a victory confirmed.

26 November 1944

Early in the morning 1,137 heavy bombers, B-24s and B-17s, took off from English airfields, together with 732 P-51 and P-47 escort fighters. The weather was good as the bombers set course for their targets: Bielefeld, Miesburg and Hanover.

For *III./JG 301* at Stendal the day was like any other at that time of year: in the morning the airfield was socked in – "Even the birds are walking!" – and the pilots took chessboards and playing cards out of the drawer in anticipation of a long wait. Others busied themselves with the ever-popular deflection shooting game.

As the hours passed, communications traffic between the fighter control center and the *Geschwader* command post increased, and the weather improved visibly. Seeing this, the pilots put aside their games and each busied himself putting his flight suit in order. Mission fever had most pilots firmly in its grasp again. A cigarette was a good way to pass the time, and because fighter pilots are all superstitious, everyone avoided taking the third light. The weather improved steadily, and when the visibility suddenly picked up everyone became convinced that the mission was going to go ahead.

Within minutes the dispersal rooms emptied and the aircraft became scenes of hectic activity. Everywhere one looked, the "Black Men" were helping pilots into their aircraft, and soon the first machines were taxiing into takeoff formation. The takeoff order was not long coming, and at 1140 hours the first of *III./JG 301*'s aircraft took off from Stendal. The other two *Gruppen* of the *Geschwader* received the takeoff order at about the same. None of *III./JG 301*'s pilots could know that the *Jagdgeschwader* was about to fight the biggest battle in its history to date.

Immediately after takeoff there was the usual radio traffic between the Döberitz fighter control center and the formation leader, and on this day the fighters were ordered to head west. As *III./JG 301* climbed out over Gardelegen, the aircraft of *II./JG 301* were already in the air from Sachau. *I./*

JG 301 took off later from Salzwedel. The controller reported "Fat Autos" with many "Indians" in grid squares GO-GP-GQ, heading east: the enemy was thus directly in front of us.

As *JG 301* overflew the Gifhorn area it was instructed to turn southwest, taking it precisely between Brunswick and Hanover. Visibility was excellent and the endless condensation trails from the bombers were already visible, but it was also impossible to miss the many shorter, thinner vapor trails around the bombers made by the escort fighters. Soon afterwards the formation leader gave the order to jettison external tanks: contact was imminent. *II./JG 301* was first to run into the American escort fighters, and seconds later *I./JG 301* reported engaging Mustangs. Once contact with the enemy was made, radio silence was lifted, and in one's headset there was suddenly a cacophony of voices. It was often impossible to tell an order from a warning.

III./JG 301 joined battle somewhat more favorably, for it found a formation of about twenty-five to thirty B-24s directly in front and attacked immediately. What followed was a fascinating sight for the observer: within a few minutes the formation of Liberators had been reduced to a few aircraft, all the rest had been riddled by fire from the Fw 190s and shot down. Everywhere pieces of aircraft whirled through the air, and there were so many crashing aircraft that one could not take them all in with one look. On the ground there was a row of fires from crashed aircraft – and the battle had only just begun. Elements of *I.* and *II./JG 301* which had avoided combat with the escort fighters joined the attack on the B-24s and also attacked a group of B-17s.

Radio communications between the American fighters and bombers were obviously functioning flawlessly again, for suddenly escort fighters poured into the combat area from every direction, and the air battle really got going. A few of the *Jagdgeschwader*'s aircraft still managed to attack the bomber formations, but as the battle went on it became almost exclusively a contest between opposing fighters.

Completely unaffected, the bombers coming up from behind continued on towards the target, the hydrogenation plant at Miesburg near Hanover.

Both sides were now fighting a bitter battle for sheer survival, and one did not always know who was behind him. Looking back, I saw no sign of my "*Kaczmarek*", *Unteroffizier* Berliner. Bitter combats raged over large areas of northern Germany, and for many, especially the young pilots on their first or second mission, there was no escape from such a fierce battle.

Locked in a running fight with P-51 escort fighters, I had failed to locate my wingman, and calls on the radio were unsuccessful. In such situations it often takes just a few seconds to settle the fate of a pilot who a short time earlier had taken off with such confidence. It was impossible to fathom the fates that were played out up above – in the end only those who made it back in one piece could provide the answers. With much effort and some luck I was able to extract myself from this fighter battle and at 1319 hours I landed at Stendal with several bullet holes in the fuselage of my Fw 190 A-8. As I taxied to the *9. Staffel* dispersal my spirits lifted: parked there was the aircraft of *Unteroffizier* Berliner, my wingman.

It was a long time before all the aircraft of *JG 301* that had escaped undamaged returned to their home airfields. Our initial assessment of the battle seemed to suggest a victory, but in the days that followed we came to realize the scope of the bloodletting that had taken place in that air battle over Hildesheim.

Experienced pilots were of course able to increase their victory totals, but some pilots on their first mission were also successful. *Unteroffizier* Rudolf Michaelis, who had been transferred to the *12. Staffel* in Alperstedt, was able to shoot down his first Liberator. In the ensuing air battle his Fw 190 A-8 was so badly shot up by Mustangs that he subsequently had to make a forced landing.

Fähnrich Jonny Wiegeshoff of the *12. Staffel* and *Unteroffizier* Julius Berliner of the *9. Staffel*, both on their second combat mission, each shot down a B-24 Liberator. *JG 301* scored all of its victories in the Hildesheim – Hanover area between 1230 and 1310 hours.

These victories are listed below:

Oberfeldwebel Anton Benning	*10./JG 301*	B-24 and P-51
Oberfeldwebel Walter Blickle	*I./JG 301*	B-24
Feldwebel Heinrich Dörr	*11./JG 301*	two B-17s
Unteroffizier Heinrich Dürr	*12./JG 301*	B-17
Unteroffizier Willi Greiner	*12./JG 301*	two B-24s
Oberfeldwebel Josef Keil	*10./JG 301*	two B-24s
Feldwebel Willi Reschke	*9./JG 301*	B-24
Unteroffizier Christoph Blum	*9./JG 301*	B-24
Unteroffizier Walter Scheller	*12./JG 301*	B-17
Oberfeldwebel Herbert Seifert	*8./JG 301*	B-17
Oberfeldwebel Hans Todt	*8./JG 301*	B-24
Oberfeldwebel Hans Müller	*2./JG 301*	three B-24s
Fähnrich Jonny Wiegeshoff	*12./JG 301*	B-24
Oberleutnant Hermann Stahl	*10./JG 301*	B-24
Unteroffizier Rudolf Michaelis	*12./JG 301*	B-24
Unteroffizier Julius Berliner	*9./JG 301*	B-24

This list of victories by *JG 301* is probably not complete, however it is impossible to confirm any others. It reasonable to assume that some of the pilots killed in this action accounted for additional enemy aircraft.

The Americans admitted the loss of forty-two four-engined bombers and eleven escort fighters in this air battle.

JG 301's casualties were extremely heavy, making this the costliest day in the *Geschwader*'s history to that point. The air battle over Germany had reached a stage that should properly be called "The Bleeding to Death of the Fighter Arm". The enemy's numerical superiority, which often exceeded ten to one, was itself enough to ensure that each battle became costlier for the German fighter arm. Statements by the *Reichsmarschall* were read out to the assembled *Jagdgeschwader*, accusing the German fighter pilots of cowardice and claiming that they could not compare with the pilots of 1940. On hearing this, one brave young *Leutnant* had the courage to reply, "*Herr Reichsmarschall*, many of the decorated fighter pilots from those days wouldn't get the Iron Cross, Second Class in the Defense of the Reich!" His statement was not meant to diminish the accomplishments of earlier days, he just wanted to point out that conditions were now completely different.

Above: Feldwebel Willi Reschke while serving with 9./ JG 301.

Above right: Oberfeldwebel Walter Blickle, 2., then 4./ JG 301.

Right: Unteroffizier Julius Berliner, 9./JG 301.

Left: Unteroffizier Walter Kircheiß. 1./JG 301, killed in action near Hameln on 26 November 1944. Right: Unteroffizier Willi Huke, 3./JG 301, shot down and killed near Hameln on 26 November 1944. This photo was taken when Huke was still a Gefreiter.

In the air battle over the Hildesheim area on 26 November 1944, *Jagdgeschwader 301* lost forty pilots killed or wounded, roughly one-third of all those who took off that day. Most of these losses were inflicted by the escort fighters, who skillfully exploited their advantages: the primary target of the German fighters was, after all, the bombers, and the escort fighters could wait near the bombers and pick off the German fighters as they broke away after completing their firing passes. Witnesses who watched this battle from the ground later sad that, as a rule, the German fighters were pursued by several American fighters and only a few stood any chance of survival. The following is a detailed summary of the *Geschwader*'s losses:

Geschwaderstab:
Fähnrich Werner Raygrotzki was shot down and killed by P-51s near Einbeckhausen. He had recently been attached to the *Stab* from *4. Staffel*. (Fw 190 A-8, WNr. 170 234). He was buried in the Wunstorf cemetery.

I./JG 301, 1. Staffel:
Leutnant Fritz Brinkmann was shot down near Einbeckhausen at the very start of the battle (Fw 190 A-9, WNr. 202 242). Brinkmann was buried in Wunstorf cemetery (Section IX r, Row 2, No. 10).

    Unteroffizier Kurt Gabler was shot down near Einbeckhausen at about the same time (Fw 190 A-9, WNr. 206 039). He, too, was buried in Wunstorf cemetery (Section IX r, Row 2, No. 9).

Unteroffizier Walter Kircheiß was shot down and killed near Hameln (Fw 190 A-9, WNr. 202 366). He was buried in Wunstorf cemetery (Section IX r, Row 2, No. 8).

Gefreiter Siegfried Meier was shot down and killed by P-51s near Minden (Fw 190 A-8, WNr. 176 063). He was buried in the New Cemetery in Minden.

2. *Staffel*:

Oberfeldwebel Heinz Günther was shot down and killed near Vietze. One of the *Staffel*'s more experienced pilots, he nevertheless succumbed to superior numbers (Fw 190 A-9, WNr. 206 108). He was buried in Hameln cemetery.

Unteroffizier Ernst Peiz had been a member of the *Geschwader* since autumn 1943 and had flown night-fighter missions. He was shot down and killed near Brunswick (Fw 190 A-9/R11, WNr. 202 362). Peiz was buried in the military cemetery in Brunswick (B II, 2/34).

3. *Staffel*:

Unteroffizier Willi Huke was shot down and killed near Hessisch-Oldendorf (Fw 190 A-9/R11, WNr. 202 590). He was buried in Wunstorf cemetery (Section IX r., Row 2, No. 7).

Oberfeldwebel Josef Löffler lost his life in combat with P-51s near Nettelrede (Fw 190 A-9/R11, WNr. 202 406). He was buried in Wunstorf cemetery (IX r., Row 2, No. 12).

Feldwebel Werner Meyer was shot down and killed near Einbeckhausen (Fw 190 A-8, WNr. 176 051). Meyer had only recently joined the *3. Staffel*. He was buried in Wunstorf cemetery (IX r., Row 3, No. 4).

Oberfeldwebel Erich Meyer joined the *Gruppe* during its rest and reorganization period and was killed in action near Pohle (Fw 190 A-9/R11, WNr. 202 361). He was buried in Wunstorf cemetery (IX r., Row 3, No. 3).

Feldwebel Erwin Seifert was shot down and killed by Mustangs near Hessisch-Oldendorf (Fw 190 A-9/R11, WNr. 202 373). He was buried in Wunstorf cemetery.

4. *Staffel*:

Feldwebel Emil Schubert was wounded in action near Bückeberg. He rejoined his *Staffel* after a brief convalescence (Fw 190 A-9/R11, WNr. 202 565).

Unteroffizier Gottfried Hellriegel was also wounded in combat and made a forced landing near Niendorf (Fw 190 A-9/R11, WNr. 202 370).

Unteroffizier Adolf Schäpers was wounded in combat near Bredenbeck and was taken to hospital. He returned to the *Staffel* after recovering from his wounds (Fw 190 A-8, WNr. 176 059).

Unteroffizier Anton Schmidt was shot down and killed in combat with escort fighters near Völksen (Fw 190 A-9/R11, WNr. 202 377). He was buried in Wunstorf cemetery (Section IX r., Row 2, No. 4).

II./JG 301, 5. *Staffel*

Unteroffizier Siegfried Baer was killed in air combat near Holtensen (Fw 190 A-9/R11, WNr. 260 085). He was buried in Holtensen-Wülfinghausen cemetery.

Feldwebel Otto-Georg Müller was wounded in combat with P-51s over Gronow but was able to parachute to safety (Fw 190 A-9/R11 "White 4", WNr. 202 430).

Oberleutnant Alfred Vollert, *Kapitän* of the *5./JG 301*, lost his life in air combat near Rethen (Fw 190 A-9/R11 "White 1", WNr. 206 160). He was buried in the family plot in Freilitsch near Hof.

6. Staffel:

Feldwebel Alfred Arens was shot down in combat with several P-51s near Sarstedt (Fw 190 A-8 "Red 29", WNr. 733 693). He was buried in Hildesheim.

Oberleutnant Rudolf Schick, *Staffelkapitän*, was killed near Dahlenburg after a lengthy battle with several Mustangs (Fw 190 A-9 "Red 1", WNr. 206 152). He was buried in Lünebeck. On 22 November Schick had written to the parents of Ernst Hobby, informing them of their son's death in combat on 21 November. Now he had suffered a similar fate.

7. Staffel:

Gefreiter Fritz Doßmann was shot down and killed near Mellendorf (Fw 190 A-9/R11 "Yellow 12", WNr. 206 156). He was buried in the military cemetery in Brunswick (B II, 2/35).

Leutnant Heinz-Ludwig Günther was killed in air combat near Hestenbeck (Fw 190 A-9/R11 "Yellow 8", WNr. 202 447). Günther, who led a *Schwarm* on this day, was buried in Salzwedel.

Feldwebel Helmut Handel was shot down and killed near Mellendorf. He was buried in the military cemetery in Brunswick (B II, 2/37).

Oberfeldwebel Franz Menzel was badly wounded in combat with escort fighters, but was able to bail out, coming down near Peine (Fw 190 A-9/R11 "Yellow 3", WNr. 202 126). Menzel, who did not return to the *Staffel*, was one of the few pilots to have survived *II./JG 301*'s retreat from Romania. He shot down three B-24s over Romania.

Feldwebel Friedrich Röglsperger was also wounded in combat with escort fighters over Peine and abandoned his aircraft (Fw 190 A-9/R11 "Yellow 4", WNr. 202 433). Röglsperger succumbed to his serious wounds on 5 December 1944 and was buried in the military cemetery in Peine.

Unteroffizier Heinz Schulz was wounded in combat and had to force-land his machine near Meerdorf (Fw 190 A-9 "Yellow 17", WNr. 202 415).

Unteroffizier Paul Stargardt was pursued by P-51s. Wounded, he was forced to abandon his aircraft over Bledeln and came down safely by parachute (Fw 190 A-9 "Yellow 5", WNr. 202 429).

8. Staffel:

Unteroffizier Kurt Dörr fought off several attacks by enemy fighters but was wounded. Despite his wounds he bailed out over Hamelspringe and landed safely (Fw 190 A-9/R11 "Blue 7", WNr. 176 071).

Gefreiter Josef Henning was shot down and killed near Bad Münder (Fw 190 A-8 "Blue 15", WNr. 172 059). He was buried in Wunstorf cemetery. *Feldwebel* Helmut Thiemann was shot down near Sarstedt while leading a *Schwarm*. Thiemann abandoned his aircraft and opened his parachute, but he died before reaching the ground (Fw 190 A-8 "Blue 2", WNr. 172 437). He was initially buried in Wunstorf cemetery, but in 1946 his remains were moved to Wuppertal-Barmen.

Left: Obergefreiter Erich Steidel of 9./JG 301. He was killed in action near Hanover on 26 November 1944.
Right: Fähnrich Hans Voigt, 10./JG 301, shot down and killed near Wunstorf on 26 November 1944.

III./JG 301, 9. *Staffel*:

Oberfeldwebel Heinz Dademarsch was wounded while attacking a formation of bombers near Wunstorf. Dademarsch, who had joined the *Gruppe* at Stendal in October, did not return to the unit (Fw 190 A-8 "White 16", WNr. 682 004).

Gefreiter Erich Steidel was shot down and killed by P-51s near Wahrendahl (Fw 190 A-8 "White 4", WNr. 176 104). Steidel joined *I./JG 302* at Götzendorf in July 1944 and after it was disbanded became a member of *III./JG 301*. In July 1944 he shot down a B-17. He was buried in Wunstorf cemetery (IX r., Row 2, No. 5).

10. *Staffel*:

Leutnant Georg Frenzel was wounded in combat over Brunswick. He had joined the *Gruppe* in Alperstedt and this was his second combat mission (Fw 190 A- 8 "Red 7", WNr. 682 301).

Leutnant Rudolf Karioth was also wounded in action over Brunswick. Nothing is known of his subsequent fate, as he did not return to the *Gruppe*. This was his second combat mission (Fw 190 A-8 "Red 8", WNr. 172 093).

Fähnrich Reinhold Hummel was wounded while attacking a formation of B-24s over Hildesheim. He returned to the *Gruppe* after a lengthy stay in hospital. He probably survived the war, however nothing could be learned about his subsequent fate. (Fw 190 A-8 "Red 10", WNr. 691 990).

Fähnrich Hans Voigt was shot down and killed by Mustangs over Wunstorf. Voigt joined the *Gruppe* at Alperstedt and was on his second combat mission. His family later had his remains moved to their home town of Haynrode in the southern Harz. (Fw 190 A-8 "Red 15", WNr. 172 358).

11. Staffel:

Fähnrich Ludwig Bracht was wounded while attacking a formation of Liberators. Unable to get back to the airfield, he abandoned his Fw 190 not far from Stendal. This was his second combat mission. Bracht returned to the *Gruppe* after recovering from his wounds. (Fw 190 A-8 "Yellow 3", WNr. 172 350).

According to other members of the unit, *Unteroffizier* Adolf Bellinghausen (Fw 190 A-8 "Yellow 16", WNr. 682 026) and *Oberfähnrich* Hubert Ludwig (Fw 190 A-8 "Yellow 7", WNr. 681 966) collided during an attack on a formation of Liberators and subsequently crashed. Both were buried in the north cemetery in Hildesheim.

An evaluation of this mission revealed two notable feats that deserve to be acknowledged:

First: the shooting down of three B-24 Liberators by *Oberfeldwebel* Hans Müller of the *2. Staffel*, a feat seldom equaled in the history of the *Reichsverteidigung*. Experienced pilots will recognize this, for they know what it means to shoot down even one four-engined bomber.

Second: the *12. Staffel* suffered no losses while claiming several of the enemy. This feat was regarded with great respect by the other *Staffeln* of the *Gruppe*. This unit had, however, served as *I./ JG 302*'s high-altitude *Staffel* and was more accustomed to air combat against the escort fighters.

An extremely negative aspect revealed by this post-mission evaluation was the fact that *JG 301* had lost sixty pilots killed or wounded in its last two missions, equivalent to half its combat strength. For the *Geschwader* command and the individual *Gruppen* this was a depressing realization, and in fact there was no way out of this misery. Replacement aircraft and pilots could no longer keep pace with losses, and the American bomber and fighter fleets continued to grow.

During the subsequent evaluation of the pictures taken by my gun camera, it was possible to follow precisely my attack on the B-24 Liberator. Although I constantly reminded myself, it was obvious that I had still opened fire too soon. Nevertheless, the tracers showed that my shells were on target from the start.

As I closed in on the B-24, it was possible to see large pieces of the left wing coming off and the spreading fire in the inner motor. The film even revealed the imminent separation of the wing.

The unfavorable weather at this time of year had a major impact on flying and thus the operational readiness of the *Geschwader*. Training flights during the reorganization period had shown that some pilots encountered difficultly climbing through low cloud in formation. Because of the heavy losses and the associated intake of new pilots, consideration was given to the formation of an all-weather unit made up of pilots with instrument training. All the pilots attended a meeting held in *III./JG 301*'s officers mess, where the idea of forming an all-weather unit was discussed. The idea was quickly dropped, however, as it would have required a complete change in the entire *Gruppe*: all of the less-experienced pilots would have been eliminated from operations in bad weather, while the number of experienced pilots was steadily diminishing. On the whole, the shortage of experienced

Above: Unteroffizier Adolf Bellinghausen. He was killed over Hanover on 26 November 1944.

Above right: Oberfeldwebel Hans Müller of 2./JG 301.

Right: Oberfähnrich Hubert Ludwig of 11./JG 301, photograph at the unit's dispersal at Stendal in November 1944. He was killed in the Hanover-Brunswick area on 26 November.

formation, *Staffel* and *Schwarm* leaders was making itself felt anyway, and as there was no hope that the situation would improve, formation of an all-weather unit would only have worsened this hopelessness.

27 November 1944

Weather was again the reason why only part of the *Geschwader* saw action on this day. While the *I.* and *II. Gruppe* were able to get airborne from Salzwedel and Sachau, at Stendal the *III. Gruppe* was grounded by low ceilings and poor visibility.

American bombers were heading for Bingen and Offenburg. This was not apparent at first, as the bombers came in farther north and only later made a right turn toward their actual targets.

The mission order sent the two *Jagdgruppen* somewhat farther south than on the previous day and contact was made with the enemy southwest of a line Brunswick-Kassel. In this action the pilots of *I.* and *II./JG 301* only got to see the bombers' condensation trails, for they were intercepted by the escort fighters while still far away. Once again there was a massive dogfight with swarms of Mustangs, and the enemy's numerical superiority was growing by the day. Even worse, however, was the inner sense of inferiority in training and inadequate experience in fighter-versus-fighter combat. One could not help but admire the courage of our pilots, who readily accepted combat against such odds. It was especially difficult for the young pilots to stay under control and overcome the hurdle of their first victory: often this meant overcoming one's own inferiority complex. The losses suffered on 27 November, however, further reduced the number of operational pilots available to *JG 301*.

I./JG 301, 1. Staffel:

Unteroffizier Otto Bissinger, born in Landhausen near Eppingen on 1 April 1922, was seriously wounded in combat. He landed near Nordhausen and did not return to the *Staffel* (Fw 190 A-8, WNr. 733 758).

Unteroffizier Heinz-Josef Maximini, born in Saarburg on 9 February 1923, was wounded in combat with P-51s near Elze. After recovering from his wounds he returned to the *Staffel* (Fw 190 A-9, WNr. 206 188).

Oberfähnrich Gerhard Golze was born in Großräschen on 29 September 1924. His aircraft was shot up by enemy fighters and he was forced to bail out. Golze landed safely, suffering only minor injuries, and was able to return to action (Fw 190 A-9, WNr. 202 372).

This was the last mission for *Unteroffizier* Hans Zaren, born in Königsberg on 26 December 1920. His crippled machine crashed near the small town of Wetteborn an der Leine. Zaren managed to bail out, but he was too low and his parachute failed to open in time (Fw 190 A-9/R11, WNr. 202 375).

Unteroffizier Artur Appelt, born in Friedland in the Sudetenland on 26 June 1922, was shot down near Göttingen (Fw 190 A-9/R11, WNr. 202 394).

2. Staffel:

Obergefreiter Siegfried Schulz, born in Jüterbog on 18 September 1923, was wounded in combat near Broizen, but after a short hospital stay he returned to his *Staffel* (Fw 190 A-8, WNr. 176 062).

Unteroffizier Gustav Wimmer, born in Munich on 23 February 1921, was shot down and killed by P-51s near Küllstedt (Fw 190 A-9/R11, WNr. 202 418).

4. Staffel:

Unteroffizier Alfred Bokr, born in Holthausen on 7 March 1923, was shot down and killed by Mustangs near Hörsum an der Leine (Fw 190 A-9/R11, WNr. 202 386).

Stab II./JG 301:

Oberfeldwebel Josef Nierhaus, born in Kohlscheid near Aachen on 4 August 1913, was pursued by several Mustangs. He was finally shot down and killed near Edemissen, northwest of Brunswick (Fw 190 A-9/R11, WNr. 206 056).

5. Staffel:

Oberfähnrich Siegfried Bonitz, born in Dresden on 7 October 1924, went down with his aircraft near Greene after aerial combat (Fw 190 A-9/R11 "White 15", WNr. 206 138).

Feldwebel Kurt Klemm, born in Veldenz on the Moselle on 19 December 1919, failed to return from this mission. Where he crashed is not known. Klemm was buried in Göttingen on 8 December 1944. (Fw 190 A-9/R11 "White 17", WNr. 206 038).

6. Staffel:

Unteroffizier Heinz Sturm was born in Herdingen, Westphalia on 4 May 1922. When the mission was over he attempted to land at Stendal but crashed just short of the airfield. The cause of the crash that claimed Sturm's life is not known (Fw 190 A-8 "Red 13", WNr. 734 397).

Although *JG 301*'s losses are well-documented, there are gaps in the records when it comes to victories, as is the case concerning the mission on 27 November 1944. The reason for this one-sided bookkeeping is not known. To those who were there, however, it is difficult to believe that the two *Jagdgruppen* that took part in this battle, at the cost of twelve pilots killed or wounded, did not claim a single victory, especially when the enemy himself admitted the loss of sixteen escort fighters in this action.

At the end of November 1944 the *Gruppenkommandeur* of *III./JG 301*, *Hauptmann* Wilhelm Fulda, was transferred to *JG 400* (Me 163 *Komet* rocket fighter), where he assumed command of that unit's *I. Gruppe*. In the final days of 1944 *III./JG 301* was temporarily commanded by *Hauptmann* Karl-Heinz Dietsche. After the death of *Hauptmann* Burggraf on 21 November 1944, *I./JG 301* was also temporarily led by one of the *Gruppe*'s more experienced officers.

In the last days of November 1944 *Hauptmann* Paul Quednau arrived to take command of the *9. Staffel*. A native of East Prussia, Quednau was a converted bomber pilot. One morning, totally unexpectedly, he arrived in the *9. Staffel* ready room, where his first words were, "I'm the new *Staffelkapitän*." He then added, "I'm sure we'll get along." The pilots, however, were not so sure at first, for there was a cold edge to the silence that ensued. *Hauptmann* Quednau saw this and immediately went to each pilot to shake his hand and exchange a few words. Quednau had the ability to be a *Staffelkapitän* and comrade at the same time, and this soon earned him the trust of the *Staffel*.

The *Geschwaderstab* under *Oberstleutnant* Auffhammer, previously based at Stendal and then Salzwedel, had taken up permanent residence in Stendal. The recent air battles had also left gaps in the *Stabsschwarm*'s ranks. It was a standing rule that only experienced pilots flew in the *Stabsschwarm*, and this time it was *Oberfeldwebel* Heinz Gossow who was transferred there. His comrades in the *9. Staffel* and even Gossow himself had mixed feelings about this, but orders are orders and so he and his kit moved into headquarters.

2 December 1944

On this day *JG 301* took part in an operation which began quite late. It seems that for quite some time the fighter control center was uncertain as to whether it should take off at all. *III./JG 301* was finally ordered off at 1240 hours, but thin cloud at high altitude reduced visibility and prevented it from linking up with the *II.* and *III. Gruppe*. *III./JG 301*'s initial heading was changed several times, and from the beginning there was uncertainty among the pilots, and the poor visibility only intensified this feeling.

The enemy formation reported by the controller was still far to the west, and we could not see how we would ever get there on our heading. The course changes had caused *III./JG 301* to become spread out, and only a few aircraft, flying on the outside of the formation, reported contact with the enemy. There was no significant combat, however. The majority of the *Geschwader*'s pilots never saw the enemy on this day, and at 1344 hours most of *III./JG 301* landed back at Stendal.

Feldwebel Gerhard Wieck of the *8. Staffel* was killed in a crash near Hennef, however it is not known if this was related to the mission.

We were becoming convinced that the quality of the fighter control in central Germany was not as good as what we had been used to in the Vienna – Munich area. The orders issued to the fighter formation often followed no clear line, and the pauses for thought between orders were too long, causing the formation to fly farther than it had to. Perhaps the controllers had already become overtaxed by this time: the enemy incursions were growing in size from day to day, while at the same time available resources in day and night fighter units were steadily dwindling.

The nature of the combats in this area was also different. In the airspace over southern Germany the bomber formations had always been the number one target and a maximum effort was made against them. As there were fewer escorts, fighter-versus-fighter combat was of lesser importance. Here it was exactly the opposite: attacking the bombers was now seen as the lesser problem, as enemy fighters posed by far the greater danger. They surrounded almost every bomber formation like a bell, and it was becoming ever more difficult to even get to the bombers. Every mission against the bombers was now the same: combat with the escort fighters, possible attack on the bombers, combat with the escort fighters again. Fighter-versus-fighter combat also caused most of our losses. The offensive tactics employed by the German fighters and the resulting combats made it difficult for pairs to remain together. As a result, German fighter pilots in the *Reichsverteidigung* more and more became lone fighters. This development in the air battles over Germany was a fateful one, especially for the newer pilots. During their first missions it was vital that they remain part of a *Schwarm* or *Rotte*, but this was now rarely the case. In fact, the experienced pilots should have taken the new pilots, who were so desperately needed as replacements, under their wing and gradually introduced them to air combat. But this was no longer possible, and we watched them go down one after the other.

The "Rosarius Circus" at Stendal in December 1944. In the foreground is a Supermarine Spitfire, behind it a P-38 Lightning.

Fw 190 A-8, standard equipment of the "Wilde Sau" Geschwader from September 1944.

Only so-called "Training Missions" allowed the newer pilots to gain experience while flying as part of the *Geschwader*. In reality, however, these training missions were actual missions, in which there was no contact with the enemy as a result of poor control.

III./JG 301 took off on one such mission on 3 December 1944. In anticipation of an attack on central Germany, the *Gruppe* took off at 1420 hours. For the next hour and forty minutes it was vectored back and forth between Harz and Brunswick without encountering the enemy.

On the afternoon of 4 December 1944 Stendal air base received a visit from the "Rosarius Circus". Its equipment consisted of captured enemy aircraft, a P-38 Lightning, a P-51 Mustang and a Spitfire. These aircraft went round the *Jagdgeschwader* making comparison flights. Their purpose was to allow combat pilots to fly mock engagements with the enemy fighters and discover their strengths and weaknesses. The *Gruppe* used Fw 190 A-8 and D-9 aircraft for these comparison flights, flown by experienced pilots.

5 December 1944

The comparison flights with aircraft of the "Rosarius Circus" began in the early morning, however they subsequently had to be terminated when the approach of large numbers of enemy aircraft was reported. A series of conflicting orders followed, but finally the *Gruppe* was ordered to scramble. This took only a few minutes, for the pilots had all been standing at their dispersals, watching the mock dogfights. The pilots who took part in the comparison flights did not have time to go on this mission, and as a result they were granted an unexpected respite.

Inbound from England were 591 four-engined bombers, B-17s and B-24s, and 901 P-51 and P-47 escort fighters. Their targets were Münster and Berlin.

All three *Gruppen* of JG 301 took off at about the same time, and the mission was led by the *Kommodore*, *Oberstleutnant* Auffhammer. The *Geschwader* formed up early, over Gardelegen, and there it was issued a new heading by fighter control, north toward Berlin.

In their headphones the pilots heard a steady stream of reports from the fighter control center: "Fat Autos with many Indians approaching Berlin." On hearing this, many wingmen moved closer to their *Schwarm* or *Rotte* leader, for it seemed very likely that they were in for another hot day.

First contact with the enemy occurred in the airspace north of Berlin, and the ensuing air battle gradually spread out over Mecklenburg and beyond into the Göttingen area. Once again the fighters had to tackle the escorts first, making it impossible for the *Geschwader* to make a formation assault on the bombers. Only a few aircraft managed to break through the screen of escort fighters to attack a formation of B-17s. Most of the fighters became involved with the Mustangs, but lessons had been learned from previous battles against this type and, in spite of their numerical superiority, many of the American fighter pilots found themselves in trouble. JG 301's battle with the American fighters and bombers lasted almost an hour and produced the following results:

1049	*Oberfeldwebel* Anton Benning	*10./JG 301*	P-51	N Berlin	14th
1050	*Leutnant* Reiche	*12./JG 301*	P-51	N Berlin	7th
1050	*Oberleutnant* Schuch	*7./JG 301*	B-17	N Berlin	1st
1053	*Feldwebel* Gerhard Koch	*1./JG 301*	P-51	near Neustrelitz	7th
1054	*Leutnant* Leonhard Renicke	*9./JG 301*	B-17	N Berlin	4th

1055	*Oberleutnant* Schuch	*7./JG 301*	P-51	Mecklenburg	2nd
1100	*Unteroffizier* August Hölscher	*5./JG 301*	P-51	Mecklenburg	1st
1100	*Unteroffizier* Albert Hoffmann	*5./JG 301*	P-51	N Berlin	1st
1100	*Feldwebel* Karl Rienth	*11./JG 301*	P-51	over Mecklenburg	1st
1100	*Unteroffizier* Gerhard Leeb	*8./JG 301*	P-51	N Berlin	1st
1132	*Oberstleutnant* Fritz Auffhammer	*Stab*	P-51	N Berlin	1st
1137	*Oberstleutnant* Fritz Auffhammer	*Stab*	P-51	N Berlin	2nd

This mission also cost *JG 301* heavily, and the widely-scattered loss sites show just how spread-out this battle had become. Total casualties were twenty-one pilots killed or wounded, details of which follow:

I./JG 301, 1. Staffel:

Feldwebel Gerhard Koch was wounded over Neustrelitz after a running battle with Mustangs and was forced to land. He returned to action a short time later (Fw 190 A-9, WNr. 202 443).

Oberfähnrich Gerhard Golze had not fully recovered from wounds suffered on 27 November 1944, yet he took part in this mission. Attacked by several Mustangs, he was finally shot down and killed near Göttingen (Fw 190 A-9, WNr. 202 404).

Feldwebel Ernst Leyer was shot down and killed by Mustangs near Fürstensee (Fw 190 A-9, WNr. 202 387).

4. Staffel:

Leutnant Max Creil had rejoined the *Gruppe* after recovering from wounds suffered over The Hague on 20 July 1944. It would be his last air battle, and where he died remains a mystery. (Fw 190 A-9 "Yellow 1", WNr. 202 362) *Oberfähnrich* Karl-Heinz Ripper was killed in action near Altstrelitz. Rippe had joined the *Gruppe* in September 1944. (Fw 190 A-9, WNr. 206 084).

Stab II./JG 301:

Gruppenkommandeur Hauptmann Rolf Jacobs was killed n combat with American escort fighters near Zirtow. Jacobs thus became the second *Gruppe* commander lost by *JG 301* in the space of a few days. His remains were taken in an urn to Bad Wiessee on the Tegernsee. (Fw 190 A-9, WNr. 206 157).

5. Staffel:

Staffelkapitän Oberleutnant Werner Poppenburg was shot down by Mustangs over Angermünde (Fw 190 A-9 "White 2", WNr. 209 913).

7. Staffel:

Oberfeldwebel Paul Becker was shot down near Prenzlau and failed to get out of his crippled aircraft (Fw 190 A-8 "Yellow 23", WNr. 175 169).

Fahnenjunker-Feldwebel Hans Ryba was overwhelmed by enemy fighters and fell in the Prenzlau area. The exact location of his loss in not known. (Fw 190 A-9 "Yellow 11", WNr. 206 176)

Unteroffizier Horst Thorwirth went down with his machine near Königsstedt (Fw 190 A-8 "Blue 5", WNr. 176 089).

8. *Staffel*:

Feldwebel Hans Pflüger went down with his Fw 190 near Blankenförde (Fw 190 A-8 "Blue 6", WNr. 176 069).

Unteroffizier Willi Sander was shot down and killed near Düsterförde (Fw 190 A-8 "Blue 9", WNr. 172 379).

9. *Staffel*:

Stabsfeldwebel Rolf Böhme began flying Fw 189 reconnaissance aircraft, and after converting to fighters joined *III./JG 301* at Alperstedt in September 1944. He was shot down and killed by Mustangs near Finow (Fw 190 A-8, WNr. 682 002).

Oberfeldwebel Heinz Döpel was from Erfurt and joined *III./JG 301* when the *Gruppe* was established at Alperstedt. His body was found in his parachute near the village of Brodowin, east of Chorin. There were no obvious injuries, just an area of discoloration around his heart. It is thought that he may have suffocated in the thin air after bailing out at high altitude. (Fw 190 A-8, WNr. 682 007).

10. *Staffel*:

Oberfähnrich Alfons Hörnig had been transferred to *II./JG 301* with a group of officer candidates. He was shot down by Mustangs in a one-sided combat near Finow (Fw 190 A-8 "Red 10", WNr. 681 882).

Unteroffizier Rudolf Marquardt joined the *Jagdgruppe* at Alperstedt and was also shot down and killed near Finow (Fw 190 A-8 "Red 5", WNr. 681 869).

Feldwebel Heinz Thierling joined the *Gruppe* during its rest and reorganization period. He was seriously wounded and forced to land his machine near Schorfheide. Thierling never returned to the *Staffel*. (Fw 190 A-8, WNr. 682 014).

Fahnenjunker-Feldwebel Helmut Tschorn also joined the *Gruppe* at Alperstedt, having previously served as an instructor with A/B 9 in Grottkau an der Neisse. He did not return from this mission, falling in the Finow area north of Berlin (Fw 190 A-8 "Red 17", WNr. 176 109).

Feldwebel Hans Viehbeck was wounded in combat over Finow and returned to the *Gruppe* after recovering from his wounds (Fw 190 A-8, WNr. 681 878).

11. *Staffel*:

Unteroffizier Karl Alt was from Sömmerda in Thuringia and joined the *Jagdgruppe* at Alperstedt. He was shot down and killed by Mustangs near Prenzlau (Fw 190 A-8, WNr. 681 357).

12. *Staffel*:

Oberfeldwebel Walter Bäker also joined the *Jagdgruppe* at Alperstedt, having previously served outside the fighter arm. He did not return from this mission, and it is not known where he was killed. (Fw 190 A-8 "Black 9", WNr. 682 005)

Stendal, November 1944. From left: Unteroffizier Heinz Warnicke, posted missing in March 1945; Feldwebel Heinrich Dörr, killed in action over Tessin near Rostock on 31 December 1944; and Oberfeldwebel Walter Bäcker, shot down and killed over Prenzlau on 5 December 1944.

Most of *JG 301*'s losses in this action had been inflicted by enemy fighters. The size of the battle zone is reflected in the widely-varying loss sites. This was no engagement by a fighter group under the command of a formation leader, rather it was a series of isolated combats by pilots desperately trying to cope with an enemy vastly superior in numbers. What kind of men were these, who again and again climbed into their machines, wounds from previous battles barely healed, to fly and fight against the enemy when there was no hope of a victorious outcome? They were men who loved their country and did whatever they could to stem the almost daily bombardment of German cities. They were lone heroes never mentioned in the *Wehrmacht* communiqués, but who gave their utmost out of concern for and loyalty to family and country: their lives.

In the days just before 10 December 1944 I made an official trip to the *Luftwaffe* testing station at Rechlin. My mission: to examine and be briefed on Focke-Wulf's latest development, the Ta 152. The fighter aircraft I saw there resembled the Fw 190 D-9 but had a much bigger wing, five meters greater in span. Even though I had been sent there, the information given by the test personnel was extremely sparse. Gradually I realized that they would rather have seen someone of higher rank, and they were unwilling to admit that experienced pilots of any rank were becoming scarce in the fighter arm. I was never allowed to fly the aircraft personally, and all I was told was that it had a maximum speed of 750 km/h and that its huge wing made it more maneuverable than the Spitfire. That all sounded good, but in the end I had no idea why I had gone to Rechlin. It made no sense to go there just to see a new fighter aircraft. The next day, when I made my report to commanding officer *Oberstleutnant* Auffhammer, he was unable hide his amazement. I was on my way out when the

Kommodore picked up the phone and spoke to Rechlin, but I did overhear that we would be receiving these aircraft in the not too distant future.

On 12 December 1944, *Unteroffizier* Walter Konrad of the *11. Staffel* crashed near Stendal airfield while ferrying a Fw 190 A-8, suffering serious injuries. He subsequently did not return to the *Staffel*.

There were also changes in *III./JG 301*'s personnel during this period. *Fahnenjunker-Feldwebel* Herbert Göbel, who had flown with the *I./JG 302* in the Vienna area, was promoted to the rank of *Leutnant*. He was later transferred to *JG 7* to fly the Me 262. *Oberfeldwebel* Heinz Gossow of the *Stabsschwarm* went the same way. His flying career saw him progress from the He 111 via the Bf 109 and Fw 190 to the Me 262. *Oberfeldwebel* Hans Todt of the *8. Staffel* later went to Lechfeld for training on the Me 262. *Oberfeldwebel* Anton Benning of the *10. Staffel* was sent to a unit leaders course in Königsberg-Neumark. He returned to *JG 301* as a *Leutnant* and at the beginning of January 1945 became *Kapitän* of the *1. Staffel*.

The officer corps was bolstered by the addition of several young *Leutnants*, who were assigned to the various *Staffeln*. *Leutnant* August-Wilhelm Hagedorn, nickname Archi, went to the *9. Staffel*, *Leutnant* Horst Reinhold to the *11. Staffel* and *Leutnant* Rolf Rüth to the *12. Staffel*. A *Leutnant* Spiess was also then a member of *III./JG 301*, however nothing is known of his subsequent fate. Still with the *Gruppe* command were the two command post clerks *Unteroffizier* Theo Jürgen-Limbke and *Obergefreiter* Horst Dietsche, brother of *Staffelkapitän* Karl-Heinz Dietsche. Having held these posts since the formation of *JG 302*, both men were intimately familiar with the needs of the combat pilots and also maintained their log books.

Former *Gruppenkommandeur Hauptmann* Heinrich Wurzer, who had been transferred, spent a few days with the *Gruppe*, then left again toward the end of the month.

With everything in short supply, the officers were issued bicycles with removable handlebars for official use. When a bicycle was left in front of the mess with the handlebars in place, it was not uncommon for it to be seen later the same evening in Stendal or Osterburg. The lower-ranking personnel had "just borrowed it" and the next morning it was back again.

"Mustang", formerly the *Staffel* mascot of *1./JG 302* and now of *9./JG 301*, was fully conscious of his status, after all he was an Hungarian sheepdog and as big as a calf. The entire airfield was his territory, but his favorite places were in front of the kitchen and mess.

In mid-December 1944 the situation became even more dramatic for the fighter units of the *Reichsverteidigung*. All available *Jagdgeschwader* were transferred to airfields near the Western Front to support the imminent offensive in the Ardennes. This left just *JG 300* and *JG 301*, based on airfields south and west of Berlin, to defend against daylight bombing raids. The airfields used by these two *Jagdgeschwader* were becoming prime targets for the enemy's tactical aircraft, which we nicknamed "Choppers". To counter these attacks, *Schwarm*-strength patrols were kept in the air over our bases; a relief *Schwarm* was held at cockpit readiness. This measure was short-lived, however, as fuel supplies dwindled steadily.

17 December 1944

JG 301 was scrambled at 1055 hours, and immediately after takeoff the *Geschwader* was vectored southwest into the Hanover area. There the fighters encountered a small formation of Liberators heading south. The bombers were escorted by P-47s and P-51s. The *Geschwader* had been scrambled because this group of bombers was heading straight toward its airfields. In contrast to previous missions, the bombers were attacked within a matter of minutes. Elements of the *I.* and *II. Gruppe* were once again immediately engaged by the escort fighters, but the *III. Gruppe*, which was flying lower in the formation, exploited the resulting gap in the fighter cover and attacked the Liberators. During attacks like this, the area directly behind the four-engined bombers was always free of escort fighters – it could have been seen as a neutral zone, were it not for the bombers' defensive fire.

In *III./JG 301* – and this had been retained from *I./JG 302* – it was an unwritten rule that following an attack on a bomber formation the fighters always broke away up and to the left or right rather than downwards.

This tactic made it possible to immediately begin a second attack on the bomber formation. For an attacking pilot, pressing the firing buttons was always a relief: hearing the pounding of the guns and seeing the effects of one's fire had a calming effect. During this phase it was impossible to pay any notice to what was happening to the left and right.

My brain had been preprogrammed to move in as close as possible when attacking the Liberator, and the first tracers confirmed that the deflection was correct. Seconds became minutes, and I often had the feeling that the speed of my shells on their way to the target was much too low. But the effects of my shells striking the Liberator's left wing were immediately visible, and soon I saw the familiar sight of pieces of wing coming away. The thought of my gun camera had a calming effect.

We broke up and to the left, and there were the escort fighters again, making a second attack on the bombers out of the question. We often had the feeling that they watched us attack the bombers, so that they could intercept us when our attack ended. After this attack I was again greeted by a Mustang. A quick look back was enough to confirm that my new wingman *Unteroffizier* Schalk was nowhere to be seen. I still remembered well my last unpleasant encounter with Mustangs, and as well I still owed them something for shooting at my parachute. No one knows at the start of an air battle; it is always a life and death struggle.

During the course of this engagement I had to do some hard maneuvering to reach a favorable position behind the Mustang, and it quickly became even better. The Mustang pilot probably felt the same fear I had felt when attacked in my parachute. One always makes mistakes when frightened: when he tried to escape by reversing his turn, I hit him with a burst from my guns. It was enough to send the Mustang down. I only hoped that the pilot got out of the aircraft. The battle was far from over, however, for once caught up in the whirlpool of fighter-versus-fighter combat, it naturally happens that one is passed from one combat to the other. My ammunition was soon gone, however, and it was time for me to find a way out of the fracas.

The gun camera film confirmed my two victories: one B-24 Liberator and one P-51 Mustang. The results of my subsequent bursts were uncertain. The final evaluation of this mission produced the following results:

Feldwebel Willy Reschke of the *9. Staffel* shot down a B-24 Liberator and a P-51 Mustang in the area south of Göttingen, his 17th and 18th victories.

Oberfeldwebel Hans Todt of the *8. Staffel* shot down a P-47 Thunderbolt in the same area, his 6th victory.

Unteroffizier Helmut Brenner of the *6. Staffel* shot down a B-24 Liberator in the area between Hanover and Kassel. It was his 2nd victory.

The loss report indicates that *Leutnant* Walter Tauscher of the *11. Staffel* was wounded in action over Göttingen. There is no indication that he subsequently returned to the *Staffel*. (Fw 190 A-8 "Yellow 10", WNr. 682 001).

Unteroffizier Walter Döbele of the *8. Staffel* crashed near Sachau airfield. It is not known to what degree this loss, which is actually dated the day before, was related to the mission.

There are also names of pilots which suddenly disappear at this time and do not reappear. It is most likely that these comrades were killed or wounded in action on this day – only their names appear in no loss list. Attempts to track them down have proved fruitless.

Inexplicably, Stendal airfield had not yet been hit by a single bomb. In those days the technical services worked round the clock in the three big hangars to the left and right of the control tower. The flow of replacement machines from the factories was slowing to a trickle, therefore any damage which might take an aircraft out of action had to be repaired as quickly as possible. It was due to the efforts of *Oberfeldwebel* Prell and his men that no pilot had to remain on the ground for lack of aircraft. If an engine change had to be carried out, there was no rest until the aircraft was on the test stand. The armorers under *Feldwebel* Herrcher also worked tirelessly. As soon as an aircraft landed and taxied to the dispersal, the armorers checked to see if there were any problems with the guns. If there were, the problem was seen to immediately. Most of the returning aircraft had empty magazines and the belts had to be reloaded with various types of ammunition. When a weapon was replaced, it had to be bore-sighted in the alignment stand, and no errors were permitted.

There was no doubt: the pilots could rely on their technicians. Often a pilot came out to his aircraft in the morning after a good night's sleep to find that the mechanics had been up all night. They were silent heroes who have received too little formal recognition, but who made a vital contribution to the success of the fighters.

24 December 1944

On this day the 8th Air Force launched 2,046 B-17s and B-24s from its airfields in England, escorted by 853 P-47s and P-51s. Their targets were the industrial regions of western and central Germany. The *1. Jagddivision* had just *JG 300* and *JG 301* with which to respond, as all other *Jagdgeschwader* were waiting to take part in the Ardennes offensive.

JG 301 received the takeoff order at 1405 hours, and as soon as the fighters became airborne there began a lively exchange of radio traffic between the *1. Jagddivision* in Döberitz and the formation leader, *Oberstleutnant* Auffhammer. Initially vectored northwest, the formation was subsequently turned, flying over Brunswick into the Hanover – Hildesheim area. Very soon the familiar dense condensation trails from the bombers became visible, followed by the thinner trails produced by the escort fighters. The fighters quickly turned in the direction of *JG 301* as it closed with the bombers.

JG 301's high-altitude *Staffel*, which was by now equipped with the Fw 190 D-9 "Longnose", soon reported engaging the escort fighters. As a rule, from that point on it became impossible for the formation leader to maintain tight control over his aircraft. In such situations everything depended on timely action by experienced *Staffel* or *Gruppe* leaders, for there was no fixed plan for joining such a combat, nor could there be an orderly attack on the bombers as had happened in the past.

III./JG 301, once again flying as the "Heavy *Gruppe*", battered its way through the screen of escort fighters and took up position for an attack on a formation of B-17s.

The *9. Staffel* again led the attack on the bombers. With it was *Hauptmann* Paul Quednau, *Kapitän* of the *9. Staffel*, on his second mission. Quite automatically the first attack wedge spread out and only minor course corrections were needed until each pilot had a target in his sight.

As I closed in on my B-17, it required only a brief burst of tracer from my two MG 151s to confirm my aim before opening up with the MK 108s, which would inflict the decisive strikes. The defensive fire from the bombers made it impossible to spend much time searching for the proper deflection. Once again my tracers sought out the tail gunner's position and then wandered forward slowly to the right wing root. Staring through the gunsight, I waited for the effect of the shells on the wing. It was the same as before: first the impacting shells made small black holes in the wing, then pieces of skin came off, and the inner motor began to burn, the flames rapidly increasing in intensity. While still under fire, the B-17 veered left and dropped out of formation in flames.

Soon after I broke off the attack my wingman *Unteroffizier* Schalk was at my side. There was always a lot of radio chatter during such air battles, thus there was no contact between us. Schalk may also have had radio problems, for he moved in closer and tried to tell me something using hand signals. I tried to contact him by radio again, but received no response. I signaled by hand that we would attack again and he nodded his head in acknowledgement. Several other of the *Geschwader*'s aircraft joined us in this second attack. Again shells from all my weapons struck the tail turret and then the wings and motors of the B-17, and when the second attack was over the demise of another B-17 was just a matter of time.

I had expended all my ammunition in the two firing passes, further evidence of what it took to bring down a B-17, a fact known by every pilot. My wingman Schalk was nowhere to be seen after the second attack on the B-17 formation, and as it was a good idea to avoid combat with escort fighters with empty magazines, I descended quickly and at 1540 hours landed back at Stendal.

When I shut down the motor at the *9. Staffel* dispersal, *Obergefreiter* August Napiwotzki, my crew chief, was already waiting, happy that "his" Fw 190 had come back. But his expression became rather serious when he began counting the holes in the wings and fuselage; after all, it was Christmas Eve!

Unteroffizier Schalk eventually landed his Fw 190 at Stendal, having landed somewhere else first. It turned out that his radio had been hit, making it impossible for him to communicate with me.

The pilots of *JG 301* sat together in small groups that Christmas Eve. At such times no one wanted to be alone in his room; everyone sought companionship and the closeness of comrades. Though the atmosphere was cheery, looking at the Christmas tree brought thoughts of home and of comrades who could no longer be with us.

Another excellent tradition in *III./JG 301* was that all pilots, from officers to enlisted men, spent their free time together in the officers' mess. The *Gruppe*'s pilots got together there at least once a day. There was no better opportunity to familiarize the pilots with the latest orders and information or discuss present or past events. It was there that new pilots were introduced to the entire *Gruppe*, and it was also where the aircrew gathered to remember those killed or wounded in recent missions. One who joined this circle a few days before Christmas was *Feldwebel* Rudolf Driebe, who was assigned to the *11. Staffel*.

Hauptmann Paul Quednau, *Kapitän* of the *9. Staffel*, scored his first victory during the mission on 24 December. It was Quednau who saw to it that the film was removed from gun cameras as quickly as possible and developed. We viewed them together, and there was no doubt that both B-17s attacked by *Feldwebel* Reschke had gone down. They crashed in the Hanover area at 1455 and 1503 hours. Another victory went to *Unteroffizier* August Hölscher of the *5. Staffel*, who shot down a Mustang in the same area at 1500 hours. It was his second victory.

The surviving records make no further reference to possible victories by the *Geschwader* on this day, although the American 8th Air Force admitted the loss of twenty-five four-engined bombers and twelve escort fighters.

The *Geschwader* records also contain no loss lists for the period from mid-December up to and including 24 December 1944. But the names of many pilots disappear at this very time and never return. It must therefore be assumed that they were killed or wounded.

These names, by *Staffel*, are:

9./JG 301: *Unteroffizier* Albrecht, *Feldwebel* Over and *Feldwebel* Müller. Müller had been with *I./ JG 302* at Götzendorf and joined *9./JG 301* in September 1944. He was last seen in the days before Christmas 1944 and the records contain no hint as to his subsequent fate.

10./JG 301: *Unteroffiziere* Ballwans, Bandit and Reuter and *Feldwebel* Schnier and Teubner.

11./JG 301: *Oberfähnrich* Fähnrich and *Unteroffiziere* Moneta, Richter and Heinz Warnicke.

12./JG 301: *Unteroffizier* Walter Kugler. Kugler was a native of Vienna and had been a member of *I./JG 302* at Götzendorf. He was a very experienced pilot and had done well with the high-altitude *Staffel*.

Unteroffizier Walter Scheller of the same *Staffel* likewise failed to return from a mission at some time and his fate remains a mystery. He was one of the *Unteroffizier* trio of Prawitz, Greiner and Scheller. None of the three had ever been seen alone, but now Scheller was gone. The other two survived the war.

The fates of *Feldwebel* Beck and *Unteroffiziere* Fellner, Friedrich and Schendera are also unknown.

After several days of rest, on 29 December *JG 301* took off on what was subsequently recorded as a "Practice Mission". It is not certain whether the entire *Geschwader* took part, but at 1250 hours *III./JG 301*, at least, was ordered to take off. For more than eighty minutes it was vectored back and forth between Salzwedel and Erfurt without engaging the enemy. The *Gruppe* then returned to Stendal. While on approach to land, *Oberfähnrich* Siegfried Aschendorf crashed to his death near Aschendorf (Fw 190 A-8 "White 10", WNr. 176 167).

Aschendorf was in radio contact with the airfield moments before his crash, the cause of which remains a mystery. Approaching the airfield from the west, at about 500 meters from the landing surface one had to cross a railway embankment, and this was his undoing. Exactly why the crash occurred is not known, however. Aschendorf was an experienced pilot and had joined *I./JG 302* at

Unteroffizier Walter Scheller of 4./JG 302. He was last attached to 12./JG 301 and was killed during a mission at the turn of the year 1944-45. The exact date of his death and where he was lost are not known.

Götzendorf on 20 June 1944. Wounded on 30 June, he had rejoined the *Gruppe* after a brief stay in hospital. He flew on every mission until his death.

31 December 1944

There was an excited mood among the pilots as they breakfasted together in the mess. No one expected a mission on the last day of the year 1944, and everyone had his own plans for the year's last few hours.

There were only a few hours left in the 1944, but in those final hours *JG 301* took part in a mission that took the *Geschwader* to the Hamburg – Bremen area, almost to the North Sea coast.

1,315 B-17 Flying Fortress and B-24 Liberator bombers had taken off to attack targets in Mainz, Kaiserslautern and Kassel. The bombers were accompanied by 785 American escort fighters, P-51 Mustangs and P-47 Thunderbolts. The *Geschwader* was ordered into the air at 1050 hours, and immediately after taking off the fighters were vectored northwest toward the German Bight. The *Gruppen* subsequently rendezvoused in the area north of Gardelegen-Salzwedel.

From its bases south of Berlin, *JG 300* took off at almost the same time and was vectored toward the northwest. The fighter control center stated that the "Fat Autos" were over the German Bight, allowing the conclusion to be drawn that contact would be made over northern Germany – an area where *JG 301* had never seen action. The number of fighters in the battle formation was visibly reduced: the most recent air battles had left their mark. The formation did, however, have a relatively strong high-altitude *Staffel*. The Fw 190 D-9s flew above and in front of the main force.

While the interceptors were still far from the bombers, the first condensation trails from the escort fighters turned toward them. Flying mainly in pairs, they flew past the fighter formation at a slightly higher altitude and gave no indication that they were about to attack. For me, the first surprise had come immediately after takeoff: I switched on the gunsight, but there was no reflected light on the windscreen. I never considered turning back, for I did have a backup sight. It was mounted somewhat lower, forcing me to duck my head to take aim.

Contact with the enemy was made in grid square DU-CU, and the *Geschwader* headed straight for the front of the bomber formation, which consisted of B-24 Liberators. The enemy apparently was not expecting such an early attack, for while most of the escort fighters could be seen approaching, they had not yet reached the front of the bomber formation. We began our attack from a right turn with a height superiority of about 600 meters. As a result, the aircraft of the first wedge attacked at a relatively sharp angle. Estimating the deflection using my backup gunsight, my tracers were slightly in front of the Liberator, but with the help of the tracer this was easily corrected. With the Liberator closing rapidly and becoming ever larger, I no longer needed the backup sight and relied solely on the tracer. As soon as the MK 108 rounds struck the wing and fuselage, the bomber's fate was sealed. One could not help but be impressed by the effect of these rounds every time, something confirmed by subsequent evaluation of the gun camera film. I broke off my attack and for a few seconds flew alongside the formation. From there I observed the aircraft breaking up in the air. Those few seconds were almost the end of me, however: from the center of the formation I saw a bright spot coming toward my machine, and a feeling of forewarning said that the direction was

Sachau, December 1944. A Fw 190 D-9 of 6./JG 301 with the name "Glykol" on the engine cowling.

right. Immediately afterwards something hit my cockpit hard, and almost automatically I rolled my Fw 190 over and dove away. Looking back, I saw entry and exit holes in my canopy, right behind my head.

By this time the escort fighters had reached the combat zone, but for several of the Liberators they were too late. The first Mustangs were intercepted by the Fw 190 D-9 pilots of *II./JG 301*. As so often happened, however, whenever the escort fighters appeared, they came in such numbers that the few German high-altitude fighters were simply overwhelmed. In most cases the Fw 190 pilots became the hunted and desperately tried to escape the pursuing pack. Oh to have been a fighter pilot when the odds were still even! The pilots of *JG 301* never experienced that – they had always been seriously outnumbered. These men knew no other kind of combat, and it had always been extremely difficult for them to hold their own.

The arrival of the escort fighters caused the air battle to become spread out, and the heavy bombers were able to reach their targets – the refineries in Harburg and the hydrogenation plant in Miesburg – with little interference. *JG 300* had joined the air battle at almost the same time. Somewhat farther south, near Rotenburg, *II./JG 300* came upon a formation of B-17s and attacked it with success. The fighters were then heavily engaged by P-51 Mustangs, but the high-altitude fighters of *III./JG 300* intervened and shot down four. *Gruppenkommandeur Major* Kamp was killed in this action. This was the second grievous loss suffered by *JG 300* in two days, for on 24 December 1944 *Oberleutnant* Bretschneider, leader of the *Sturmgruppe*, had failed to return.

After being hit in the canopy, I descended my shot-up machine, but even at that altitude the fighter-versus-fighter battle was still raging and I was drawn in again. These were anxious moments for me, for without a reflector sight I was as good as blind, and the strange howling sound behind my head made the situation even more uncomfortable. The Mustangs had by now been joined by Thunderbolts, and I devoted all my efforts to keeping my tail clear and escaping this witch's cauldron at a suitable moment. I fired my guns repeatedly, but more to calm myself down, for without a reflector sight I could do little. I finally withdrew from the air battle and landed at Lüneburg at 1210 hours.

While the aircraft was being refueled I discovered that in addition to the hole in my canopy, there were others in the wing and fuselage. I was extremely fortunate that the Americans were not using our ammunition. The bullet that hit the canopy had missed my head by inches.

At 1250 hours I took from Lüneburg, but because of P-47 fighter-bombers in the area I was unable to fly directly to Stendal. When I did land at Stendal, I of course wanted my crew chief, *Unteroffizier* August Napiwotzki, to explain to me why the reflector sight had failed. His face became flushed. Then he walked to the hangar, and when he returned he had the gunsight bulb in his hand. During his morning checks the bulb in his flashlight had burned out, and since another was not immediately available, he had taken the bulb from the reflector sight. He then forgot to replace it. More than anything, he probably felt like crawling off into a hole somewhere, and when he saw my shot-up canopy he turned white as a sheet. He slept little the following night, for, even though it was New Year's Eve, by next morning my Fw 190 A-8 "White 8" was completely serviceable again and all of the holes had been patched. I truly had an outstanding crew chief!

Although the American 8th Air Force admitted the loss of twenty-seven four-engined bombers and eleven escort fighters in this battle, *JG 301*'s records claim just three victories. On the other hand, there are photographs from that time showing pilots with the Iron Cross, First Class whose names appear in no victory list. They were mainly younger pilots who had been transferred to the *Geschwader* during its rest period. The *Geschwader*'s victory and loss records are obviously incomplete. Exactly why remains a mystery to this day.

Successes by *JG 301* on 31 December 1944

Feldwebel Rudolf Driebe of the *11. Staffel* shot down a P-51 Mustang south of Hamburg, his 1st victory.

Oberfeldwebel Josef Keil of the *10. Staffel* also shot down a Mustang in the same area, his 3rd victory.

Feldwebel Willi Reschke of the *9. Staffel* shot down a Liberator northeast of Rotenburg at 1135 hours. It was his 21st victory.

Losses by *JG 301* on 31 December 1944:

I./JG 301, 2. Staffel:
Führer Ulrich Leopold was wounded in combat with Mustangs and forced to abandon his aircraft near Celle (Fw 190 A-9, WNr. 205 963).

Gefreiter Lothar Sattler was forced to abandon his aircraft during the air battle, reason unknown. Two days later his body was found by a farmer on the Pietz Moor, southeast of Schneverdingen. Sattler was sitting on his parachute, leaning against a tree. He was buried in Schneverdingen. (Fw 190 A-9, WNr. 206 163).

4. Staffel:
Unteroffizier Manfred Hillert was wounded in combat with escort fighters. He bailed out successfully and came down near Rotenburg (Fw 190 A-9, WNr. 202 428).

II./JG 301:
Gruppenkommandeur and Knight's Cross wearer *Hauptmann* Herbert Nölter was wounded in combat with Mustangs south of Hamburg. He also abandoned his aircraft and after a brief stay in hospital returned to action at the head of his *Jagdgruppe* (Fw 190 D-9, WNr. 210 916).

5. Staffel:
Staffelkapitän Oberleutnant Helmut Ostendorp went down with his Fw 190 near Jävenitz. The crash may have been the result of a collision (Fw 190 A-9 "White 9", WNr. 206 097). Ostendorp was buried in the Gardelegen military cemetery (Grave No. 54).

Leutnant Karl Kapril was overwhelmed by the Mustangs and shot down. His Fw 190 struck the ground at a shallow angle on the outskirts of Kalbe and he was thrown from the aircraft. The engine flew another 100 meters and buried itself in the ground. Kapril was buried in Stade. (Fw 190 A-9 "White 4", WNr. 205 914).

Gefreiter Wenzel Marschik was shot down and killed near Rotenburg (Fw 190 A-9 "White 1", WNr. 206 167).

Feldwebel Rudi Driebe in the cockpit of his Fw 190 A-8 at Stendal in late 1944.

6. *Staffel*:

While flying with the high-altitude *Staffel*, *Unteroffizier* Alfred Heindl was shot down by Mustangs near Lüneburg (Fw 190 D-9 "Red 12", WNr. 210 914). He was buried in Military Cemetery II in Lüneburg (Row 2, Grave 53).

Oberfeldwebel Otto Wallner was also a member of the high-altitude *Staffel*. Pursued by several Mustangs, he was unable to escape. He and his aircraft came down near the village of Scharnebeck (Fw 190 D-9 "Red 6", WNr. 210 906). He was buried in Military Cemetery II in Lüneburg (Row 2, Grave 4).

8. *Staffel*:

Unteroffizier Ottmar Christoph was shot down and killed south of Braten (Fw 190 D-9 "Red 2", WNr. 210 902). He was buried in Military Cemetery II in Lüneburg (Row 2, Grave 52).

Unteroffizier Erich Leeb was wounded in combat and bailed out near the village of Eichholz (Fw 190 A-9 "Blue 6", WNr. 205 060).

III. Gruppe:

The *III. Gruppe* suffered the heaviest losses, as a result of its attack on the Liberator bombers and subsequent combat with escort fighters.

9. Staffel:

The unit lost its *Staffelkapitän, Hauptmann* Paul Quednau. He had only been transferred to the *Staffel* in December and shot down his first heavy bomber on 24 December. Quednau was in the first wedge during the attack on the Liberator formation and was wounded by return fire. He subsequently broke off the attack and headed for Fassberg air base. It would appear that, his strength failing, he was unable to reach the runway and instead made a forced landing just short of the airfield boundary. Several other of the *Gruppe*'s pilots observed this while waiting to land, and after reaching the ground rushed to the scene. They found a Fw 190 that had made a perfect belly landing, but *Hauptmann* Quednau was dead, the stick still grasped firmly in his hand. (Fw 190 A-8 "White 14", WNr. 176 096).

Unteroffizier Johann Fröhler, who had been transferred to the *Gruppe* at Alperstedt in September 1944, was shot down by defensive fire during the first pass on the Liberator formation. The wreckage of Fröhler's aircraft was found in the Sellhorner Forest near Behringen. He had been thrown from the aircraft (Fw 190 A-8 "White 4", WNr. 682 030). Fröhler's parachute was found in 1982, charred but still in original condition, just beneath the surface of the forest floor. He is buried in Schneverdingen cemetery.

10. Staffel:

Leutnant Max Müller was shot down by Mustangs over Stade. He had also joined the *Gruppe* at Alperstedt. Müller was a combat veteran, having previously served in a *Zerstörer* unit based on the Channel coast. He crashed just a few hundred meters from where *Leutnant* Kapril had come down. It would seem that his aircraft broke up in the air, for witnesses stated that the wreckage was scattered over a wide area. (Fw 190 A-8 "Red 4", WNr. 175 948). He is buried in Stade.

Fahnenjunker-Feldwebel Hans Penzin arrived from a flying school in September 1944, joining the *Gruppe* at Alperstedt. He survived his first few missions without difficulty. On this day he was wounded over Rotenburg. He did not return to the *Staffel*. (Fw 190 A-8 "Red 3", WNr. 175 960).

Oberleutnant Hermann Stahl, acting *Staffel* commander, was wounded in combat over Rotenburg. He spent a brief period in hospital but did not return to the *Gruppe*. (Fw 190 A-8 "Red 19", WNr. 176 058).

According to eyewitnesses, *Oberfähnrich* Arthur Schindehütte was pursued by three American fighters but for a considerable time held them off with skillful flying. The combat, which had begun at a height of 3000 meters, gradually moved lower. Over Bispingen his Fw 190 was hit and lost a wing. It went straight down and hit the ground in a field near the present-day autobahn. He was buried in Schneverdingen cemetery.

11. Staffel:

Unteroffizier Rolf Burghardt was killed in action near Tessin east of Rostock after his aircraft was hit by defensive fire from the Liberator formation. (Fw 190 A-8 "Yellow 6", WNr. 176 095).

Feldwebel Heinrich Dörr was killed near Tessin. After making a firing pass at the Liberator formation, he was himself attacked and shot down by Mustangs. Dörr came from *I./JG 302* and at the time of his death had six victories to his credit. (Fw 190 A-8 "Black 18", WNr. 682 009).

Feldwebel Ernst Otto, who had only been transferred to the *Staffel* at Stendal in December, was shot down and killed near Düssin. (Fw 190 A-8 "Yellow 4", WNr. 172 357).

Feldwebel Karl Rienth did not survive combat with the escort fighters and was shot down near Boitzenburg. (Fw 190 A-8 "Yellow 7", WNr. 175 917).

12. Staffel:

Unteroffizier Franz Schrack was wounded in combat over Lüneburg and after a brief hospital stay returned to the *Staffel*. (Fw 190 A-8 "Black 4", WNr. 682 027).

JG 301's *9. Staffel* was once again without a commanding officer, and again *Leutnant* Reinicke stepped in to lead the *Staffel*. His command lasted but a few hours, however, for in the first few hours of the new year the new *Staffelkapitän* arrived. His name was *Hauptmann* Gerhard Posselmann.

Hauptmann Heinrich Wurzer, who had assumed command of the *Gruppe* following *Hauptmann* Fulda's transfer, was assigned to other duties. His place as *Gruppenkommandeur* was taken by *Major* Guth.

Of course New Year's Eve 1944 gave little cause for celebration, and the mess filled up very late on this evening. Those pilots who had survived the air battle earlier in the day landed at other airfields, spent the first part of the evening with the technical personnel there. For some unknown reason a ban had been imposed on alcohol for the night. For most this was an inexplicable measure, for no one in the mess yet knew that "Operation Bodenplatte" was to begin the following morning. Most of the activity on this night centered around the three billiard tables in the anteroom. Those waiting to play stood by and gave advice, the others sat in small groups at the tables and relived the day's fighting. Some had ceased to believe in the oft-promised light on the horizon. The situation had deteriorated on every front, but no one wanted to think about the possibility of defeat. Many sat lost in thought, weighing their chances of survival – the odds they faced were becoming greater every day.

A little more than a year had passed since the formation of *JG 301*, and if one looked closely at the names of the pilots in the various *Staffeln* only a very few would be found who had been present when the *Geschwader* was formed and lived through the period of the single-engined night-fighters. Of these few, there was probably no one who had come through completely unscathed: everyone had suffered injuries or wounds in combat. And yet, in every *Staffel* there was a hard core of "Old Hares". This fact confirmed the general view that surviving the first few missions and combats increased one's chances of survival.

In late December 1944 rumors spread that a *IV./JG 301* was to be formed at Gardelegen. In reality, this process had been underway since 15 October 1944, using mainly personnel from the disbanded *III./KG 51 "Hindenburg"*. The bomber unit had been based at Fassberg, where it flew the He 177. In October 1944 the unit's ground personnel were given training on how to maintain the Bf 109 at Schönwalde air base, while at the same time the *Gruppe*'s pilots learned to fly the Bf 109 G-10 at Wittstock. During this period the *Gruppe* was renamed *II./JG 77*, but then in November 1944 it received its ultimate designation, *IV./JG 301*.

Gruppenkommandeur of *IV./JG 301* was *Hauptmann* Wilfried Schmitz, and the *Gruppe* consisted of three *Staffeln*:

13. Staffel: *Staffelkapitän Oberleutnant* Johann Patek,
14. Staffel: *Staffelkapitän Leutnant* Günter Förster,
15. Staffel: *Staffelkapitän Oberleutnant* Otto Schöppler.

The *Gruppe* flew its first missions as part of *JG 301* in February 1945.

1 January 1945

1945 was only a few hours old, but on the very first day of the year *JG 301*'s familiar routine began anew: 850 B-17 and B-24 bombers had taken off from bases in England to attack Magdeburg, Kassel and Coblenz. With them was an escort of 725 P-47 Thunderbolts and P-51 Mustangs.

The badly-battered *Jagdgeschwader 301* received the takeoff order at about 1100 hours, and the first Fw 190s of *III./JG 301* lifted off from their airfield at 1102. This mission was unusual in that the three *Gruppen* did not see action together; instead, each attacked the bombers more or less on its own. *I./JG 301*, which had received the mission order somewhat earlier than the others, was engaged east of Salzwedel airfield while still climbing to altitude.

III./JG 301, which took off from Stendal, assembled over its airfield. As the unit's fighters climbed, the fighter controller repeatedly requested them to climb faster and instructed them to head west.

This was an indication that the bombers attacking Magdeburg had almost reached the fighters' location. *III./JG 301* had just reached a height of 7,500 meters when the first condensation trails were sighted in the west.

II./JG 301, which had taken off from Sachau at the same time, also had to struggle to reach altitude. Those *Staffeln* equipped with the Fw 190 D-9 reached altitude faster and were already above the main formation. The two *Jagdgruppe* had established a loose contact when through our headphones we heard: "Jettison external tanks – attack now!"

The consequences of this order must have produced fear among the civilians at times, for the drop tanks were sometimes mistaken for bombs, causing those on the ground to believe that an air raid was imminent.

Leading the incoming bombers were smaller formations of B-17s with, for that time, an astonishingly small number of escort fighters. Our high-altitude *Staffeln* were now equipped exclusively with the Fw 190 D-9, which caused the American escort fighters some problems. As a result, their attacks on the rest of the formation were rather tentative, especially as their numerical superiority was not all that great.

The attack wedge formed quickly, without serious interference from the escort fighters. The first wave was already firing into the bombers at the rear of the formation as the last wave rolled in to attack. Our targets were B-17s which, as is well known, could absorb a great deal of punishment. The hail of bullets I directed at my B-17 must have been on target from the very start, however, because it was burning fiercely even before I completed my attack. I could scarcely believe what I was seeing: in all my attacks on four-engined bombers I had never seen one burn so quickly. The fire spread rapidly and the B-17 was soon one big fireball. I wanted to get a close-up look at the burning bomber, and without thinking I flew past its left side, very close. The entire aircraft was a blazing torch and it could only be seconds before it went down. The only areas untouched by the fire

This photograph was allegedly shot from an American bomber over Gardelegen on 1 January 1945. It shows a German pilot bailing out of his burning aircraft. Willi Reschke of 9./JG 301 abandoned his burning Fw 190 A-8 over Gardelegen on 1 January 1945.

were the so-called "Cheese-Dish Cover" (dorsal turret) and part of the fuselage. Most crews in similar situations would have already abandoned their aircraft, but suddenly a burst of fire came from the part of the B-17 still untouched by fire and struck the engine of my Fw 190 A-8. Seconds later it, too, was in flames. I was later told by those in the command post on the airfield that I had transmitted: "Aircraft on fire! Bailing out! Do you understand?" I must have done that subconsciously, for I certainly didn't wait around for an answer to my question.

There was only one thing to do: get out of the aircraft as quickly as possible. I undid my straps, tore off my oxygen mask, disconnected the radio leads to my helmet, jettisoned the canopy, pushed the stick forward and out I went.

As the feeling of leaving the machine was not new to me, I decided to stretch out my arms and legs and let myself fall to a height of 4,000 meters before opening my parachute. Memories of my last parachute jump had come flooding back, and on this day too the American fighters were especially active at my altitude. But something was different this time, for after a short while I became sick, and my hand reached for the ripcord much sooner than I had hoped. After the chute opened everything on me felt like lead, and soon afterwards I threw up while hanging in my parachute.

At first I could not find an explanation for it, but after a while I felt a little better and decided to try and find out what was making the strange sound. I looked up and saw what was wrong: my parachute had opened alright, but two of the panels were torn, causing me to come down lopsided and producing the strange sound.

What had happened? After thinking about it, I could only come up with one explanation: it was the first time I had jumped from a Fw 190, and the fin of a Fw 190 was taller than that of the Bf 109.

As a result, I had probably hadn't applied enough forward pressure on the stick when I bailed out, causing me to leave the machine at too shallow an angle. My parachute had then struck the fin, damaging it. In the Fw 190 the pilot wore a back parachute, whereas in the Bf 109 he wore a seat pack. Because the parachute was on my back, it softened the impact with the fin. If this had happened when wearing a seat parachute, the consequences would likely have been much worse. As I was still above 4,000 meters, I had sufficient time to observe the area below me. I was floating above a huge forested area, and not all that far away I could see Gardelegen and the airfield. It was already quite obvious to me that I would be coming down somewhere in this wooded area. I had never landed in a forest before, and with my increased rate of descent on account of my damaged parachute, I had concerns about my safety. But perhaps the forest might also be my salvation.

The treetops approached quickly, and when they were right beneath me I raised my arms to cover my face. Then I dropped into the branches. I waited for a hard landing, but it never came. I did feel solid ground beneath my feet, however, and when I lowered my arms I saw that though I was still hanging in my parachute my feet were touching the ground. Above me was a huge tree, and my torn parachute was hanging in it. It was probably thanks to this tree that I was still alive: at the last moment it had slowed my excessive descent rate.

From above I had seen a forest road not far away, and without recovering my parachute I began walking in that direction. My progress was slow, for I now became aware of pain in my back and hip. It turned out that it was only a few hundred meters to the road, and while I was trying to decide which way to go, I heard the sound of an automobile engine. Before long I saw a Volkswagen *Kübel* (utility vehicle) coming my way. The occupants, a *Feldwebel* and an *Unteroffizier*, both members of the *Luftwaffe*, eyed me somewhat critically. The *Feldwebel* asked it I had just come down by parachute, and I replied that I had. Their looks became even more skeptical: they probably couldn't imagine that someone could land safely there. Together we walked the short distance back to my parachute, and the two saw it hanging high in the tree. The men then told me that they had watched the air battle from Gardelegen airfield, and on seeing the partially opened parachute they had immediately set off toward it. Both then insisted on recovering my parachute from the top of the tree.

I returned to Stendal the same day, and my first stop was to see medical officer Czaja. His examination revealed severe bruising on my hip and back beneath the shoulder blades.

The plate of the back parachute had taken the brunt of the impact with the fin and had distributed the force over my entire back. If I had made a similar bail-out from a Bf 109, it could have cut me in two!

I was a little sad over the loss of my Fw 190 A-8 "White 6" and with it the gun camera. I would have liked to see the film of that victory: perhaps I could have discovered by whom I was shot down.

JG 301's attack on the bombers on 1 January 1945 took place over the Colbitz-Letzlinger Heath, just a few kilometers south of the *Geschwader's* bases. *I./JG 301*, which took off from Salzwedel, did not get through to the bombers, as it was intercepted by escort fighters while still climbing. It became involved in a dogfight with P-47s and P-51s, but suffered only minor losses.

The *I. Gruppe's* early air battle cleared the way for the *II.* and *III. Gruppe* to attack the bombers bound for Magdeburg. Although the first attack was made without interference from enemy fighters, it was not as successful as it might have been. Heavy bomber specialists were in short supply in both *Jagdgruppen*, and the bloodletting within the fighter arm was not over.

On this day *Oberfeldwebel* Josef Keil of *10./JG 301* shot down two B-17s in the airspace south of Gardelegen and Stendal, his 5th and 6th victories.

Feldwebel Willi Reschke of *9./JG 301* shot down a B-17 southeast of Gardelegen at 1200 hours, however he was subsequently forced to abandon his crippled machine. It was his 22nd victory.

Oberfeldwebel Hans Todt of *8./JG 301* shot down another B-17 in the same area, recording his 7th victory.

Compared to those of previous air battles, losses on this occasion were bearable, but as few replacements were being received, every pilot lost meant a reduction in operational strength.

I./JG 301, 2. Staffel:

Unteroffizier Heinz Nicolaus was wounded in combat with P-51s south of his airfield. He attempted to reach Salzwedel air base, but was obliged to make a forced landing just short of the airfield. (Fw 190 A-9, WNr. 205 969)

4. Staffel:

Unteroffizier Benno Berkler was shot down and crashed with his machine southwest of Stendal (Fw 190 A-9, WNr. 202 170).

Leutnant Otto Frank did not return from this mission. He was shot down and killed by escort fighters near the town of Groß-Schwarzlosen southwest of Stendal (Fw 190 A-9, WNr. 205 908). He is buried in Stendal cemetery.

II./JG 301, 8. Staffel:

Fahnenjunker-Oberfeldwebel Georg Schöneich went down with his machine near the village of Belkau northwest of Stendal following aerial combat (Fw 190 A-9 "Blue 2", WNr. 205 966).

III./JG 301, 9. Staffel:

Leutnant Leonhard Reinicke, in temporary command of the *Staffel*, was wounded while attacking B-17s and tried to reach Stendal airfield. His strength ran out just short of the airfield, and while attempting a forced landing his machine grazed the roof of a barn. Nothing is known of Reinicke's subsequent fate. He did not return to the *Gruppe* and a postwar investigation revealed nothing. (Fw 190 A-8 "White 5", WNr. 172 346)

Feldwebel Willi Reschke was forced to abandon his crippled and burning aircraft after attacking a formation of B-17s. He came down in the Colbitz-Letzlinger Heath. (Fw 190 A-8, "White 6")

10. Staffel:

Feldwebel Kurt Born was wounded in action and had to force-land his aircraft near Stendal. Born did not return to the *Gruppe*. (Fw 190 A-8 "Red 1", WNr. 175 958)

11. Staffel:

Feldwebel Friedrich Winter's aircraft was badly damaged by enemy fire during an attack on a formation of B-17s and he was wounded. Winter made a forced landing south of Stendal. His wounds proved to be serious and he was left permanently disabled. (Fw 190 A-8 "White 11", WNr. 175 912)

12. Staffel:

Feldwebel Heinrich Wißmann was also wounded in combat and failed to reach Stendal airfield. His subsequent fate is not known. (Fw 190 A-8 "Black 12", WNr. 682 031)

The rumor mill was again hard at work in the first days of January, and fanfares of orders and counter-orders flew in all directions. Reports of a transfer to the Eastern Front proved untrue, but the rumor that *III./JG 301* was to convert to the fast Ta 152, a development of the Fw 190 with a liquid-cooled engine, proved to be more factual. Little could be learned at the mission debriefings, which were usually held in the mess immediately after landing, even from command officers. It was becoming increasingly clear that the clear-cut policy in the command of fighter units, to which we had become accustomed, no longer existed.

This was due in large part to Commander-in-Chief of the *Luftwaffe* Hermann Göring's performance before the commanders of the *Luftwaffe*'s fighter *Gruppen* and *Geschwader*. Although it was always toned down by superiors, his declaration that the fighters had not achieved the desired success and that he was of a mind to replace them with the flak eventually filtered down to the pilots in the fighter units. These pilots already had reason enough to doubt the command decisions made by the *Luftwaffe*. Nevertheless, they continued to climb into their aircraft, engage an enemy whose numerical superiority was growing steadily, and – all too often – pay with their lives. The fighter pilots in the Defense of the Reich never experienced the feeling of superiority that existed in the west at the beginning of the war and later over the Eastern Front. They always had to fight against crushing numerical superiority and prove their courage each and every day. Young, inexperienced and often lacking the necessary training, they were thrown into the hellfire of these air battles – but they never gave up or resigned themselves. Only a few of these men survived the end of the war, and only a few know the names of those who sacrificed their lives.

The *Geschwader*'s airfields had still been spared bombing attacks, even though the bombers frequently passed overhead en route to Berlin. But such an attack might come at any hour, and therefore on 4 January 1945 *JG 301* was moved into the area north of Dresden. *IV./JG 301*, which was still in the formation process at Gardelegen and not yet committed to combat, was unaffected.

The *Geschwaderstab* and *II./JG 301* moved to Welzow, *I./JG 301* to Finsterwalde and *III./JG 301* to Alteno near Luckau. *III./JG 301*'s transfer from Stendal to Alteno was carried out one *Staffel* at a time, something unique in the history of the *Geschwader*. The *9. Staffel* took off from Stendal at 1044 hours and landed at Alteno at 1125.

The facilities at Alteno were similar to those at Alperstedt. The few barracks were surrounded by blast walls, and the technical personnel had just one small hangar in which to carry out repairs. The dispersals for the individual *Staffeln* were located on the east, south and west sides of the airfield and bordered a wood. As there were only enough barracks for the ground personnel, the pilots were billeted in the Park Hotel in Luckau; and because the airfield was several kilometers away, a vehicle was provided to transport the pilots mornings and evenings.

With the move to Alteno, the rumors about *III./JG 301*'s conversion to the Ta 152 intensified from day to day, only no one could really imagine where these machines might come from. At first, though, we continued flying the Fw 190 A-8, and even carried out practice missions with new pilots, something that should have been done earlier. Most were flown in pairs, although some *Schwarm*-strength sorties were also carried out.

On 7 January 1945 I went on one such training sortie with *Oberfähnrich* Karl Hänsel. We couldn't believe our eyes when we ran into three P-38 Lightnings east of Herzberg. We knew this type of escort fighter well from our days in Austria, but had not yet them encountered them in the Berlin area. There followed a brief dogfight and I hit one of the P-38s with a burst from my guns. The enemy fighter dove away immediately and disappeared. As the other P-38s were still in front of us, we were unable to pursue the machine I had fired at. Actually this ended the engagement, for all we could do from that point was admire the P-38's rate of climb. We simply couldn't keep up in our Fw 190 A-8s, but we also had no great interest in doing so.

During one of these practice missions on 13 January 1945, *Leutnant* Karl Strohmeier of the *8. Staffel* was killed in a landing accident at Welzow. He was flying Fw 190 A-9 "Blue 10", WNr. 207 171.

14 January 1945

The *Gruppe* had flown no combat missions since moving into the area southeast of Berlin. The orders that reached the *Gruppen* in those days gave rise to suspicions that new tasks lay ahead of the

IV./JG 301 at Gardelegen in the spring of 1945. Second from the left in the first row is Unteroffizier Fritz Kolb, while fourth from the left is Oberfeldwebel Tiedke.

Geschwader. These suspicions were quickly put to rest, however, when the *Geschwader* was placed on combat alert late on the morning of 14 January. The order to take off came at 1150 hours and the target was not announced until the units were airborne.

Incoming were 911 B-17s and B-24s of the American 8th Air Force, screened by 860 P-47 and P-51 escort fighters. Their targets were industrial districts in northern and western Germany and a fuel dump at Derben-Ferchland. Ground control fed us a steady stream of position reports on the bombers and their escorts.

On this occasion the formation was given few course changes after forming up, and we flew past Berlin on a northwest heading. Because of the distance to the target, the *Geschwader* should have had plenty of time to reach the assigned altitude of 8,000 meters, but climbing in formation takes longer, and the Fw 190 A-8's rate of climb dropped off badly above 6,000 meters. As a result, we were still climbing when we reached the operational area. The visibility was good on that January day, and both sides could see the other long before battle was joined. As *JG 301* approached the airspace east of Rathenow, a large force of Mustangs came toward our fighters on a reciprocal heading, though the enemy had a height advantage of 500 meters. The two groups of fighters met in grid square EF. Only the fighter control centers in Treuenbrietzen or Döberitz could know if this encounter was avoidable. But with *JG 301*'s formation at a height disadvantage, the inevitable happened.

On this day the majority of *JG 301*'s pilots only saw the bombers from far away, for the Mustangs dove on our formation like a swarm of hornets. Leading the "Heavy *Gruppe*" was *Oberleutnant* Herzog, whose flight was ahead and to the left of mine. He was the first victim of the Mustang attack. His aircraft was only about fifty meters from mine, and I saw it shake as it was struck by a burst of fire and then fall away steeply. The same thing happened to many of *JG 301*'s aircraft, and we had to overcome this initial, paralyzing shock. For many pilots this meant the end of the mission, or even the end forever.

The Mustang that had fired the burst into *Oberleutnant* Herzog's machine was able to use its high speed to climb up in front of our aircraft, but in doing so it gave me the opportunity to fire a burst at it with my two MG 151 (20mm) cannon. The tracers flashing past the Mustang must have had an effect, for it rolled to the left and dove away. This maneuver helped me, for I was able to pick up speed I did not have before. Ignoring everything happening around me, I set off after the Mustang and took advantage of each maneuver to close the range. The pilot of the Mustang was also aware that the man in the Fw 190 behind him had the advantage and could choose the shorter path in every flight maneuver. He tried every trick in the book to shake me, but I stayed with him and continued to close the range. It was a bitter struggle between two pilots, each trying to improve his position. The battle was fought out to the bitter end as if we were completely alone in the sky. When the Mustang pulled up into a left turn I hit it with a burst and the P-51 shook exactly as *Oberleutnant* Herzog's Fw 190 had done a short time before. This pilot would have no chance to file his victory claim.

Only then did I again check my surroundings, with the first look to the rear as always. There was no sign of my wingman, but everywhere fighters twisted and turned. It was impossible to tell whether they were friend or foe. I used every halfway good opportunity to fire bursts at P-51s in threatening positions behind my own comrades and force them to break off. I also repeatedly found myself in threatening positions and had to look after my own safety. In the course of the air battle I lost a great deal of altitude. Below me I could see pillars of smoke rising from the ground – friend or foe I could not tell – an indication of the battle's ferocity.

I had made up my mind to extricate myself from the air battle and find a place to land, but then I was drawn into combat again. While in a right turn I ran into two P-47 Thunderbolts. I had not seen this type in the battle higher up, but their offensive intentions were obvious. At a height of 2,000 meters my Fw 190 clearly turned better, and I quickly got behind the two Thunderbolts and put a burst into one of them. Pouring smoke, it quickly left the combat area. The second Thunderbolt seemed more interested in heading west than continuing the battle. At 1315 hours I landed at Königsberg-Neumark airfield, east of the combat zone. It was there, almost exactly four years before, that I had made my first contact with the *Luftwaffe* as a raw recruit.

For several reasons, 14 January 1945 was a day of fighting unique in the history of this *Jagdgeschwader* in the Defense of the Reich. On the one hand, only a few aircraft were able to carry out the unit's primary mission, to attack the heavy bombers, and on the other the *Geschwader* was vectored straight into the American fighters, which also enjoyed a height advantage. This air battle in the airspace north of Berlin went down as one of the costliest in the history of the *Geschwader*.

The successes achieved were out of all proportion to the losses suffered: *Hauptmann* Helmut Suhr, *Kapitän* of the *8. Staffel*, shot down a B-17 over Mecklenburg, his 9th victory.

Fähnrich Schäfer of the *4. Staffel* was flying one of his first missions on this day and shot down a Boeing in the same area for his 1st victory.

Feldwebel Willi Reschke of the *9. Staffel* shot down a P-51 Mustang at 1245 hours and a P-47 over Kyritz at 1255 hours, his 23rd and 24th victories.

JG 301's casualties on 14 January 1945:

Geschwaderstab:

Unteroffizier Albert Hoffmann was shot down and killed by Mustangs near Strohdeme an der Havel (Fw 190 D-9 "Black 2", WNr. 210 276).

I./JG 301, 1. Staffel:

Hauptmann Wolfgang Hankamer, Knight's Cross wearer and *Staffelkapitän*, was shot down in a fierce battle with Mustangs east of Kyritz (Fw 190 A-9 "White 1", WNr. 206 198). Hankamer had come from *KG 2*, having seen action in the Balkans, Russia and over England. He had received the Knight's Cross on 29 October 1944 after 264 combat missions, 157 of them over England. Transferred to fighters during the disbandment of the bomber force, he had become *Staffelkapitän* of *1./JG 301* on 9 November 1944.

2. Staffel:

Gefreiter Reinhard Kleinstück was wounded in combat with P-51s, but was able to parachute to safety near Kyritz (Fw 190 A-9, WNr. 206 154).

Oberfeldwebel Hans Schäfer was forced to abandon his Fw 190 over Kyritz and came down by parachute. After treatment of his wounds he returned to the *Staffel*. (Fw 190 A-9, WNr. 206 185)

Unteroffizier Willi Schmidt was shot down in flames. Wounded, he came down by parachute near Breddin. Schmidt returned to action a short time later. (Fw 190 A-9, WNr. 205 906).

Feldwebel Otto Sturm was pursued by several Mustangs and finally shot down and killed over Barenthin west of Kyritz (Fw 190 A-9, WNr. 205 068).

3. *Staffel*:

Fähnrich Wilfried Hacheney was wounded in combat and forced to bail out. He landed safely near Kyritz. Hacheney did not return to the unit. (Fw 190 A-9, WNr. 205 977).

4. *Staffel*:

Unteroffizier Hans Pieschel was wounded in combat over Kyritz and subsequently did not return to the *Staffel* (Fw 190 A-9, WNr. 205 930).

Feldwebel Walter Schmidt was shot down and killed by Mustangs near Barenthin (Fw 190 A-9, WNr. 206 189).

Feldwebel Emil Schubert was wounded over Kyritz and had to make a forced landing. He was taken to hospital and never returned to the unit. (Fw 190 A-9, WNr. 203 386).

Fähnrich Horst Strauß was shot down and killed near Gumtow northwest of Kyritz (Fw 190 A-9, WNr. 206 191).

II./JG 301, 5. *Staffel*:

Feldwebel Herbert Schaar was shot down by P-51s and went down with his Fw 190 near the town of Gumtow (Fw 190 A-9 "White 16", WNr. 205 961).

6. *Staffel*:

Feldwebel Werner Ebert was shot down over Kyritz. He and his machine came down near the city (Fw 190 D-9 "Red 16", WNr. 210 260).

Unteroffizier Franklin Höhne was engaged by Mustangs over Pritzwalk northwest of Neuruppin and was shot down there (Fw 190 D-9 "Red 15", WNr. 210 977).

Leutnant Walter Kropp was wounded in combat over Brandenburg and forced to bail out. He returned to the *Gruppe* soon afterwards and became acting *Staffel* commander in place of *Oberleutnant* Gerhard Walter, who had been killed on 31 December. (Fw 190 D-9 "Red 7", WNr. 210 907)

Feldwebel Clemens Schmoll was shot down and killed near Lohm, west of Neustadt an der Dosse (Fw 190 D-9 "Red 13", WNr. 210 913).

8. *Staffel*:

Feldwebel Heinz Riedel was overwhelmed by Mustangs and shot down near Havelburg (Fw 190 A-9, WNr. 206 173). He was buried in Perleburg cemetery near Wittenberge.

Unteroffizier Heinrich Fischer was hit while attacking four-engined bombers and crashed to his death south of Havelburg (Fw 190 A-9 "Blue 9", WNr. 205 946). He is buried in Perleburg cemetery.

Feldwebel Hans-Dieter Jander flew into the ground near Kyritz following air combat (Fw 190 A-9 "Blue 7", WNr. 207 201). Jander is buried in Wittstock cemetery.

Obergefreiter Günter Angermann of 9./JG 301, killed in action near Neustadt an der Dosse on 14 January 1945.

Unteroffizier Heinz Kettmann was shot down by Mustangs southwest of Stendal and went down with his machine near the town of Wittenmoor (Fw 190 A-9 "Blue 8", WNr. 207 169). He is buried in Military Cemetery II in Stendal.

Unteroffizier Gustav Kilzer was shot down and killed by Mustangs northwest of Rübhorst (Fw 190 A-9 "Blue 2", WNr. 207 177). He is buried in the Rathenow Military Cemetery (Row 8, Grave 4).

III./JG 301, 9. Staffel:

Obergefreiter Günter Angermann was shot down in the initial attack by the Mustangs and crashed near Neustadt an der Dosse (Fw 190 A-8 "White 3", WNr. 176 075). Angermann was from Zielenzig east of Frankfurt an der Oder. He had joined *I./JG 302* at Götzendorf in June 1944 and continued to serve with that *Gruppe* even after it was renamed *III./JG 301*. He took part in every mission during that time and was awarded the Iron Cross, Second Class for his actions. In action as in private, he was always a reliable comrade. Only on the promotion list did he fall to the bottom, as he had a tendency to speak before thinking.

Oberfähnrich Karl Hänsel was shot down and killed by P-51s neat the town of Lohm west of Neustadt an der Dosse (Fw 190 A-8 "White 13", WNr. 175 920). He died just a few days after our battle with the P-38s in which he had fought so bravely.

10. Staffel:

Feldwebel Hubert Blomert allegedly did not return from this mission, however where he was lost is not known. There are indications, however, that Blomert was killed at a later date. On this day he flew Fw 190 A-8 "Red 9", WNr. 682 006).

11. Staffel:

Oberleutnant Christoph Herzog, *Staffelkapitän*, was shot down and wounded by a P-51. He bailed out and landed safely near Kyritz. After leaving hospital he did not return to the *Gruppe*. (Fw 190 A-8 "Yellow 3", WNr. 175 925).

Oberfeldwebel Kurt Kabler crashed to his death during the fighting over Barenthin in Mecklenburg (Fw 190 A-8 "Yellow 4").

12. Staffel:

Obergefreiter Egon Straub was wounded in combat with P-51s over Kyritz and forced to make a crash-landing. He subsequently did not return to the *Staffel*. (Fw 190 A-8 "Black 10", WNr. 172 355)

And so 14 January 1945, a Sunday, had been another black day for *JG 301*. Its casualties, twenty killed and eight wounded, were equal to one third of all its available pilots. The *Geschwader* had lost just over 150 pilots killed or wounded in the brief period between 21 November 1944 and 14 January 1945. While a solid core remained in each *Staffel*, the steady flow of replacements meant that the faces were becoming ever younger, and there was almost no opportunity to make the newcomers feel part of the *Staffeln*.

The *9. Staffel* had for all intents and purposes been without a commanding officer since 1 January 1945. *Hauptmann* Gerhard Posselmann arrived to fill the post in early January and the pilots had to get to know him too. From experience we knew that on the ground this relationship developed quickly in the course of our regular routine, but in the air there were sometimes problems, for every *Staffelkapitän* wanted to – and indeed was supposed to – be recognized as the leader. If everything did no go as expected in action, the new leader came in for justifiable criticism from the pilots, for their number included some aces who were more than just takers of orders.

At the briefing the next morning we were shown the situation map with the latest positions of the fronts in the east and west. For the first time one of the pilots remarked out loud that we were losing the war badly. A hush fell over the room and even the presenting officer, *Hauptmann* Dietsche, did not know what to say at first. Everyone present knew that these words were all too true, but the remark should not have been made in that room. The same pilot broke the silence, declaring that his outburst had been a spontaneous reaction to the situation at the front. As the comment had been made among his comrades, that was the end of it. Nevertheless, it did nothing to brighten the troubled faces staring at the situation map. Although the existing situation on land, sea and air gave no cause for optimism, from time to time there were still events that kept the sparks of optimism glowing. One was the persistent rumor that *III./JG 301* was to be taken out of action and reequipped with the new Ta 152. At that time initial preparations were being made to transfer some Fw 190s to the other *Staffeln* of the other two *Gruppen*, but no new machines reached from the factories still producing aircraft.

20 January 1945

In the midst of this rumored type conversion came a thunderbolt: the three *Gruppen* of *JG 301* were to be moved to the Eastern Front! The *Geschwader* was to fly fighter-bomber missions against Russian forces that had broken through to Silesia and West Prussia. The *Gruppen* were transferred to airfields at Sagan, Sorau, Posen and Schroda, southwest of Posen. In the end, however, almost no fighter-bomber missions were carried out, because at that time of year the weather was too bad. As well, the rapidly-advancing Soviets soon made these airfields untenable. The aircraft based at Posen and Schroda had to take off in bad weather to avoid being overrun by the advancing Soviet front. The pilots were universally critical of these fighter-bomber missions: they were unfamiliar with such operations, wasted a lot of fuel, and there were casualties – the missions were a failure. The few *Staffeln* that did fly fighter-bomber missions had an inadequate knowledge of the front and moreover had no idea where friend and foe might be. On 26 January 1945 most of the aircraft sent east returned to their original airfields. Losses suffered in these missions, which often differed little one from another, were:

20 January 1945

Unteroffizier Dieter Göthel of the *9. Staffel* was wounded in action and crashed near Helerau not far from Dresden. He did not return to the *Staffel*. (Fw 190 A-8 "Red 11", WNr. 681 992).

Oberfeldwebel Heinz Brand of the *10. Staffel* was shot down and killed near Heiligenkreuz (Fw 190 A-8 "Red 5", WNr. 175 921).

Unteroffizier Josef Idstein of the *1. Staffel* crashed to his death after air combat near Taucha (Fw 190 A-9, WNr. 202 402).

Unteroffizier Gottfried Hellriegel of the *4. Staffel* was shot down during an air battle near Dreihaken (Fw 190 A-9, WNr. 205 089).

Unteroffizier Karl Schweger of the *5. Staffel* was shot down and killed near Kohau (Fw 190 A-9 "White 3", WNr. 206 086). He was buried in the Marienbad cemetery (Section A, Grave No. 48).

Leutnant Erich Reinke of the *3. Staffel* and *Feldwebel* Werner Gemmer of the *2. Staffel* were both killed on 21 January 1945 during the retreat from Schroda while fighting with the infantry. Both had flown fighter-bomber missions against Russian positions from Schroda. Unable to fly out because their aircraft were damaged, they were caught between the fronts. Members of the technical personnel also found themselves in that situation. Some were assigned to other units while others made their way back to the *Geschwader* via circuitous routes.

Gefreiter Harald Himmelstoss of the *3. Staffel* was killed in action on 23 January 1945; the type of mission and location of his loss are not known. On 24 January 1945 *Oberleutnant* Christian Straßburger, *Kapitän* of the *3. Staffel*, was shot down while on a fighter-bomber mission (Fw 190 A-9, WNr. 207 172).

Fähnrich Günter Hoffmann of the *1. Staffel* was wounded while attacking ground targets near Posen on 25 January 1945. His subsequent fate is not known. (Fw 190 A-9, WNr. 205 010)

It is impossible to provide anything more than a general description of the fighter-bomber missions flown by *JG 301*, as there are few surviving eyewitnesses and written records are sketchy. They do suggest, however, that the *Geschwaderstab* did not take part in these operations, indicating that the individual *Gruppen* were probably attached to different commands. The records also show that the *Gruppen* were deployed in different areas, which is probably why they operated separately.

In the general disarray it is also impossible to say exactly what fighter-bomber missions were flown, for with the *Gruppen* separated there was no centralized recording of missions. It is impossible to say to what degree the following casualties were associated with these missions.

On 26 January 1945 elements of *III./JG 301* were again in action, and on that day *Oberleutnant* Wolfgang Dreier, acting commander of the *11. Staffel*, was posted missing in action (Fw 190 A-8 "Yellow 12", WNr. 682 055).

Leutnant Rolf Lüth of the *12. Staffel* was wounded in the same action, however he was able to parachute to safety over Lübben (Fw 190 A-8, WNr. 175 955).

It is known with certainty that *JG 301*'s fighter-bomber period on the Eastern Front ended on 26 January 1945. Most of the aircraft deployed in the east returned to their home airfields. There is no detailed information as to the sense and purpose of this deployment, and information on the losses suffered by pilots and ground personnel is far from complete.

Several days before this transfer took place, on 18 January 1945, *Hauptmann* Karl-Heinz Dietsche, *Staffelkapitän* of *10./JG 301*, was transferred to *JG 3 "Udet"* on the Eastern Front. There he was placed in command of that unit's *7. Staffel*. Dietsche, who had served as a strategic reconnaissance pilot in northern Norway from 19 January 1942 until 15 September 1943, joined *I./JG 300* at Altenburg on 29 October 1943, arriving by way of Instrument Flying School 110. On 20 November 1943 he assumed command of the *2. Staffel* at Jüterbog and remained in that position until the *Staffel* was renamed *10./JG 301* in September 1944. He attended a unit leaders course in Bad Wörishofen from 1 March to 15 April 1945, and on 16 April became *Gruppenkommandeur* of *II./JG 300* at Holzkirchen.

Chapter Nine

Into Action with the Ta 152 H-1

On 27 January 1945 *III./JG 301* was withdrawn from operations. What no one believed possible was about to happen – the *Gruppe* was to reequip on the fabulous Ta 152. The decision had probably been made a few days earlier, for an order from the *Luftwaffe* High Command dated 23 January 1945 states in Paragraph I, Article 2:

"Instead of the planned expansion of the Ta 152 test detachment, *III./JG 301* will be equipped with the Ta 152 H-1 as an operational trials unit. As well, the *Gruppe* will continue to operate its current equipment until further notice."

The order contained one other significant provision: "Effective immediately, the Ta 152 test detachment formed on 2 November 1944 is redesignated *Stabsstaffel JG 301*." The unit referred to was *Erprobungskommando Ta 152* under *Hauptmann* Stolle, based at Rechlin. At no time, however, were Stolle and his test detachment under the command of *JG 301*, which led to some mix-ups later.

In the early morning hours of 27 January 1945 some of the *Gruppe*'s pilots were taken by truck to the Neuhausen aircraft factory near Cottbus. Their orders were to take charge of Ta 152 aircraft and fly them to Alteno near Cottbus. In spite of earlier talk, the order had taken all of the pilots in the truck somewhat by surprise, and all nervously awaited their first contact with the high-altitude fighter. The vehicle finally arrived at Neuhausen airfield and the pilots were allowed to leave the hard benches in the back of the truck. Before them they saw twelve Ta 152s parked in three rows.

They were a strange sight at first, for with their enormous wingspan and long noses these aircraft did not even look like fighters. With a critical eye and an uneasy feeling, the pilots walked along the rows of aircraft, after which the first questions and answers were exchanged with the ground crews responsible for the machines. After a general technical briefing, which lasted barely more than half an hour, the Ta 152s were turned over to the pilots and the transfer to Alteno could begin.

At 1108 hours I made my first takeoff in a Ta 152 from Neuhausen and at 1128 I landed it at Alteno.

The first Ta 152s were received by III./JG 301 at the end of January 1945.

My initial impressions:

- Acceleration was so great on takeoff that one's body was pressed against the seat back.
- The Ta lifted off after only a few hundred meters.
- Initial climb rate was enormous.
- I had never flown an aircraft with such a tremendous wingspan.
- Control forces appeared to be good.
- All-round view from and freedom of movement in the cockpit were also good.
- The landing speed was rather lower and thus unfamiliar.

That same afternoon the twelve Ta 152s were sitting on Alteno airfield, and they were surrounded by the pilots and technical staff of the *Staffeln*. Plans called for the *Gruppe* to be equipped with thirty-five of these aircraft and, after a brief familiarization period, take them into action. In the days that followed, however, deliveries of aircraft stopped. Important facilities like Marienburg in East Prussia were overrun by the Soviets, seriously hampering production. As a result, in the first days of the conversion the pilots of *III./JG 301* never had more than sixteen Ta 152 H-0 and H-1 aircraft available. This total was never increased in the period that followed.

Ta 152 H-0 and H-1 Specification
Power Plant: Jumo 213 E-1 twelve-cylinder, liquid-cooled engine producing 1,750 h.p. for takeoff and 2,050 h.p. with MW 50 methanol-water injection.
Performance: maximum speed 750 km/h at 9,000 m. **Initial climb rate:** 17 m/s to about 5,000 m.
Wingspan: 14.82 m. Length: 14.82 m.

Service Ceiling: with pressurized cockpit 14,000 m, without 12,000 m (the H-0 was flown without a pressurized cockpit).

Fuel Capacity: 1,000 liters (plus 300-liter external tank).

Propeller: 3-blade, maximum blade width 60cm.

Armament: one MK 108 automatic cannon (30mm) firing through the propeller hub with ninety rounds of ammunition, plus two MG 151 automatic cannon (20mm) in the wing roots, each with 175 rounds of ammunition.

The Ta 152 H High-Altitude and Escort Fighter

Work on jigs and tools for the construction of the first prototypes of the new Ta 152 H-0 did not begin until early 1944. The third proposed variant of the Tank fighter, the Ta 152 H was designed as a high-altitude and escort fighter. It differed from the Ta 152 A and B mainly in having a much larger wing with an area of 23.5 m≈ and a span of 14.82 m.

Front and rear views of the Ta 152. Note the intake for the three-stage supercharger on the right side of the fuselage and the broad propeller blades.

213

In keeping with the requirements of high-altitude combat operations, a GM system (nitrous oxide injection for improved engine performance) was installed and armament was restricted to one MK 108 engine-mounted cannon and two MG 151/20 cannon in the wing roots. Provision was made for specialized versions with additional armament in the fuselage or wings. Selected to power the aircraft was the Jumo 213 standard power plant, which had by then become available. The DB 603 G was seen as a backup power plant.

With this ultimate development of the Ta 152, Focke-Wulf in fact overtook the enemy's temporary lead in fighter design. It was representative of the ultimate stage of piston-engined fighter design achieved by the end of the war. Today one can scarcely imagine what that meant in a nation that was being carpet-bombed day and night.

III./JG 301 was equipped with Ta 152 H-0 and H-1 series aircraft. While the H-0 lacked cockpit pressurization, the H-1 was equipped with a functioning pressurization system. The cockpit was sealed by a tubular bladder partly filled with foam rubber, which was inflated by a compressed air bottle to 2.5 atmospheres. The bladder had to be deflated and the canopy lock released before the canopy could be jettisoned. The canopy consisted of two layers of plexiglass to prevent fogging. Silica-gel capsules kept the air between the two layers dry.

Today there is uncertainty as to whether the pilots were ever briefed on the canopy jettisoning procedure. Based on the memories of surviving Ta 152 pilots it probably never happened. It is therefore doubtful that an attempted bail-out would have succeeded.

Although the first Ta 152s were at Alteno and initial flights were being made, it was still difficult to understand why an entire fighter *Gruppe* had been withdrawn from action to reequip on a new fighter type that was not available in sufficient numbers. It was also difficult to understand because *III./JG 301* had always been employed as a "Heavy *Gruppe*", whose main purpose was to shoot down bombers.

In future operations with the Ta 152 high-altitude fighter, exactly the opposite would be required of the *Gruppe*, for it would fly cover for the other *Gruppen*. Whether this would work out remained to be seen.

First Impressions of the Ta 152

The first unpredictable surprises occurred during practice flights over the airfield in the Ta 152, when aircraft from other *Staffeln* were encountered. Such encounters often proved problematic, for the outline of the Ta 152 was virtually unknown to German pilots. In such encounters pilots also reacted very differently. The vast majority immediately displayed defensive reactions or offensive intentions, but there were also pilots who reacted to the encounter with panic and tried to flee to safety. The pilots of the Ta 152 had to deal with these reactions until the end of the war.

On climbing into the Ta 152 one immediately noticed the great freedom of movement in the cockpit. The all-round view was excellent with the canopy closed, and the great freedom of movement allowed an unusually good view to the rear.

Even while taxiing one got a sense of the tremendous power produced by the Jumo 213 E. Pushing the throttle full forward resulted in tremendous acceleration which pressed one hard against the seat back. The force was such that pilots were hesitant to apply full power for the first few takeoffs. The aircraft lifted off effortlessly at about 210 km/h after a short takeoff run. One scarcely

In the center Leutnant Schallenberg, technical officer, right Oberleutnant Schröder, adjutant of III./JG 301.

noticed the retraction of the undercarriage and flaps. This was a big difference from other versions of the Fw 190, which sagged noticeably when the flaps were raised. The enormous thrust of the propeller with its broad 60cm blades and the great wingspan were positively noticeable. Rate of climb was 17.5 m/s to a height of 5,000 meters. It took twelve minutes to reach a height of 10,000 meters, which was equivalent to an average rate of climb of 14.2 m/s.

During a high-altitude test flight in a Ta 152 H-0 the three-stage supercharger worked flawlessly, but it should be mentioned that later on operations there were occasional problems with the third stage.

At an altitude of 10,000 meters the Ta 152 still reacted perfectly to control inputs, by comparison at that height the Fw 190 A-8 was already unstable and reacted rather sluggishly to control inputs. Not until a height of 12,000 meters did one feel that the limit of performance had been reached.

During the conversion program comparison flights were carried out with the *Gruppe*'s remaining Fw 190 A-8s, with mock combats playing a prominent role. This provided an opportunity to test the performance capabilities of the Ta 152 and to see if this fighter aircraft was really as good as was claimed. These mock combats repeatedly showed that the Ta 152 was much superior in a dogfight. Especially at heights from 6,000 to 8,000 meters, where most fighter combats took place, one had the impression that the Ta 152 could turn on the spot.

During the period from the beginning until the middle of February 1945 all of *III./JG 301*'s pilots got the opportunity to fly the Ta 152. This process could have been speeded up if we had received aircraft more quickly.

The *Gruppe* retained some Fw 190 A-8s as a precaution, preserving the unit's operational strength for the future. Everything now depended on how rapidly additional Ta 152s were delivered to the *Gruppe*. Here the first doubts arose, and they were reinforced daily by the slow pace of deliveries. The *Gruppe* never achieved its planned strength of thirty-five aircraft during the conversion phase and fifty machines for operations. The aircraft was built by a decentralized production organization and several factories, such as the one in Marienburg that built the wings, had fallen into enemy hands, causing production at Neuhausen to come to a halt.

We lost our first Ta 152 during the conversion phase: on 1 February 1945 *Unteroffizier* Hermann Dürr was killed when his Ta 152, WNr. 150 037, crashed about one kilometer east of Alteno airfield.

In those days it was customary that whenever a Ta 152 was in the air many of the pilots would gather at the edge of the landing field and observe the flight. Dürr carried out his program at a height of 2,000 to 3,000 meters, and none of the pilots watching saw any sign of danger. Quite suddenly, however, the aircraft went from a steep left turn into a flat spin. The Ta 152 was still at a height of more than 2,000 meters, and the pilots were all sure that he would be able to recover. But, as the onlookers held their breath, the Ta 152 drew ever closer to the ground. In the end there was just a pillar of smoke from the crash scene. Only when the fire and rescue vehicles raced across the field to the crash site was the silence among the pilots broken.

A flat spin, in which the aircraft falls from the sky like a dry leaf, is known to be a dangerous maneuver. Dürr was an experienced pilot and knew how to react in such a situation. But it was impossible to ask what had happened, and the cause of this tragic accident was never explained.

As February went on, it became obvious that *III./JG 301*'s planned conversion to the Ta 152 was not going as planned. The anticipated number of thirty-five Ta 152s was not reached, consequently the *Gruppe* was left with a mixture of Ta 152 H-0s and H-1s plus Fw 190 A-8s.

The other *Gruppen* of *JG 301* continued to fly combat during the *III. Gruppe*'s conversion. The *Geschwader* was bolstered by the addition of *IV./JG 301*, which began operations at the beginning of February 1945. The enemy air attacks were now concentrated on the fuel industry and transportation hubs, but large cities like Berlin and Dresden were also bombed by the British and Americans. During *III./JG 301*'s conversion to the Ta 152 the *Luftwaffe* high command had issued an order to the fighter units that they were only to take off when there were prospects of success. At that time, however, such occasions were very rare indeed. As a result, fighter operations dwindled away, nevertheless losses remained high. The great bloodletting continued, and *JG 301* also suffered in the early days of February 1945.

1 February 1945

Feldwebel Bernhard Ikier of the *1. Staffel* developed engine trouble and was injured in a crash-landing near Finsterwalde (Fw 190 A-9, WNr. 176 050).

Unteroffizier Kurt Woldt of the *5. Staffel* was forced to abandon his aircraft near Kahnsdorf and was injured in the process. Why he bailed out is not known. (Fw 190 A-9, WNr. 206 071).

Leutnant Hermann Helm of the *6. Staffel* was shot down by anti-aircraft fire during a mission over the Eastern Front and did not survive (Fw 190 A-9 "Red 12", WNr. 205 067).

Leutnant Peter Kratzsch of the *8. Staffel* was killed during a mission over the Eastern Front, however exactly where he was lost is not known (Fw 190 A-9 "Blue 1", WNr. 207 176).

Unteroffizier Ferdinand Loth, also of the *8. Staffel*, crashed on landing at Drewitz airfield near Potsdam and was injured. The reason for the crash is not known. (Fw 190 A-9 "Blue 10", WNr. 206 060)

Leutnant Peter Kratzsch of the *8. Staffel* was killed during a mission over the Eastern Front, location unknown (Fw 190 A-9 "Blue 1", WNr. 207 176).

Unteroffizier Ferdinand Loth, also of the *8. Staffel*, was injured in a landing crash at Drewitz airfield near Potsdam. The cause of the crash is not known. (Fw 190 A-9 "Blue 10", WNr. 206 060).

On 1 February 1945 *Oberfeldwebel* Hans Todt of the *8. Staffel* claimed a Polikarpov U-2 light bomber shot down during a mission over the Eastern Front.

2 February 1945

Unteroffizier Herbert Haas of the *4. Staffel* crashed to his death during an air battle near Kamenz. The type of mission is not known.

Unteroffizier Friedrich Jokiel of the *5. Staffel* was shot down and killed by friendly anti-aircraft fire east of Schwerin (Fw 190 A-9 "White 15", WNr. 206 141).

Oberfeldwebel Herbert Schüller of the *8. Staffel* was injured when his aircraft overturned during a crash-landing at Neuhausen (Fw 190 A-9 "Blue 14", WNr. 206 157).

On 3 February *Feldwebel* Max Schleifenheimer of the *1. Staffel* was wounded in action over Bärwalde while intercepting a raid on Berlin. He rejoined the *Staffel* a short time later. (Fw 190 A-8, WNr. 175 918)

4 February 1945

The establishment of *IV./JG 301* had been underway at Gardelegen since the end of 1944. Unlike the other three *Gruppen*, which operated versions of the Fw 190, the new unit was equipped with the Bf 109 G-10. Although the main body of the *Geschwader* was based in Lusatia (the area between the Elbe and Oder Rivers), *IV./JG 301* remained at Gardelegen and flew its first major operation on this day. Instead of intercepting enemy bombers, however, the *Gruppe* was ordered against the advancing Soviet ground forces. The area of operations was east of Frankfurt on the Oder on a line between Ziebingen and Crossen on the Oder. While attacking Soviet positions the Messerschmitts ran into Russian fighters and close-support aircraft, resulting in dogfights. The majority of the *Gruppe*'s pilots were retrained bomber pilots with very little experience in aerial combat. Flying from Finsterwalde and Welzow, the *I.* and *II. Gruppe* were also active against ground targets on the Eastern Front on this day, however it is no longer possible to determine whether their area of operations was the same as *IV./JG 301*'s. There is no information on the nature of these missions or their outcome, but the records do contain some information on losses:

I./JG 301:

Feldwebel Gerhard Zimmermann of the *2. Staffel* failed to return and was declared dead. It is not known where he was lost. (Fw 190 A-9, WNr. 207 203).

Feldwebel Franz Domhöfer of the *3. Staffel* also failed to return from this mission. It is relatively certain that he was shot down over the fronts, but the exact location is not known. (Fw 190 A-9, WNr. 202 403).

II./JG 301:

Unteroffizier Georg Gude of the *6. Staffel* was also declared dead after this mission, where he was lost is not known. (Fw 190 A-9 "Red 3", WNr. 205 938)

Fähnrich August Bader of the *8. Staffel* failed to return from this mission and was subsequently declared dead. Once again, the location of this loss is unknown. (Fw 190 A-9 "Blue 6", WNr. 207 188)

Leutnant Otto Schwarz, also of the *8. Staffel*, failed to return from this mission. Where he went down is not known. (Fw 190 A-9 "Blue 2", WNr. 207 195)

IV./JG 301:

Hauptmann Wilfried Schmitz was killed during his very first mission as *Gruppenkommandeur*. He was shot down by anti-aircraft fire ten kilometers south of Ziebingen while attacking Soviet positions. (Bf 109 G-10 "Green 21", WNr. 491 157). *Leutnant* Günter Förster of the *14. Staffel* met the same fate, falling to Soviet anti-aircraft fire. Where he was shot down is not known. (Bf 109 G-10 "Red 5", WNr. 157 440)

All of these pilots fell east of the Oder and Neisse Rivers, and in most cases the exact location of their loss is not known. These operations were very different from what the pilots were used to, exposing them to anti-aircraft fire and attacks by enemy fighters and close-support aircraft operating near the front. In the years after the war it was impossible to investigate further, and consequently the fates of may pilots shot down there remain a mystery.

7 February 1945

On this day the Eastern Front was once again the number one priority; the interception of enemy bombers was increasingly relegated to second place. It is known that *IV./JG 301* flew several missions over the front east of Frankfurt on the Oder, however they were flown in *Staffel* rather than *Gruppe* strength. It had been learned in previous missions that formations were too unwieldy for attacks on ground targets and failed to produce the desired results. It is not clear whether *IV./JG 301* flew these first missions from Wittstock or Gardelegen, for a brief memo exits which states that the *Gruppe* was based at Wittstock from 6 to 12 February 1945. *II./JG 301* also took part in operations over the Eastern Front, however its area of operations was farther to the south. There is no record of operations by *I./JG 301* on this day. *Leutnant* Gerhard Lippold of the *5. Staffel* was hit while attacking Soviet positions. He attempted to nurse his damaged Fw 190 back to Welzow but crashed while attempting to land and was killed. (Fw 190 A-9 "White 16", WNr. 206 116)

Oberfeldwebel Horst Wolf of the *6. Staffel* was wounded in action and was forced to crash-land his machine. The location of his forced landing is not known. (Fw 190 A-9 "White 1", WNr. 205 414)

Oberleutnant Otto Schöppler, acting commanding officer of the 15. *Staffel*, was wounded when his aircraft was hit by flak east of Küstrin (Bf 109 G-10 "Yellow 1", WNr. 491 238).

8 February 1945

The German Army committed all available forces in an effort to stem the westward advance by Soviet forces, but it received inadequate support from the *Luftwaffe*. As most bomber units had been disbanded by this time and their pilots retrained as fighter pilots, there were just a few fighter units to support the fighter troops on the Eastern Front. Their efforts were far too weak to bring any significant relief, however. The front-line units were also feeling the drastic effects of the fuel shortage: for some time already, the fighters units had been using oxen to tow their aircraft to and from their blast pens. While this makeshift solution was often laughed at, it had become a regular part of life and operations on an airfield.

The following pilots did not return or were wounded in action on 8 February 1945:

II./JG 301:

Unteroffizier Ullrich Filipp of the *5. Staffel* was shot down and killed over the Eastern Front, location unknown (Fw 190 A-9 "White 13", WNr. 206 148). *Unteroffizier* Heinz Fürste, also of the *5. Staffel*, did not return from this mission and was declared dead (Fw 190 A-9 "White 17", WNr. 202 365). Since this mission *Unteroffizier* Helmut Brenner of the *6. Staffel* has been listed killed in action, location unknown (Fw 190 D-9 "Red 9", WNr. 210 909).

IV./JG 301:

The *Gruppe* suffered the following losses during operations northeast of Frankfurt an der Oder: *Obergefreiter* Wilhelm Herfel of the *13. Staffel* was shot down by Russian anti-aircraft fire near Küstrin (Bf 109 G-10 "White 1", WNr. 150 801). *Leutnant* Günter Hautschik of the *14. Staffel* was wounded by Russian anti-aircraft fire six kilometers east of Drossen (Bf 109 G-10 "Red 16", WNr. 150 726).

Unteroffizier Robert Vögele of the *15. Staffel* was wounded on this mission; his subsequent fate is not known.

9 February 1945

During the mid-morning formations of four-engined bomber flew into the airspace over Thuringia and Saxony with the objective of destroying the Lützkendorf hydrogenation plant located west of Merseburg. *Jagdgeschwader 300* and *301*, both stationed in that area, took off to intercept. *JG 301* put just two *Gruppen* into the air, both of which had been seriously weakened by previous losses. The *Geschwader*'s aircraft did not get through to the bombers, as they were intercepted and engaged by escort fighters. There are no reports of success from this mission, which once again raises the question of how and where the operational reports by the *Geschwader* and *Gruppen* were written and evaluated. The surviving reports contain an almost complete record of losses, while victories are scarcely mentioned. Proof that successes continued to be recorded is found in photos of the *Geschwader*'s young pilots wearing decorations – their names, however, are not recorded anywhere. On this day *Oberleutnant* Walter Burghoff of the *4. Staffel* was wounded in combat with escort fighters. While bailing out of his Fw 190 his feet struck the tail surfaces, breaking both legs below the knee. In great pain, he managed to pull the ripcord. Fortunately for the injured pilot, his parachute became caught in a tree. This saved his life, and firemen who rushed to the scene got him down. In hospital both legs were amputated, one below and one above the knee. After the war he lived in his home town of Apolda, where he worked as a salesman. Walter Burgdorff died there in the mid-1980s. *Oberfeldwebel* Max Sulzgruber of the *6. Staffel* was wounded in combat over Grieben and compelled to make a forced landing near the town (Fw 190 D-9 "Red 5", WNr. 210 905). *Leutnant* Karl-Heinz Müller of the *8. Staffel* was shot down and killed by escort fighters. The exact location where he crashed is not known. (Fw 190 A-9 "Blue 5", WNr. 207 202)

14 February 1945

During the night of 13-14 February British Lancaster and Mosquito bombers launched a major raid on Dresden, whose railway stations and streets were filled with refugees from the German eastern territories. Later that same morning the Saxon metropolis was attacked again, this time by the Americans with several hundred B-17 Flying Fortresses. The bombers were screened by a force of almost 800 Mustang escort fighters, and once again it was *JG 300* and *JG 301* which bore most of the burden of intercepting the raid. Only the *I.* and *II. Gruppe* of *JG 301* saw action, as the *III. Gruppe* was still converting to the Ta 152 high-altitude fighter and *IV. Gruppe* was still engaged in ground attacks against the advancing Soviets.

Contact was made between Leipzig and Dresden, and once again the fighters were able to penetrate to the bombers. The escort fighters had by now become so powerful that the bombers had little reason to fear attacks by German fighters.

The crews of these bombers knew nothing of the nervous strain faced by earlier crews. From mid-1943 until early 1944 the escort fighters lacked the range to escort the bombers much farther than the German Bight, leaving them to fight their way to and from the target under constant attack from German fighters and *Zerstörer*. Those crews that did not voluntarily extend their tours of duty were transferred elsewhere after a certain number of missions.

German airmen knew no such operational limits, beyond which they were taken off combat flying: they flew until they were killed or grounded as a result of wounds. Only a very few were transferred to less dangerous roles such as headquarters service or instructor. The majority, provided they lived, fought on until the end of the war.

The air battle caused the following losses:

Obergefreiter Heino Krause of the *1. Staffel* was shot down and killed by Mustangs over Dresden (Fw 190 A-8, WNr. 682 300).

Oberfeldwebel Willi Frank of the *7. Staffel* was overwhelmed by escort fighters over Leipzig and went down with his aircraft (Fw 190 D-9 "Yellow 10", WNr. 210 919)

Oberfeldwebel Helmut Stöber of the *7. Staffel* was shot down in the same area, however it is not known where his aircraft crashed (Fw 190 A-9 "Yellow 10", WNr. 208 378).

Leutnant Hans Stuck of the *7. Staffel* was wounded in combat over Leipzig. There is no clue as to his subsequent fate. (Fw 190 D-9 "Yellow 16", WNr. 210 238)

III./JG 301 was on the ground during the attack on Dresden. Explosions could be heard as far away as Alteno.

No further Ta 152s had been received by the *Gruppe*. On 14 February 1945 the *Gruppe* sent a report to the *Luftwaffe* High Command on testing of the Ta 152.

"The *III. Gruppe* of *JG 301*, which has been tasked with the front-line evaluation of the Ta 152 H-0, is based at Alteno, having previously flown in the Defense of the Reich with the Fw 190 A-8/ R11 and R12. At the beginning of the Russian offensive the *Gruppe* was transferred east to an airfield that proved to be behind enemy lines and had to be hastily abandoned. In spite of fog, most

I./JG 301 at roll call, Salzwedel, spring 1945.

aircraft were able to take off again, while the rest had to be blown up. The aircraft that managed to escape were incorporated into other units."

Note: some authors who have written about the Ta 152 describe this incident in such a way that it appears that Ta 152s took part in the flight to the airfield behind Russian lines. This is definitely not true, for the *Gruppe* did not receive its first Ta 152s until 27 January 1945.

"The *Gruppe* therefore has only the Ta 152 H-0s delivered for trials, eleven aircraft with the *Werknummer* 001, 002, 025, 032 and 034 to 040. Of these, 037 sustained 98% damage in a crash, and 022 was damaged in a crash-landing and subsequently repaired. Average serviceability is 75% and has only temporarily fallen to 30% as a result of water in the fuel and subsequent injection pump seizures.

The technical personnel and aircrew are well-trained. Almost all of the pilots are experienced and are very eager to go into action. They are approaching the testing of the Ta 152 with a positive attitude, consequently the aircraft are in good hands with the *Gruppe*.

The personnel complement is:

Gruppenkommandeur, Major Guth
Adjutant, *Lt.* Schröder
Technical Officer, *Hptm.* Hölzer (transferred to the *I. Gruppe* on 14 Feb. 1945. His successor, *Oblt.* Schallenberg, former technical officer of the *II. Gruppe*, has already arrived).

The approach of the front has made Alteno airfield a front-line base for fighter and close-support *Gruppen*. To prevent any interruption in testing activities, the *Gruppe* will soon be moving to Alperstedt near Erfurt."

Note: the *Gruppe* in fact moved to Sachau near Gardelegen.

Assessment of the Ta 152 H-0 by the Unit

"*III./JG 301* gave the Ta 152 H-0 the best evaluation the undersigned has ever seen given to a piece of equipment by a front-line unit. The aircraft's turning ability came in for especially high praise. The number of complaints received is well below the level expected for a new design. With the exception of the undercarriage hydraulics, they are not fundamental problems which could jeopardize the immediate introduction of the type into service.

Those shortcomings that needed to be addressed immediately in the interest of maximum serviceability were attended to by the *Gruppe* itself. It is expected, however, that these complaints will be eliminated from the next aircraft to be delivered, especially since they do not require extensive modifications. Anticipating that the problems will be addressed quickly, the *Gruppe* has not passed these complaints on to a higher level. Instead it has transmitted only a good overall impression with the note that all shortcomings found will be eliminated in direct agreement with the manufacturer.

A) Flight Characteristics

Compared to the Fw 190 A-8, the Ta 152 H-0 has a smaller turning radius with less tendency to stall, and the stall develops at a lower airspeed (approx. 250 km/h). Recovery from a resulting spin is easily effected after about 500 to 600 meters. In mock combat with a Fw 190 A-8, the latter, flown by a very good pilot, was easily outturned by the H-0, which was flown by a pilot with just two flights on type. To date most handling trials have taken place from ground level to about 3,000 meters."

There followed further figures on rates of climb, speeds at various altitudes, on the wing, power plant and load factors. Overall it was a positive test report, from which could be concluded

The Tank Ta 152 H-0.

III./JG 301 during infantry training in the forest near Sachau.

Oberleutnant Sauer reports to Major Guth.

Oberfeldwebel Jupp Keil at Sachau in January 1945.

that *III./JG 301* had recognized the enormous advantages of this aircraft. This was corroborated by subsequent statements.

On 19 February 1945 the situation at the fronts forced *JG 301* to abandon its airfields and return to its former bases west of Berlin.

The *Geschwaderstab* and *II. Gruppe* moved to Stendal, the *I. Gruppe* to Salzwedel and the *III. Gruppe* to Sachau west of Gardelegen. The *IV. Gruppe*, which had been based at Stendal with the *II. Gruppe* for a few days, moved back to Gardelegen and remained there until its disbandment in early April. Sachau was a secondary airfield located at the northwestern edge of the Colbitz-Letzlinger Heath. The airfield was bordered by forest north and south, and the *Staffel* dispersals and aircraft were well-camouflaged among the trees. The command post and barracks were located in the south wood. The runway was laid out in an east-west direction, with clear approaches to both ends. Like all secondary airfields, which were built after the start of the war, it had only a few hangars and blended well into the terrain.

Soon after the *Gruppe*'s arrival at Sachau, the *Kapitän* of the *9. Staffel*, *Hauptmann* Gerhard Posselmann, was transferred to *I./JG 301* at Salzwedel to become *Gruppenkommandeur*. *Oberleutnant* Hermann Stahl was named *Staffelkapitän* of *9./JG 301*. He was the last surviving member of the former *12./JG 51*, which in June 1944 had been attached to *I./JG 302* as its high-altitude *Staffel*.

At Sachau *III./JG 301* never had more than sixteen Ta 152s. Fw 190 A-8s and A-9s were flown in for the rest of the *Gruppe*. The plan to send an entire *Jagdgruppe* equipped with Ta 152s into action had now come to an end. A maximum effort would therefore have to be made to keep the few available Ta 152s serviceable, so that no aircraft were left on the ground in the event of a mission.

Another Ta 152 was written off during the *Gruppe*'s first few days at Sachau. The starting situation was very different from that of the crash at Alteno on 1 February, but once again it proved impossible to determine the exact cause of the accident.

Oberfähnrich Jonny Wiegeshoff had taken off on a practice flight and after completing his program he flew low over the airfield in preparation for landing. Though straight and level, airspeed was very low during the pass over the airfield. To observers on the ground it appeared as if some force was holding the aircraft back. At the end of the airfield he pulled up the Ta's nose at much too low a speed. The aircraft stalled out of a left turn and dropped like a stone, striking the ground in a small group of trees not far from the airfield.

This accident was the topic of discussion among those in the know for some time. No one could explain the slow pass over the airfield or why the pilot had tried to carry out a reversal at such a low speed.

Oberfähnrich Wiegeshoff was certainly not an experienced pilot, but he was also not a so-called "Three-Day Pilot". He had joined the *Jagdgruppe* at Alperstedt in September 1944 and had performed extremely well in the missions that followed. Wiegeshoff had been awarded the Iron Cross, First Class and had scored four or five victories, although his name appeared in the success list only once. Under the existing rules he should have been buried without military honors, but his comrades intervened decisively and he was buried with full military honors in Gardelegen cemetery.

On 20 February 1945 *Oberfeldwebel* Jupp Keil of the *10. Staffel* claimed a B-17 shot down, which suggests that the *Gruppe* saw action on this day. There is no mention of this in the records, however.

Only after the *III. Gruppe* moved to Sachau did the members of the *Gruppe* have increased contact with their new commanding officer, *Major* Guth, a converted bomber pilot. It was Guth's plan to strictly separate the pilots according to rank when off duty, but this met with energetic resistance and was subsequently withdrawn. Beyond this, we of course asked ourselves about the point of such a measure: it was certainly no way to win a war.

25 February 1945

On this day the bulk of *JG 301* saw action for the first time after its transfer back into the area west of Berlin. The 8th Air Force's targets were railway junctions in the Salzwedel – Wittenberge – Stendal triangle.

For the *Geschwader* this was an ill-fated mission which was as confused as the overall situation. Only the first three *Gruppen* took to the air – why the *Geschwader*'s *IV. Gruppe* was not ordered to take off is not clear. Although *JG 301* had only left this area of operations a few weeks earlier, the balance of forces had once again shifted in favor of the Americans. In addition to the bombers and their fighter escort, the Americans were now sending fighter sweeps ahead of the bombers to catch German fighters as they were taking off. The *II.* and *III. Gruppe* took off without incident, but at Salzwedel an incident occurred during the *I. Gruppe*'s takeoff which demonstrated that the Americans now had full control of the air and were capable of attacking their enemy on his airfields.

Unteroffizier Heinrich Panno of the *1. Staffel*, who had served for a long time as a ferry pilot for *I./JG 301*, described one such attack:

Officers of III./JG 301 at Sachau, thirty-five kilometers east of Wolfsburg, in March 1945. Front row, from left: Government Advisor Bartholomäus, Oberleutnante Schröder and Stahl, Major Guth, Oberleutnant Sauer and Leutnante Reiche, Reinhold and Hagedorn. Second row: Oberzahlmeister Heun, Leutnante Volkmann and Frenzel, Government Inspector Maiwald, Stabsarzt Czaja and Leutnante Spiess and Schallenberg. Visible in the back row are: Oberfähnriche Bee, Ludwig, Rödhammer, Hummel, Zeidler and Wiegeshoff and Leutnante von Alven, Göbel and Nabakowski.

March 1945 at Stendal: Leutnant Rudolf Wurf of 6./JG 301 in front of his Fw 190 D-9.

"On 25 February 1945, a day I will never forget, I arrived from our former base near Breslau in Silesia. I was unable to land as the *Gruppe* was in takeoff position on the airfield, one aircraft next to the other, even on the landing runway. I had monitored the reports of approaching enemy aircraft and knew that escort fighters were lurking about, so I kept a damned good lookout. I expected that the *Gruppe* would be taking off soon and planned to wait until then to land.

But instead of taking off, two aircraft moved off the runway. A green flare went up, clearance for me to land. I brought my kite down between the two machines and taxied to the maintenance hangar. I was on my way to flight control when the takeoff order came and I, of course, stopped to watch the *Gruppe*'s departure. The aircraft of the *1. Staffel* had just lifted off and were in the process of raising undercarriage and flaps – the most defenseless position one could imagine – when four American Mustangs raced in from behind and opened fire on the four aircraft suspended in front of them. One Fw 190 dropped onto the airfield and went up in flames, another caught fire, a third trailed smoke, and later one could see two columns of smoke some distance from the airfield."

A few days earlier *Leutnant* Anton Benning had joined to the *Gruppe* after attending a unit leaders course in Königsberg. He had previously served for a long time with *III./JG 301* and now commanded the *1. Staffel*. As a veteran combat pilot, he led the *Gruppe*'s fighters on this day. They were heavily engaged by Mustangs in the Salzwedel area and prevented from getting to the bombers. *I./JG 301*'s formation was split up and involved in individual combats. Once again a number of the *Gruppe*'s pilots paid with their lives: the circle of pilots was becoming ever smaller.

II./JG 301, which took off from Stendal, was also engaged by the American escort fighters flying well ahead of the bombers, and this *Jagdgruppe* was also prevented from attacking the bombers. In the ensuing dogfights *Obergefreiter* Hans Todt of the *8. Staffel* shot down a P-51 Mustang for his ninth victory.

III./JG 301 took off from Sachau with ten to twelve Ta 152 H-0s and H-1s. The rest of the *Gruppe*'s pilots flew Fw 190 A-8s or A-9s. The formation was initially vectored in the direction of Brunswick, then there was a course change to the north. *Major* Guth reported that he had engine trouble and was going to try to get back to Sachau. As the airspace in that area was full of Mustangs, *Unteroffizier* Blum and *Feldwebel* Reschke provided an escort for the *Gruppenkommandeur*. All three reached Sachau safely.

The resulting change in command caused some unrest in the Ta 152 group, but that was probably not the reason why there was no significant enemy contact. In the evening one saw groups of pilots sitting around wearing contemplative expressions: the Ta 152's great test under fire had not taken place, and in the opinion of the pilots the chaos had become even worse after the break in operations. The days when large numbers of fighters were concentrated against the American raids were gone forever.

JG 301's losses in this operation:

Fähnrich Hans Gebauer of the *1. Staffel* was shot down by Mustangs while taking off from Salzwedel and crashed just beyond the airfield perimeter (Fw 190 A-8, WNr. 176 111).

Unteroffizier Otto Dischinger of the *1. Staffel* was also shot down by Mustangs while taking off from Salzwedel. He and his aircraft went down just beyond the airfield (Fw 190 A-8, WNr. 205 965).

Feldwebel Gerhard Koch, a flight leader in the *1. Staffel*, suffered the same fate. His aircraft was shot up during takeoff and crashed just outside the perimeter of Salzwedel airfield. (Fw 190 A-8, WNr. 683 323)

Koch was one of the *Gruppe*'s most successful pilots, with six night and one day victories to his credit. He died with no chance of defending himself.

Feldwebel Gerhardt Schmidt of the *2. Staffel* was also shot down by Mustangs and crashed near Salzwedel airfield (Fw 190 A-9, WNr. 202 427).

Unteroffizier Kurt Funke of the *5. Staffel* crashed while attempting to nurse his shot-up aircraft back to the airfield. His engine failed and he crashed to his death near Arnim. (Fw 190 D-9 "Red 6", WNr. 500 404)

2 March 1945

From its airfields in the United Kingdom, the American 8th Air Force launched 1,232 B-17 and B-24 four-engined bombers with an escort of 774 P-47s and P-51s. Their targets were chemical plants in Böhlen and Chemnitz and industrial facilities in the Magdeburg area.

Again *JG 301* put all available aircraft into the air in an attempt to make the enemy's approach to the target area as difficult as possible. On this day the newly-formed *IV./JG 301* flew its first major mission against enemy bombers as part of the *Geschwader*. Equipped with the Bf 109 G-10, these *Staffeln* initially caused some confusion.

The *I.* and *II. Gruppe*, which took off from Salzwedel and Stendal, had not yet received replacements for their most recent losses and were therefore forced to take off with far fewer aircraft than usual. It wasn't much different for the *III. Gruppe*, which took off from Sachau. The *Gruppe* had sufficient pilots available, but because of delays in the delivery of sufficient numbers of Ta 152s to completely reequip the *Gruppe*, it had less than a full complement of aircraft. The *Gruppe* put a mixed group of fighters into the air, twelve Ta 152s and about the same number of Fw 190 A-8s and A-9s.

For the Ta 152 pilots, this mission brought a reversal of roles. They had formerly flown in the "Heavy *Gruppe*", whose main target was always the bombers, but now the small force of Ta 152s would have to form part of the fighter escort. The pilots were looking forward to their first encounters with the Mustang, for many had a score to settle with the escort fighters. The reality was much different, however.

Immediately after takeoff the fighters were vectored almost due south, toward the Harz region, and radio traffic revealed that the other *Gruppen* of the *Jagdgeschwader* were also heading in that direction. The Ta 152s, which were led by *Oberleutnant* Stahl, climbed to altitude very quickly and flew far above the rest of the formation. The *Geschwader* formed up loosely on reaching grid square "Heinrich-Cäsar". The Ta 152s were flying at a height of just over 8,000 meters, and there they encountered a formation of Bf 109s. The pilots of the Ta 152s were certainly not upset by this unexpected reinforcement, especially as the aircraft wore the same yellow and red fuselage band.

But seconds later we could not believe our eyes: the group of Bf 109s opened up on us and the first tracers flashed by. *Unteroffizier* Blum was the first to be attacked, and his immediate warning made us realize the situation we were suddenly in. There was immediate confusion and the radio traffic that followed did nothing to change the situation. The leader of the Ta *Staffel* received the

Stendal in March 1945: II./JG 301 at fifteen minute readiness.

Stendal in March 1945. Hauptmann Nölter, Gruppenkommandeur of II./JG 301, reads out the order of the day.

order to, "Climb up and stay with the formation!" But even this did no good, for the *Geschwader*'s own Bf 109s continued to pursue and attack. It was also not possible to determine whether it was just Bf 109s of our own unit that were chasing us or if there were also fighters from other units. The Ta 152 pilots found themselves in a situation which words can scarcely describe: we were all fleeing from our own comrades, whom we did not want to shoot down. Many came to realize just how small and pitiful one feels when he is unable to defend himself. The Ta 152s were thus scattered to the four winds by our own fighters and took no further part in the mission.

This incident illustrates the breakdown in communications that affected the *Luftwaffe* at that time. There were gaps in information even within our own unit. Many fighter pilots were completely unfamiliar with the Ta 152 and, thinking them to be enemy aircraft, naturally attacked. The complicated communications system between *Jagdgeschwader* further added to the confusion.

The incident was also the triggering mechanism for the disaster that overwhelmed the pilots of *JG 301* in the following minutes. A large group of P-51s took advantage of the confusion to take our fighters unawares, and for *IV./JG 301* the tragedy quickly took its course. Combats rapidly spread over large areas of central Germany, extending beyond Dresden as far as Bohemia. *II./JG 301*, in particular, became heavily involved with the American escort fighters south of Dresden.

As the pilots of the *IV. Gruppe* were on their first mission against the bomber formations and in part on their own, they proved unequal to the overpowering enemy and paid a high price in blood. This disaster would probably never have happened had not so many unforeseen conditions been encountered at the same time, had their been a better exchange of information between the fighter control center and the fighter units, and, not least, had all parts of our own *Geschwader* been better informed about our own intentions.

2 March 1945 was the last time *JG 301* flew a major defensive mission against the enemy's four-engined bombers. It also marked the end of a once powerful *Jagdgeschwader* in the Defense of the Reich. For the Ta 152 *Staffel*, which was attacked by friendly fighters, the mission was one great debacle. While it was demonstrated that the Ta 152 could easily climb away from our other fighters, the anticipated encounter with the Mustangs did not happen. The *Staffel* suffered no losses, but on the other hand it also claimed no successes. The misunderstandings had also resulted in the entire fighter unit becoming separated and facing overwhelming numbers of the enemy in different areas.

JG 301 suffered the following losses on 2 March 1945:

I./JG 301:

During the course of the air battle this *Gruppe* was forced far to the south, where the *2. Staffel* under *Oberleutnant* Oskar Schenk bore the brunt of the fighting.

Unteroffizier Gerhard Güttel of the *2. Staffel* failed to return from this mission and was declared missing. His fate remains a mystery. (Fw 190 A-9, WNr. 207 193).

Oberfeldwebel Hans Schäfer of the *2. Staffel* was also listed missing on this day, and his fate remains unknown (Fw 190 A-9, WNr. 207 193).

Fähnrich Heinrich Lieb of the *2. Staffel* was shot down and killed in combat with Mustangs over Bohemia (Fw 190 A-9).

Right: Fähnrich Helmut Rix of 8./JG 301 was wounded in combat near Aussig and bailed out.

Below: Pilots of IV./JG 301 "Hindenburg" at Gardelegen in March 1945. Standing, from the left: Unteroffizier Archibald Rahn, Oberfähnrich Jost Bezdeka, Oberfähnrich Hermann Schmidt, Unteroffizier Hans Brüggler (KIA near Gotha on 4 April 1945), Feldwebel Alois Hasenkopf (WIA near Burg on 2 March 1945), Oberfähnrich Jochen Damaske, Leutnant Müller, unidentified Unteroffizier, Unteroffizier Robert Vögele (WIA near Stendal on 22 February 1945), Oberfeldwebel Wolf (probably).

Bf 109 G-10. In November of 1944 JG 301's IV. Gruppe was equipped with aircraft of this type.

II./JG 301: Leutnant Spies and Leutnant Hagedorn reconnoitering the terrain around Sachau airfield.

II./JG 301:

As the air battle widened, this *Jagdgruppe* was also forced into the airspace south of Dresden as far as Aussig. Unable to get through to the bombers, it was constantly engaged with enemy fighters.

Unteroffizier Günter Schulz of the *5. Staffel* was shot down and killed west of Schlanstedt (Fw 190 D-9 "White 14", WNr. 500 569).

Fähnrich Hans Geban of the *6. Staffel* went down with his Fw 190 near Störbke. The cause of the crash is unexplained.

Fahnenjunker-Unteroffizier Walter Gescheit of the *6. Staffel* was shot down over Dresden (Fw 190 D-9 "Red 2", WNr. 500 419).

Unteroffizier Egbert Müller of the *6. Staffel* was shot down by Mustangs over Dresden (Fw 190 D-9 "Red 11", WNr. 500 429).

Unteroffizier Jürgen Dietrich of the *8. Staffel* crashed to his death near Fleyh, cause unknown (Fw 190 D-9 "Blue 10", WNr. 206 169).

Unteroffizier Wolfgang Ehrlich of the *8. Staffel* was shot down and killed over Dresden (Fw 190 A-9 "Blue 9", WNr. 206 164).

Unteroffizier Helmut Heger of the *8. Staffel* was overwhelmed and shot down near Dresden-Klotzsche (Fw 190 A-9 "Blue 4", WNr. 980 582).

Leutnant Walter Kropp, acting commander of the *8. Staffel*, was shot down and killed near Wörkwitz (Fw 190 D-9 "Red 1", WNr. 500 431).

Fahnenjunker-Unteroffizier Helmut Rix of the *8. Staffel* was shot down by Mustangs over Aussig. He bailed out and landed safely. (Fw 190 D-9 "Red 4", WNr. 500 111).

III./JG 301:

In addition to the Ta 152s, this *Gruppe* also put approximately ten to twelve Fw 190 A-8s and A-9s into the air. They were attacked by Mustangs over and south of Magdeburg following a failed attempt to attack the bombers and suffered heavy losses.

IV./JG 301:

The majority of the pilots of this *Jagdgruppe* came from the disbanded *III./KG 77 "Hindenburg"*, having flown the He 177 on operations. For all of them it was their first mission in the *Reichsverteidigung* against the American fighters and bombers. The fighting west and northwest of Magdeburg had just one possible outcome, a bitter defeat.

Oberfähnrich Walter Rummel of the *13. Staffel* was shot down by escort fighters over Burg at the very beginning of the air battle (Bf 109 G-10 "White 12", WNr. 150 787).

Oberfähnrich Josef Bäcker of the *13. Staffel* was wounded in combat over Burg, however he made a successful forced landing near his home airfield Bf 109 G-10 "Green 4", WNr. 491 152).

Feldwebel Helmuth Hasenkopf of the *13. Staffel* was wounded in combat over Burg but was able to parachute to safety (Bf 109 G-10 "White 9", WNr. 491 186).

Unteroffizier Vinzenz Heilberger of the *13. Staffel* was shot down near the town of Regendorf (Bf 109 G-10 "White 4", WNr. 150 715).

Oberleutnant Johann Patek, *Staffelkapitän* of *13./JG 301*, led his *Staffel* into battle against superior numbers of enemy fighters over Burg. He was subsequently shot down and crashed near the city (Bf 109 G-10 "White 5", WNr. 151 515).

Unteroffizier Otto Zietlow of the *13. Staffel* suffered the same fate and fell near Burg (Bf 109 G-10 "White 11", WNr. 150 812).

Unteroffizier Alfred Appel of the *14. Staffel* was shot down by Mustangs. He and his machine crashed onto Burg airfield (Bf 109 G-10 "Red 4", WNr. 610 100).

Unteroffizier Otto Bayerl of the *14. Staffel* was shot down and wounded. He managed to escape his doomed fighter near Altengrabe (Bf 109 G-10, WNr. 150 745).

Fähnrich Harald Ruh of the *15. Staffel* was shot down by enemy fighters and went down with his machine near the town of Stresow (Bf 109 G-10 "Yellow 7", WNr. 491 200).

Unteroffizier Siegfried Hornschuh of the *15. Staffel* was shot down and bailed out over Burg (Bf 109 G-10 "Yellow 6", WNr. 491 240).

Fähnrich Fritz Blechschmidt of the *15. Staffel* was also wounded in combat near Burg and parachuted to safety (Bf 109 G-10 "Yellow 8", WNr. 151 621).

Unteroffizier Leonhard Keil of the *15. Staffel* also crashed to his death near Burg during the fighting (Bf 109 G-10 "Yellow 1", WNr. 151 087).

Unteroffizier Rudolf Welsch of the *15. Staffel* was shot down by escort fighters and went down with his aircraft near the town of Racksdorf (Bf 109 G-10 "Yellow 17", WNr. 151 556).

IV./JG 301 never recovered from this blow. The heavy losses suffered on this day began a process that resulted in the unit being disbanded in early April 1945. Its remaining pilots were reassigned to the other three *Gruppen*. Like those of many other units, the *Gruppe*'s ground personnel were transferred to the infantry.

The air battle of 2 March 1945 covered a vast area from Burg northwest of Magdeburg almost to Prague. The loss reports indicate that their was fighting throughout the entire area. Small numbers of the *Geschwader*'s fighters must have stayed to together long enough to attack the bombers. The records contain claims of B-17s shot down in the Magdeburg area by *Oberfeldwebel* Hans Todt of the 8. *Staffel* and *Leutnant* August-Wilhelm Hagedorn of the 9. *Staffel*. It seems highly likely that these were not the only successes by the *Geschwader*'s pilots, for the American 8th Air Force admitted the loss of fifteen four-engined bombers and fifteen escort fighters. Proving this is extremely difficult, however an appendix to the victory list contains the following entry:

Oberstleutnant Fritz Auffhammer, *Stab*, three fighter kills missing.
Hauptmann Wilhelm Burggraf, eight other victories missing.
Hauptmann Wilhelm Fulda, one four-engined bomber kill missing.
Leutnant Anton Benning, five fighter and nine four-engined bomber kills missing.
Major Gerhard Posselmann, three daylight victories missing.
Hauptmann Helmut Suhr had three more victories.
Hauptmann Erich Wegener, five additional victories.
Leutnant Max Kreil, four additional victories are missing.
Oberfeldwebel Willi Kropf, six victories missing.
Unteroffizier Willi Greiner had three more victories.
Unteroffizier August Hölscher, two four-engined bomber and one P-51 kill missing.
Oberfeldwebel Erich Meyer, five victories missing.
Oberfeldwebel Heinz Gossow, three more four-engined bomber kills missing.

For *JG 301*, the mission on 2 March 1945 was its last major operation against enemy bombers. From then on its primary role was ground attack missions in support of hard-pressed army units on the Eastern and Western Fronts. The enemy's fighters and bombers now controlled the airspace over Germany at all altitudes. This fact is graphically illustrated by what happened to *Unteroffizier* Heinrich Panno of *I./JG 301* on 8 March 1945 while ferrying a repaired Fw 190 A-9 from Brunswick to Salzwedel. While on approach to land at Salzwedel, he was attacked by American fighters and shot down from a height of seventy meters. He was fortunate to crash near the fire hall, as fire-fighters reached the scene immediately and pulled the badly wounded pilot from his aircraft. He was taken to hospital in Munsterlager and was not released until September 1945.

Formation of a Staff Flight Equipped with the Ta 152

III./JG 301's complement of Ta 152s had not increased, and as there was little hope of receiving additional aircraft, the surviving aircraft were passed on to the *Geschwaderstab* and used to form a *Stabsschwarm*, or staff flight. Effective 13 March 1945 the following pilots were transferred to the *Geschwaderstab*:

Oberfeldwebel Sepp Sattler, *10. Staffel*,
Oberfeldwebel Josef Keil, *10. Staffel*,
Feldwebel Willi Reschke, *9. Staffel*,
Unteroffizier Christoph Blum, *9. Staffel*.

On that same day *Feldwebel* Reschke flew Ta 152 H-1 "Black 13" from Sachau to Stendal, departing at 1615 hours and landing at Stendal at 1625. There were two reasons for *Feldwebel* Reschke's flight to Stendal: on this day he was awarded the German Cross in Gold by *Oberstleutnant* Auffhammer, the *Geschwaderkommodore*.

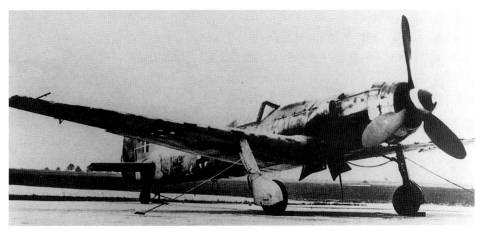

Ta 152 H-1. The entire III. Gruppe of JG 301 was supposed to have been equipped with this type. Lack of aircraft prevented this plan from being implemented, however, and only the Stabsschwarm was equipped with this outstanding fighter aircraft.

The main reason for the quick ferrying of a Ta 152 to Stendal, however, was an inspection of the *Geschwaderstab* by *General* Dietrich Peltz. The former Commanding General of Bombers, Peltz had recently taken the place of *General der Jagdflieger* Adolf Galland, who left the post following differences with Hermann Göring. Galland subsequently formed *JV 44*, a fighter unit equipped with the Me 262 jet, and assembled a group of ace pilots to fly with him. This change was a clear indication that the *Luftwaffe* command had completely abandoned the bomber force and was now devoting all its resources to maintaining its few remaining fighter units. The pilots in the *Jagdstaffeln* were not unaware of the differences within the *Luftwaffe* command, however, and *Reichsmarschall* Göring lost all respect among the fighter pilots after relieving *General der Jagdflieger* Galland.

We were never told the exact purpose of *General* Peltz's inspection of the *Geschwaderstab* and *II./JG 301*, but it is noteworthy that the general climbed into the cockpit of a Ta 152 and took the aircraft up on a test flight. Unfortunately we never learned his impressions of this fighter aircraft.

The *Gruppen* of *JG 301* were now frequently committed separately, and from this time on the *Stabsschwarm* often flew fighter cover for *II./JG 301*, which operated from the same airfield. It also took part in missions by the other *Gruppen*, however, and there were days when the *Stabsschwarm* participated in several missions. The ground personnel had their hands full keeping the Ta 152s serviceable as various technical problems arose. The most serious difficulties were caused by the supercharger's third stage and malfunctioning weapons.

Late one afternoon I was sent up from Stendal in a Ta 152 to intercept a Mosquito flying reconnaissance high over Berlin. There were two radars near the *Geschwaderstab*'s dispersal, a *Freya* and a *Würzburg*, and I received excellent guidance, sighting the Mosquito over Genthin. It was on its way home, flying at a height of more than 9,000 meters. As I was still a few hundred meters lower, I tried to at least reach the same altitude while closing the distance.

Although the Mosquito was an extremely fast aircraft at high altitude, I was able to overtake it very rapidly even though I was in a shallow climb. In my Ta 152 everything was ready: I had the Mosquito in the illuminated reticle of my gunsight and my fingers were on the firing levers. I had already informed ground control, with which I was in constant contact, that I was about to attack. Suddenly a jolt shook the Ta 152 and my speed dropped: the third stage of the supercharger had cut out, even though it had functioned well when it engaged at about 7,000 meters. The Mosquito continued on its way unharmed, its crew probably unaware that they had barely escaped destruction.

Such or similar technical malfunctions were quite rare, and the mechanics had actually become adept at fixing them. It was simply a fighter aircraft that was still in the test stage, but which received very high marks from the test pilots. For this reason we were always searching for aircraft that had left the manufacturer in a serviceable state. Unfortunately our efforts were largely in vain: further deliveries of Ta 152s had been cut off.

The pilots of the *Stabsschwarm* now had little contact with their former comrades of *III./JG 301*. The latter was still based at Sachau, flying missions over the Eastern and Western Fronts – like the other *Gruppen*. JG 301's last encounter with the heavy bombers took place on 15 March 1945, although only part of the *Geschwader* was involved. *Hauptmann* Helmut Suhr reported a B-17 shot down over northwestern Germany, *JG 301*'s last victory over a four-engined bomber. Most subsequent missions were directed against enemy positions on both fronts, using guns and sometimes bombs

Stendal, 14 March 1945. From left: Oberstleutnant Auffhammer, Generalleutnant Peltz and – with his back to the camera – Hauptmann Nölter.

Generalleutnant Peltz and Hauptmann Nölter review the assembled personnel of II./JG 301. In the background is the Ar 96 which Oberfeldwebel Reschke and Feldwebel Blum flew to Erfurt on 8 April 1945 to collect two Ta 152 H-1s.

Above: Generalleutnant Peltz in conversation with pilots of II. and III./JG 301. In the background are Unteroffiziere Schalk, Warnicke and Scheller of III./JG 301. Born in Gera on 9 June 1914, Dietrich Peltz became a general at 28 and at 29 the youngest commanding general in the German armed services. He had a decisive influence on the development of the bomber arm. On 23 July 1943 he became the 31st member of the Wehrmacht to receive the Knight's Cross with Swords and Oak Leaves. On 1 January 1945, during the Ardennes offensive, he assumed command of the II. Jagdfliegerkorps and on 1 March took over the entire Defense of the Reich. When the war ended he was commanding general of the I. Fliegerkorps. After the war he worked for Krupp and Telefunken, becoming manager of the latter's factory in Konstanz.

Right: Stendal, March 1945: Generalleutnant Peltz climbs into the cockpit of Ta 152 "Black 13".

carried beneath the fuselage. In a matter of days the fighter unit had become a fighter-bomber unit, a situation that was to remain unchanged until the end of the war. For the *Geschwader* the days of large-scale air battles were over, but also the days of heavy losses. There were still losses during missions over the Eastern and Western Fronts, but most were the result of the changed role of the enemy's escort fighters. With little reason to fear attacks on the bombers by German fighters, they were free to take on other missions.

Instead of sitting idle on their airfields in England, the long-range fighters increasingly turned to fighter-bomber role. We called these low-flying attackers "Choppers". Small formations of enemy fighter-bombers, American P-47s and P-51s and British Spitfires and Tempests, were to be found everywhere over Germany, especially at low altitude. The attacks by the fighter-bombers always came by surprise and pilots of *JG 301* were among those who lost their lives as a result.

One such was *Obergefreiter* Herbert Kölsch of the *1. Staffel*, who was attacked by a flight of fighter-bombers in the Langenhagen area during a transfer flight. He suffered serious wounds and died in hospital on 27 March 1945. (Fw 190 A-8, WNr. 683 335)

Unteroffizier Otto Taubert of the *2. Staffel* was shot down and killed by enemy fighters over Salzwedel airfield on 27 March (Fw 190 A-9, WNr. 980 548). *Feldwebel* Herbert Müller of the *2. Staffel* was shot down and killed over his own airfield on the same day (Fw 190 A-9, WNr. 202 408).

At the end of March 1945 *Unteroffizier* Heinz Warnicke of the *12. Staffel* was killed on another of these missions, whose objective was unknown to us. To this day it is not known where his Fw 190 A-8 went down. Warnicke joined the *Geschwader* in autumn 1944 and subsequently earned the Iron Cross, First Class, but his name appears in no victory list.

Other members of the *Geschwader* lost at the end of March were *Fähnrich* Ulrich Leopold and *Gefreiter* Konrad Witzgall, both of the *2. Staffel*. Where they went down remains a mystery.

March 1945 at Stendal: pilots of III./JG 301. In the background a team of oxen is seen pulling a Fw 190 to a Staffel dispersal.

At the end of March 1945 *Feldwebel* Rudi Driebe of *III./JG 301* wrote the following poem at the *11. Staffel*'s dispersal between missions over the Eastern Front:

We never knew
if we were flying for the last time,
German heart beating in our breasts,
urging us to attack, to prevail.
Never did we lay wreaths
or shed tears for the pilots,
we laughed through it all
and the dead laughed with us.
Always filled with cheer and strength
we swung the torch,
and from the dark night freed
the devil himself and god of old.

2 April 1945, Easter Sunday

Oberfähnrich Ludwig Bracht of *III./JG 301*, whose home is in Korbach, wrote the following in his diary about 1 and 2 April 1945:

"The aircraft were prepared for a mission over our own country. Area of operations Kassel-Hersfeld-Eschwege-Witzenhausen. We attacked American columns from low level using 250kg bomb dispensers loaded with one-kg anti-personnel bombs.

Oberfähnriche Ludwig Bracht and Hans Fay of III./JG 301.

240

March 1945 at Gardelegen. Oberfähnrich Jochen Damaske with the ground crewman responsible for his aircraft. Damaske was killed near Eschwege on 2 April 1945.

2 April 1945. Three missions today in the Kassel area with fragmentation bombs, my Fw 190 was hit. A piston seized as I was approaching to land at Salzwedel, but I was able to make a belly landing beside the airfield to avoid endangering the other aircraft taking off and myself. Hit my head on the gunsight. Commanding officer at Salzwedel *Major* Posselmann."

On that 2 April the entire *Geschwader* launched waves of attacks against American tanks and infantry advancing west of Eisenach. All of the aircraft carried a 250kg fragmentation bomb instead of an external fuel tank. Attacks on that sector of the front went on almost all day. To what degree they slowed the American advance is not known, but the *Geschwader*'s pilots displayed great dedication to duty in carrying them out.

The following did not return from these missions:

Unteroffizier Siegfried Schulz of the *2. Staffel*. From Jüterbog, Schulz was declared killed in action, though it is not known where he died. Not until 1996 were the remains of his Fw 190 A-9 discovered in excavations near Ifta. An identity disk found in the wreckage identified the pilot as Schulz. Also found during the excavation was Schulz's Iron Cross. First Class. His name never appeared in any victory list. The remains of *Unteroffizier* Siegfried Schulz were buried in the military cemetery in Herleshausen, with many of the local population in attendance.

The Fw 190 A-9 flown by *Leutnant* Horst Reinhold of the *11. Staffel* was hit by ground fire during one of these missions, and he attempted to reach the airfield at Erfurt-Bindersleben. As he was coming in to land, with his undercarriage down, Reinhold was attacked and shot down by a Mustang. He was buried in the main cemetery in Erfurt.

According to statements by comrades, *Oberleutnant* Friedrich Kranke of the *12. Staffel* met an airman's death. Kranke had only recently joined *III./JG 301*; it is not known where he was lost. He is one of the many German fighter pilots who still lie with their machines, buried in unknown locations beneath German soil.

Fähnrich Friedrich Redlein of the *13. Staffel* was shot down while attacking American armored units near Eschwege. He died when his Bf 109 G-10 struck the ground.

Oberfeldwebel Erwin Bunk of the *14. Staffel* and his Bf 109 G-10 were reported missing after a ground-attack mission.

The attack by the American armored spearheads continued in the days that followed, for *Feldwebel* Max Schleifenheimer of the *1. Staffel* was killed in the Eisenach-Gotha area on 3 April 1945.

Oberfeldwebel Hans Müller of the *2. Staffel* was wounded during a ground attack mission on 5 April but was able to fly his machine back to his base at Salzwedel.

Unteroffizier Adolf Schäpers of the *4. Staffel* also took part in this mission and was wounded. He wrote: "My last mission was on 5 April 1945, from Salzwedel in the direction of Thuringia. We were supposed to attack American armored forces. I was wounded in the right arm by anti-aircraft during a low-level attack. I could only move my left arm, but with a great deal of luck I managed a

Left: Unteroffizier Siegfried Schulz of 2./JG 301, killed in action west of Eisenach on 2 April 1945. Right: Oberleutnant Friedrich Kranke of 12./JG 301, killed near Eisenach in early April 1945.

The Dietsche brothers: Horst Dietsche was an Obergefreiter and worked in the command post, Karl-Heinz Dietsche was a Hauptmann and Staffelkapitän in I./JG 302 and III./JG 301. In the center is their mother.

smooth forced landing near Weimar. I was subsequently taken to hospital in Weimar. The Americans entered the city several days later."

The fronts were now closing in from both sides and it was becoming ever more difficult for the *Jagdgruppen* to take off from their own airfields. Enemy fighters, mainly P-47s, often appeared over *JG 301*'s bases in the early morning hours to prevent the *Gruppe* from taking off or landing. This always meant a tough time for the pilots assigned to the airfield protection flights, whose mission was to cover the rest of the *Gruppe*. As a rule only experienced pilots were assigned to the protection flights.

These experienced "Old Hares" were becoming fewer in number, most having fallen in earlier battles. But it was in the hell fires of these increasingly difficult air battles that the experienced pilots were at their best. Of course they were not invulnerable and stood a chance of being shot down.

In those days the airfield protection flights were also unable to prevent *III./JG 301*'s base at Sachau from being attacked by a group of P-47 fighter-bombers, which showered the airfield with bombs. One bomb struck the *Gruppe* command post, killing *Unteroffizier* Horst Dietsche, a clerk working there. He was the brother of the former *Staffelkapitän* of *10./JG 301*, *Hauptmann* Karl-Heinz Dietsche, who had since been transferred.

One day a group of Mustangs strafed Stendal airfield. As our aircraft were well concealed in earth-walled revetments in the surrounding forest, the enemy concentrated on the hangars. One Mustang pilot swooped down, headed straight for the open door of one hangar, and fired at the aircraft inside. He pulled up a fraction of a second too late, however, and the roof of the hangar tore off the entire underside of the Mustang. We later found the remains of the aircraft and its pilot lying on the sports field just beyond the hangar.

Unteroffizier Moneta of the *11. Staffel* was also involved in a collision with an object on the ground. Flying a Fw 190 equipped with an external tank, he struck a workshop vehicle during a low

Left: Fähnrich Herbert Evers of I./JG 301. Evers was killed on 7 April 1945, probably while flying escort for the Elbe mission. He is buried in Zimmernsupra in Thuringia. Right: Unteroffizier Heinz Sonntag of 11./JG 301 was killed in action over Bokelskamp on 8 April 1945. Pilot and aircraft were not recovered until years later. His gravesite is in the Wienhausen cemetery.

pass. Unlike the American pilot, however, Moneta made a successful forced landing. His subsequent fate is unknown, but he was probably killed on a later mission.

One day in early April 1945 a group of B-24 Liberator bombers flew over Stendal on their way back from Berlin. One must have had bombs left, and these were dropped on the airfield. They were probably jettisoned rather than aimed and they merely created a few craters at the edge of the airfield.

In the last days of March one could observe more and more pilots arriving at Stendal who did not belong to *JG 301*. I spoke to some of them but was unable to find out why they had gathered at the airfield.

One evening – it may have been 4 or 5 April 1945 – I ran into *Unteroffizier* Suckrow in the mess. We had both been at flying school A/G 9 in Grottkau in early 1943. He told me that he was one of the pilots I had been seeing everywhere on the airfield for the past few days and that they were part of "Operational Detachment Elbe", which was to undertake ramming attacks against enemy bombers. Sitting with him was his fiancé, who had come in from Berlin, and I recalled that Suckrow had been born in Berlin. A very interesting conversation developed, the main topic of which, of course, was the coming mission by "*Kommando Elbe*". As I had once rammed an enemy

On 7 April 1945 Gefreiter Reinhard Kleinstück of 2./JG 301 was shot down by American fighters near Deilmissen...

... he attempted a belly landing but something went wrong, with fatal consequences. His aircraft came down on the road from Deilmissen to Esbeck.

Right: Unteroffizier Herbert Kordas' pilot identity card dated 18 February 1945.

Below: Taken in 1942, this photo shows the later Feldwebel Friedrich Winter, back row second from the left, and Oberfeldwebel Helmut Krönke, back row second from the right. Both joined III./ JG 301 in December 1944.

bomber, I was able to describe to him the sound produced by the collision of two aircraft, something that stayed with one for days and weeks afterward. The evening prior to 7 April 1945 we met again in the mess, where most of those present were pilots I had never seen before. The majority of these pilots had no combat experience and had spent all their time at schools. Suckrow, too, had been transferred from one school to another, even though it had always been his desire to fly with a combat unit.

He told me that his apartment in Berlin had been reduced to soot and ashes and that he wanted to take this opportunity to do his part to defend the homeland. He was thirsting for action and on 7 April 1945 he took off under waving war flags. I do not know if he survived this mission.

There was a secret order within the *Luftwaffe* concerning *"Kommando Elbe"* and its ramming operation, calling on the units to support the mission. This order was to be read out to the assembled aircrew by commanders of *Gruppen* and *Geschwader*, after which it was to be destroyed.

It is difficult to say to what extent this directive was followed by the various *Jagdgeschwader*. The pilots of *JG 301* certainly did not join *"Kommando Elbe"*, but one can assume that elements of the *Geschwader* flew escort for the ramming mission.

Fähnrich Herbert Evers of *I./JG 301*, who had joined the *Gruppe* at Finsterwalde in February 1945, did not return from this mission. He and his Fw 190 D-9 were shot down by Mustangs near Zimmernsupra in Thuringia. He was buried in Zimmernsupra the same day.

According to eyewitnesses, *Gefreiter* Reinhard Kleinstück of the *2. Staffel* was shot down by American fighters near Deilmissen and attempted a forced landing. He managed to put the fighter down, but then it slid across a road and was completely wrecked. Kleinstück's body was recovered from the wreckage. This very green pilot had flown only a few missions.

Unteroffizier Franz Schrack of the *12. Staffel* was killed in the fighting near Lüneburg.

Always on the lookout for Ta 152s that had left the factory serviceable, we discovered that two were waiting to be collected at the REWE production works in Erfurt-North. Early on 8 April 1945 *Oberfeldwebel* Reschke and *Feldwebel* Blum – both had been promoted on 1 April – flew from Stendal to Erfurt-North in an Ar 96 to pick up the two Ta 152s.

Knowing that low-flying enemy aircraft were constantly active over steadily shrinking Germany, we stayed low, exploiting every bit of cover, and reached Erfurt. We taxied the Ar 96 right up to the hangar, in front of which sat the two Ta 152s. The handover was completed quickly and the two-seat Ar 96 trainer left sitting in front of the hangar. Both Ta 152s were fueled and fitted with armament, but had not been armed. We would therefore be taking off with no ammunition. As we taxied for takeoff the air raid sirens began wailing, signaling the approach of fighter-bombers supporting the American armored spearheads. We had very fast fighter aircraft, but without ammunition we could not really defend ourselves if things got serious. But everything went well, and we landed safely at Stendal. The *Geschwaderstab* now had two more Ta 152 H-1s.

According to statements by *Unteroffizier* Herbert Kordas of *II./JG 301* at Sachau, at that time a radio message was received from Celle air base saying that eighteen Ta 152s could be collected immediately. When the pilots got to Celle they could not believe their eyes: standing before the aircraft they saw that the tailwheels of all the Ta 152s had been destroyed, rendering them unflyable.

The *Geschwader* flew further missions on 8 April, all against American armored spearheads in the Kassel-Eisenach area. Ground troops were also attacked with bombs and guns, however the enemy's fighter-bombers were always in the forefront. At this time the pilots often had the feeling that every *Gruppenkommandeur* had become his own general, using his own judgment to select the timing for missions. All missions were now "Twilight Missions", flown in the early evening and increasingly the early morning.

Unteroffizier Heinz Sonntag of the *11. Staffel* failed to return from one such mission. As it was not known where he was lost, he was initially listed missing in action. It was not until many years after the war that his aircraft was discovered near Celle. *Unteroffizier* Sonntag was buried in Wienhausen cemetery near Celle.

On the same day *Oberfeldwebel* Herbert Krönke of the *12. Staffel* was shot down and killed while attacking American ground troops near Ammern in Thuringia.

Chapter Ten

JG 301's Last Transfer

All day long on 10 April 1945 the thunder of guns could be heard more clearly from *JG 301*'s airfields. During the night that followed, the members of the *Geschwaderstab* and *II. Gruppe* at Stendal failed to get a single hour of sleep. Under cover of darkness all serviceable aircraft were positioned for takeoff. The bulk of the technical personnel and those pilots without aircraft left Stendal during the night and headed in the direction of Neustadt-Glewe air base near Ludwigslust in Mecklenburg. A few technicians stayed behind to help prepare the aircraft for takeoff. Some squeezed into the aircraft with their pilots. It was a proper "Dawn Takeoff". Coming from the south, the American armored spearheads had reached the environs of the air base.

The *I.* and *II. Gruppe* probably moved a few days later. This is confirmed by an entry in the logbook of *Oberfeldwebel* Artur Groß, who together with his *Schwarm* flew cover over Gardelegen on 15 April. Groß subsequently flew to Schwerin on 18 April. It is believed that from that date on the *Geschwader* was concentrated in a relatively small area once again: the *Geschwaderstab* and *II. Gruppe* at Neustadt-Glewe and the *I.* and *II. Gruppe* at Hagenow.

The air base at Neustadt-Glewe was completely surrounded by forest, and the aircraft were dispersed around the airfield in well-camouflaged positions at the forest's edge. This was vitally important, for enemy aircraft kept the airfield under observation throughout the day. The technical personnel and pilots were housed in wooden barracks, and the command post was a wooden hut. Only at the northwest edge of the airfield were there small metal hangars. Nearby, at the south edge of the airfield close to the bank of a small stream, there was a caravan, well-hidden beneath trees. From this time forward *Hauptmann* Cescotti and *Oberleutnant* Sievers were quartered in one half of the caravan, with *Oberfeldwebel* Sattler and Reschke in the other.

Neustadt-Glewe airfield had another advantage: positioned around the airfield were twin-barreled 20mm anti-aircraft guns with a clear field of fire in all directions. In the coming days the pilots would come to value their support.

I once had a comrade... II./JG 301 in April 1945: funeral for a fallen fighter pilot at the Neustadt-Glewe cemetery near Parchim. The identity of the deceased pilot cannot be determined. Giving the funeral oration is Leutnant Haudeck, n the foreground is HFW Mohrmeiser.

On the day prior to this transfer *Gruppenkommandeur* and Knight's Cross wearer *Hauptmann* Herbert Nölter had been seriously wounded during a mission by *II./JG 301* near Halberstadt. He was taken to hospital in Rendsburg, where he died of his injuries on 13 May 1945.

Hauptmann Nölter had received the Knight's Cross for his actions as a bomber pilot while serving with *I./KG 3*, where he flew more than 300 combat missions. On his final bombing mission he was forced to bail out after suffering engine failure and three days later made his way back to the German lines. In the summer of 1944 he retrained as a fighter pilot and at the beginning of December assumed command of *II./JG 301*. He probably had no victories to his credit.

After the loss of Nölter, *Hauptmann* Robert Cescotti, who had previously served in the *Geschwaderstab*, assumed command of the *II. Gruppe*.

At that time almost all of the remaining fighter units were concentrated in northern Germany. As a result, *Oberst* Karl-Gottfried Nordmann, commanding the *1. Jagddivision* and responsible for fighter operations over the Eastern Front, sometimes controlled these from Neustadt-Glewe.

The *Geschwaderstab* and *II./JG 301* had not yet settled into Neustadt-Glewe when the first mission order came. The target was Stendal airfield: American motorized units on the airfield were to be attacked with guns. It was a strange feeling to know that *JG 301*'s home base was in enemy hands and that we were to attack it from the air. We knew every building, every path, every square meter from so well that it was hard to squeeze the triggers. The expected concentration of American vehicles was not found, however, and the pilots of the *II. Gruppe* took pains to only shoot at vehicles that did not belong there. No buildings were fired at, as none of the pilots could bring himself to put his gunsight on them.

The *Stabsschwarm*, which was to provide top cover with its Ta 152s, had little difficulty carrying out its mission. There was a brief encounter with several P-47 fighter-bombers, one of which was immediately shot down by *Oberfeldwebel* Jupp. This put a quick end to the combat.

In the coming days the *Geschwader* did not operate as a unit, instead the *Gruppen* were given individual combat assignments. The enemy was now watching our airfields round the clock, which made it impossible for a mass takeoff by the entire *Geschwader*. The *Gruppen* based at Neustadt-Glewe and Hagenow were increasingly forced to fly "Twilight Missions". Takeoffs were made as late in the evening as possible to avoid interference by enemy fighters. This tactic succeeded only rarely, for the enemy had long since moved his bases into western Germany and was always close by. While the *Gruppen* did fly some missions against targets on the west bank of the Elbe between Lauenburg and Boizenburg, where the English front was advancing, the main effort was against the Eastern Front around the Berlin area.

On 13 April 1945 *Leutnant* Anton Benning, *Staffelkapitän* of *1./JG 301*, was awarded the Knight's Cross for his actions in the Defense of the Reich. He had been a member of the *Luftwaffe* since 1938 and served for a long time as a flight instructor. He flew transports into the Stalingrad pocket and in early 1943 retrained as a fighter pilot. From September 1943 he served with both *JG 302* and *JG 301*. At the beginning of January 1945 he was named commander of the *1. Staffel*. While serving as a fighter pilot he shot down twenty-eight enemy aircraft by day and night, including eighteen four-engined bombers.

As the *Stabsschwarm* and its Ta 152s were based with *II./JG 301* at Neustadt-Glewe, the fates of the two units' pilots were closely linked in the final days of the war. It was quite natural that the *Stabsschwarm* should provide high cover for the *Gruppe*. At this time the *Stabsschwarm* was bolstered by the addition of *Oberfeldwebel* Walter Loos, who had served successfully in *JG 300*. For a long time he had flown as wingman to *Oberst* Walter Dahl, *Geschwaderkommodore* of *JG 300*.

These were difficult days for the *Stabsschwarm*, for British and American fighters began circling overhead Neustadt-Glewe as soon as the sun came up. Spitfires and Tempests were especially active, keeping the airfield under close surveillance. They stayed at medium altitudes, however, for any attempt to go lower or overfly the airfield from one side was met by heavy, accurate fire from the 20mm anti-aircraft guns. The flak provided covering fire for takeoffs by the *Stabsschwarm* and *Gruppe*, with the *Stabsschwarm* always taking off first to provide top cover. *Oberleutnant* Hermann Stahl, former *Kapitän* of the *9. Staffel*, was transferred to the *Stabsschwarm* to help it perform this mission. The *Stabsschwarm* was increased in size to two flights of three aircraft (*Ketten*), but it was still no easy task to fend off the enemy fighters with these few machines. Though always outnumbered, the *Stabsschwarm* never lost an aircraft in these battles over the airfield. This can be attributed both to the quality of the Ta 152 and the skill and experience of the pilots. The *Stabsschwarm* was also very successful in enabling the *Gruppe* to take off and land without interference. During all of these missions just one pilot, an *Unteroffizier* of the *II. Gruppe*, was shot down in his Fw 190 D-9 while attempting to land. Unfortunately I have been unable to discover the pilot's name.

The *Stabsschwarm* always took off and landed under the protection of the base flak. Here, too, the special flight characteristics of the Ta 152 made themselves apparent: on takeoff it was possible to retract the undercarriage and flaps as soon as the aircraft left the ground, for unlike other types there was no loss of altitude. This made it possible for the aircraft to gain a great deal of speed at low level, and in such situations airspeed meant immediate readiness for combat.

Above: Leutnant Anton Benning, last Staffelkapitän of 1./JG 301. He was awarded the Knight's Cross on 13 April 1945.

Above left: Oberfeldwebel Walter Loos was transferred from JG 300 to JG 301 in the final weeks of the war. He was assigned to the Stabsschwarm where he flew the Ta 152.

Right: Oberfeldwebel Sepp Sattler. He was transferred from I./JG 302 to 10./JG 301 in September 1944. From March 1945 he flew the Ta 152 as a member of the Geschwader Stabsschwarm. On 14 April 1945 he was killed in a combat with Tempests near Ludwigslust.

On landing it was possible to make a very tight approach, which shortened the landing process considerably.

One day during this period *Feldwebel* Blum of the *Stabsschwarm* was extremely fortunate. As he came in to land, a Spitfire positioned itself behind him. The pilot of the Spitfire probably wanted to be very certain of his kill and shoot down the Ta 152 just before it landed. There can be no other explanation, for the enemy aircraft followed Blum through his entire approach without firing. The anti-aircraft gunners positioned around the airfield also observed the approach, but – like so many others – assumed that it was two of our aircraft about to land. When the error was discovered, all guns were of course turned on the Spitfire. Almost at once, the entire tail of the enemy aircraft was blown off. The Spitfire made a half roll, hit the ground inverted and slid after the Ta 152 as it landed. Blum landed his aircraft gingerly and while taxiing in was at a loss as to why there were now pieces of wreckage on the runway.

It was thanks to the gun crews manning the flak positions around the airfield that the aircraft were able to take off and land with a reasonable degree of safety, which gave our pilots a feeling of security. The enemy showed a great deal of respect for the guns and usually remained at a safe height. Whenever they ventured lower, it usually cost them at least one of their number. On another occasion two Spitfires attacked the airfield at low level. One was hit by anti-aircraft fire and crashed near the Elbe.

14 April 1945

Although weather conditions were less than ideal, the *Geschwader* flew a morning mission, with a simultaneous takeoff by all *Gruppen*. The target was Soviet positions on the Oder front.

The fighters initially flew at 2,000 meters, but near Berlin the weather improved and they were able to climb to 3,000 meters. According to the latest situation reports, the Red Army had crossed the Oder near Küstrin and was advancing on Berlin.

JG 301 had just overflown Oranienburg when heavy anti-aircraft forced the *Gruppe* to spread out. The tracer's red color meant that the fire was coming from Soviet flak positions. The front line was in fact farther east than anticipated, but as it could not be clearly identified, the Soviet anti-aircraft positions were attacked with guns. It was extremely difficult, if not impossible, to identify the front: as well, the pilots lacked experience in attacking ground targets.

The *Stabsschwarm* contributed six Ta 152s which were to protect the rest of the *Geschwader* from enemy fighter attack. They had no opportunity to take part in the action, as no enemy aircraft were encountered. There is no record of any losses resulting from this mission.

Attacks by enemy fighter-bombers became more frequent in the areas around the airfields, and Tempests were seen more frequently. From Neustadt-Glewe we could see them hanging in the air like hawks, ready to swoop down on anything that moved. During the late afternoon hours on 14 April 1945 two of these aircraft were seen attacking the railway line from Ludwigslust to Schwerin, which passed just a few kilometers from the airfield. Immediately three Ta 152s took off flown by *Oberstleutnant* Auffhammer, *Oberfeldwebel* Sattler and *Oberfeldwebel* Reschke.

As our takeoff was in the same general direction as the railway line, we reached the Tempests' attack area shortly after takeoff. I was flying as number three in the formation, and as we reached the area where the Tempests were I saw Sattler's Ta 152 go down for no apparent reason. Now it was two against two, and the low-level battle began.

The Tempest was known to be a very fast aircraft, with which the English had been able to catch and shoot down the V 1. In this engagement, however, speed played a less important role: at low level an aircraft's maneuverability was more important. As I approached, my opponent pulled up from a low-level attack and I attacked from out of a left-hand turn.

Both pilots realized that this was a fight to the finish, and from the outset both used every tactical and piloting ploy in an attempt to gain an advantage. At that height neither could afford to make a mistake, and for the first time I was to see what the Ta 152 could really do.

Twisting and turning, never more than fifty meters above the ground, I closed the range on the Tempest. At no time did I get the feeling that my machine had reached the limit of its performance. The Tempest pilot quite understandably had to undertake risky maneuvers to avoid a fatal burst from my guns. As my Ta 152 closed in on the Tempest, I could see that it was on the verge of rolling the other way: an indication that it could not turn any tighter. The first burst from my guns struck the Tempest in the rear fuselage and tail. The Tempest pilot reacted by immediately flicking his aircraft into a right-hand turn, which increased my advantage even further. There was no escape for the Tempest now. I pressed the firing buttons again, but my guns remained silent. Recharging them did no good: my guns refused to fire even a single shot. I can't remember whom and what I cursed at that moment. Luckily the Tempest pilot was unaware of my bad luck, for he had already had a sample. He continued to twist and turn, and I positioned my Ta 152 so that he always had a view of my machine's belly. Then came the moment when the Tempest went into a high-speed stall: it rolled left and crashed into a wood. This combat was certainly unique, having been played out at heights which were often just ten meters above the trees and rooftops. Throughout I never had the feeling that my Ta 152 had reached its performance limit, instead it reacted to the slightest control input, even though we were practically at ground level. *Oberstleutnant* Auffhammer also gained the upper hand against his Tempest, but in the end the enemy succeeded in escaping to the west. As the combat had taken place just a few kilometers from the airfield, in the late afternoon we drove out to the scene and discovered that *Oberfeldwebel* Sattler's Ta 152 and my Tempest had crashed within 500 meters of each other. The treetops had absorbed some of the force of the crash and the Tempest looked like it had made a forced landing. The damage inflicted by my cannon shells was clearly visible on the tail and rear fuselage and the pilot was still strapped in the cockpit. It turned out that he was a New Zealander, Warrant Officer O.J. Mitchell of No.486 Squadron, Royal Air Force. The next day the two fallen pilots were buried with military honors in the Neustadt-Glewe cemetery.

For a long time that evening the crash of *Oberfeldwebel* Sattler occupied the minds of the pilots and the many witnesses who had observed the combat from the airfield. The engagement had not even begun when Sattler went down, as both Tempest pilots were still busy with their low-level attacks on the railway line and incapable of posing any threat to the Ta 152s. Moreover he was too experienced a fox to place himself in a disadvantageous position in such a situation. We could not find an explanation for his crash, which will remain a mystery forever. This was the third crash of a Ta 152, and all were unexplained. For the *Gruppen* of *JG 301* the days that followed were filled with missions over every front within Germany. Although it was becoming ever more difficult just to get off the ground, the *Gruppen* sometimes flew missions over all three fronts on the same day. During one such mission from Hagenow by the *I.* and *II. Gruppe, Oberfeldwebel* Hugobert Langelotz of the *11. Staffel* was ordered to lead a flight of three fighters to provide top cover. Ignoring well-

Left: Oberfeldwebel Walter Loos flew the Ta 152 with the Stabsschwarm in the final weeks of the war. Loos was awarded the Knight's Cross on 20 April 1945. Right: Oberfeldwebel Willi Reschke of the Stab of JG 301. He was awarded the Knight's Cross on 20 April 1945.

intentioned advice from his comrades to stay low and begin climbing once clear of the airfield, Langelotz tried to climb his formation over the airfield. Having observed the takeoff, waiting enemy fighters swooped down on the Fw 190s and shot down all three.

Oberfeldwebel Hugobert Langelotz had joined *I./JG 302* at the end of 1943. He had also been a member of *Einsatzkommando Helsinki* under *Hauptmann* Lewens and *Hauptmann* Dietsche. He shot down four enemy aircraft during *I./JG 302*'s missions over Austria and Hungary but was wounded and spent a long time in hospital. In late autumn 1944 he returned to duty with *III./JG 301* and was killed shortly before the end of war. *Leutnant* Hermann Engelhardt of the *3. Staffel* was killed during a mission by *I./JG 301* on 15 April 1945. He had only just recovered from the wounds suffered over Pößneck on 21 November 1944.

On the morning of 16 April 1945 a lone enemy aircraft appeared over Hagenow airfield and circled there at about 2,000 meters. The commander of the *I. Gruppe*, *Hptm.* Posselmann, ordered six of the *Gruppe*'s aircraft to take off and shoot down this intruder. Within a few minutes a large number of enemy aircraft – probably Spitfires – had gathered over Hagenow and these attacked the Fw 190s from above. According to an eyewitness report by *Lt.* Willi Swetz, all of our aircraft were shot down in the ensuing combat. One of the pilots was *Lt.* Lothar Ettmüller, born on 28 April 1924. *Feldwebel* Bernhard Ikier of the *1. Staffel* failed to return from a mission by *I./JG 301* on 19 April. He was lost while attacking enemy ground forces. On 17 April, during a ferry flight in a Fw 190 D-9, *Leutnant* Robert Mietsche of *II./JG 301* was shot down by a number of Spitfires near Ludwigslust. Mietsche had survived nineteen missions in the Defense of the Reich. He was buried in the parish cemetery in Ludwigslust (Honor Section, Row 1, Grave No. 16). On 20 April 1945 *Oberfeldwebel* Walter Loos and Willi Reschke, both pilots in the *Stabsschwarm JG 301*, were awarded the Knight's Cross for their actions in the Defense of the Reich. The two pilots had very different backgrounds. *Oberfeldwebel* Walter Loos had joined *III./JG 3* in January 1944 and soon afterwards was transferred to *IV./JG 3*, the famous *Sturmgruppe*. In May 1944 he transferred to *JG 300*, where for a long time he flew as wingman to *Geschwaderkommodore Major* Walter Dahl. For a brief period in October 1944 he served as a fighter instructor with *Ergänzungsgruppe Ost*. In April 1945 he joined the *Geschwaderstab* of *JG 301*. Loos scored thirty-eight victories in sixty-six combat missions and was shot down nine times.

Oberfeldwebel Willi Reschke joined *I./JG 302* on 20 June 1944, taking part in missions against American bombers flying from Italy until the end of August.

The *Gruppe* was disbanded and subsequently renamed *III./JG 301*. In early September 1944 it returned to action against American raids in western Europe. In March 1945 he was transferred to the *Geschwaderstab* of *JG 301*. He scored twenty-seven victories in approximately forty-eight combat missions. He was shot down eight times and forced to take to his parachute four times.

21 April 1945

The day had scarcely begun when the first aircraft taxied out for takeoff at Neustadt-Glewe. Once again the Ta 152s of the *Stabsschwarm* were the first to take off. *II./JG 301* had been ordered to support the army on the Oder front southeast of Berlin, using guns and bombs.

All of the *II. Gruppe*'s aircraft carried a single bomb under the fuselage. The five Ta 152s providing fighter cover for the *Gruppe* carried no external load.

Oberfeldwebel Jupp Keil. He came to 10./JG 301 from I./JG 302 in September 1944. From March 1945 he flew the Ta 152 as a member of the Geschwaderstab.

When the *Jagdgruppe* flew past the Reich capital, all was quiet on the ground and in the air. This changed abruptly when it reached the area between Storkow and Beeskow, however. From this area with its many lakes, the first tracers rose toward the *Gruppe*'s aircraft. Once again the pilots of the *II. Gruppe* found it difficult to pinpoint the exact location of the front line, so they concentrated their attacks on Soviet anti-aircraft positions. Many of the bombs were well wide of the mark, for the *Jagdgeschwader*'s pilots had no experience dropping bombs.

The repeated low-level attacks caused the *Gruppe* to become spread out, which complicated the *Stabsschwarm*'s task of fending off attacks by enemy fighters. As the *Gruppe* withdrew there was a brief encounter with Soviet Yak-9 fighters, two of which were shot down by *Oberfeldwebel* Jupp Keil. It was our first meeting with Russian fighter aircraft, and as the engagement lasted only a very short time, it was impossible to draw any conclusions or compare the Yak-9 to American aircraft.

24 April 1945

JG 301 once again succeeded in getting all of its units into the air to bomb and strafe Russian positions near Zossen southeast of Berlin. The *Stabsschwarm* and *II./JG 301* took off from Neustadt-Glewe at 0800 hours, and the *I.* and *III. Gruppe* got airborne from Hagenow at about the same time. All of aircraft together equaled the strength of a regular *Gruppe*, for the individual *Staffeln* were now down to about *Schwarm* strength.

As usual, the *Stabsschwarm* took off before the *II. Gruppe*, putting up one flight of three and a flight of two. The pair consisted of *Oberleutnant* Stahl and *Oberfeldwebel* Reschke, the flight of three *Oberfeldwebel* Loos and Keil and *Feldwebel* Blum. The cloud base on this day was only about 1,500 meters above the ground, which prevented the *Stabsschwarm* from taking up position above the formation. For this reason the flight of three (*Kette*) positioned itself on the right of the formation and the pair (*Rotte*) to the left. There was no interference from the enemy during the flight to the target area, and as there was almost no information on the location of the front, the pilots had to orient themselves by means of enemy ground fire. This was not all that difficult, for the Russian tracer was red, while ours was yellow.

The weather in the target area was no better than it had been during the flight, consequently conditions were less than ideal for *JG 301*. The area around Zossen contained numerous lakes and forests, making it difficult to make out our own and the enemy's positions. In the end each pilot was his own general and attacked what he thought was the correct target. It is difficult to say whether the bombing achieved much, but the strafing runs were certainly more successful. There was no sign of Russian fighters over this sector of the front, and the attacks on the Russian positions were conducted without interference from the air.

During the pre-mission briefing the Ta 152s had been given a special assignment: carry out a reconnaissance flight following the *Geschwader*'s mission near Zossen. To reconnoiter the front positions around Berlin, it had been decided that the *Kette* would make its return south of Berlin and the *Rotte* north of the capital. When the *Geschwader*'s aircraft had completed their attacks on this sector of the front and headed for home, the *Stabsschwarm* split up and the two formations took up their assigned courses.

Ta 152 H-1 Werknummer 150 168, part of display of captured enemy aircraft at Farnborough, England in 1946. Formerly "Green 9" of the Stabsschwarm of JG 301, this was the aircraft flown by Oberfeldwebel Willi Reschke on 24 April 1945 on his mission near Zossen south of Berlin.

Oberleutnant Stahl and I flew past the transmitter towers of Königs-Wusterhausen, in order to fly round the east side of Berlin and then set course for Neustadt-Glewe. Red tracers occasionally rose toward us from the lake area between Königs-Wusterhausen and Erkner, and indication that the Russians were already quite close to Berlin. We were flying about 200 meters apart and the cloud base was still at about 1,500 meters with scattered cloud below. We occasionally lost sight of one another in this scattered cloud and the visibility in general was severely limited. It was probably for this reason that we failed to spot Russian fighter aircraft crossing our path from the right. The Soviets ended up at our four o'clock and immediately turned toward the Ta 152 flown by *Oberleutnant* Stahl, who was on my right. I alerted Stahl to the presence of the enemy fighters by radio and turned toward them. Stahl's reaction took me by surprise, for instead of initiating any sort of defensive maneuver he simply put the nose down and dove away. I radioed warnings and urged him to climb up into the clouds, because the first red tracers were already flashing past his Ta 152, but there was no reaction and he continued his shallow dive.

I was in firing position behind a Yak-9 when tracer went by my machine. I had concentrated on *Oberleutnant* Stahl's critical situation so much that I only now realized that mine wasn't much better. I immediately put my Ta 152 into a hard left turn and for the time being shook off the Yak-9 behind me. Only then did I realize that it was an entire flight of unfamiliar aircraft. As I had lost some altitude following Stahl, I began turning with the Russians. Having never encountered Russian fighters before, I was unfamiliar with their tactics, but figured that if I got in trouble I could still climb up into the clouds. The Russians held their tight formation, consequently I was at first unable to turn as tightly as I would have liked. I soon went from being in front of the enemy fighters to behind them, further proof of the Ta 152's maneuverability. Only after I shot down the number four aircraft did the Russian formation split up, and each tried to get me on his own. Only one of the Russians had the will to carry on, however, and the other two withdrew. The remaining pilot was probably the leader of this small fighter unit, but his Yak-9 was hopelessly inferior to my Ta 152. In the end, he went down trailing smoke. The combat took place in the area north of Erkner in the direction of Neuenhagen.

I had of course lost all contact with *Oberleutnant* Stahl during the engagement, and so I called him again on the radio. There was no answer. Looking down, I saw many fires burning around Berlin. Allocating one of these smoke columns to a particular aircraft was impossible.

The *Geschwader* was still in the air and the flight of three Ta 152s from the *Stabsschwarm* was engaged with Soviet fighters south of Berlin. The frequency was a babble of voices, making it more difficult to contact *Oberleutnant* Stahl. I still hoped that he might be on his way home, and the radio traffic revealed that the *Gruppen* had reached their bases.

I landed my Ta 152 H-1 "Green 9", WNr. 150 168, at Neustadt-Glewe air base at 0915 hours. This was my last air engagement and my last combat mission in this war.

Lütjenholm, May 1945. Hauptmann Rickert shakes the hands of his men, who thus swear allegiance to Grand Admiral Dönitz, the new head of state. On the far right is Fähnrich Rix.

The Ta 152 had been my life insurance in the final weeks of the war: without this fighter's outstanding performance my chances of surviving the war would have been much poorer.

Oberleutnant Hermann Stahl did not return from the mission and is still listed as missing. A postwar investigation turned up nothing.

The *Stabsschwarm* shot down four Yak-9s in dogfights with Russian fighters in the airspace around Berlin on 24 April 1945. I shot down two Yaks in the Erkner area, while *Oberfeldwebel* Walter Loos accounted for the other two south of Berlin.

For a pilot of the *Reichsverteidigung*, used to engaging American and English fighter aircraft, this one battle was actually no yardstick for comparison: fighting the Soviets in the air was more like a fair fight man against man, but against the Anglo-Saxons it was always a struggle of man and aircraft against overwhelming numbers. For this reason alone the two are scarcely comparable.

Oberfeldwebel Sattler and *Oberleutnant* Stahl, both experienced pilots, were lost in the final days of the war. They were flying an aircraft that must be acknowledged as the best piston-engined fighter of the Second World War. Neither showed any sign of inferiority as fighters or pilots – and yet both times men and machines were lost. Each time competent witnesses were present, who saw what happened and were even in the same situation. It is curious that there were no outward signs that might shed light on the causes of these inexplicable crashes. Was the Ta 152 hiding a secret that can never be explained?

JG 301 was now increasingly caught between the pincers of the front. What was left of the *Geschwader* flew its last mission on 30 April 1945, taking part in the Battle of Berlin. The records reveal nothing about the success of this mission against Russian ground forces. Enemy fighters were encountered, and two Yak-9s were shot down, one by *Oberfeldwebel* Walter Loos in a Ta 152 and the other by *Unteroffizier* Willi Greiner of the *12. Staffel* flying a Fw 190 A-9.

The *Geschwader* carried out its final move immediately after this mission. It was not as orderly as in the past, instead it was a race against time. The destination, Leck airfield in Schleswig-Holstein could only still be reached through a narrow corridor. On orders from above, the remaining aircraft of the *Geschwaderstab* and *II./JG 301* were to be handed over to *JG 11*, which had moved to Neustadt-Glewe the day before. This *Jagdgeschwader* had pilots, but scarcely any aircraft, and when *JG 301* arrived at Leck, its own Ta 152s and Fw 190 A-8s and A-9s were already there.

What remained of the German fighter arm had gathered at the Leck and Lütjenholm airfields with the aircraft that had escaped the hell fires of aerial combat. The remnants of various *Jagdgeschwader* had escaped to Northern Germany, but a few days later the war ended for them too.

The *Geschwaderstab* of *JG 301* was located in the small town of Sande near Leck. It remained there until the surrender on 8 May 1945. Then, for a short time, it shared quarters with *II./JG 301* on the Lütjenholm airfield and from there the unit's personnel were subsequently transported to release camps. For the pilots of the *I.* and *III. Gruppe* and a few of the technical personnel, the end of the line was the Reich Labor Service camp at Leck air base. Most of the technical personnel of the two *Gruppen* had been pressed into service as infantry and not all of them survived the end of the war.

I can credit the English with treating us fairly as prisoners of war.

Using the documents available to me and my own experiences, I have tried to retell the story of *JG 301* and *JG 302* and their service in the Defense of the Reich during the entire period of their existence. I did this because of my own experiences and from the point of view of a pilot in these two units. I do not, therefore, make any claims to completeness – there are surely certain events that I did not include.

There were, for example, pilots who served with these two *Jagdgeschwader* whose names I did not mention. Over the course of times I have forgotten many names, and some were with the units for so brief a period that their names did not sink in.

I dedicate these lines to all my comrades who gave their lives for the Fatherland in good faith, but whose names should and never will be forgotten. The years after the war have proved that, for the members of both *Jagdgeschwader*, comradeship and solidarity were always foremost. Once every year we meet and spend hours together in memory of our comrades who were killed in the war or have died since.

This solidarity will exist until the last *Horrido* rings out!

Chapter Eleven

Final Thoughts on *JG 301*

From the beginning of *JG 301*'s formation in autumn 1943 until the beginning of October 1944, the three *Gruppen* of the *Jagdgeschwader* were only under the command of a *Geschwaderstab* for a very brief time. The *Gruppen* were often based at airfields far apart from one another, and after the second disbandment of *III./JG 301* at the beginning of 1944 the *Geschwaderstab* was also disbanded. *I./JG 301* was subsequently transferred to France, where it was employed in the single-engined night-fighter role, while *II./JG 301* was sent to Romania to defend against American daylight raids from the south. In mid-August 1944 the two depleted *Jagdgruppen* were withdrawn from operations and transferred into the area west of Berlin to rest and reequip.

With the reestablishment of *III./JG 301* at Alperstedt near Erfurt in September 1944, the *Jagdgeschwader* was once again given a *Geschwaderstab*. Based at Stendal, Salzwedel and Sachau, the *Gruppen* for the first time operated under the unified command of a *Geschwaderstab*. The *Geschwader* was kept together even after subsequent transfers and remained so until the end of the war. *IV./JG 301* formed part of the *Geschwader* for only a brief period.

During this time the *Geschwader* or elements of the *Geschwader* took part in about seventy missions, losing at least 258 pilots killed in combat or crashes. 141 pilots were wounded or injured and at least nine are still listed as missing.

Losses among the technical personnel during this time totaled 125 killed, wounded or missing. The greatest loss of ground personnel occurred during *II./JG 301*'s retreat from Romania.

In its missions against the bomber formations, *JG 301* shot down 156 four-engined bombers and claimed another ten damaged and forced to leave formation. The *Geschwader* also shot down thirty-eight enemy fighter aircraft.

As the records of missions during the final weeks of the war were lost, there were probably successes by certain pilots and additional losses that are not included in this chronicle.

Appendices

Aerial Victories of *JG 301* and *JG 302*

Rank	Name	Unit	Date	Time	Type	Area	Victory#	Night/Day
Lt	Alven v., Heinrich	I./301	30 Jan 44	—	4-Eng.	—	1.	Day
Lt	Alven v., Heinrich	I./301	20 Feb 44	—	B-17	—	2.	Day
OGefr	Angermann, Günther	1./302	19 Jul 44	09.55	B-17	SW-Munich	1. HSS*	Day
Maj	Auffhammer, Fritz	Stab/301	5 Dec 44	11.32	P-51	N-Berlin	1.	Day
Maj	Auffhammer, Fritz	Stab/301	5 Dec 44	11.37	P-51	N-Berlin	2.	Day
Uffz	Bamberg, K.-Heinz	2./302	26 Jun 44	10.10	B-24	Sopron	1.	Day
Uffz	Bamberg, K.-Heinz	2./302	26 Jun 44	10.20	B-24	Raab	2.	Day
Fw	Bausch, —	2./302	2 Jul 44	10.28	B-24	Budapest	1. e.V.**	Day
Fw	Bausch, —	2./302	19 Jul 44	9.51	B-17	Munich	2.	Day
Fw	Bausch, —	2./302	21 Jul 44	10.45	B-17	Wels	3.	Day
Fw	Becker, Kurt	5./302	2 Dec 44	20.34	4-Eng.	—	1.	Night
Fw	Benning, Anton	1./302	22 Sep 43	22.29	Lancaster	—	1.	Night
Fw	Benning, Anton	1./302	22 Sep 43	22.35	Lancaster	—	2.	Night
Ofw	Benning, Anton	1./302	16 Dec 43	19.48	Lancaster	—	3.	Night
Ofw	Benning, Anton	I./302	24 Mar 44	22.40	Lancaster	—	4.	Night
Ofw	Benning, Anton	I./302	10 May 44	11.26	B-24	—	5.	Day
Ofw	Benning, Anton	I./302	10 May 44	11.38	B-24	—	6.	Day
Ofw	Benning, Anton	2./302	29 May 44	9.54	B-24	—	7.	Day
Ofw	Benning, Anton	2./302	9 Jun 44	10.04	B-24	Landshut	8. HSS	Day
Ofw	Benning, Anton	2./302	9 Jun 44	10.09	B-24	Landshut	9.	Day
Ofw	Benning, Anton	2./302	13 Jun 44	10.15	B-24	Pfaffenhofen	10.	Day
Ofw	Benning, Anton	2./302	26 Jun 44	10.40	P-51	Neusiedler See	11.	Day
Ofw	Benning, Anton	10./301	26 Nov 44	14.00	B-24	Hildesheim	12.	Day
Ofw	Benning, Anton	10./301	26 Nov 44	14.00	P-51	Hildesheim	13.	Day
Ofw	BenningvAnton	10./301	5 Dec 44	10.49	P-51	Berlin	14.	Day
Uffz	Berliner, Julus	9./301	26 Nov 44	14.00	B-24	Hildesheim	1.	Day
Uffz	Berlinska, W.	2./302	2 Jul 44	10.25	B-24	Budapest	1.	Day
Uffz	Berlinska, W.	2./302	2 Jul 44	10.28	B-24	Budapest	2. e.V.	Day
Uffz	Berlinska, W.	2./302	16 Jul 44	10.25	B-24	—	3.	Day
Lt	Bernhard, Gerd	I./301	23 Sep 43	—	Lancaster	—	1. rammed	Night
Lt	Bernhard, Gerd	I./302	10 May 44	11.32	B-24	—	2. HSS	Day
Lt	Bernhard, Gerd	I./302	24 May 44	10.13	P-51	—	3.	Day
Lt	Bernhard, Gerd	I./302	24 May 44	10.20	B-24	—	4.	Day
Ofw	Blickle, Walter	I./301	26 Nov 44	14.00	B-24	Hildesheim	1.	Day
Fw	Blomert, Hubert	3./302	26 Jul 44	11.15	B-17	Bückfeld	1.	Day
Gefr	Blum, Christoph	1./302	26 Jul 44	11.40	B-17	Neusiedler See	1.	Day
Gefr	Blum, Christoph	1./302	5 Aug 44	12.42	B-17	Magdeburg	2.	Day
Gefr	Blum, Christoph	1./302	7 Aug 44	12.35	B-24	Raab	3. HSS	Day
Uffz	Blumv, Christoph	1./302	22 Aug 44	10.05	B-24	Pápa	4.	Day
Uffz	Blumv, Christoph	1./302	24 Aug 44	12.37	P-51	Böhmen-Mäh.	5.	Day
Uffz	Blumv, Christoph	9./301	26 Nov 44	14.00	B-24	Hildesheim	6.	Day
Lt	Bolduanv, Fritz	3./302	2 Jul 44	10.25	B-24	Budapest	1.	Day
Lt	Bolduan, Fritz	3./302	25 Jul 44	10.33	B-24	Mariazell	2.	Day
Fw	Böwer, Herbert	1./301	8 Jul 44	01.10	4-Eng.	France	1.	Night
Fw	Böwer, Herbert	1./301	8 Jul 44	01.44	4-Eng.	France	2.	Night
Ofhr	Brenner, Peter	6./301	6 May 44	11.45	B-24	—	1. HSS	Day
Uffz	Brenner, Helmut	6./301	24 Jun 44	09.32	B-24	—	1.	Day
Uffz	Brenner, Helmut	6./301	17 Dec 44	12.05	B-17	Kassel	2.	Day
Uffz	Breuers, Hans	5./302	24 May 44	11.08	B-17	—	1.	Day
Lt	Brinkmann, Fritz	1./301	8 Jul 44	01.39	4-Eng.	France	1.	Night
Lt	Brinkmann, Fritz	1./301	8 Jul 44	01.43	4-Eng.	France	2.	Night
Hptm	Burggraf, Wilhelm	I./301	8 Jul 44	01.12	Lancaster	France	1.	Night
Hptm	Burggraf, Wilhelm	I./301	8 Jul 44	01.21	Lancaster	France	2.	Night
Uffz	Burghardt, Rolf	3./301	29 Mar 44	13.44	B-17	—	1.	Day
Uffz	Burghardt, Rolf	3./301	13 Apr 44	12.55	B-24	—	2.	Day
Uffz	Burghardt, Rolf	3./301	13 Apr 44	13.11	B-24	—	3.	Day
Uffz	Burghardt, Rolf	3./302	16 Jun 44	10.40	B-24	Lake Constance	4.	Day
Uffz	Diecke, Rudolf	3./302	10 May 44	11.50	B-24	—	1.	Day

Rank	Name	Unit	Date	Time	Type	Area	Victory#	Night/Day
Uffz	Diecke, Rudolf	3./302	9 Jun 44	10.15	B-24	Salzburg	2.	Day
Uffz	Diecke, Rudolf	3./302	16 Jun 44	09.50	B-24	Raab	3. HSS	Day
Ofw	Dieckmann, Fritz	1./302	29 May 44	09.54	B-24	Markersdorf	1.HSS	Day
Ofw	Dieckmann, Fritz	1./302	8 Jul 44	10.41	B-24	Vienna	2.HSS	Day
Ofw	Dieckmann, Fritz	1./302	17 Jul 44	10.20	B-24	—	3.	Day
Fw	Dienst, Werner	3./302	29 Apr 44	11.30	B-17	—	1.	Day
Hptm	Dietschev K.-Heinz	2./302	22 Nov 43	21.14	4-Eng.	—	1.	Night
Hptm	Dietsche, K.-Heinz	2./302	23 Nov 43	21.43	4-Eng.	—	2.	Night
Hptm	Dietsche, K.-Heinz	2./302	8 Mar 44	13.30	B-17	Magdeburg	3. HSS	Day
	EinsKdo Helsinki	2./302	16 Feb 44	—	—	—	2 victories	Night
	EinsKdo Helsinki	2./302	26 Feb 44	—	—	—	4 victories	Night
Fw	Dörr, Heinrich	4./302	19 Jul 44	10.15	B-17	Starnberg	1. HSS	Day
Fw	Dörr, Heinrich	4./302	21 Jul 44	10.45	B-17	Wels	2. HSS	Day
Fw	Dörr, Heinrich	4./302	25 Jul 44	10.53	B-24	Mariazell	3. HSS	Day
Fw	Dörr, Heinrich	4./302	29 Jul 44	10.20	B-17	Linz	4.	Day
Fw	Dörr, Heinrich	11./301	26 Nov 44	13.00	B-17	Hildesheim	5.	Day
Fw	Dörrv Heinrich	11./301	26 Nov 44	13.10	B-17	Hildesheim	6.	Day
Fw	Dreesmann, Rudolf	4./302	9 Jun 44	10.10	P-51	Landshut	10.	Day
Fw	Dreesmann, Rudolf	4./302	13 Jun 44	—	B-24	—	11.	
Fw	Dreesmann, Rudolf	4./302	16 Jun 44	09.40	P-51	Preßburg	12.	Day
Fw	Dreesmann, Rudolf	4./302	26 Jun 44	09.10	P-51	Preßburg	13.	Day
Fw	Dreesmann, Rudolf	4./302	27 Jun 44	—	B-17	—	14.	—
Fw	Dreesmann, Rudolf	4./302	2 Jul 44	10.40	P-51	Tata	15.	Day
Fw	Driebe, Rudi	11./301	31 Dec 44	—	P-51	Hamburg	1.	—
Uffz	Dürr, Hermann	4./302	22 Aug 44	09.47	P-38	Balaton	1.	Day
Uffz	Dürr, Hermann	4./302	22 Aug 44	10.05	B-24	Balaton	2.	Day
Uffz	Dürr, Hermann	4./302	24 Aug 44	—	B-17	—	3.	—
Uffz	Dürr, Hermann	4./302	24 Aug 44	—	B-17	—	4.	—
Uffz	Dürr, Hermann	12./301	26 Nov 44	12.40	B-17	Hildesheim	5.	Day
Fw	Ebel, Fritz	10./301	10 Jun 44	08.58	P-38	—	1.	Day
Fw	Ebel, Fritz	10./301	3 Jul 44	12.10	B-24	—	2.	Day
Fw	Emanuel, —	1./301	22 Oct 44	21.16	4-Eng.	—	1.	Night
Fw	Emanuel, —	1./301	2 Apr 44	11.37	B-24	—	2. HSS	Day
Fw	Emanuel, —	1./301	8 Jul 44	01.25	Lancaster	—	3.	Night
Ofw	Emler, Kurt	1./302	3 Oct 43	22.04	Stirling	Hannover	1.	Night
Ofw	Emler, Kurt	1./302	9 Oct 43	01.17	Stirling	Funkf. Mar.	2.	Night
Ofw	Emler, Kurt	1./302	9 Oct 43	01.32	Stirling	—	3.	Night
Ofw	Emler, Kurt	1./302	22 Nov 43	—	4-Eng.	—	4.	Night
Ofw	Emler, Kurt	1./302	22 Nov 43	—	4-Eng.	—	5.	Night
Ofw	Emler, Kurt	1./302	16 Dec 43	20.12	4-Eng.	—	6.	Night
Ofw	Emler, Kurt	1./302	24 Dec 43	04.20	Lancaster	Berlin	7.	Night
Fw	Engfer, Hans	1./301	5 Jul 44	01.19	4-Eng.	France	1.	Night
Fw	Engfer, Hans	1./301	8 Jul 44	01.20	Lancaster	France	2.	Night
Fw	Engfer, Hans	1./301	8 Jul 44	01.42	4-Eng.	France	3.	Night
Lt	Esche, Willi	1./301	12 Apr 44	12.22	B-24	—	1.	Day
Lt	Esche, Willi	1./301	5 Jul 44	01.26	Lancaster	France	2.	Night
Lt	Esche, Willi	1./301	5 Jul 44	01.58	Lancaster	France	3.	Night
Lt	Esche, Willi	1./301	6 Jul 44	03.56	4-Eng.	France	4.	Night
Lt	Esche, Willi	1./301	8 Jul 44	01.38	Lancaster	France	5.	Night
OLt	Fischer, Ernst	2./301	5 Jul 44	01.35	Lancaster	France	1.	Night
OLt	Fischer, Ernst	2./301	5 Jul 44	01.39	Lancaster	France	2.	Night
Ofw	Freckmann, —	I./301	29 May 44	—	B-24	—	1. HSS	—
Lt	Fries, —	8./302	20 Feb 44	02.40	Lancaster	—	1.	Night
Fw	Gaißmayer, Anton	7./302	8 Apr 44	13.44	B-24	—	1. HSS	Day
Hptm	Gerlach, —	5./302	31 Mar 44	01.03	4-Eng.	—	1.	Night
Lt	Glaass, —	8./301	20 Feb 44	04.20	Lancaster	—	1.	Night
Lt	Glaass, —	8./301	28 Apr 44	02.38	4-Eng.	—	2.	Night
Lt	Glass, —	9./302	24 Mar 44	22.50	Lancaster	—	1.	Night
Fw	Gniffke, Fritz	5./302	11 Apr 44	11.24	B-24	—	1.	Day
Ofw	Göbel, Hubert	3./302	16 Jul 44	10.21	B-24	Vienna	1. e.V.	Day
Ofw	Gossow, Heinz	1./302	22 Sep 43	22.30	Lancaster	Bremen	1.	Night
Ofw	Gossow, Heinz	1./302	16 Jun 44	09.58	B-24	Komarom	2. HSS	Day
Ofw	Gossow, Heinz	1./302	5 Aug 44	12.41	B-17	Magdeburg	3.	Day
Ofw	Gossow, Heinz	1./302	16 Aug 44	10.00	B-17	Kassel	4.	Day
Ofw	Gossow, Heinz	1./302	20 Aug 44	09.45	B-17	Budapest	5.	Day

Rank	Name	Unit	Date	Time	Type	Area	Victory#	Night/Day
Ofw	Gossow, Heinz	1./302	21 Aug 44	10.25	B-24	Debrecen	6. HSS	Day
Ofw	Gossow, Heinz	1./302	22 Aug 44	10.05	B-24	Pápa	7.	Day
Hptm	Gottuck, Hans	II./301	18 Oct 43	20.24	4-Eng.		1.	Night
Uffz	Grätz, —	3./301	5 Jul 44	01.15	4-Eng.	France	1.	Night
Uffz	Greiner, Willi	4./302	21 Jul 44	10.45	B-17	Wels	1.	Day
Uffz	Greiner, Willi	4./302	20 Aug 44	09.45	B-17	Budapest	2. HSS	Day
Uffz	Greiner, Willi	4./302	22 Aug 44	10.00	B-24	Pápa	3. HSS	Day
Uffz	Greiner, Willi	12./301	26 Nov 44	12.25	B-24	Hildesheim	4.	Day
Uffz	Greiner, Willi	12./301	26 Nov 44	12.35	B-24	Hildesheim	5.	Day
Uffz	Greiner, Willi	12./301	30 Apr 45	—	Jak-9	Berlin	6.	—
Fw	Gromoll, Manfred	3./301	8 Jul 44	01.36	Lancaster	France	1.	Night
Fw	Gromoll, Manfred	3./301	8 Jul 44	01.48	Lancaster	France	2.	Night
Ofw	Groß, Artur	2./302	22 Sep 43	22.54	Lancaster	Hannover	1.	Night
Ofw	Groß, Artur	2./302	23 Sep 43	23.15	Lancaster	Mannheim	2.	Night
Ofw	Groß, Artur	2./302	11 Apr 44	—	4-Eng.	—	3.	—
Ofw	Groß, Artur	2./302	19 Apr 44	—	4-Eng.	—	4.	—
Ofw	Groß, Artur	2./302	29 Apr 44	—	4-Eng.	Brunswick	5.	Night
Ofw	Groß, Artur	2./302	24 May 44	10.14	B-24	St. Pölten	6.	Day
Ofw	Groß, Artur	2./302	24 May 44	10.16	B-24	St. Pölten	7.	Day
Ofw	Groß, Artur	2./302	9 Jun 44	10.04	B-24	Landshut	8. HSS	Day
Ofw	Groß, Artur	2./302	9 Jun 44	10.08	B-24	Landshut	9. HSS	Day
Ofw	Groß, Artur	2./302	9 Jun 44	10.12	B-24	Landshut	10. HSS	Day
Lt	Grumme, Ernst	4./302	13 Jun 44	09.55	P-38	Landau/Isar	21.	Day
Lt	Grumme, Ernst	4./302	14 Jun 44	11.25	P-38	Lake Constance	22.	Day
Lt	Grumme, Ernst	4./302	16 Jun 44	10.03	P-38	Budapest	23.	Day
Lt	Grumme, Ernst	4./302	26 Jun 44	10.20	B-24	Neusiedler See	24. HSS	Day
Lt	Grumme, Ernst	4./302	27 Jun 44	10.25	B-17	Budapest	25.	Day
Lt	Grumme, Ernst	4./302	2 Jul 44	10.20	B-24	Budapest	26. HSS	Day
Lt	Grumme, Ernst	4./302	7 Jul 44	12.00	B-24	Preßburg	27. HSS	Day
Lt	Grumme, Ernst	4./302	14 Jul 44	09.58	P-51	Budapest	28.	Day
Ofw	Günther, Heinz	2./301	8 Jul 44	02.26	B-26	France	1.	Night
Ofw	Haase, Ernst	1./302	22 Oct 43	—	Lancaster	Kassel	1.	Night
Ofw	Haase, Ernst	1./302	26 Nov 43	20.56	Lancaster	—	2.	Night
Ofw	Haase, Ernst	1./302	2 Dec 43	20.26	Lancaster	Berlin	3.	Night
Ofw	Haase, Ernst	1./302	24 Mar 44	—	Halifax	Berlin	4.	Night
Ofw	Haase, Ernst	1./302	9 Apr 44	—	B-24	—	5.	Day
Ofw	Haase, Ernst	1./302	11 Apr 44	—	B-17	—	6.	—
Ofw	Haase, Ernst	1./302	29 Apr 44	—	B-17	Brunswick	7.	—
Ofw	Haase, Ernst	1./302	26 Jun 44	09.59	B-24	Neusiedler See	8. HSS	Day
Ofw	Haase, Ernst	1./302	27 Jun 44	—	B-17	Budapest	9.	—
Ofw	Haase, Ernst	1./302	27 Jun 44	—	B-17	Budapest	10. HSS	—
Ofw	Haase, Ernst	1./302	2 Jul 44	10.30	B-24	Tordas	11.	Day
Ofw	Haase, Ernst	1./302	2 Jul 44	10.34	B-24	Tordas	12.	Day
Ofw	Haase, Ernst	1./302	19 Jul 44	09.56	B-17	Munich	13. HSS	Day
Ofw	Haase, Ernst	1./302	21 Jul 44	10.49	B-17	Wels	14.	Day
Ofw	Haase, Ernst	1./302	25 Jul 44	10.58	B-24	Vienna	15. HSS	Day
Ofw	Haase, Ernst	1./302	29 Jul 44	10.20	B-17	Linz	16. HSS	Day
Lt	Hagedorn, A.W.	9./301	2 Mar 45	—	B-17	Magdeburg	1.	—
Fw	Hähnel, Joachim	3./301	8 Jul 44	01.28	Lancaster	France	1.	Night
Lt	Hallenberger, W.	4./302	16 Jun 44	10.40	B-24	Galanta	2.	Day
Lt	Hallenberger, W.	4./302	27 Jun 44	—	B-17	Budapest	3.	—
Lt	Hallenberger, W.	4./302	2 Jul 44	12.15	B-17	Balaton	4.	Day
Lt	Hallenberger, W.	4./302	7 Jul 44	12.00	B-24	Preßburg	5. HSS	Day
Lt	Hallenberger, W.	4./302	7 Jul 44	12.25	B-24	Komarom	6. HSS	Day
Lt	Hallenberger, W.	4./302	19 Jul 44	10.06	B-17	Munich	7.	Day
Lt	Hallenberger, W.	4./302	21 Jul 44	—	B-17	Wels	8.	—
Fw	Hartl, Andreas	6./301	27 Sep 43	23.08	4-Eng.	—	1.	Night
Fw	Hartl, Andreas	6./301	27 Sep 43	23.24	4-Eng.	—	2.	Night
Fw	Hartl, Andreas	6./302	2 Dec 43	20.20	4-Eng.	Berlin	3.	Night
Fw	Hartl, Andreas	6./302	2 Dec 43	20.38	4-Eng.	Berlin	4.	Night
Fw	Hartl, Andreas	6./302	2 Jan 44	02.56	Lancaster	—	5.	Night
Fw	Hartl, Andreas	6./302	6 Jan 44	03.41	Lancaster	—	6.	Night
Fw	Hartl, Andreas	6./302	21 Jan 44	23.15	4-Eng.	—	7.	Night
Fw	Hartl, Andreas	6./302	24 Mar 44	22.37	4-Eng.	Berlin	8.	Night
Fw	Hartl, Andreas	6./302	24 Mar 44	—	4-Eng.	Berlin	9.	Night
Fw	Hartl, Andreas	6./302	24 Mar 44	—	4-Eng.	Berlin	10.	Night
Fw	Hartl, Andreas	6./302	24 Mar 44	—	4-Eng.	Berlin	11.	Night

Rank	Name	Unit	Date	Time	Type	Area	Victory#	Night/Day
Gefr	Heerdegen, L.	1./302	7 Jul 44	10.25	B-17	Preßburg	1. HSS	Day
Fw	Herre, Herbert	1./302	2 Dec 43	20.39	4-Eng.	Berlin	1.	Night
Lt	Hiller, Alfred	3./301	8 Jul 44	01.33	Lancaster	France	1.	Night
OLt	Hocker, Otto-E.	III./301	25 Apr 44	00.43	Lancaster	—	1.	Night
Uffz	Hoffmann, A.	5./301	5 Dec 44	11.00	P-51	Berlin	1.	Day
Uffz	Hölscher, August	5./301	5 Dec 44	11.00	P-51	Berlin	1.	Day
Uffz	Hölscher, August	5./301	24 Dec 44	15.00	P-51	Hannover	2.	Day
Ofw	Ippoldt, Hubert	10./301	5 Apr 44	15.44	B-17	Norddeutschland	1.	Day
Ofw	Jaacks, Egbert	3./302	2 Dec 43	20.56	Halifax	Berlin	1.	Night
Uffz	Jakobi, Klaus	2./301	8 Jul 44	01.43	Lancaster	France	1.	Night
Ofw	Janke, —	3./302	24 May 44	10.08	B-24	Mitterndorf	1.	Day
Fw	Jäschke, Herbert	2./302	24 May 44	10.19	B-24	St. Pölten	1.	Day
Fw	Jäschke, Herbert	2./302	24 May 44	10.22	B-24	St. Pölten	2. e.V.	Day
Fw	Jäschke, Herbert	2./302	29 May 44	09.48	B-24	St. Pölten	3.	Day
Lt	Jüngling, Richard	1./302	2 Jul 44	10.30	B-24	Budapest	1.	Day
Lt	Kapp, —	St./302	27 Jul 44	09.30	P-51	Balaton	1.	Day
Lt	Kapp, —	St./302	27 Jul 44	09.33	P-51	Balaton	2.	Day
Ofw	Keil, Josef	10./301	26 Nov 44	12.30	B-24	Hildesheim	1.	Day
Ofw	Keil, Josef	10./301	26 Nov 44	12.38	B-24	Hildesheim	2.	Day
Ofw	Keil, Josef	10./301	31 Dec 44	—	P-51	Hamburg	3.	—
Ofw	Keil, Josef	10./301	1 Jan 45	—	B-17	Gardelegen	4.	—
Ofw	Keil, Josef	10./301	1 Jan 45	—	B-17	Stendal	5.	—
Ofw	Keil, Josef	10./301	20 Feb 45	—	B-17	Berlin	6.	—
Ofw	Keil, Josef	10./301	1 Mar 45	—	P-51	Reichsgebiet	7.	—
Ofw	Keil, Josef	St./301	10 Apr 45	—	P-47	Kassel	8.	—
Ofw	Keil, Josef	St./301	21 Apr 45	—	Jak-9	Berlin	9.	—
Ofw	Keil, Josef	St./301	21 Apr 45	—	Jak-9	Berlin	10.	—
Uffz	Kemmerling, H.	2./302	30 Jun 44	10.00	B-24	Spittel	1.	Day
Uffz	Kemmerling, H.	2./302	2 Jul 44	12.40	B-24	Györ	2.	Day
Fw	Kiehling, Ernst	10./301	31 May 44	10.06	P-38	Rumania	1.	Day
Lt	Kirchner, Horst	2./302	2 Jul 44	10.27	B-24	Budapest	8. HSS	Day
Lt	Kirchner, Horst	2./302	8 Jul 44	10.27	B-24	Vienna	9.	Day
Lt	Kirchner, Horst	2./302	16 Jul 44	10.22	B-24	Vienna	10. HSS	Day
Lt	Kirchner, Horst	2./302	21 Jul 44	10.40	B-17	Wels	11.	Day
Uffz	Klärner, Adolf	4./302	21 Jul 44	10.42	B-17	Wels	1.	Day
Uffz	Klammer, —	4./302	19 Jul 44	10.15	B-17	Starnberg	1. HSS	Day
Fw	Koch, Gerhard	1./301	14 Mar 44	23.25	Lancaster	—	1.	Night
Fw	Koch, Gerhard	1./301	14 Mar 44	23.35	Lancaster	—	2.	Night
Fw	Koch, Gerhard	1./301	5 Jul 44	01.30	Lancaster	France	3.	Night
Fw	Koch, Gerhard	1./301	6 Jul 44	00.38	4-Eng.	France	4.	Night
Fw	Koch, Gerhard	1./301	6 Jul 44	00.45	4-Eng.	France	5.	Night
Fw	Koch, Gerhard	1./301	8 Jul 44	02.50	4-Eng.	France	6.	Night
Fw	Koch, Gerhard	1./301	5 Dec 44	10.53	P-51	Berlin	7.	Day
Ofhr	Kolbe, Günter	3./302	8 Jul 44	10.42	B-24	Götzendorf	1.	Day
Ofhr	Kolbe, Günter	3./302	8 Jul 44	10.55	B-17	Preßburg	2.	Day
Uffz	Koller, Ludwig	3./302	8 Jul 44	10.30	B-24	Vienna	1.	Day
Lt	Körver, Alfred	7./302	2 Dec 43	21.11	Lancaster	Berlin	1.	Night
Lt	Körver, Alfred	7./302	18 Apr 44	14.32	B-17	—	2.	Day
OLt	Kray, Ferdinand	4./302	13 Jun 44	10.42	P-51	Landau/Isar	17.	Day
OLt	Kray, Ferdinand	4./302	16 Jun 44	10.45	P-51	Neusiedler See	18.	Day
OLt	Kray, Ferdinand	4./302	26 Jun 44	09.40	B-24	Vienna	19.	Day
OLt	Kray, Ferdinand	4./302	2 Jul 44	10.50	P-51	Budapest	20.	Day
OLt	Kray, Ferdinand	4./302	16 Jul 44	10.15	B-24	Vienna	21.	Day
OLt	Kray, Ferdinand	4./302	16 Jul 44	10.45	P-38	Vienna	22.	Day
OLt	Kray, Ferdinand	4./302	19 Jul 44	09.58	B-17	Munich	23.	Day
OLt	Kray, Ferdinand	4./302	19 Jul 44	10.05	B-17	Starnberg	24. HSS	Day
OLt	Kray, Ferdinand	4./302	21 Jul 44	10.48	B-17	Wels	25.	Day
Lt	Kreil, Max	4./301	8 Jul 44	01.16	Lancaster	France	1.	Night
OLt	Kretschmer, H.	10./301	17 Apr 44	11.26	B-24	Rumania	1.	Day
OLt	Kretschmer, H.	10./301	21 Apr 44	12.57	B-24	Rumania	2.	Day
Ofw	Krista, Adolf	8./301	12 Apr 44	12.23	B-24	—	1.	Day
Ofw	Kroker, Eberhard	6./302	24 Mar 44	22.42	4-Eng.	Berlin	1.	Night
Ofw	Kroker, Eberhard	6./302	9 Apr 44	11.38	B-24	—	2.	Day
Ofw	Kroker, Eberhard	6./302	9 Apr 44	11.45	B-24	—	3. HSS	Day
Ofw.	Kroker, Eberhard.	6./302	11.Apr.44	11:19	B-24	—	4. HSS	
Ofw	Kroker, Eberhard	6./302	18 Apr 44	14.35	B-17	—	5.	Day
Ofw	Kroker, Eberhard	6./302	19 Apr 44	10.34	B-17	—	6. HSS	Day

Rank	Name	Unit	Date	Time	Type	Area	Victory#	Night/Day
Ofw	Kroker, Eberhard	6./302	29 Apr 44	10.12	B-24	Brunswick	7.	Day
Ofw	Kroker, Eberhard	6./302	8 May 44	10.12	B-17	—	8. HSS	Day
Ofw	Kropf, Willi	7./301	29 Mar 44	13.45	B-17	—	1.	Day
OLt	Kucharsowsky, —	9./301	29 Jan 44	03.21	4-Eng.	—	1.	Night
OGefr	Kugler, Walter	3./302	16 Jun 44	10.00	B-17	Kassel	1.	Day
Lt	Kummer, —	II./301	9 Oct 43	01.24	Lancaster	—	1.	Night
Uffz	Laborenz, Jakob	2./302	25 Jul 44	10.53	B-24	Mariazell	1. HSS	Day
Ofw	Langelotz, Hubert	3./302	11 Jan 44	12.37	4-Eng.	—	1.	Day
Ofw	Langelotz, Hubert	3./302	20 Feb 44	13.10	B-17	Seesen	2. e.V.	Day
Ofw	Langelotz, Hubert	3./302	9 Jun 44	10.05	B-24	Landshut	3. HSS	Day
Ofw	Langelotz, Hubert	3./302	13 Jun 44	10.32	B-24	Weidenbach	4. HSS	Day
Fw	Laubenheimer, F.	1./301	15 Mar 44	23.28	Lancaster	—	1.	Night
Uffz	Leeb, Gerhard	8./301	5 Dec 44	11.00	P-51	Berlin	1.	Day
Hptm	Lewens, Richard	I./302	24 May 44	10.16	B-24	Viennaer Neustadt	1.	Day
Hptm	Lewens, Richard	I./302	30 Jun 44	10.07	P-38	Balaton	2.	Day
Ofw	Löffler, Josef	3./301	8 Jul 44	02.46	Lancaster	France	1.	Night
Ofw	Loos, Walter	St./301	24 Apr 45	—	Jak-9	Berlin	1.	—
Ofw	Loos, Walter	St./301	24 Apr 45	—	Jak-9	Berlin	2.	—
Ofw	Loos, Walter	St./301	30 Apr 45	—	Jak-9	Berlin	3.	—
Uffz	Maeser, Günter	7./302	8 Apr 44	13.10	B-17	—	1.	Day
Ofw	Menzel, Franz	10./301	15 Apr 44	12.15	B-24	Rumania	1.	Day
Ofw	Menzel, Franz	10./301	5 May 44	14.08	B-24	Rumania	2.	Day
Ofw	Menzel, Franz	10./301	28 Jun 44	09.55	B-24	Rumania	3.	Day
Lt	Merz, German	7./302	24 Mar 44	22.32	Halifax	Berlin	1.	Night
Lt	Merz, German	7./302	8 Apr 44	13.44	P-51	—	2.	Day
Lt	Merz, German	7./302	27 Apr 44	02.59	4-Eng.	—	3.	Night
Lt	Mess, —	7./302	8 Apr 44	13.44	B-24	—	1. HSS	Day
Fw	Mett, Gerhard	10./301	4 Apr 44	14.00	B-24	Rumania	1. HSS	Day
Fw	Mett, Gerhard	10./301	5 Apr 44	14.35	B-24	Rumania	2. HSS	Day
Fw	Mett, Gerhard	10./301	5 Apr 44	14.40	B-24	Rumania	3.	Day
Fw	Mett, Gerhard	10./301	11 Jun 44	09.25	B-24	Rumania	4.	Day
Fw	Mett, Gerhard	10./301	3 Jul 44	11.51	B-24	Rumania	5.	Day
Uffz	Michaelis, R.	11./301	26 Nov 44	14.00	B-24	Hildesheim	1.	Day
Uffz	Müller, —	I./301	15 Mar 44	23.23	Lancaster	—	1.	Night
Ofw	Müller, Hans	2./301	4 Jul 43	01.31	Stirling	Cologne	1.	Night
Ofw	Müller, Hans	2./301	1 Sept 43	00.58	Lancaster	Berlin	2.	Night
Ofw	Müller, Hans	2./301	24 Feb 44	12.55	B-17	Steyr	3.	Day
Ofw	Müller, Hans	2./302	24 Apr 44	13.45	P-51	Ebersberg	4.	Day
Ofw	Müller, Hans	2./301	6 Jul 44	00.44	Halifax	Ärmelkanal	5.	Night
Ofw	Müller, Hans	2./301	26 Nov 44	13.45	B-24	Brunswick	6.	Day
Ofw	Müller, Hans	2./301	26 Nov 44	13.46	B-24	Brunswick	7.	Day
Ofw	Müller, Hans	2./301	26 Nov 44	13.47	B-24	Brunswick	8.	Day
Fw	Müller-Leutert, —	2./301	25 Feb 44	13.30	B-24	—	1.	Day
Fw	Nightigall, Kurt	3./302	9 Jun 44	10.07	B-24	Landshut	1.	Day
Fw	Nightigall, Kurt	3./302	16 Jun 44	10.04	B-24	Neusiedler See	2.	Day
Ofw	Nevack, Heinz	1./302	29 Aug 44	10.55	B-17	Brünn	1.	Day
Lt	Prenzel, Horst	1./301	6 Jul 44	01.36	Lancaster	France	1.	Night
Lt	Prenzel, Horst	1./301	6 Jul 44	01.48	Lancaster	France	2.	Night
Fw	Pritzel, Otto	5./302	29 Dec 43	—	4-Eng.	Berlin	1.	Night
Fw	Pritzel, Otto	5./302	24 May 44	11.08	B-17	—	2. HSS	Day
Fw	Pritzel, Otto	5./302	24 May 44	11.18	B-17	—	3.	Day
Fw	Pritzel, Otto	5./302	29 May 44	—	B-24	—	4.	—
Lt	Reiche, —	3./302	2 Jul 44	10.20	B-24	Budapest	1.	Day
Lt	Reiche, —	3./302	8 Jul 44	10.45	B-24	Vienna	2. HSS	Day
Lt	Reiche, —	3./302	21 Jul 44	10.47	B-17	Wels	3. HSS	Day
Lt	Reiche, —	3./302	29 Jul 44	10.20	B-17	Linz	4.	Day
Lt	Reiche, —	3./302	16 Aug 44	10.00	B-17	Kassel	5.	Day
Lt	Reiche, —	3./302	24 Aug 44	12.40	B-24	Neuhaus	6.	Day
Lt	Reiche, —	12./301	5 Dec 44	10.50	P-51	Berlin	7.	Day
Lt	Reinicke, Leonhard	1./302	20 Aug 44	09.58	B-24	Budapest	1.	Day
Lt	Reinicke, Leonhard	1./302	21 Aug 44	10.25	B-24	Debrecen	2. HSS	Day
Lt	Reinicke, Leonhard	1./302	22 Aug 44	12.50	B-17	Balatonsee	3. HSS	Day
Lt	Reinicke, Leonhard	9./301	5 Dec 44	10.54	B-17	Berlin	4.	Day
Uffz	Reschke, Willi	1./302	2 Jul 44	10.25	B-24	Budapest	1.	Day
Uffz	Reschke, Willi	1./302	2 Jul 44	10.29	B-24	Budapest	2.	Day
Uffz	ReschkevWilli	1./302	7 Jul 44	11.55	B-24	Preßburg	3.	Day
Uffz	Reschke, Willi	1./302	13 Jul 44	10.45	B-17	Neusiedler See	4.	Day

Rank	Name	Unit	Date	Time	Type	Area	Victory#	Night/Day
Uffz	Reschke, Willi	1./302	14 Jul 44	09.55	B-24	Budapest	5.	Day
Uffz	Reschke, Willi	1./302	18 Jul 44	10.53	B-24	Munich	6.	Day
Uffz	Reschke, Willi	1./302	18 Jul 44	11.10	P-51	Munich	7.	Day
Uffz	Reschke, Willi	1./302	19 Jul 44	09.57	B-17	Starnberg	8.	Day
Uffz	Reschke, Willi	1./302	16 Aug 44	10.00	B-17	Kassel	9.	Day
Uffz	Reschke, Willi	1./302	20 Aug 44	09.45	B-17	Budapest	10.	Day
Uffz	Reschke, Willi	1./302	20 Aug 44	09.52	B-17	Budapest	11. HSS	Day
Uffz	Reschke, Willi	1./302	22 Aug 44	12.50	B-17	Balaton	12.e.V.	Day
Uffz	Reschke, Willi	1./302	24 Aug 44	12.40	B-24	Neuhaus	13.	Day
Uffz	Reschke, Willi	1./302	29 Aug 44	10.50	B-17	Ung. Brod	14.	Day
Fw	Reschke, Willi	9./301	21 Nov 44	12.05	B-17	Magdeburg	15.	Day
Fw	Reschke, Willi	9./301	26 Nov 44	12.45	B-24	Hildesheim	16.	Day
Fw	Reschke, Willi	9./301	17 Dec 44	11.20	B-24	Kassel	17.	Day
Fw	Reschke, Willi	9./301	17 Dec 44	11.25	P-51	Kassel	18.	Day
Fw	Reschke, Willi	9./301	24 Dec 44	14.55	B-17	Hannover	19.	Day
Fw	Reschke, Willi	9./301	24 Dec 44	15.03	B-17	Hannover	20.	Day
Fw	Reschke, Willi	9./301	31 Dec 44	11.35	B-24	Hamburg	21.	Day
Fw	Reschke, Willi	9./301	1 Jan 45	12.00	B-17	Gardelegen	22.	Day
Fw	Reschke, Willi	9./301	14 Jan 45	12.45	P-51	Mecklenburg	23.	Day
Fw	Reschke, Willi	9./301	14 Jan 45	12.55	P-47	Kyritz	24.	Day
Ofw	Reschke, Willi	St./301	14 Apr 45	19.20	Tempest	Ludwigslust	25.	Day
Ofw	Reschke, Willi	St./301	24 Apr 45	08.45	Jak-9	Berlin	26.	Day
Ofw	Reschke, Willi	St./301	24 Apr 45	08.48	Jak-9	Berlin	27.	Day
Fw	Resech, —	I./302	24 May 44	10.19	B-24	Vienna	1. HSS	Day
Uffz	Reuter, Heinrich	2./302	7 Jul 44	12.36	B-24	Györ	1.	Day
Uffz	Reuter, Erich	3./302	8 Jul 44	11.05	B-17	Götzendorf	1. HSS	Day
Uffz	Richter, Günter	3./302	2 Jul 44	10.30	B-24	Budapest	1.	Day
Fw	Rienth, Karl	11./301	5 Dec 44	11.00	P-51	Berlin	1.	Day
Ofw	Ries, Eduard	2./302	1 Jan 44	—	4-Eng.	—	1.	Night
Ofw	Ries, Eduard	2./302	27 Jan 44	—	4-Eng.	—	2.	Night
Ofw	Ries, Eduard	2./302	27 Jun 44	10.25	B-17	Budapest	3.	Day
Ofhr	Rödhammer, W.	1./302	8 Jul 44	10.45	B-24	Vienna	1.	Day
Uffz	Ropers, Heinz	1./302	29 May 44	09.52	B-24	Markersdorf	1.	Day
Ofw	Rusche, Dieter	2./302	9 Jun 44	10.00	B-24	Freising	1. HSS	Day
Ofw	Rusche, Dieter	2./302	9 Jun 44	10.13	B-24	Regensburg	2.	Day
Ofw	Rusche, Dieter	2./302	2 Jul 44	10.27	B-24	Budapest	3.	Day
Ofw	Rusche, Dieter	2./302	21 Jul 44	10.45	B-24	Wels	4. HSS	Day
Ofw	Rusche, Dieter	2./302	25 Jul 44	10.53	B-24	Mariazell	5. HSS	Day
Ofw	Sattler, Josef	2./302	9 Jun 44	10.06	B-24	Munich	1. HSS	Day
Ofw	Sattler, Josef	2./302	26 Jun 44	09.22	B-24	Deutsch-Wagram	2.	Day
Ofw	Sattler Josef	2./302	26 Jun 44	09.26	P-51	Deutsch-Wagram	3.	Day
OLt	Sauter, —	II./301	27 Sep 43	—	Lancaster	—	1.	Night
Ofw	Schäfer, Ernst	2./302	16 Jun 44	10.55	B-24	Neusiedler See	1.	Day
Ofw	Schäfer, Ernst	2./302	2 Jul 44	10.25	B-24	Budapest	2.	Day
Ofw	Schäfer, Ernst	2./302	8 Jul 44	11.20	B-17	Neusiedler See	3.	Day
Ofw	Schäfer, Ernst	2./302	16 Jul 44	10.20	B-24	Vienna	4.	Day
Ofw	Schäfer, Ernst	2./302	16 Jul 44	10.40	B-24	Vienna	5. e.V.	Day
Ofw	Schäfer, Ernst	2./302	21 Jul 44	10.43	B-17	Wels	6.	Day
Fhr	Schäfer, —	4./301	14 Jan 45	12.30	B-17	Mecklenburg	1.	Day
Fw	Scharein, Georg	1./301	5 Jul 44	01.52	Lancaster	France	1.	Night
Fw	Scharein, Georg	1./301	8 Jul 44	02.14	B-26	France	2.	Night
Fw	Scharein, Georg	1./301	8 Jul 44	02.44	B-26	France	3.	Night
Uffz	Scheller, Walter	4./302	16 Jul 44	10.20	B-24	Vienna	1. HSS	Day
Uffz	Scheller, Walter	12./301	26 Nov 44	12.50	B-17	Hildesheim	2.	Day
Fw	Schellner, H.-W.	2./302	16 Jun 44	09.50	B-24	Komarom	1. HSS	Day
Fw	Schellner, H.-W.	2./302	16 Jun 44	09.55	B-24	Komarom	2. HSS	Day
Ofw	Schellner, H.-W.	2./302	7 Jul 44	09.45	B-17	Komarom	3.	Day
Ofw	Schellner, H.-W.	2./302	16 Jul 44	10.20	B-24	Vienna	4.	Day
Ofw	Schellner, H.-W.	2./302	16 Jul 44	—	P-38	Vienna	5.	—
Ofw	Schellner, H.-W.	2./302	25 Jul 44	11.05	B-24	Vienna	6. HSS	Day
Ofw	Schellner, H.-W.	2./302	28 Jul 44	10.05	P-51	Hof	7.	Day
Ofw	Schellner, H.-W.	2./302	22 Aug 44	12.55	B-17	Vasegerszeg	8.	Day
Lt	Schölta, Erich	2./302	2 Dec 43	20.43	Stirling	Berlin	1.	Night
OLt	Schuch, —	7./301	5 Dec 44	10.50	B-17	Berlin	1.	Day
OLt	Schuch, —	7./301	5 Dec 44	10.55	P-51	Berlin	2.	Day
Fw	Schulze, Martin	1./301	5 Jul 44	01.17	4-Eng.	France	1.	Night
Fw	Schulze, Martin	1./301	5 Jul 44	01.28	4-Eng.	France	2.	Night

Rank	Name	Unit	Date	Time	Type	Area	Victory#	Night/Day
Fw	Schulze, Martin	1./301	8 Jul 44	03.05	B-26	France	3.	Night
Lt	Schwamb, Otto	8./302	24 Mar 44	22.25	Lancaster	—	1.	Night
Lt	Schwamb, Otto	8./302	23 Apr 44	01.15	4-Eng.	—	2.	Night
Lt	Schwamb, Otto	8./302	23 Apr 44	01.20	4-Eng.	—	3.	Night
OLt	Seeler, Karl-H.	1./301	9 Oct 43	01.27	Halifax	—	1.	Night
OLt	Seeler, Karl-H.	5./302	24 Mar 44	22.57	4-Eng.	Berlin	2.	Night
OLt	Seeler, Karl-H.	5./302	11 Apr 44	11.20	B-24	—	3. HSS	Day
OLt	Seeler, Karl-H.	5./302	29 Apr 44	11.04	B-17	Brunswick	4. HSS	Day
OLt	Seeler, Karl-H.	5./302	13 May 44	14.21	B-17	—	5.	Day
OLt	Seeler, Karl-H.	5./302	23 May 44	02.16	4-Eng.	—	6.	Night
OLt	Seeler, Karl-H.	5./302	23 May 44	02.27	4-Eng.	—	7.	Night
OLt	Seidel, Heinz	3./302	4 Mar 44	—	B-17	—	1.	—
OLt	Seidel, Heinz	3./302	9 Apr 44	—	B-17	—	2.	—
OLt	Seidel, Heinz	3./302	19 Apr 44	—	B-17	—	3.	—
OLt	Seidel, Heinz	3./302	29 Apr 44	—	B-17	Brunswick	4.	—
OLt	Seidel, Heinz	3./302	29 Apr 44	—	P-51	Brunswick	5.	—
OLt	Seidel, Heinz	3./302	7 May 44	—	B-17	—	6.	—
OLt	Seidel, Heinz	3./302	8 May 44	—	B-17	—	7.	—
OLt	Seidel, Heinz	3./302	24 May 44	10.13	B-24	St. Pölten	8.	Day
OLt	Seidel, Heinz	3./302	9 Jun 44	10.04	B-24	Landshut	9. HSS	Day
OLt	Seidel, Heinz	3./302	9 Jun 44	10.15	B-24	Landshut	10.	Day
OLt	Seidel, Heinz	3./302	13 Jun 44	—	B-24	Landau	11.	—
Ofw	Seifert, Herbert	8./301	29 Jan 44	03.20	Lancaster	—	1.	Night
Ofw	Seifert, Herbert	8./301	26 Nov 44	13.55	B-24	Hildesheim	2.	Day
Fw	Siegfahrt, Robert	7./301	24 Mar 44	22.37	Lancaster	—	1.	Night
OLt	Stahl, Hermann	10./301	26 Nov 44	12.55	B-24	Hildesheim	3.	Day
Gefr	Steidel, Erich	1./302	28 Jul 44	10.50	B-17	Neustadt/Do.	1.	Day
Ofw	Stephan, Herbert	1./302	27 Jun 44	10.26	B-17	Budapest	1.	Day
Ofw	Stephan, Herbert	1./302	2 Jul 44	10.28	B-24	Budapest	2.	Day
Ofw	Stephan, Herbert	1./302	8 Jul 44	10.33	B-24	Vienna	3.	Day
Ofw	Stephan, Herbert	1./302	16 Jul 44	10.22	B-24	Vienna	4. HSS	Day
Ofw	Stephan, Herbert	1./302	25 Jul 44	10.58	B-24	Vienna	5. HSS	Day
Ofw	Stephan, Herbert	1./302	29 Jul 44	10.15	B-17	Linz	6. HSS	Day
Ofw	Stephan, Herbert	1./302	20 Aug 44	09.45	B-17	Budapest	7.	Day
Ofw	Stephan, Herbert	1./302	22 Aug 44	10.05	B-24	Pápa	8.	Day
Ofw	Streuff, Paul	1./302	24 May 44	10.15	B-24	St. Pölten	1. HSS	Day
Ofw	Streuff, Paul	1./302	29 May 44	09.55	B-24	St. Pölten	2. HSS	Day
Hptm	Suhr, Helmut	7./301	4 Oct 43	22.43	Stirling	—	1.	Night
Hptm	Suhr, Helmut	7./301	20 Jan 44	19.47	Lancaster	—	2.	Night
Hptm	Suhr, Helmut	7./301	30 Mar 44	—	Lancaster	—	3.	Night
Hptm	Suhr, Helmut	1./301	2 Apr 44	11.17	B-17	—	4.	Day
Hptm	Suhr, Helmut	1./301	12 Jun 44	—	Wellington	France	5.	Night
Hptm	Suhr, Helmut	1./301	12 Jun 44	—	Wellington	France	6.	Night
Hptm	Suhr, Helmut	1./301	8 Jul 44	02.22	Lancaster	France	7.	Night
Hptm	Suhr, Helmut	1./301	26 Aug 44	—	P-61	France	8.	Night
Hptm	Suhr, Helmut	8./301	14 Jan 45	12.35	B-17	Mecklenburg	9.	Day
Hptm	Suhr, Helmut	8./301	15 Mar 45	—	B-17	Norddeutschland	10.	—
Ofw	Sulzgruber, Max	6./301	31 May 44	10.54	B-24	—	1.	Day
Ofw	Sulzgruber, Max	6./301	23 Jun 44	09.40	P-51	—	2.	Day
Ofw	Sulzgruber, Max	6./301	28 Jun 44	09.48	B-24	—	3.	Day
Ofw	Todt, Hans	2./301	24 Mar 44	22.41	4-Eng.	—	1.	Night
Ofw	Todt, Hans	2./301	24 Mar 44	—	4-Eng.	—	2.	Night
Ofw	Todt, Hans	2./301	14 Jul 44	—	Lancaster	France	3.	Night
Ofw	Todt, Hans	2./301	8 Aug 44	—	Halifax	France	4.	Night
Ofw	Todt, Hans	8./301	26 Nov 44	12.55	B-24	Hildesheim	5.	Day
Ofw	Todt, Hans	8./301	17 Dec 44	11.30	P-47	Kassel	6.	Day
Ofw	Todt, Hans	8./301	1 Jan 45	12.00	B-17	Gardelegen	7.	Day
Ofw	Todt, Hans	8./301	1 Feb 45	—	U-2	Norddeutschland	8.	—
Ofw	Todt, Hans	8./301	25 Feb 45	—	P-51	Reichsgebiet	9.	—
Ofw	Todt, Hans	8./301	2 Mar 45	—	B-17	Magdeburg	10.	—
Uffz	Toldrian, Walter	6./301	31 May 44	10.25	B-24	—	1. HSS	Day
Fw	Unger, Karl	10./301	15 Apr 44	12.15	B-24	Rumania	1.	Day
Fw	Vetter, Karl	3./302	26 Jun 44	09.38	B-24	Vienna	1.	Day
Uffz	Voss, Werner	1./302	24 May 44	10.13	B-24	St. Pölten	1.	Day
Uffz	Voss, Werner	1./302	9 Jun 44	10.10	B-24	Landshut	2.	Day
Uffz	Walter, Gerhard	2./302	13 Jun 44	10.10	B-24	Ingolstadt	1.	Day
Uffz	Walter, Gerhard	2./302	2 Jul 44	10.25	B-24	Budapest	2.	Day

Rank	Name	Unit	Date	Time	Type	Area	Victory#	Night/Day
Lt	Weber, Hans-J.	6./301	6 May 44	11.35	B-24	—	1.	Day
Lt	Weber, Hans-J.	6./301	18 May 44	11.15	B-17	—	2. HSS	Day
Lt	Weber, Hans-J.	6./301	31 May 44	10.25	B-24	—	3. HSS	Day
Hptm	Wegner, Erich	2./301	8 Jul 44	01.21	4-Eng.	France	1.	Night
Oberstl.	Weinreich, Helmut	St./301	18 Nov 43	20.35	4-Eng.	—	1.	Night
Gefr	Weinzierl, Walter	3./302	2 Jul 44	10.25	B-24	Budapest	1.	Day
Gefr	Weinzierl, Walter	3./302	2 Jul 44	10.50	B-24	Budapest	2.	Day
Gefr	Weinzierl, Walter	3./302	19 Jul 44	10.13	B-17	Starnberg	3.	Day
Gefr	Weinzierl, Walter	3./302	21 Jul 44	10.55	P-38	Brügg	4.	Day
Gefr	Weinzierl, Walter	3./302	26 Jul 44	11.20	B-17	Aspern	5.	Day
Ofw	Welter, Kurt	5./301	22 Sep 43	23.04	4-Eng.	—	1.	Night
Ofw	Welter, Kurt	5./301	22 Sep 43	23.12	4-Eng.	—	2.	Night
Ofw	Welter, Kurt	5./301	3 Oct 43	22.29	Halifax	—	3.	Night
Ofw	Welter, Kurt	5./301	3 Oct 43	22.41	Halifax	—	4.	Night
Ofw	Welter, Kurt	5./301	22 Oct 43	21.04	4-Eng.	—	5.	Night
Ofw	Welter, Kurt	5./301	22 Oct 43	21.14	4-Eng.	—	6.	Night
Ofw	Welter, Kurt	5./301	22 Oct 43	21.24	4-Eng.	—	7.	Night
Ofw	Welter, Kurt	5./301	2 Jan 44	02.55	4-Eng.	—	8.	Night
Ofw	Welter, Kurt	5./301	5 Jan 44	03.46	4-Eng.	—	9.	Night
Ofw	Welter, Kurt	5./301	11 Jan 44	04.11	4-Eng.	—	10.	Night
Ofw	Welter, Kurt	5./301	28 Jan 44	—	4-Eng.	—	11.	Night
Ofw	Welter, Kurt	5./301	20 Feb 44	03.27	Lancaster	—	12.	Night
Ofw	Welter, Kurt	5./301	20 Feb 44	04.16	Lancaster	—	13.	Night
Ofw	Welter, Kurt	5./301	18 Mar 44	—	Lancaster	—	14.	Night
Ofw	Welter, Kurt	5./301	18 Mar 44	—	Lancaster	—	15.	Night
Ofw	Welter, Kurt	5./301	24 Mar 44	22.44	Lancaster	—	16.	Night
Ofw	Welter, Kurt	5./301	24 Mar 44	—	Lancaster	—	17.	Night
Uffz	Wernecke, Horst	4./301	16 Jul 44	10.30	B-17	Vienna	1.	Day
Uffz	Werner, Paul	3./301	8 Jul 44	02.28	B-26	France	1.	Night
Ofw	Wick, Ernst	1./302	9 Apr 44	—	B-24	—	1.	—
Fhr	Wiegeshoff, Jonny	12./301	26 Nov 44	13.05	B-24	Hildesheim	1.	Day
Uffz	Witt, Gerhard	2./301	22 Oct 43	21.14	4-Eng.	—	1.	Night
OLt	Wolfsberger, Josef	5./302	22 Oct 43	21.06	Lancaster	—	1.	Night
Lt	Wurff, Rudolf	6./301	30 Apr 44	09.40	B-24	—	1.	Day
Lt	Wurff, Rudolf	6./301	6 Jun 44	09.40	B-24	—	2. HSS	Day
Lt	Wurff, Rudolf	6./301	21 Apr 45	—	Tempest	Dammer See	3.	—
Hptm	Wurzer, Heinrich	1./302	22 Nov 43	—	Lancaster	—	1.	Night
Hptm	Wurzer, Heinrich	1./302	20 Jan 44	19.24	Halifax	—	2.	Night
Hptm	Wurzer, Heinrich	1./302	30 Jan 44	—	B-17	—	3.	Day
Hptm	Wurzer, Heinrich	1./302	10 Feb 44	—	B-24	—	4.	—
Hptm	Wurzer, Heinrich	1./302	20 Feb 44	—	B-17	Seesen	5.	—
Hptm	Wurzer, Heinrich	1./302	22 Feb 44	—	B-17	—	6.	—
Hptm	Wurzer, Heinrich	1./302	24 Feb 44	—	B-24	—	7.	—
Hptm	Wurzer, Heinrich	1./302	6 Mar 44	12.30	B-17	Berlin	8.	Day
Hptm	Wurzer, Heinrich	1./302	6 Mar 44	—	B-17	—	9.	—
Hptm	Wurzer, Heinrich	1./302	8 Mar 44	13.30	B-24	Magdeburg	10.	Day
Hptm	Wurzer, Heinrich	1./302	8 Mar 44	13.35	B-24	Magdeburg	11.	Day
Hptm	Wurzer, Heinrich	1./302	5 Apr 44	—	P-51	—	12.	—
Hptm	Wurzer, Heinrich	1./302	9 Apr 44	—	B-17	—	13.	—
Hptm	Wurzer, Heinrich	1./302	9 Apr 44	—	B-17	—	14.	—
Hptm	Wurzer, Heinrich	1./302	10 May 44	11.32	B-24	Neusiedler See	15.	Day
Hptm	Wurzer, Heinrich	1./302	10 May 44	11.50	B-24	Viennaer Neustadt	16.	Day
Hptm	Wurzer, Heinrich	1./302	24 May 44	10.10	B-24	St. Pölten	17.	Day
Hptm	Wurzer, Heinrich	1./302	24 May 44	10.17	B-24	Vienna	18.	Day
Hptm	Wurzer, Heinrich	1./302	29 May 44	09.54	B-24	St. Pölten	19. HSS	Day
Hptm	Wurzer, Heinrich	1./302	29 May 44	09.59	B-24	St. Pölten	20. HSS	Day
Hptm	Wurzer, Heinrich	1./302	9 Jun 44	09.58	B-24	Landshut	21. HSS	Day
Hptm	Wurzer, Heinrich	1./302	9 Jun 44	10.10	B-24	Landshut	22.	Day
Hptm	Wurzer, Heinrich	1./302	16 Jun 44	09.57	B-24	Komarom	23. HSS	Day
Hptm	Wurzer, Heinrich	1./302	16 Jun 44	10.02	B-24	Komarom	24.	Day
Hptm	Wurzer, Heinrich	1./302	8 Jul 44	10.50	B-24	Vienna	25.	Day
Hptm	Wurzer, Heinrich	1./302	8 Jul 44	10.51	B-24	Vienna	26. HSS	Day
Fj-Ofw	Yung, Fritz	1./301	18 Oct 43	22.43	Lancaster	—	1.	Night
Fj-Ofw	Yung, Fritz	1./301	22 Oct 43	20.59	4-Eng.	—	2.	Night
Fj-Ofw	Yung, Fritz	1./301	22 Oct 43	21.12	4-Eng.	—	3.	Night
Fj-Ofw	Yung, Fritz	1./301	18 Nov 43	—	Lancaster	—	4.	Night
Fj-Ofw	Yung, Fritz	1./301	21 Feb 44	—	Lancaster	—	5.	Night

Rank	Name	Unit	Date	Time	Type	Area	Victory#	Night/Day
Fj-Ofw	Yung, Fritz	1./301	24 Feb 44	—	4-Eng.	—	6.	Night
Fj-Ofw	Yung, Fritz	1./301	26 Feb 44	01.30	Halifax	—	7.	Night
Fj-Ofw	Yung, Fritz	1./301	3 Mar 44	—	Spitfire	—	8.	Day
Fj-Ofw	Yung, Fritz	1./301	18 Mar 44	—	P-38	—	9.	—
Fj-Ofw	Yung, Fritz	1./301	18 Mar 44	—	P-38	—	10.	—
Fj-Ofw	Yung, Fritz	1./301	13 Apr 44	14.37	P-51	—	11.	—
Uffz	Zarm, Hans	1./301	5 Jul 44	01.50	4-Eng.	France	1.	Night
Fw	Zeisler, Gerhard	10./301	5 Apr 44	14.55	B-24	Rumania	1. HSS	Day
Fw	Zeisler, Gerhard	10./301	5 Apr 44	15.05	B-24	Rumania	2. HSS	Day
Fw	Zeisler, Gerhard	10./301	6 Jun 44	09.15	B-24	Rumania	3.	Day

This list was compiled by the author from available records and makes no claim to completeness.

*HSS = Damaged and forced to leave formation
**e.V. = Finished off damaged aircraft.

Appendix 2
JG 301/JG 302 Loss List

JG 301

Date	Unit	Aircraft Type	WerkNr/Code	Cause	Location	Rank	Name	Fate
1943								
3 Sep 43	2./301	Bf 109 G-6		crashlanding	Werneuchen	Fw.	Hans Müller	injured
20 Sep 43	2./301	Bf 109		crash	Neubrandenburg	Fw.	Richard Meyer	Killed Fly.Acc.
20 Sep 43	2./301	Bf 109		crash	Airfield Briest	Lt.	Hans Kirsch	injured
22 Sep 43	1./301	Bf 109		friendly flak	Verden	Ofw.	Xaver Neumaier	WIA
22 Sep 43	3./301	Bf 109		collision Bf 109	Verden	Uffz.	Werner Dienst	injured
22 Sep 43	6./301	Fw 190 A-4	142 347	air combat	Wittmundhafen	Fw.	Wilhelm Marten	KIA
22 Sep 43	7./301	Bf 109		air combat	Wunstorf	Ofw.	Adolf Wiedermann	KIA
23 Sep 43	4./301	Fw 190 A-5	410 273	crash	S. of Husum	Uffz.	Gerhard Zirrgiebel	Killed Fly.Acc.
23 Sep 43	5./301	Fw 190 A-6	470 04.	crash	near Husum	Uffz.	Herbert Kreuchen	Killed Fly.Acc.
27 Sep 43	III./301	Bf 109		air combat	near Celle	Olt.	Schür	WIA
27 Sep 43	1./301	Bf 109 G-6		air combat	Hannover	Fw.	Heinz Radloff	KIA
27 Sep 43	6./301	Fw 190 A-4	140 607 "Yellow 4"	air combat	Wunstorf	Fw.	Alfred Riediger	KIA
27 Sep 43	7./301	Bf 109 G-6		air combat	Oldenburg	Fw.	Erich Reitberger	KIA
13 Oct 43	Stab/301	Fw 190 A-6	530 354	crash	Mchn-Riem	Olt.	Friedrich Amsink	injured
18 Oct 43	I./301	Bf 109 G-6	20 274	crashlanding	Gardelegen	Hptm.	Richard Kamp	injured
18 Oct 43	I./301	Bf 109 G-6	18 848	crashlanding	Gardelegen	Lt.	Benno Rehfeld	injured
20 Oct 43	1./301	Bf 109 G-6		air combat	NW. of Gardelegen	Uffz.	Rudi Fischer	KIA
20 Oct 43	1./301	Bf 109 G-6		air combat	Breslau?	Fw.	Heinz Hürdler	KIA
20 Oct 43	2./301	Bf 109 G-6		air combat	Peckfitz	Lt.	Ludwig Wißgens	KIA
20 Oct 43	3./301	Bf 109 G-6		air combat	Solpke	Uffz.	Kurt Groß	KIA
22 Oct 43	7./301	Bf 109 G-6		crash	near Kassel	Fw.	Kurt Degenkoll	Killed Fly.Acc.
22 Oct 43	8./301	Bf 109 G-6		crash	Göttingen	Fw.	Horst Neumann	Killed Fly.Acc.
18 Nov 43	7./301	Bf 109 G-6		air combat	Fischbach	Lt.	Rolf-Dieter Nedden	KIA
18 Nov 43	7./301	Bf 109 G-6		air combat	Lachen-Speiersd.	Lt.	Arno Schmidt	KIA
18 Nov 43	Stab/ 301	Fw 190 A-5	151 482	crash	Zeppelinheim	Major	Helmut Weinreich	Killed Fly.Acc.
25 Nov 43	1./301	Bf 109 G-6	410 224	air combat	E. of Gardelegen	Uffz.	August Deumlich	KIA
26 Nov 43	3./301	Fw 190 A-9	202 373	air combat	Krückeberg	Fhj.Fw.	Erwin Seifert	KIA
26 Nov 43	7./301	Bf 109 G-6		air combat	Mespelbrunn	Fw.	Heinz Schwarz	KIA
26 Nov 43	8./301	Bf 109 G-6		air combat	Rohrbrunn	Uffz.	Ullrich Braun	KIA
26 Nov 43	8./301	Bf 109 G-6		air combat	Kreidach	Uffz.	Ernst Krieg	KIA
2 Dec 43	8./301	Bf 109 G-6		crash	Hennef	Fw.	Gerhard Wieck	Killed Fly.Acc.
11 Dec 43	9./301	Bf 109 G-6		crash	Frankfurt/Main	Fw.	Wilh. Falkenberg	Killed Fly.Acc.
16 Dec 43	9./301	Bf 109 G-6		crash	Lohrhaupten	Olt.	Georg Sucker	KFA
20 Dec 43	8./301	Bf 109 G-6		shotdown, bailed out	Wesermünde	Uffz.	Walter Scheller	WIA
21 Dec 43	3./301	Bf 109 G-6		crash-start	Germersheim	Ofw.	Josef Löffler	injured
30 Dec 43	4./301	Bf 109 G-6		crash	Seyring	Lt.	Josef Mester	injured
1944								
4 Jan 44	3./301	Bf 109 G-6	20 445	crash	Unterzimmering	Uffz.	Gerhard Koch	Killed Fly.Acc.
5 Jan 44	8./301	Bf 109 G-6		shotdown, bailed out	St. Truiden	Gefr.	Ernst Peitz	WIA
7 Jan 44	7./301	Bf 109 G-6		shotdown,	Heidelberg	Fw.	Leonhard Stark	WIA
7 Jan 44	7./301	Bf 109 G-6		air combat	Worms	Fw.	Fritz Utermark	KIA
9 Jan 44	III./301	Bf 109 G-6		crash	Frankfurt/M.	Hptm.	Klaus Kossmos	Killed Fly.Acc.
11 Jan 44	3./301	Bf 109 G-6	411 213	crashlanding	Brandis	Uffz.	Heinz Grube	injured
14 Jan 44	9./301	Bf 109 G-6		friendly flak shotdown, bailed out	Halle	Uffz.	Paul Hengel	KIA
20 Jan 44	9./301	Bf 109 G-6		air combat	Jüterbog	Fw.	Eugen Bauer	KIA
21 Jan 44	Stab 301	Fw 190 A-7	430 178<3+	crash	N. of Kehlheim	Olt.	Franz Amsink	Killed Fly.Acc.
21 Jan 44	Stab 301	Fw 190 A-7		crash	Welzow	Ofw.	Heinz Stahlhut	injured

Date	Unit	Aircraft Type	WerkNr/Code	Cause	Location	Rank	Name	Fate
28 Jan 44	1./301	Bf 109 G-6		air combat	Södingen	Ofw.	Ernst Cimmek	KIA
28 Jan 44	1./301	Bf 109 G-6		air combat	W. of Finsterwalde	Lt.	Albert Wolter	KIA
30 Jan 44	7./301	Bf 109 G-6		air combat	unknown	Fw.	Kurt Zschoche	KIA
30 Jan 44	9./301	Bf 109 G-6		air combat	Deelen	Ofw.	Rudolf Kirchner	KIA
8 Feb 44	8./301	Bf 109 G-6		crash	near Magdeburg	Fw.	Gerhard Friedrich	Killed Fly.Acc.
8 Feb 44	7./301	Bf 109 G-6	411 136	crash	Barby	Fw.	Heinz Hoppe	Killed Fly.Acc.
14 Feb 44	3./301	Bf 109 G-6		shotdown, bailed out	unknown	Fw.	Theo Estermann	WIA
19 Feb 44	8./301	Bf 109 G-6	410 773	crash	Dütschow	Fw.	Herbert Seifert	injured
20 Feb 44	I./301	Bf 109 G-6	411 228	crash	Germersheim	Maj.	Walter Brede	injured
20 Feb 44	2./301	Bf 109 G-6	411 226	friendly flak, bailed out	Göppingen	Olt.	Ernst Fischer	WIA
20 Feb 44	3./301	Bf 109 G-6		air combat	unknown	Fw.	Friedrich Brüssel	KIA
22 Feb 44	1./301	Bf 109 G-6	411 270	shotdown, bailed out	N. of Salzburg	Olt.	Walter Burghoff	WIA
22 Feb 44	2./301	Bf 109 G-6	411 244	shotdown, bailed out	Penk	Uffz.	Heinrich Block	WIA
24 Feb 44	1./301	Bf 109 G-6	411 225	air combat	Almkogel	Ofw.	Max Röhricht	KIA
25 Feb 44	I./301	Bf 109 G-6	161 192	shotdown, bailed out	Ludwigsburg	Uffz.	W. Waldenberger	WIA
25 Feb 44	2./301	Bf 109 G-6	411 455	crash-start	Neubiberg	Fw.	Hans Müller	injured
28 Feb 44	7./301	Bf 109 G-6		air combat	Zerbst	Fw.	Hans Engfer	WIA
12 Mar 44	7./301	Bf 109 G-6	160 059	crash	Magdeburg	Uffz.	Horst Wöstenberg	Killed Fly.Acc.
15 Mar 44	2./301	Bf 109 G-6	161 137	air combat	Steinbronn	Uffz.	Gerhard Witt	KIA
15 Mar 44	3./301	Bf 109 G-6	411 516	crash-start	Neuburg, Do.	Fhj.Fw.	Heinz Grube	injured
18 Mar 44	1./301	Bf 109 G-6	162 373	air combat	Ebersberg	Fw.	Fr. Laubenheimer	injured
18 Mar 44	3./301	Bf 109 G-6	411 238	air combat	Harthausen	Ofw.	Karl Hausmann	KIA
18 Mar 44	3./301	Bf 109 G-6	411 735	air combat	Haar	Fw.	Ludwig Schmutz	WIA
18 Mar 44	4./301	Bf 109 G-6	15 478	air combat	W. of Reichenau	Ofw.	Josef Grauvogel	WIA
21 Mar 44	5./301	Bf 109 G-6	18 478	crash	Seyring	Lt.	Waldem. Göttert	injured
22 Mar 44	1./301	Bf 109 G-6	411 232	air combat crashlanding	Neuburg, Do.	Fhj.Fw.	Fritz Brinkmann	WIA
22 Mar 44	3./301	Bf 109 G-6	411 205	air combat	Rohrenfels	Olt.	Wilhelm Burggraf	WIA
22 Mar 44	7./301	Bf 109 G-6		air combat	unknown	Uffz.	Geo. Schleenbecker	MIA
23 Mar 44	10./301	Bf 109 G-6	20 441	crash	Targsoroul, Rom.	Ofw.	Egon Gerz	Killed Fly.Acc.
24 Mar 44	8./301	Bf 109 G-6		air combat	Berlin	Olt.	Kurt Medinn	KIA
29 Mar 44	7./301	Bf 109 G-6		air combat	Gardelegen	Ofw.	Willi Kropf	WIA
29 Mar 44	7./301	Bf 109 G-6		air combat	Magdeburg	Fw.	Robert Siegfahrt	KIA
29 Mar 44	9./301	Bf 109 G-6		air combat	Colbitz	Ofw.	Walter Blickle	WIA
31 Mar 44	9./301	Bf 109 G-6		Crash	Straguth	Ofw.	Willi Rose	Killed Fly.Acc.
1 Apr 44	I./301	Bf 109 G-6	161 392	engine failure, bailed out	Sonnen	Lt.	Max Kreil	WIA
12 Apr 44	4./301	Bf 109 G-6	160 809	air combat	W of Neustadt	Uffz.	Rudolf Schneider	KIA
12 Apr 44	4./301	Bf 109 G-6	412 042	air combat	SW. of Eisenstadt	Ofw.	Tad.Wakonigg	KIA
12 Apr 44	6./301	Bf 109 G-6	410 088	air combat-B-24	Oberpullendorf	Fw.	Kurt Lamm	WIA
12 Apr 44	6./301	Bf 109 G-6	410 305	air combat P-38	Ödenburg, Burgl.	Uffz.	Stefan Zeitlinger	WIA
13 Apr 44	1./301	Bf 109 G-6	162 412	shotdown, bailed out	Augsburg	Fw.	Georg Scharein	WIA
13 Apr 44	3./301	Bf 109 G-6	411 721	air combat	NW. of Kirchdorf	Ofw.	Hans Dornhoff	WIA
13 Apr 44	4./301	Bf 109 G-6	411 375	air combat B-24	S. of Budapest	Olt.	Kurt Jäger	KIA
15 Apr 44	10./301	Bf 109 G-6	160 089 "Black 4"	takeoff crash	Bucuresti	Ofw.	Rudolf Walther	WIA
17 Apr 44	10./301	Bf 109 G-6	20 424 "Black 7"	takeoff crash	Bucuresti	Ofw.	Hubert Ippoldt	WIA
24 Apr 44	3./301	Bf 109 G-6		shotdown, bailed out	Erding	Olt.	Hans Tschauder	WIA
24 Apr 44	1./301	Bf 109 G-6	163 060	shotdown, bailed out	Mkt. Schwaben	Ofw.	Hans Schäfer	WIA
24 Apr 44	1./301	Bf 109 G-6		air combat bailed out	Mkt. Schwaben	Fhj.Fw.	Fritz Yung	WIA
24 Apr 44	2./301	Bf 109 G-6		air combat	Erding	Fhj.Fw.	Ar. Müller-Leutert	KIA
24 Apr 44	3./301	Bf 109 G-6		air combat	Mkt. Schwaben	Fw.	Herbert Kunzinger	KIA
24 Apr 44	3./301	Bf 109 G-6	411 245	air combat	Piusheim	Ofw.	Ludwig Schmutz	KIA
24 Apr 44	I./301	Bf 109 G-6		air combat	Holzkirchen	Major	Walter Brede	WIA
25 Apr 44	7./301	Bf 109 G-6	411 377	air combat	Mannheim	Fw.	Paul Dettmar	KIA
25 Apr 44	7./301	Bf 109 G-6	163 046	crash	Linz a. Rhein	Lt.	Gustav Mohr	Killed Fly.Acc.
25 Apr 44	8./301	Bf 109 G-6	440 990	air combat	Großsachsenheim	Uffz.	Werner Albers	KIA

Date	Unit	Aircraft Type	WerkNr/Code	Cause	Location	Rank	Name	Fate
3 Mai 44	10./301	Bf 109 G-6	20 189	air combat	unknown, Rom.	*Uffz.*	Josef Niedermeyer	KIA
7 Mai 44	7./301	Bf 109 G-6	441 153	crash	Heimdingen	*Lt.*	Hans Kohler	Killed Fly.Acc.
31 Mai 44	10./301	Bf 109 G-6	163 089	air combat	Rumanesti, Rom.	*Uffz.*	Waldemar Blazek	KIA
31 Mai 44	10./301	Bf 109 G-6	20 144 "Black 8"	air combat	Bultea, Rom.	*Fw.*	Fritz Gehrmann	KIA
31 Mai 44	10./301	Bf 109 G-6	412 236 "Black 5"	air combat	N. of Bucharest	*Olt.*	Hans Kretschmer	WIA
31 Mai 44	10./301	Bf 109 G-6	162 126	air combat	NW. of Bukarest	*Fw.*	Kurt Witschel	KIA
6 Jun 44	10./301	Bf 109 G-6	412 255	air combat	unknown, Rom.	*Fw.*	Gerhard Zeisler	KIA
11 Jun 44	5./301	Bf 109 G-6	410 085	air combat P-51	W. of Bodewgrod	*Fw.*	Paul Becker	WIA
11 Jun 44	5./301	Bf 109 G-6	162 644	air combat	NW. of Belowgrad	*Uffz.*	Hermann Erchen	WIA
11 Jun 44	5./301	Bf 109 G-6	162 309	air combat P-51	SW. of Samokow	*Uffz.*	Heinz Gerling	KIA
11 Jun 44	5./301	Bf 109 G-6	411 988	air combat P-51	Bodewgrad	*Fw.*	Günter Iffert	KIA
14 Jun 44	3./301	Bf 109 G-6		shotdown, bailed out	Etampes, France	*Fw.*	Theo Estermann	WIA
23 Jun 44	10./301	Bf 109 G-6	163 422 "Black 10"	air combat	unknown, Rom.	*Uffz.*	Friedr. Röglsperger	WIA
27 Jun 44	2./301	Bf 109 G-6	441 114	shotdown, bailed out	Lallaing, France	*Fw.*	Paul Hengel	WIA
28 Jun 44	10./301	Bf 109 G-6	160 211 "Black 3"	air combat	unknown, Rom.	*Ofw.*	Franz Menzel	WIA
28 Jun 44	10./301	Bf 109 A-6	161 432 "Black 10"	air combat	unknown, Rom.	*Fw.*	Karl Unger	WIA
4 Jul 44	6./301	Bf 109 G-6	163 492 "Yellow 10"	air combat	N. of Ibanezti	*Ofw.*	Max Sulzgruber	WIA
4 Jul 44	6./301	Bf 109 G-6	410 068 "Yellow 7"	shotdown, bailed out	S. of Hermannst.	*Uffz.*	Walter Toldrian	WIA
7 Jul 44	1./301	Bf 109 G-6	163 236	shotdown, bailed out	Crecy, France	*Olt.*	Ernst Fischer	WIA
7 Jul 44	3./301	Bf 109 G-6	163 509	shotdown, bailed out	Jeuvoi, France	*Uffz.*	Paul Werner	WIA
9 Jul 44	6./301	Bf 109 G-6	163 208 "Yellow 5"	air combat P-51	Mizil, Rom.	*Uffz.*	Wilhelm Esser	WIA
9 Jul 44	10./301	Bf 109 G-6	165 043 "Black 3"	air combat	unknown, Rom.	*Fw.*	Ernst Kiehling	KIA
9 Jul 44	10./301	Bf 109 G-6	163 632 "Black 1"	air combat	unknown, Rom.	*Olt.*	Otto Kobert	KIA
9 Jul 44	10./301	Bf 109 G-6	412 236 "Black 8"	air combat	unknown, Rom.	*Fw.*	Gerhard Mett	WIA
14 Jul 44	3./301	Bf 109 G-6	412 662	air combat	NE. of Dovai, Fr.	*Fw.*	Joachim Hähnel	WIA
18 Jul 44	1./301	Bf 109 G-6	412 632	air combat	Changry, France	*Fw.*	Hans Engfer	WIA
20 Jul 44	3./301	Bf 109 G-6	163 411	air combat	unknown, France	*Lt.*	Max Kreil	WIA
21 Jul 44	1./301	Bf 109 G-6	412 951 "White 16"	air combat	unknown	*Lt.*	Horst Prenzel	KIA
21 Jul 44	3./301	Bf 109 G-6	163 240 "Yellow 8"	air combat	unknown	*Fw.*	Manfred Gromoll	KIA
31 Jul 44	10./301	Bf 109 G-6	412 237 "Black 12"	air combat	unknown, Rom.	*Fw.*	Fritz Ebel	WIA
8 Aug 44	2./301	Bf 109 G-6	412 441	air combat	St. Pol-sur-Mer	*Lt.*	Willi Esche	KIA
8 Aug 44	2./301	Bf 109 G-6	162 236	air combat	Ledeghem	*Lt.*	Alfred Miller	KIA
18 Aug 44	1./301	Bf 109 G-6	166 229 "White 7"	air combat	unknown, France	*Fw.*	Enno Hansen	KIA
26 Aug 44	6./301	Bf 109 G-6		ground-attack	Targsoroul, Rom.	*Olt.*	Friedr. Seyffert	KIA
27 Aug 44	1./301	Bf 109 G-6		shotdown bailed out	Cambrai, France	*Fw.*	Martin Schulze	WIA
23 Sep 44	1./301	Fw 190 A-8	732 272	crash	Solpke	*Fw.*	Hans Engfer	Killed Fly.Acc.
23 Sep 44	2./301	Fw 190 A-8	175 179	crash	Recklingen	*Fw.*	Georg Ertel	Killed Fly.Acc.
9 Oct 44	3./301	Fw 190 A-9	201 376	crash	Salzwedel	*Olt.*	Kurt Dittmann	Killed Fly.Acc.
11 Oct 44	9./301	Fw 190 A-8	682 011	crash	unknown	*Ofw.*	Karl Petersen	MIA
13 Oct 44	8./301	Fw 190 A-8	734 039 CP+UX	crash	Sachau	*Uffz.*	Werner Malz	Killed Fly.Acc.
16 Oct 44	1./301	Fw 190 A-9	202 398	crash	Salzwedel	*Fw.*	Georg Scharein	Killed Fly.Acc.
16 Oct 44	6./301	Fw 190 A-8	350 236 TV+WD	collision near start	Sachau	*Uffz.*	Heinz Sturm	injured
21 Oct 44	12./301	Fw 190 A-8	681 801 "Black 1"	crash	Stendal	*Olt.*	Karl Völker	Killed Fly.Acc.
3 Nov 44	9./301	Fw 190 A-8	682 308 "White 8"	collision	Airfield Stendal	*Uffz.*	Dieter Ratzow	Killed Fly.Acc.

Date	Unit	Aircraft Type	WerkNr/Code	Cause	Location	Rank	Name	Fate
3 Nov 44	9./301	Fw 190 A-8	681 897 "White 7"	collision	Airfield Stendal	*Uffz.*	Johann Schweiger	Killed Fly.Acc.
7 Nov 44	8./301	Fw 190 A-8	176 080 "Blue 13"	crash	N. of Rathenow	*Uffz.*	Ludwig Vogel	Killed Fly.Acc.
7 Nov 44	3./301	Fw 190 A-9	202 431	air combat bailed out	Brixleben	*Fw.*	Werner Meyer	WIA
19 Nov 44	1./301	Fw 190 A-9	202 384	Crash	Stendal	*Fw.*	Franz Modrow	Killed Fly.Acc.
19 Nov 44	5./301	Fw 190 A-9	205 083 "White 17"	Unfall	Airfield Sachau	*Uffz.*	Anton Obermaier	Killed Fly.Acc.
19 Nov 44	6./301	Fw 190 A-9	206 150 "Red 2"	Crash	Solpke	*Lt.*	Harry Winkelhöfer	Killed Fly.Acc.
21 Nov 44	1./301	Fw 190 A-9	206 072	air combat	Jena	*Hptm.*	Wilhelm Burggraf	KIA
21 Nov 44	1./301	Fw 190 A-9	202 374	air combat-crash	Stendal	*Fw.*	Herbert Böver	WIA
21 Nov 44	1./301	Fw 190 A-9	202 435	shotdown, bailed out	Gr. Möhring	*Gefr.*	Johann Meindl	WIA
21 Nov 44	2./301	Fw 190 A-9	202 419	air combat P-51	Langensalza	*Fw.*	Viktor Gstrein	KIA
21 Nov 44	2./301	Fw 190 A-9	202 379	air combat P-51	Bröckau	*Uffz.*	Klaus Jakobi	KIA
21 Nov 44	2./301	Fw 190 A-9	202 319	air combat P-51	Röhrensee	*Uffz.*	Willy Peterreit	KIA
21 Nov 44	2./301	Fw 190 A-9	206 040	shotdown, bailed out	Zeitz	*Uffz.*	Alfredf Scholz	WIA
21 Nov 44	3./301	Fw 190 A-9	202 444	shotdown, bailed out	Pößnek	*Lt.*	Hermann Engelhardt	WIA
21 Nov 44	3./301	Fw 190 A-9	202 421 "Yellow 15"	air combat P-51	near Jena	*OGefr.*	Franz Harrer	KIA
21 Nov 44	3./301	Fw 190 A-9	202 434	air combat P-51	Langensalza	*Lt.*	Klaus Pagel	KIA
21 Nov 44	3./301	Fw 190 A-9	202 448	shotdown, bailed out	Kl. Lochmar	*Olt.*	Heinz Weise	KIA
21 Nov 44	4./301	Fw 190 A-9	206 047	air combat	near Sanne/Stend.	*Uffz.*	Harry Rauch	KIA
21 Nov 44	5./301	Fw 190 A-9	206 153 "White 7"	shotdown, bailed out	Bendeleben	*Lt.*	Siegfried Heise	WIA
21 Nov 44	5./301	Fw 190 A-8	350 238	air combat	unknown, Thüringen	*Uffz.*	Willi Heidenreich	KIA
21 Nov 44	6./301	Fw 190 A-9	206 137 "Red 12"	air combat	Eisenberg	*OGefr.*	Ernst Hobbie	KIA
21 Nov 44	6./301	Fw 190 A-9	202 424 "Red 7"	air combat	Könitz	*Ofw.*	Hans Wagler	WIA
21 Nov 44	7./301	Fw 190 A-9	206 170 "Yellow 16"	air combat	Goldbach	*OGefr.*	Willy Kempf	KIA
21 Nov 44	8./301	Fw 190 A-8	176 071 "Blue 12"	engine failure	Neustadt	*Uffz.*	Herbert Barteniek	injured
21 Nov 44	9./301	Fw 190 A-8	682 008 "White 5"	air combat	Waldeck	*OGefr.*	Rudolf Bender	WIA
21 Nov 44	10./301	Fw 190 A-9	208 112 "Yellow 1"	air combat P-51	Wenigenlumpnitz	*Olt.*	Hans Kretschmer	KIA
26 Nov 44	St./301	Fw 190 A-8	170 234	air combat	Münder	*Fhr.*	Werner Raygrotzki	KIA
26 Nov 44	1./301	Fw 190 A-9	202 442	air combat P-51	Münder	*Lt.*	Fritz Brinkmann	KIA
26 Nov 44	1./301	Fw 190 A-9	206 039	air combat P-51	Münder/Einbeck	*Uffz.*	Kurt Gabler	KIA
26 Nov 44	1./301	Fw 190 A-9	202 366	air combat P-51	Hameln	*Uffz.*	Walter Kircheiß	KIA
26 Nov 44	1./301	Fw 190 A-8	176 063	air combat	near Minden	*Gefr.*	Siegfried Meier	KIA
26 Nov 44	2./301	Fw 190 A-9	206 108	air combat	near Vietze	*Ofw.*	Heinz Günther	KIA
26 Nov 44	2./301	Fw 190 A-9	202 363	air combat	near Prentzen	*Uffz.*	Ernst Peitz	KIA
26 Nov 44	3./301	Fw 190 A-9	202 590	air combat	near Hameln	*Uffz.*	Willy Huke	KIA
26 Nov 44	3./301	Fw 190 A-9	202 406	air combat	near Nettelrede	*Ofw.*	Josef Löffler	KIA
26 Nov 44	3./301	Fw 190 A-8	176 051	air combat	Einbeckhausen	*Fw.*	Werner Meyer	KIA
26 Nov 44	3./301	Fw 190 A-9	202 361	air combat	near Pohle	*Ofw.*	Erich Meyer	KIA
26 Nov 44	4./301	Fw 190 A-9	202 565	air combat	Bückeburg	*Fw.*	Emil Schubert	WIA
26 Nov 44	4./301	Fw 190 A-9	202 570	air combat	Niendorf	*Uffz.*	Gottfried Hellriegel	WIA
26 Nov 44	4./301	Fw 190 A-8	176 049	air combat	Bredenbeck	*Uffz.*	Adolf Schäpers	WIA
26 Nov 44	4./301	Fw 190 A-9	202 377	air combat	near Völksen	*Uffz.*	Anton Schmidt	KIA
26 Nov 44	5./301	Fw 190 A-9	206 085 "White 2"	air combat	Holthusen	*Uffz.*	Siegfried Baer	KIA
26 Nov 44	5./301	Fw 190 A-9	202 430 "White 4"	shotdown, bailed out	Grenow	*Fw.*	Otto-Georg Müller	WIA
26 Nov 44	5./301	Fw 190 A-9	206 160 "White 1"	air combat	Rethem	*Olt.*	Alfred Vollert	KIA
26 Nov 44	6./301	Fw 190 A-8	733 693 "Red 29"	air combat P-51	Saarstedt	*Fw.*	Alfred Arens	KIA

276

Date	Unit	Aircraft Type	WerkNr/Code	Cause	Location	Rank	Name	Fate
26 Nov 44	6./301	Fw 190 A-9	206 152 "Red 1"	air combat P-51	Dahlenburg	*Olt.*	Rudolf Schick	KIA
26 Nov 44	7./301	Fw 190 A-9	206 156 "Yellow 12"	air combat	Mellendorf	*Gefr.*	Fritz Doßmann	KIA
26 Nov 44	7./301	Fw 190 A-9	202 447 "Yellow 8"	air combat	Hertenbeck	*Lt.*	Heinz-Ludw. Günther	KIA
26 Nov 44	7./301	Fw 190 A-9	206 142 "Yellow 14"	air combat P-51	Mellendorf	*Fw.*	Helmut Handel	KIA
26 Nov 44	7./301	Fw 190 A-9	206 126 "Yellow 3"	shotdown, bailed out	Peine	*Ofw.*	Franz Menzel	WIA
26 Nov 44	7./301	Fw 190 A-9	202 433 "Yellow 4"	shotdown, bailed out	Peine	*Fw.*	Friedr. Röglsperger	WIA
26 Nov 44	7/301	Fw190 A-9	202 415 "Yellow 17"	shotdown, bailed out	Meerdorf	*Uffz.*	Heinz Schulz	WIA
26 Nov 44	7./301	Fw 190 A-9	202 429 "Yellow 5"	shotdown, bailed out	near Bledeln	*Uffz.*	Paul Stargardt	WIA
26 Nov 44	8./301	Fw 190 A-8	176 071 "Blue 7"	shotdown, bailed out	Hammelspringe	*Uffz.*	Kurt Dörr	WIA
26 Nov 44	8./301	Fw 190 A-8	172 059 "Blue 15"	air combat P-51	Münder	*Gefr.*	Josef Henning	KIA
26 Nov 44	8./301	Fw 190 A-8	172 437 "Blue 2"	shotdown, bailed out	Saarstedt	*Fw.*	Helmut Thiemann	KIA
26 Nov 44	9./301	Fw 190 A-8	682 004 "White 16"	air combat	Wunstorf	*Ofw.*	Heinz Dademarsch	WIA
26 Nov 44	9./301	Fw 190 A-8	176 102 "White 4"	air combat P-51	Wahrendahl	*Gefr.*	Erich Steidel	KIA
26 Nov 44	10./301	Fw 190 A-8	682 301 "Red 7"	air combat	Braunschweig	*Lt.*	Georg Frenzel	WIA
26 Nov 44	10./301	Fw 190 A-8	691 990 "Red 10"	air combat	Hildesheim	*Fhr.*	Reinhold Hummel	WIA
26 Nov 44	10./301	Fw 190 A-8	172 093 "Red 8"	air combat	Braunschweig	*Lt.*	Rudolf Karioth	WIA
26 Nov 44	10./301	Fw 190 A-8	172 358 "Red 15"	air combat	Wunstorf	*Fhr.*	Hans Voigt	KIA
26 Nov 44	11./301	Fw 190 A-8	682 026 "Yellow 16"	air combat	Hannover	*Ofhr.*	Adolf Bellinghaus.	KIA
26 Nov 44	11./301	Fw 190 A-8	172 350 "Yellow 3"	air combat	Stendal	*Fhr.*	Ludwig Bracht	WIA
26 Nov 44	11./301	Fw 190 A-8	681 966 "Yellow 7"	air combat	Marschsee	*Ofhr.*	Hubert Ludwig	KIA
27 Nov 44	St./301	Fw 190 A-9	206 056 < 3 +	air combat	Edemissen	*Ofw.*	Josef Nierhaus	KIA
27 Nov 44	1./301	Fw 190 A-8	733 758	air combat	Nordhausen	*Uffz.*	Otto Bissinger	WIA
27 Nov 44	1./301	Fw 190 A-9	202 372	air combat	Göttingen	*Ofhr.*	Gerhard Golze	WIA
27 Nov 44	1./301	Fw 190 A-9	206 188	air combat P-51	near Elze	*Uffz.*	Heinz Maximini	WIA
27 Nov 44	1./301	Fw 190 A-9	202 375	shotdown, bailed out	near Wetteborn	*Uffz.*	Hans Zarm	KIA
27 Nov 44	2./301	Fw 190 A-8	176 062	air combat	Broitzem	*Ogfr.*	Siegfried Schulz	WIA
27 Nov 44	2./301	Fw 190 A-9	202 418	air combat P-51	Küllstedt	*Uffz.*	Gustav Wimmer	KIA
27 Nov 44	4./301	Fw 190 A-9	202 386	air combat P-51	near Hörsum	*Uffz.*	Alfred Bokr	KIA
27 Nov 44	5./301	Fw 190 A-9	206 138 "White 15"	air combat	near Greene	*Ofhr.*	Siegfried Bonitz	KIA
27 Nov 44	5./301	Fw 190 A-9	206 083 "White 17"	air combat	unknown	*Fw.*	Kurt Klemm	KIA
27 Nov 44	6./301	Fw 190 A-8	734 397 "Red 31"	crash	Airfield Stendal	*Uffz.*	Heinz Sturm	Killed Fly.Acc.
2 Dec 44	8./301	Fw 190 A-8		crash	Hennef	*Fw.*	Gerhard Wieck	Killed Fly.Acc.
5 Dec 44	II./301	Fw 190 A-9	206 157 << +	air combat	near Zirtow	*Hptm.*	Rolf Jacobs	KIA
5 Dec 44	1./301	Fw 190 A-9	202 404	air combat	Göttingen	*Ofhr.*	Gerhard Golze	KIA
5 Dec 44	1./301	Fw 190 A-9	202 387	air combat	Fürstensee	*Fw.*	Ernst Leyer	KIA
5 Dec 44	1./301	Fw 190 A-9	202 443	air combat	Neustrelitz	*Fw.*	Gerhard Koch	WIA
5 Dec 44	4./301	Fw 190 A-9	202 362 "Yellow 1"	air combat	unknown	*Lt.*	Max Kreil	KIA
5 Dec 44	4./301	Fw 190 A-9	206 084	air combat	Altstrelitz	*Ofhr.*	Karl-Heinz Ripper	KIA
5 Dec 44	5./301	Fw 190 A-9	209 913 "White 2"	air combat P-51	Angermünde	*Olt.*	Werner Poppenburg	KIA

Date	Unit	Aircraft Type	WerkNr/Code	Cause	Location	Rank	Name	Fate
5 Dec 44	7./301	Fw 190 A-8	175 169 "Yellow 23"	air combat P-51	Prenzlau	*Ofw.*	Paul Becker	KIA
5 Dec 44	7./301	Fw 190 A-9	206 176 "Yellow 11"	air combat P-51	near Sonnenberg	*Fhj.Fw.*	Hans Ryba	KIA
5 Dec 44	7./301	Fw 190 A-8	176 089 "Yellow 5"	air combat P-51	Königsstedt	*Uffz.*	Horst Thorwirt	KIA
5 Dec 44	8./301	Fw 190 A-8	176 069 "Blue 6"	air combat	Blankenförde	*Fw.*	Franz Pflüger	KIA
5 Dec 44	8./301	Fw 190 A-8	172 379 "Blue 9"	air combat	Düsterförde	*Uffz.*	Willi Sander	KIA
5 Dec 44	9./301	Fw 190 A-8	682 002	air combat	Finow	*StFw.*	Rolf Böhme	KIA
5 Dec 44	9./301	Fw 190 A-8	682 007	air combat	Brodowin	*Ofw.*	Heinz Döpel	KIA
5 Dec 44	10./301	Fw 190 A-8	681 882 "Red 1"	air combat	Finow	*Ofhr.*	Alfons Hörnig	KIA
5 Dec 44	10./301	Fw 190 A-8	681 869 "Red 5"	air combat	Finow	*Uffz.*	Rudolf Marquart	KIA
5 Dec 44	10./301	Fw 190 A-8	682 014	air combat	Schorfheide	*Fw.*	Heinz Thierling	WIA
5 Dec 44	10./301	Fw 190 A-8	176 109 "Red 17"	air combat	Raum-Finow	*Fhj.Fw.*	Helmut Tschorn	KIA
5 Dec 44	10./301	Fw 190 A-8	681 878	air combat	Raum-Finow	*Fw.*	Hans Viehbeck	WIA
5 Dec 44	11./301	Fw 190A-8	681 357	air combat	Prenzlau	*Uffz.*	Karl Alt	KIA
5 Dec 44	12./301	Fw 190 A-8	682 005 "Black 9"	air combat	Mecklenburg	*Ofw.*	Walter Bäcker	KIA
12 Dec 44	11./301	Fw 190 A-8		crash	Stendal	*Uffz.*	Walter Konrad	injured
15 Dec 44	8./301	Fw 190 A-8	734 035 "Blue 5"	crash	Sachau	*Uffz.*	Bernhard Döbele	Killed Fly.Acc.
18 Dec 44	11./301	Fw 190 A-8	682 001 "Yellow 10"	air combat	Göttingen	*Lt.*	Walter Tauscher	WIA
29 Dec 44	9./301	Fw 190 A-8	176 167 "White 10"	crash	Stendal	*Ofhr.*	Siegfr. Aschendorf	Killed Fly.Acc.
31 Dec 44	2./301	Fw 190 A-9	205 963	shotdown, bailed out	Celle	*Fhr.*	Ulrich Leopold	WIA
31 Dec 44	2./301	Fw 190 A-9	206 163	air combat	Pietzmoor	*Gefr.*	Lothar Sattler	KIA
31 Dec 44	4./301	Fw 190 A-9	202 428	shotdown, bailed out	Rotenburg	*Uffz.*	Manfred Hillert	WIA
31 Dec 44	II./301	Fw 190 D-9	210 916	shotdown, bailed out	S. of Hamburg	*Hptm.*	Herbert Nölter	WIA
31 Dec 44	5./301	Fw 190 A-9	206 097 "White 9"	crash	Jävenitz	*Olt.*	Helmut Ostendorp	Killed Fly.Acc.
31 Dec 44	5./301	Fw 190 A-9	205 914 "White 4"	air combat	Celbe	*Lt.*	Karl Kapriel	KIA
31 Dec 44	5./301	Fw 190 A.9	206 167 "White 1"	air combat	Rotenburg	*Gefr.*	Wenzel Marschik	KIA
31 Dec 44	6./301	Fw 190 D-9	210 914 "Red 12"	air combat	Lüneburg	*Uffz.*	Alfred Heindl	KIA
31 Dec 44	6./301	Fw 190 D-9	210 906 "Red 6"	air combat	Scharnebeck	*Ofw.*	Otto Wallner	KIA
31 Dec 44	8./301	Fw 190 D-9	210 902 "Red 2"	air combat	S. of Braten	*Uffz.*	Otmar Christoph	KIA
31 Dec 44	8./301	Fw 190 A-9	205 060 "Blue 6"	shotdown, bailed out	Eichholz	*Uffz.*	Franz Leeb	WIA
31 Dec 44	8./301	Fw 190 A-9	205 989 "Blue 1"	air combat	Tessin	*Olt.*	Gerhard Walter	KIA
31 Dec 44	9./301	Fw 190 A-8	176 096 "White 14"	air combat	Fassberg	*Hptm.*	Paul Quednau	KIA
31 Dec 44	10./301	Fw 190 A-8	175 948 "Red 4"	air combat P-51	Tiste near Stade	*Lt.*	Max Müller	KIA
31 Dec 44	10./301	Fw 190 A-8	175 960 "Red 3"	air combat	Rotenburg	*Fj.Fw.*	Hans Penzin	WIA
31 Dec 44	10./301	Fw 190 A-8		air combat	Soltau	*Ofhr.*	Artur Schindehütte	KIA
31 Dec 44	10./301	Fw 190 A-8	176 058 "Red 19"	air combat	Rotenburg	*Olt.*	Hermann Stahl	WIA
31 Dec 44	11./301	Fw 190 A-8	176 095 "Yellow 6"	air combat	Tessin	*Uffz.*	Rolf Burghardt	KIA
31 Dec 44	11./301	Fw 190 A-8	172 357 "Yellow 4"	air combat	near Düssin	*Fw.*	Ernst Otto	KIA
31 Dec 44	11./301	Fw 190 A-8	175 917 "Yellow 7"	air combat	Boitzenburg	*Fw.*	Karl Rienth	KIA

Date	Unit	Aircraft Type	WerkNr/Code	Cause	Location	Rank	Name	Fate
31 Dec 44	12./301	Fw 190 A-8	682 009 "Black 18"	air combat	near Tessin	*Fw.*	Heinrich Dörr	KIA
31 Dec 44	12./301	Fw 190 A-8	682 027 "Black 4"	air combat	near Lüneburg	*Uffz.*	Franz Schrack	WIA

1945

Date	Unit	Aircraft Type	WerkNr/Code	Cause	Location	Rank	Name	Fate
1 Jan 45	2./301	Fw 190 A-9	205 969	air combat	Salzwedel	*Uffz.*	Karl-H. Nicolaus	WIA
1 Jan 45	4./301	Fw 190 A-9	202 170	air combat	Lüderitz	*Uffz.*	Bruno Brekler	KIA
1 Jan 45	4./301	Fw 190 A-9	205 908	air combat P-51	Gr.Schwarzenlose	*Lt.*	Otto Frank	KIA
1 Jan 45	8./301	Fw 190 A-9	205 966 "Blue 2"	air combat	Belkau, Stendal	*Fj.Ofw.*	Georg Schöneich	KIA
1 Jan 45	9./301	Fw 190 A-8	172 346 "White 5"	air combat	near Stendal	*Lt.*	Leonhard Reinicke	WIA
1 Jan 45	9./301	Fw 190 A-8	"White 6"	shotdown, bailed out	E. of Gardelegen	*Fw.*	Willi Reschke	injured
1 Jan 45	10./301	Fw 190 A-8	175 958 "Red 1"	air combat	near Stendal	*Fw.*	Kurt Born	WIA
1 Jan 45	11./301	Fw 190 A-8	175 912 "White 11"	air combat	S. of Stendal	*Fw.*	Friedrich Winter	WIA
1 Jan 45	12./301	Fw 190 A-8	682 031 "Black 12"	air combat B-17	over Stendal	*Fw.*	Heinr. Wißmann	WIA
13 Jan 45	8./301	Fw 190 A-9	207 171 "Blue 10"	crash	Welzow	*Lt.*	Karl Strohmeyer	Killed Fly.Acc.
14 Jan 45	1./301	Fw 190 A-9	206 198	air combat P-51	E. of Priegnitz	*Hptm.*	Wolfg. Hankamer	KIA
14 Jan 45	1./301	Fw 190 A-9	206 188	air combat P-51	Neuruppin	*Uffz.*	Heinz Maximini	KIA
14 Jan 45	2./301	Fw 190 A-9	206 154	shotdown, bailed out	Kyritz	*Gefr.*	Reinh. Kleinstück	WIA
14 Jan 45	2./301	Fw 190 A-9	206 185	shotdown, bailed out	Kyritz	*Ofw.*	Hans Schäfer	WIA
14 Jan 45	2./301	Fw 190 A-9	205 906	shotdown, bailed out	near Breddin	*Uffz.*	Willi Schmidt	WIA
14 Jan 45	2./301	Fw 190 A-9	205 068	air combat	Barenthin	*Fw.*	Otto Sturm	KIA
14 Jan 45	3./301	Fw 190 A-9	205 977	shotdown, bailed out	Kyritz	*Fhr.*	Wilfried Hacheney	WIA
14 Jan 45	4./301	Fw 190 A-9	205 930	air combat	Kyritz	*Uffz.*	Hans Pieschel	WIA
14 Jan 45	4./301	Fw 190 A-9	206 189	air combat P-51	Barenthin	*Fw.*	Walter Schmidt	KIA
14 Jan 45	4./301	Fw 190 A-9	203 386	air combat	Kyritz	*Fw.*	Emil Schubert	WIA
14 Jan 45	4./301	Fw 190 A-9	206 191	air combat	near Gumtow	*Fhr.*	Horst Strauß	KIA
14 Jan 45	5./301	Fw 190 A-9	205 961 "White 16"	air combat	Gumtow	*Fw.*	Herbert Schaar	KIA
14 Jan 45	6./301	Fw 190 D-9	210 260 "Red 16"	air combat	Kyritz	*Fw.*	Werner Ebert	KIA
14 Jan 45	6./301	Fw 190 D-9	210 977 "Red 15"	air combat	Pritzwalk	*Uffz.*	Franklin Höhne	KIA
14 Jan 45	6./301	Fw 190 D-9	210 907 "Red 7"	shotdown, bailed out	Brandenburg	*Lt.*	Walter Kropp	WIA
14 Jan 45	6./301	Fw 190 D-9	210 913 "Red 13"	air combat	near Lohn	*Fw.*	Clemens Schmoll	KIA
14 Jan 45	8./301	Fw 190 A-9	206 173	air combat	near Havelberg	*Fw.*	Heinz Riedel	KIA
14 Jan 45	8./301	Fw 190 A-9	205 946 "Blue 9"	air combat	Havelberg	*Uffz.*	Heinrich Fischer	KIA
14 Jan 44	8./301	Fw 190 A-9	207 201 "Blue 7"	air combat	Kyritz	*Fw.*	Hans-Diet. Jander	KIA
14 Jan 45	8./301	Fw 190 A-9	207 169 "Blue 8"	air combat P-51	Wittemoor/Stend	*Uffz.*	Heinz Kettmann	KIA
14 Jan 45	8./301	Fw 190 A-9	207 177 "Blue 2"	air combat P-51	NW. of Rübhorst	*Uffz.*	Gustav Kilzer	KIA
14 Jan 45	9./301	Fw 190 A-8	176 075 "White 3"	air combat	Neustadt/Dosse	*OGefr.*	Günter Angermann	KIA
14 Jan 45	9./301	Fw 190 A-8	175 920 "White 13"	air combat P-51	near Lohn	*Ofhr.*	Karl Hänsel	KIA
14 Jan 45	10./301	Fw 190 A-8	682 006 "Red 9"	air combat	S. of Schwerin	*Fw.*	Hubert Blomert	KIA
14 Jan 45	11./301	Fw 190 A-8	175 925 "Yellow 3"	air combat P-51	Kyritz	*Olt.*	Christoph Herzog	WIA
14 Jan 45	11./301	Fw 190 A-8	"Yellow 4"	air combat P-51	Barenthin	*Ofw.*	Kurt Kabler	KIA

Date	Unit	Aircraft Type	WerkNr/Code	Cause	Location	Rank	Name	Fate
14 Jan 45	12./301	Fw 190 A-8	172 355 "Black 10"	air combat	Kyritz	OGefr.	Egon Straub	WIA
14 Jan 45	Stab/301	Fw 190 D-9	210 276 "Black 2"	air combat P-51	Strodehne	Uffz.	Albert Hoffmann	KIA
20 Jan 45	9./301	Fw 190 A-8	681 992 "Red 11"	crash	near Dresden	Uffz.	Dieter Göthel	WIA
20 Jan 45	1./301	Fw 190 A-9	202 402	air combat	Tauchau	Uffz.	Josef Idstein	KIA
20 Jan 45	4./301	Fw 190 A-9	205 089	air combat	Dreihaken	Uffz.	Gottfr. Hellriegel	KIA
20 Jan 45	5./301	Fw 190 A-9	206 086 "White 3"	air combat	near Kohau	Uffz.	Karl Schweger	KIA
20 Jan 45	10./301	Fw 190 A-8	175 921 "Red 5"	air combat	Heiligenkreuz	Ofw.	Heinz Brandt	KIA
21 Jan 45	3./301	Fw 190 A-9		ground-attack	Schroda	Lt.	Erich Reinke	KIA
21 Jan 45	2./301	Fw 190 A-9		ground-attack	Schroda	Fhr.	Werner Gemmer	KIA
22 Jan 45	5./301	Fw 190 A-9	206086 "White 3"	air combat	near Pilsen	Uffz.	Karl Schweger	KIA
23 Jan 45	3./301	Fw 190 A-9		air combat	unknown	Gefr.	Harald Himmelstoß	KIA
24 Jan 45	3./301	Fw 190 A-9	207172	air combat	Posen	Olt.	Chr. Straßburger	KIA
25 Jan 45	4./301	Fw 190 A-9	205910	air combat	near Kyritz	Uffz.	Jacob Funken	KIA
25 Jan 45	1./301	Fw 190 A-9	205010	air combat	Posen	Fhr.	Günther Hoffmann	WIA
26 Jan 45	11./301	Fw 190 A-8	682055 "Yellow 12"	unknown	near Steinau	Olt.	Wolfgang Dreier	MIA
26 Jan 45	12./301	Fw 190 A-8	175955	shotdown, bailed out	near Lüben	Lt.	Horst Lüth	WIA
1 Feb 45	1./301	Fw 190 A-8	176050	engine failure	near Finsterwalde	Fw.	Bernhard Ikier	injured
1 Feb 45	8./301	Fw 190 A-9	206060 "Blue 10"	crashlanding	near Drewitz	Uffz.	Ferdinand Loth	injured
1 Feb 45	5./301	Fw 190 A-9	206071	shotdown, bailed out	Kahnsdorf	Uffz.	Kurt Woldt	injured
1 Feb 45	6./301	Fw 190 A-9	205067 "Red 12"	Russ. Flak	Neumühl	Lt.	Hermann Helm	KIA
1 Feb 45	8./301	Fw 190 A-9	207176 "Blue 1"	air combat	unknown	Lt.	Peter Kratzsch	KIA
1 Feb 45	12./301	Ta 152 H-1	150037	crash	Alteno	Uffz.	Hermann Dürr	Killed Fly.Acc.
2 Feb 45	4./301	Fw 190 A-9		air combat	Kamenz	Uffz.	Herbert Haas	KIA
2 Feb 45	5./301	Fw 190 A-9	206 141 "White 15"	Flak	W. of Schwerin	Uffz.	Friedrich Jokiel	KIA
2 Feb 45	8./301	Fw 190 A-9	206 057 "Blue 14"	crashlanding	Neuhausen	Ofw.	Herbert Schüller	injured
3 Feb 45	1./301	Fw 190 A-8	175918	air combat	Bärwalde	Fw.	Max Schleifenheimer	WIA
4 Feb 45	IV./301	Bf 109 G-10	491157 "Green 21"	Russ. Flak	10 km S. of Ziebingen	Hptm.	Wilfried Schmitz	KIA
4 Feb 45	2./301	Fw 190 A-9	207 203	air combat	Eastern Front	Fw.	Gerh. Zimmermann	KIA
4 Feb 45	3./301	Fw 190 A-9	202403	air combat	Eastern Front	Fw.	Franz Domhöver	KIA
4 Feb 45	6./301	Fw 190 A-9	205938 "Red 13"	air combat	Eastern Front	Uffz.	Georg Gude	KIA
4 Feb 45	8./301	Fw 190 A-9	207188 "Blue 6"	air combat	Eastern Front	Fhr.	August Bader	KIA
4 Feb 45	8./301	Fw 190 A-9	207195 "Blue 2"	air combat	Eastern Front	Lt.	Otto Schwarz	KIA
4 Feb 45	14./301	Bf 109 G-10	157440 "Red 5"	Russ. Flak	Eastern Front	Lt.	Günter Förster	KIA
7 Feb 45	5./301	Fw 190 A-9	206116 "White 16"	crash	Welzow	Lt.	Gerhard Lippold	Killed Fly.Acc.
7.Feb 45	6./301	Fw 190 A-9	205414 "White 1"	air combat	Eastern Front	Ofw.	Horst Wolf	WIA
7 Feb 45	15./301	Bf 109 G-10	491238 "Yellow 1"	Russ. Flak	SE. of Schwerin	Olt.	Otto Schöppler	WIA
8 Feb 45	14./301	Bf 109 G-10	150726 "Red 16"	Russ. Flak	6 km E. of Drossen	Lt.	Günter Hautschik	WIA
8 Feb 45	5./301	Fw 190 A-9	206148 "White 13"	air combat	Eastern Front	Uffz.	Ullrich Filipp	KIA
8 Feb 45	5./301	Fw 190 A-9	202365 "White 17"	air combat	Eastern Front	Uffz.	Heinz Fürste	KIA
8 Feb 45	6./301	Fw 190 D-9	210909 "Red 9"	air combat	Eastern Front	Uffz.	Helmut Brenner	KIA
8 Feb 45	13./301	Bf 109 G-10	150801 "White 1"	Flak	near Küstrin	Ogfr.	Wilhelm Herfel	KIA

Appendices

Date	Unit	Aircraft Type	WerkNr/Code	Cause	Location	Rank	Name	Fate
9 Feb 45	6./301	Fw 190 D-9	210905 "Red 5"	air combat	Grieben	Ofw.	Max Salzgruber	WIA
9 Feb 45	8./301	Fw 190 A-8	207202 "Blue 5"	air combat	unknown	Lt.	K.-Heinz Müller	KIA
14 Feb 45	1./301	Fw 190 A-8	682300	air combat	near Dresden	OGefr.	Heino Krause	KIA
14 Feb 45	7./301	Fw 190 D-9	210919 "Yellow 13"	air combat	Leipzig	Ofw.	Willi Frank	KIA
14 Feb 45	7./301	Fw 190 A-9	208378 "Yellow 10"	air combat	Leipzig	Fw.	Helmut Stöber	KIA
14 Feb 45	7./301	Fw 190 D-9	210238 "Yellow 16"	air combat	Leipzig	Lt.	Hans Stuck	WIA
25 Feb 45	1./301	Fw 190 A-9	205965	air combat	Salzwedel	Uffz.	Otto Dischinger	KIA
25 Feb 45	1./301	Fw 190 A-8	176111	air combat	Salzwedel	Fhr.	Hans Gebauer	KIA
25 Feb 45	1./301	Fw 190 A-8	683323	air combat	Salzwedel	Fw.	Gerhard Koch	KIA
25 Feb 45	2./301	Fw 190 A-9	202427	air combat	Salzwedel	Fw.	Willi Schmidt	KIA
25 Feb 45	5./301	Fw 190 D-9	500404 "Red 6"	engine failure	Arnim	Uffz.	Kurt Funke	Killed Fly.Acc.
2 Mar 45	2./301	Fw 190 A-9	202371	air combat	unknown	Ofw.	Hans Schäfer	MIA
2 Mar 45	2./301	Fw 190 A-9	207193	air combat	unknown	Uffz.	Gerhard Güttel	MIA
2 Mar 45	2./301	Fw 190 A-9		air combat	Ruzyne	Fhr.	Heinrich Lieb	KIA
2 Mar 45	5./301	Fw 190 D-9	500569 "White 14"	air combat	Schlan W. of Prague	Uffz.	Günter Schulz	KIA
2 Mar 45	6./301	Fw 190 D-9		air combat	near Störpke	Fhr.	Hans Geban	KIA
2 Mar 45	6./301	Fw 190 D-9	500419 "Red 2"	air combat	Dresden	Uffz.	Walter Gescheidt	KIA
2 Mar 45	6./301	Fw 190 D-9	500429 "Red 11"	air combat	near Dresden	Uffz.	Egbert Müller	KIA
2 Mar 45	8./301	Fw 190 A-9	206169 "Blue 10"	crash	Fleyh	Uffz.	Jürgen Dietrich	Killed Fly.Acc.
2 Mar 45	8./301	Fw 190 A-9	206164 "Blue 9"	air combat	near Dresden	Uffz.	Wolfgang Ehrlich	KIA
2 Mar 45	8./301	Fw 190 A-9	980582 "Blue 4"	air combat-P-51	Klotzsche	Uffz	Helmut Heger	KIA
2 Mar 45	8./301	Fw 190 D-9	500431 "Red 1"	air combat	near Würkwitz	Lt.	Walter Kropp	KIA
2 Mar 45	8./301	Fw 190 D-9	500111 "Red 4"	shotdown, bailed out	Aussig	FhjUffz.	Helmut Rix	WIA
2 Mar 45	13./301	Bf 109 G-10	150 787 "White 12"	air combat-P-51	Burg	Ofhr.	Walter Rummel	KIA
2 Mar 45	13./301	Bf 109 G-10	491152 "Green 4"	air combat	Burg	Ofhr.	Josef Bäcker	WIA
2 Mar 45	13./301	Bf 109 G-10	491186 "White 9"	shotdown, bailed out	Burg	Fw.	Alois Hasenknopf	WIA
2 Mar 45	13./301	Bf 109 G-10	150715 "White 4"	air combat	near Burg/ Regendorf	Uffz.	Vinz. Heilberger	KIA
2 Mar 45	13./301	Bf 109 G-10	151515 "White 5"	air combat- P-51	Burg	Olt.	Johann Patek	KIA
2 Mar 45	13./301	Bf 109 G-10	150812 "White 11"	air combat	Burg	Uffz.	Otto Zietlow	KIA
2 Mar 45	14./301	Bf 109 G-10	610100 "Red 4"	air combat	Flp-Burg	Uffz.	Alfred Appel	KIA
2 Mar 45	14./301	Bf 109 G-10	150745	shotdown, bailed out	Altengrabe	Uffz.	Arno Beyerl	WIA
2 Mar 45	15./301	Bf 109 G-10	491200 "Yellow 7"	air combat	near Stresow	Fhr.	Harald Ruh	KIA
2 Mar 45	15./301	Bf 109 G-10	491240 "Yellow 6"	shotdown, bailed out	Burg	Uffz.	Siegfried Hornschuh	WIA
2 Mar 45	15./301	Bf 109 G-10	151621 "Yellow 8"	shotdown, bailed out	Burg	Fhr.	Fritz Blechschmidt	WIA
2 Mar 45	15./301	Bf 109 G-10	151087 "Yellow 1"	air combat	Burg	Uffz.	Leonhard Keil	KIA
2 Mar 45	15./301	Bf 109 G-10	151556 "Yellow 17"	air combat	near Raksdorf	Uffz.	Rudolf Welsch	KIA
4 Mar 45	12./301	Ta 152		crash	Sachau	Ofhr.	Jonny Wiegeshoff	Killed Fly.Acc.
8 Mar 45	1./301	Fw 190 A-9	202441	crash	Salzwedel	Uffz.	Heinrich Panno	injured

Date	Unit	Aircraft Type	WerkNr/Code	Cause	Location	Rank	Name	Fate
March 45	11./301	Fw 190 A-9		air combat	unknown	Uffz.	Heinz Warnicke	MIA
March 45	2./301	Fw 190 A-9		air combat	unknown	Fhr.	Ullrich Leopold	KIA
March 45	2./301	Fw 190 A-9		air combat	unknown	Gefr.	Konrad Witzgall	KIA
25 Mar 45	1./301	Fw 190 A-8	683335	crash	Langenhagen	OGefr.	Herbert Kölsch	injured
27 Mar 45	2./301	Fw 190 A-9	980548	air combat	Salzwedel	Uffz.	Otto Taubert	KIA
27 Mar 45	2./301	Fw 190 A-9	202408	air combat	Salzwedel	Fw.	Herbert Müller	KIA
2 Apr 45	13./301	Bf 109 G-10		air combat	Eschwege	Fhr.	Friedrich Redlein	KIA
2 Apr 45	11./301	Fw 190 A-9		air combat	Erf.-Bindersleben	Lt.	Horst Reinhold	KIA
3 Apr 45	1./301	Fw 190 A-9		air combat	Gotha-Eisenach	Fw.	Max Schleifenheimer	KIA
4 Apr 45	8./ 301	Fw 190 D-9		air combat	westl. Cochstedt	Uffz.	Helmut Helis	KIA
4Apr 45	2./301	Fw 190 A-9		air combat	near Ifta	Uffz.	Siegfried Schulz	KIA
5 Apr 45	4./301	Fw 190 A-9		air combat	near Nohra	Uffz.	Adolf Schäpers	WIA
7 Apr 45	2./301	Fw 190 D-9		air combat	Deilmissen	Gefr.	Reinh. Kleinstück	KIA
8 Apr 45	11./301	Fw 190 A-9		air combat	Wienhausen/Celle	Uffz.	Heinz Sonntag	KIA
8 Apr 45	12./301	Fw 190 A-9		air combat	Ammern/Thür.	Ofw.	Helmut Krönke	KIA
Apr 45	5./301	Fw 190 A-9		air combat	unknown	Fhr.	Heinrich Ladewig	MIA
Apr 45	7./301	Fw 190 D-9		air combat	unknown	OGefr.	Norbert Kleiber	MIA
Apr 45	10./301	Fw 190 A-9		air combat	Hagenow	Ofw.	Hubert Langelotz	KIA
Apr 45	14./301	Bf 109 G-10		air combat	unknown	Ofw.	Erwin Bunk	KIA
11 Apr 45	10./301	Fw 190 A-9		air combat	S. of Schwerin	Fw.	Hubert Blomert	KIA
14 Apr 45	St./ 301	Ta 152		air combat - Tempest	Ludwigslust	Ofw.	Sepp Sattler	KIA
17 Apr 45	II./ 301	Fw 190 D-9		air combat	Ludwigslust	Lt.	Robert Nitsche	KIA
24 Apr 45	St./301	Ta 152		air combat - Jak-9	E. of Berlin	Olt.	Hermann Stahl	MIA

JG 302

Date	Rank	Name	Unit	Fate	Cause	Location
25 Nov 43	Uffz.	Heinz Kotthaus	7./302	Killed Fly.Acc.	takeoff crash	Wehnen
25 Nov 43	Olt.	Friedr. Leimkühler	8./302	injured	friendly Flak	Dutztal
26 Nov 43	Gefr.	Hans Derksen	7./302	Killed Fly.Acc.	takeoff crash	Wehnen
26 Nov 43	Olt.	Hans Gottuck	4./302	WIA	shotdown, bailed out	S. of Bremen
02 Dec 43	Ofw.	Karl Dreißinger	5./302	injured	crashlanding	Lüneburg
02 Dec 43	Fw.	Gerhard Lenz	5./302	KIA	air combat	SO-Garlitz
03 Dec 43	Fw.	Kurt Becker	5./302	Killed Fly.Acc.	Crash	SO-Husum
03 Dec 43	Ofw.	Hans Jatzack	9./302	Killed Fly.Acc.	Crash	Wildenloh
10 Dec 43	Fw.	Günter Nehrlich	6./302	Killed Fly.Acc.	Crash	SE. of Kiel
18 Dec 43	Uffz.	Otto Kutschenreuther	8./302	Killed Fly.Acc.	takeoff crash	Kayhauserfeld
20 Dec 43	Fw.	Ernst Hautmann	7./302	Killed Fly.Acc.	takeoff crash	Bokel
20 Dec 43	Fw.	Josef Leiner	5./302	Killed Fly.Acc.	Crash	Olderbeck
20 Dec 43	Uffz.	Leonhard Palzkill	5./302	WIA	shotdown, bailed out	Schweinfurt
23 Dec 43	Uffz.	Gerhard Krögel	6./302	KIA	air combat	W. of Ludwigslust
24 Dec 43	Uffz.	Helmut Meinersberger	6./302	Killed Fly.Acc.	Crash	near Jüterbog
24 Dec 43	Fw.	Gerhard Pietsch	6./302	Killed Fly.Acc.	Crash	near Jüterbog
27 Dec 43	Uffz.	Heinrich Kairies	4./302	Killed Fly.Acc.	Crash	SW. of Ludwigslust
29 Dec 43	Ofw.	Albert Hachtel	1./302	KIA	air combat	near Clausdorf
2 Jan 44	Ofw.	Kurt Emler	1./302	KIA	air combat	near Jüterbog
5 Jan 44	Uffz.	Heinz Brändlein	6./302	KIA	air combat	S. of Stettin
5 Jan 44	Ofw.	Ernst Haase	1./302	injured	crashlanding	Stade
5 Jan 44	Uffz.	Otto Steinhagen	5./302	injured	shotdown, bailed out	near Berlinchen
6 Jan 44	Uffz.	Thomas Braun	2./302	KIA	air combat	Potsdam
6 Jan 44	Uffz.	Eduard Ries	3./302	WIA	air combat	near Küstrin
11 Jan 44	Ofw.	Heinz Gossow	1./302	WIA	shotdown, bailed out	near Nordweide
11 Jan 44	Lt.	Erich Reinke	3./302	WIA	air combat	near Osnabrück
11 Jan 44	Fw.	Walter Schermutzki	4./302	injured	Crash	Grabow
11 Jan 44	Lt.	Helmut Steinmann	2./302	WIA	air combat	near Hiller
14 Jan 44	Fw.	Herbert Herre	1./302	KIA	air combat	Markendorf
14 Jan 44	Olt.	Herbert Petersen *St.Kptn.*	1./302	KIA	air combat	near Kamenz
20 Jan 44	Ofw.	Siegfried Heintsch	1./302	KIA	air combat	near Pretzsch
27 Jan 44	Maj.	Treum. Engelhard *Gkd.*	II./302	injured	shotdown, bailed out	Pritzier
19 Feb 44	Uffz.	Walter Peuster	7./302	KIA	air combat	Düblinghausen
19 Feb 44	Olt.	Helmut Schlechter	9./302	Killed Fly.Acc.	crashlanding	Oldenburg
19 Feb 44	Uffz.	Adam Winterstein	6./302	WIA	shotdown, bailed out	Oranienburg
20 Feb 44	Fw.	Herbert Chantelau	3./302	WIA	shotdown, bailed out	near Rothleben

Date	Rank	Name	Unit	Fate	Cause	Location
20 Feb 44	Fw.	Erich Teubner	2./302	WIA	shotdown, bailed out	Bernburg
1 Mar 44	Uffz.	Gisbert Vöcking	7./302	Killed Fly.Acc.	crash	Wittmoor
4 Mar 44	Lt.	Karl Vogel	2./302	KIA	air combat	Klein-Wulkow
5 Mar 44	Uffz.	Josef Feist	3./302	KIA	air combat	near Zerkenitz
6 Mar 44	Fw.	Erich Buhrig	2./302	KIA	air combat	Hohen-Lobbese
6 Mar 44	Uffz.	Kurt Pelz	2./302	KIA	air combat	Stendal
8 Mar 44	Fw.	Karl Männer	1./302	KIA	air combat	near Oschatz
12 Mar 44	Uffz.	Otto Pritzl	6./302	injured	collision, bailed out	Stendal
12 Mar 44	Lt.	Josef Wolfsberger	5./302	injured	collision, bailed out	Stendal
20 Mar 44	Fw.	Ernst Lutz	4./302	KIA	air combat	SW. of Salzwedel
24 Mar 44	Fw	Kurt Bemme	1./302	injured	engine failure, bailed out	Niedergörsdorf
24 Mar 44	Uffz.	Wolfgang Kindhäuser	5./302	injured	takeoff crash	Ludwigslust
24 Mar 44	Fw.	Herbert Stephan	1./302	injured	crash landing	Pretzsch
29 Mar 44	Hptm.	Karl-H. Dietsche St.Kptn.	2./302	injured	crash	Stendal
30 Mar 44	Ofw.	Friedrich Hill	8./302	KIA	air combat	near Lischaid
30 Mar 44	Uffz.	Erwin Völkel	7./302	KIA	air combat	Hildburghausen
08 Apr 44	Uffz.	Günther Häser	7./302	KIA	air combat	near Drohe
08 Apr 44	Uffz.	Andreas Hartl	6./302	KIA	air combat	E. of Hannover
08 Apr 44	Uffz.	Willibald Heymann	7./302	KIA	air combat	near Schweimke
08 Apr 44	Uffz.	Günter Maeser	7./302	KIA	air combat	near Drohe
08 Apr 44	Fhj.Fw.	Gerd Setzermann	8./302	KIA	air combat	near Wettendorf
08 Apr 44	Ofw.	Ernst Wick	1./302	KIA	air combat	location unknown
17 Apr 44	Uffz.	Herbert Kordas	2./302	injured	crash	Maltershausen
19 Apr 44	Uffz.	Thilo Beetz	2./302	KIA	air combat	near Wahlhausen
19 Apr 44	Ofw.	Karl Dreißinger	4./302	KIA	air combat	near Kassel
19 Apr 44	Olt.	Willi Klein St.Kptn.	4./302	KIA	air combat	near Kassel
28 Apr 44	Hptm.	Franz Gerig	Stab./302	KIA	air combat	E. of Euskirchen
29 Apr 44	Lt.	Erich Schötta	2./302	KIA	air combat	near Celle
03 Mai 44	Fw.	Walter Schulze	9./302	Killed Fly.Acc.	crash	Braunschweig
08 Mai 44	Hptm.	Friedhelm Höschen St.Kptn.	6./302	KIA	air combat	Braunschweig
08 Mai 44	Lt.	Alfred Körver	7./302	KIA	air combat	E. of Wiesenbüttel
11 Mai 44	Uffz.	Günter Heinsen	9./302	Killed Fly.Acc.	crash	Edemissen
13 Mai 44	Uffz.	Heinrich Amerkamp	6./302	KIA	air combat	near Dargun
13 Mai 44	Fw.	Fritz Gnifke	5./302	WIA	air combat	Nienendorf
13 Mai 44	Uffz.	Werner Greskow	6./302	WIA	shotdown, bailed out	near Demmin
13 Mai 44	Uffz.	Arthur Mayer	4./302	WIA	shotdown, bailed out	SE. of Levin
17 Mai 44	Ofw.	Alfred Pelz	3./302	Killed Fly.Acc.	crash	Seyring
19 Mai 44	Uffz.	Heinz Sarnow	4./302	KIA	air combat	over Berlin
24 Mai 44	Fw.	Werner Dienst	3./302	WIA	air combat	St. Aegid
24 Mai 44	Ofw.	Egbert Jaacks	3./302	WIA	air combat	near Kindberg
24 Mai 44	Lt.	Jonny Kruse St.Fhr.	4./302	KIA	air combat	Berlin
28 Mai 44	Uffz.	Hans Brevers	5./302	WIA	shotdown, bailed out	N. of Köthen
29 Mai 44	Uffz.	Roland Bever	2./302	KIA	air combat	near St. Pölten
29 Mai 44	Olt.	Hans Uhse St.Kptn.	7./302	Killed Fly.Acc.	collision	near Völkenrode
13 Jun 44	Uffz.	Hans Ettinger	2./302	KIA	air combat	near Erding
13 Jun 44	Uffz.	Horst Sennewald	4./302	KIA	air combat	Straubing
16 Jun 44	Uffz.	Rudolf Diecke	3./302	WIA	air combat	Szekesfehervar, Hungary
16 Jun 44	Uffz.	Heinz Ropers	1./302	KIA	air combat	location unknown
16 Jun 44	Olt.	Heinr Seidel St.Kptn.	3./302	WIA	air combat	near Györ, Hungary
26 Jun 44	Lt.	Peter Altmeyer St.Fhr	2./302	KIA	air combat	Zisterdorf
26 Jun 44	Fw.	Kurt Nachtigall	3./302	KIA	air combat	Szene, Hungary
26 Jun 44	Fw.	Hans Spielhagen	1./302	KIA	air combat	Raspunka, Hungary
27 Jun 44	Lt.	Gerd Bernhardt St.Fhr.	2./302	KIA	air combat	Demesed, Hungary
27 Jun 44	Uffz.	Heinz Strissel	4./302	KIA	air combat	S. of Szekesfehervar, Hung.
30 Jun 44	Ofhr.	Siegfried Aschendorf	1./302	WIA	air combat	N. of Budapest
01 Jul 44	Uffz.	Roland Müller	3./302	KIA	air combat	Bakonywald, Hungary
02 Jul 44	Uffz.	Rolf Burghardt	3./302	WIA	air combat	Szekesfehervar
02 Jul 44	Uffz.	Kurt Kittler	4./302	KIA	air combat	Szeregelyes, Hungary
02 Jul 44	Ofw.	Adolf Krista	2./302	Killed Fly.Acc.	crash	Ercsi, Hungary
02 Jul 44	Uffz.	Hermann Lammers	3./302	KIA	air combat	Ercsi, Hungary
02 Jul 44	Ofw.	Xaver Neumeier	1./302	KIA	air combat	location unknown
02 Jul 44	Uffz.	Willi Reschke	1./302	emergency landing	air combat	near Erd, S. of Budapest
02 Jul 44	OGefr.	Max Pick	4./302	KIA	air combat	Alcheid
02 Jul 44	Uffz.	Kurt Ramlow	4./302	KIA	air combat	location unknown
02 Jul 44	Fw.	Gerhard Scholz	1./302	KIA	air combat	near Erd
02 Jul 44	Ofw.	Paul Streuff	1./302	KIA	air combat	Martonvasar, Hungary
02 Jul 44	Uffz.	Gerhard Walter	2./302	injured	air combat	near Budapest
02 Jul 44	Uffz.	Otto Wiedemann	4./302	KIA	air combat	Laszlomajor, Hungary

Date	Rank	Name	Unit	Fate	Cause	Location
03 Jul 44	*Fw.*	Karl Vetter	3./302	KIA	air combat	location unknown
06 Jul 44	*Fw.*	Rudolf Dreesmann	4./302	KIA	air combat	location unknown
07 Jul 44	*Uffz.*	Willi Reschke	1./302	injured	shotdown, bailed out	Rammst. S. of Preßburg
07 Jul 44	*Uffz.*	Karl.H. Bamberg	2./302	KIA	air combat	Malacky, Slovakia
07 Jul 44	*OGefr.*	Wilhelm Herfel	4./302	WIA	air combat	near Bruck
08 Jul 44	*Uffz.*	Heinrich Reuter	2./302	WIA	air combat	Trautmannsdorf
08 Jul 44	*Ofhr.*	Walter Rödhammer	1./302	WIA	air combat	Untersiebenbrunn
08 Jul 44	*Fw.*	Werner Voss	1./302	WIA	air combat	near Marchegg
08 Jul 44	*Hptm.*	Heinrich Wurzer *St.Kptn.*	1./302	WIA	air combat	Götzendorf
08 Jul 44	*Uffz.*	Kurt Zitzmann	2./302	KIA	air combat	location unknown
13 Jul 44	*Fw.*	Werner Mühlich	3./302	KIA	air combat	near Enzersdorf
14 Jul 44	*Lt.*	Ernst Grumme	4./302	KIA	air combat	Budaörs, Hungary
14 Jul 44	*Uffz.*	Erich Reuter	3./302	KIA	air combat	Hungary, location unknown
15 Jul 44	*Lt.*	Richard Jüngling	1./302	KIA	air combat	location unknown
16 Jul 44	*Ofhr.*	Fritz Braune	2./302	KIA	air combat	location unknown
16 Jul 44	*Ofhr.*	Günter Kolbe	3./302	KIA	air combat	Neusiedlersee
19 Jul 44	*Gefr.*	Ludwig Heerdegen	1./302	KIA	air combat	Wolfratshausen/Bay.
19 Jul 44	*Uffz.*	Paul Kraatz	1./302	WIA	air combat	Eggenfelde
19 Jul 44	*Uffz.*	Willi Reschke	1./302	WIA	air combat	Neubiberg/München
19 Jul 44	*Uffz.*	Wilhelm Menke	3./302	KIA	air combat	Gatelried/Bay.
20 Jul 44	*Uffz.*	Horst Pollak	1./302	WIA	air combat	location unknown
20 Jul 44	*Ofw.*	Fritz Dieckmann	1./302	WIA	air combat	Baisweil/Bay.
21 Jul 44	*Lt.*	Wilhelm Hallenberger	4./302	WIA	air combat	SW. of Backeringen
21 Jul 44	*Lt.*	Horst Kirchner	2./302	KIA	air combat	Straß am Attersee
25 Jul 44	*Fj.Fw.*	Hubert Göbel	3./302	WIA	air combat	near Treptitz
25 Jul 44	*Uffz.*	Hans Kemmerling	2./302	Killed Fly.Acc.	crash	near Schwarzenbach
25 Jul 44	*OGefr.*	Ludwig Koller	3./302	KIA	air combat	near Kienberg
25 Jul 44	*Olt.*	Ferdinand Kray *St.Kptn.*	4./302	KIA	air combat	St. Pölten
25 Jul 44	*Gefr.*	Heinrich Pfeifer	3./302	KIA	air combat	near Boding
25 Jul 44	*Uffz.*	Günter Richter	3./302	WIA	air combat	St. Pölten
26 Jul 44	*Uffz.*	Guido Buhl	4./302	KIA	air combat	location unknown
27 Jul 44	*Uffz.*	Herbert Eckert	4./302	KIA	air combat	location unknown
28 Jul 44	*Uffz.*	Dieter Ratzow	1./302	WIA	air combat	Neustadt/Donau
28 Jul 44	*Gefr.*	Erich Steidel	1./302	WIA	air combat	location unknown
28 Jul 44	*Gefr.*	Walter Winzierl	3./302	KIA	air combat	Neustadt/Donau
29 Jul 44	*Fw.*	Ernst Schäfer	2./302	KIA	air combat	Plauen
29 Jul 44	*Uffz.*	Horst Wernecke	4./302	KIA	air combat	Laucha/Thür.
7 Aug 44	*Lt.*	Fritz Boldnau *St.Fhr.*	1./302	WIA	air combat	Szombathely, Hungary
7 Aug 44	*Fw.*	Heinrich Dörr	4./302	WIA	air combat	Pecel, Hungary
7 Aug 44	*Uffz.*	Paul Friedrich	2./302	KIA	air combat	Györ, Hungary
7 Aug 44	*Ofhr.*	Walter Rödhammer	1./302	KIA	air combat	Szombathely, Hungary
16 Aug 44	*Lt.*	Karl-Heinz Müller	2./302	WIA	air combat	Kassel
17 Aug 44	*Uffz.*	Walter Berlinska	2./302	Killed Fly.Acc.	crash	Heiligenstedt
20 Aug 44	*Hptm.*	Richard Lewens *Gr.Kdr.*	?/302	KIA	air combat	near Papa, Hungary
20 Aug 44	*Olt.*	Heinrich Ötteking *St.Kptn.*	1./ 302	KIA	air combat	Bugyi, Hungary
22 Aug 44	*Ofw.*	Herbert Stephan	1./302	WIA	air combat	Celldömölk, Hungary
24 Aug 44	*Uffz.*	Hermann Dürr	4./302	WIA	air combat	Indrichuv
24 Aug 44	*Uffz.*	Adolf Klärner	4./302	KIA	air combat	Wostoikowitz
24 Aug 44	*Ofhr.*	Sommer	3./302	KIA	air combat	Neubistritz
29 Aug 44	*Uffz.*	Willi Reschke	1./302	emergency landing	air combat	Banov, Hungary-Brod

29 August 1944 was the final day of operations for *I./JG 302*, the sole *Gruppe* of JG 302 still operational. The *Jagdgruppe* was withdrawn from action and moved to Alperstedt near Erfurt to reequip and be brought up to strength. It was subsequently renamed *III./JG 301*.

* = Crash landing.
** = FAA Friendly anti-arcraft flak

Also from the Publisher

Focke-Wulf Ta 152
The Story of the Luftwaffe's Late-War, High-Altitude Fighter
Dietmar Harmann

One of the best fighter aircraft of the Second World War – a masterpiece produced by chief designer Kurt Tank. With a large number of photographs – some previously unpublished – and drawings, this book details the development history of the Ta 152. It also illustrates the hopelessness of Germany's efforts late in the war to deploy advanced aircraft in large numbers.

Size: 8 1/2"x11" • over 165 b/w photographs and line drawings • 144 pp.
ISBN: 0-7643-0860-2 • hard cover • $35.00

Focke-Wulf Fw 190 "Long Nose"
An Illustrated History of the Fw 190 D Series
Dietmar Hermann

This book covers the complete development history of those variants of the Focke-Wulf Fw 190 powered by inline engines. The first Fw 190 equipped with a Daimler Benz liquid-cooled engine took to the air in early 1942, followed six months later by another powered by a Jumo 213. Production of the Fw 190 C, Fw 190 D and Ta 153 was delayed by the German air ministry. Not until 1944, by which time Germany had lost control of the air, did the Fw 190 D-9, an interim fighter powered by the Jumo 213 A, enter production. The Fw 190 D-9 proved an immediate success, largely due to an excellent prototype test program under Dipl.Ing. Hans Sander. The type quickly entered service with the *Luftwaffe* and more than 1,700 examples were completed by the end of the war. The Fw 190 D-9 gave rise to a number of improved variants with the more powerful Jumo 213 F engine and a heavier armament, however only a handful of the D-11 and D-13 versions were completed. With a maximum speed of 750 km/h, the Fw 190 D-12 powered by the new Jumo 213 EB would have represented the apex of Fw 190 development. The proposed Fw 190 D-14 and D-15, both powered by improved versions of the dive-bombers 603, came too late to see service with the *Luftwaffe*.

Size: 8 1/2"x11" • over 250 black and white, drawings, charts, color aircraft profiles • 208 pages
ISBN: 0-7643-1876-4 • hard cover • $59.95

JG 54
A Photographic History of the Grunherzjäger
Werner Held, Hannes Trautloft, Ekkehard Bob

In five turbulent years the members of this highly successful *Luftwaffe* fighter unit developed into such a close-knit team that even now – almost fifty years later – that bond still exists. This unique photo history was compiled with assistance from the air and ground crews of *JG 54*. The 400+ photographs document the story of the *Grunherz-Geschwader* from its formation in the spring of 1939 to the final battles in the courland pocket in the spring of 1945. Within the timespan lay the arduous years of operations in Poland, France, the Channel Front, the Balkans, Russia, Finland and the defense of the Reich.

Size: 7"x10" • over 400 b/w photographs • 196 pp.
ISBN: 0-88740-690-4 • hard cover • $29.95

JG 7
The World's First Jet Fighter Unit 1944/1945
Manfred Boehme

Formed in August 1944, *Jagdgeschwader 7* was equipped with the revolutionary Me 262 jet fighter, which was faster than any aircraft in existence at the time. This unit experienced all of the highs and lows associated with the introduction of such a radically new design. Thus the history of *JG 7* is also the story of the Me 262, an inspired design which broke new ground in many areas of technology, and for which there was simply not enough time for thorough development. Manfred Boehme has collected many documentary sources including first hand accounts, technical records and photo archives.

Size: 6"x9" • 168 photos, line drawings • 288 pp.
ISBN: 0-88740-395-6 • hard cover • $29.95